ISBN 978-0-364-92876-9
PIBN 10251578

The Dark Entry, Canterbury.   *Frontispiece.*

Highways and Byways

in

Kent

BY WALTER JERROLD
WITH · ILLUSTRATIONS · BY
HUGH THOMSON

MACMILLAN AND CO., LIMITED
ST. MARTIN'S STREET, LONDON
1914

PREFACE

As one of the counties most crowded with varied interests, as the scene of many historic events, as the place at which invaders and more peaceful visitors have landed, as the raising ground of a strong yeomanry and of many men of great distinction from the time of the making of England to the present, as the original centre of our national church life, Kent has a peculiarly notable position among the counties of England. Many books .have been written dealing with these various aspects of the county, and with its geological features, with its flora and its fauna; others have been devoted to its history, now in large and many-volumed form, now in merest outline; its past has been presented in fiction and in archæological records, there have been many guides dealing with it as a whole, and many more dealing in special fashion with particular centres. A library of respectable dimensions might be made of books concerning Kent, so that it may seem a temerarious act to add yet another to their number. The series to which this volume belongs has, however, established a place of its own in the large class of topographical works. Between the voluminous method of a Hasted or the worthy clergyman who spent his life in collecting materials and would have written a greater history had he had a second life to do it in, and that of the compiler of the useful but necessarily compact "guide," there are many degrees. It is a position between these two extremes that a volume of the Highways and Byways Series such as this seeks to fill ; while it may answer many of the requirements of a guide book it does not pretend to supplant such a useful companion.

In dividing up a county into subjects for chapters many methods may be followed. Here I have mostly taken a district around some centre from which it may conveniently be explored, and have sought to indicate the nature of the surrounding scenery, to point out the more interesting places to be visited, and to tell something of the men and events associated with them. The object has been to indicate the various attractions of a county peculiarly rich in associations, and including within its limits much beautiful and varied scenery.

From Lambarde, who perambulated Kent nearly three centuries and a half ago, there has been a succession of writers on Kent and to a large number of them the present day writer is necessarily indebted—for he is but telling an old tale in a new way. To many who have preceded me in wandering about the highways and byways of Kent I owe much, but special mention must be made of the long series of volumes of the *Archæologia Cantiana*, a crowded repository of facts which is invaluable to all who would inquire into the past history of Kent. But if the gossiping topographer owes gratitude to predecessors who have worked in the same field he is also grateful to friends and to those acquaintances whom his work has brought him, who have assisted him in compressing much into little,—a large county into a small volume.

In the spelling of place names – in which there is occasional disagreement—I have made a rule of following that of the Ordnance Survey maps.

W. J.

October 17, 1907.

In the one-inch-to-the-mile Ordnance Survey maps Kent is comprised in the following fourteen sheets—sheet 258 includes the fringe of the Thames marshes, and sheet 320 an inconsiderable scrap—

270 Beckenham	271 Dartford	272 Rochester	273 Whitstable	274 Isle of Thanet
	287 Sevenoaks	288 Maidstone	289 Canterbury	290 Deal
	303 Tunbridge Wells	304 Tenterden	305 Hythe	306 Shakespeare's Cliff
			321 Lydd	

CONTENTS

LIST OF ILLUSTRATIONS

HIGHWAYS AND BYWAYS

IN

KENT

CHAPTER I

"O famous Kent
What county hath this isle that can compare with thee ?
That hath within thyself as much as thou canst wish :
Thy rabbits, venison, fruits, thy sorts of fowl and fish ,
As with what strength comports, thy hay, thy corn, thy wood,
Nor anything doth want that anywhere is good."

MICHAEL DRAYTON.

To invite anyone to a saunter through Kentish byways, or even to a motor-scorch along Kentish highways, is to invite them into a county that has beauty, and varied beauty, to offer to the eye at all seasons of the year ; but it is to invite them also to a county rich in matters that appeal to the imagination, a county in which the making of history has been carried on for close upon twenty centuries, and one rich even in those relics which tell of earlier unrecorded times when wild in woods the naked savage ran. From the coming of Cæsar Kent takes a prominent place as the scene of notable events ; it was ravaged successively by the neighbouring kings of Mercia and Wessex and by the Danes ; its shores welcomed the first coming of Christianity ; it has witnessed fighting, has taken part in rebellions of a serious and of an insignificant character, has welcomed the comings of some of the Kingdom's rulers and speeded the parting of

E   B others. It has been the scene of pageants and of pilgrimages, of historic love-making and of historic crime. It has, indeed, come to stand for the whole kingdom of England, for to what do the thoughts of the exile turn if it be not to the white cliffs of Albion—and it may be affirmed that for the vast majority of exiles the vision which those words conjure up is a vision of the cliffs of the south-eastern corner of Kent, the cliffs about Dover, where one was wont—if Shakespeare is to be accepted as a topographical authority—to gather samphire, dangerous trade.

From the point at which London touches Kent in the north, to Dover in the south ; from the quiet lane which marks the entrance of the old Pilgrims' Way on the west, to the holiday-maker's Merry Margate in the extreme east, the county offers an infinite variety of attractions in the towns along its highways, the villages and hamlets of its byways, the pleasure resorts along its coast, in its wide stretches of hopfields, its orchards, its strawberry fields, its woods and coppices, its meadows, streams, and riverside marshes.

An American visitor who saw the county in the time of the bridal white of its cherry-bloom thought of Kent as of one vast cherry orchard. Visiting it later in the year, when the fragrant hops were near the time of their gathering, he rubbed his eyes and wondered where all the cherry trees had gone. Yet cherries and hops cover but a small portion of the acreage of our county, and there is so much else to be seen that a man might know much of Kent yet know but little about the uplifting beauty of a cherry orchard in bloom, or even of the fragrant trailers of the hopbine. In things to be seen, and associations for stimulating the imagination, the county is so rich that to one who has wandered hither and thither about it, has sojourned for some years now in a lonely hill-top house four miles from a railway station, now in a valley in the very shelter of a railway embankment and then by the wind-blown shore, it becomes a difficult matter to know where to begin a description of what may be seen, an account of some of the many associations, historical, literary and general, with which every square mile of the county is marked. We might enter Kent from London, and, following after a long interval in the steps of Chaucer's story-telling band, reach Canterbury, and thence take radiating routes to the rest of the county ; we might follow the course of the conquering Romans; we might consider ourselves as newly come to England by that common port of entry at the base of Shakespeare's Cliff, and so work through the land to London ; or we might imagine a pleasure-seeker at one of Thanet's populous resorts determining to learn something of the Kentish hinterland, setting out from Ramsgate or Margate to explore the Kentish ways. It matters not where we begin with all the county before us, but perhaps the centre which for hundreds

Canterbury from a Distance.

of years has attracted visitors from all parts of the world will be that at which it is fittest to make a start.

Before beginning our saunterings through historic towns, by lanes and footpaths, or our more hurried journeyings along the telegraph-poled and mile-marked highways, it may be well to take a bird's-eye view of the county as a whole, to note its situation and some of its general features. Of the " scituation," saith William Lambarde, the father of English topography, " *Kent* therefore lying in the Southern Region of this Realm, hath on the North the River of Thames ; on the East the Sea, on the South the Sea and *Sussex*, and on the West *Sussex* and *Surrey*. It extendeth in length from the West of the lands in *Beckenham*, called (I will not say purposely hereof) Langley, where is the stile, as it were, over into *Surrey*, to the *Ramsgate*

A Kentish Byway.

in the Isle of Thanet, about fifty and three miles; and reacheth in breadth from the River *Rother* on the South of *Newendene* next *Sussex*, to the River of *Thames* at *Nowrheade* in the Isle of *Greane*, twenty-six miles and somewhat more: And hath in circuit 160 miles or thereabouts."

Its situation at the south-eastern corner of England, at the point nearest to the Continent, has made Kent a place of great historical importance from earliest times, whilst its position, bounded on two sides by the sea, on one by the river Thames, has given it a larger share than most other counties of the advantages which the whole country gains from its insular position. Then, too, the 1,624 square miles of its area include great tracts of the chalk downs and of the greensand hills, broad stretches of the fruitful Weald, rich pasturage, and wide sea and river marshes. Old Fuller has pointed out that the county "differeth not more from other shires than from itself, such the variety thereof." In some parts of it, the same quaint writer puts it, "health and wealth are at many miles distance, which in other parts are reconciled to live under the same roof— I mean abide in one place together." The same differentiation has been expressed in quatrain form, thus :

> " Rye, Romney, and Hythe, for wealth without health,
>   The Downs for health with poverty ;
> But you shall find both health and wealth
>   From Foreland Head to Knole and Lee."

The river marshes in the north and the Romney Marshes in the south can scarcely be cited for their healthfulness, yet of the greater part of the county it may be said that health and wealth are reconciled together, though the height of the chalky downs suggest more of health than wealth—the rich meadows of the valley of the Medway, the stretching orchards surrounding houses and farmsteads, the extensive fruit gardens in the part of the country nearer London, the many thousands of acres of swaying hops, all point to the wealthfulness of the county—its very nickname of the Garden of England suggests something of the same kind. It looks a rich country as viewed from any of the numerous heights along "the Backbone of Kent" as the southern chalk downs are named, along the northern downs of chalk and greensand, or any of the other elevations by which the whole county is marked, for there is but little level country, with the exception of the flats along the river Thames, the marshes about the estuary of the Stour and the levels recaptured from the sea in the south. Be we where we may, from Sydenham Hill to Dover Castle Hill, from Shooter's Hill to the neighbourhood of Tunbridge Wells, there

is always an eminence from which we may get an extended view
of the well diversified country, though in many parts the
extent of the woods must make the observer wonder where lie
the pasture and arable lands; in other parts orchards or hops
seem to have annexed the country-side.   Of these various hills
we shall say something as we reach their neighbourhood, but of
the Kentish rivers a few words may here be said indicating
their course.   "The river of Thames," as Lambarde terms it,

Bridge over the Medway at Teston, near Maidstone.

belongs to the country rather than to the county; but on its
Kentish banks we shall find Deptford, Greenwich, Woolwich,
Erith, Greenhithe, Gravesend—places of interest and import-
ance all.

   The river of Kent most characteristic of the county is
the "Medway, the bright flowing Medway," which passes
through the most varied scenery.   Entering the county at the
Sussex border, it meanders in a general north-easterly direction,
flows west and north of Tunbridge Wells to Tonbridge and

Maidstone, thence by the ancient battle-ground of Aylesford to the stretch of beautiful country disfigured by cement works, and so to Strood, Rochester and Chatham, and thence by broad, winding reaches to Sheerness and at the estuary of the Thames to its marriage with that river, as celebrated by Edmund Spenser and Michael Drayton. Though Spenser, in one poem, describes the nuptials of Medway and Thames, in another he makes them brethren, where he sings of

> " The salt Medway that trickling streams
> Adown the dales of Kent
> Till with his elder brother Thames
> His brackish waves be blent."

The Medway is notable for being navigable during about two-thirds of its course of sixty miles.

Next in importance to the Medway comes the Stour, or the Great Stour as it is proudly named. As a local singer puts it :

> " Let others sing the Doon and Trent,
> Yet none my lingering thoughts shall lure ;
> I love my own romantic Kent,
> And best I love—the banks of Stour."

One branch of this river rises near Lenham and flows south-easterly, the other—the East Stour—rises near Postling, within about three miles of the south coast, and flows north-westerly. These streams unite at Ashford and flow north-easterly through a picturesque valley of parks and pasture by Chilham and Chartham to Canterbury, and thence by the ancient Fordwich through pleasant country by Sarre, beyond which it is joined by the Little Stour to the Isle of Thanet, and, by a great curve in which it doubles and redoubles on itself past Richborough Castle and Sandwich, it reaches the North Sea at Pegwell Bay, immediately to the south of Ramsgate. Near Sarre the Stour used to branch, one stream going north to the sea east of Reculver, and the other following more or less closely the present course to Pegwell. These two branches from Sarre to the sea used to be known as the Wantsume, or Wantsome, and it was their course which made Thanet an island, a term since the drying up of the northern channel no longer geographically accurate. When Bede wrote this Wantsume was about three furlongs broad, with but two fordable places, but in Lambarde's time (1570) the one branch was so far silted up that it was necessary to asseverate that the persons yet living who had seen vessels pass the whole length of the Wantsume were "right credible." The Little Stour rises in the Elham valley, and after flowing north towards Canterbury turns near Bridge and goes roughly parallel with its greater neighbour until their junction near East Stourmouth.

The Darent, Spenser's

> "Still Darent, in whose waters clean
> Ten thousand fishes play,"

Nov. 5 06

Quebec House, Westerham.

rises near the western limits of the county at Westerham, and after flowing south of the North Downs, passes through a break in the hills at Otford and goes north by Farningham, Darenth and Dartford, joining the Thames a mile and a half east of Erith. The Sussex Rother during a portion of its course is in part a Kentish river, forming the boundary between the two counties for some miles, and there are many tributaries of the larger streams mentioned, and pleasant smaller rivulets which will be more fittingly noticed as we visit them.

From the streams that water our fruitful valleys we may pass to some of the general features of the stream of History as it has passed over the fair land. Of the " five great landings in English History," as Dean Stanley pointed out, the three first and most important probably took place on the shores of Kent —those which first " revealed us to the civilised world and the civilised world to us ; . . . which gave us our English fore-fathers and our English characters ; . . . which gave us our English Christianity." It was on the Kentish coast that Julius Cæsar landed with his Roman soldiery in the year 55 B.C., as every schoolboy knows—exactly where the Roman general landed even the wisest of those whose business it is to add to the schoolboy's knowledge cannot affirm with certainty. The balance of evidence is, however, so much in favour of the neighbourhood of Deal that we may look upon that district with some confidence as being that which first did lie at the proud foot of the conqueror fresh from his achievements in Gaul. Some writers, it is true, think that the landing was effected at Romney Marsh, while others would take the tradition away from Kent altogether and make Sussex the scene of Cæsar's as well as of William of Normandy's landing. The evidence adduced on behalf of the east coast, somewhere between Walmer and the Isle of Thanet, is, however, sufficiently convincing for most people. Cæsar recorded that he found the people of Kent—though they had menaced him at Dover so seriously as to make him seek a landing further north—remarkable for the civility of their manners. "Kent in the commen-taries Cæsar writ is termed the civil'st place of all the isle."

The Roman occupation of over four hundred years left many marks upon our county in the way of roads, while of remains of varied character we learn hither and yon all up and down the county. Five centuries after Cæsar's coming three ship-loads of Saxons under Hengist and Horsa landed at Ebbsfleet and set about the overthrowing of Vortigern. Incidentally it may be remembered that from the banner of the Saxon chiefs Kent takes its distinguishing mark of the rampant white horse. Another hundred and fifty years passed, and at the same spot Augustine and his missionaries landed to begin their peaceful conquest of the country, and to leave in Kent most enduring

marks of their holy zeal, though there have been writers who
refer to Reculver as Augustine's landing plaçe.

Reculver.

When William the Conqueror came and added Norman blood
and influence to the "tide of races" out of which the English

nation was to emerge, the men of Kent offered peace and faithful obedience only on condition that they were permitted to enjoy all their ancient liberties, otherwise " Warr, and that most deadly." The ancient liberties of the county thus preserved included the custom of gavelkind, by which at a man's death his lands were equally divided among his sons, the youngest of whom succeeded to the home. The story of how the men of Kent dictated their terms to the Conqueror is recorded by Lambarde as taken from Thomas Spot, "sometimes a monk and chronicler of St. Augustine at Canterbury," and, as the same quaint old topographer puts it, " I neither well may, ne will at all, stick now eftsoons to rehearse it."

" After such time (saith he) as *Duke William* the *Conqueror* had overthrown King *Harold* in the field, at Battell in *Sussex* and had received the *Londoners* to mercy, he marched with his army toward the castle of *Dover*, thinking thereby to have brought in subjection this Country of *Kent* also. But *Stigande*, the Archbishop of *Canterbury*, and *Egelsine*, the Abbot of St. *Angustines*, perceiving the danger, assembled the *Countrymen* together and laid before them the intolerable pride of the *Normanes* that invaded them and their own miserable condition if they should yield unto them. By which means they so enraged the common people, that they ran forthwith to weapon, and meeting at *Swanscombe*, elected the Archbishop and the Abbot for their Captains. This done, each man got him a green bough in his hand and beare it over his head, in such sort, as when the *Duke* approached, he was much amased therewith, thinking at the first that it had been some miraculous wood that moved toward him, But they, as soon as he came within hearing, cast away their boughs from them, and at the sound of a trumpet bewraied their weapons, and withall despatched towards him a messenger, which spake unto him in this manner :—*The Commons of Kent (most noble Duke) are ready to offer thee either Peace or Warr, at thy own choice and election : Peace with their faithfull Obedience, if thou wilt permit them to enjoy their ancient Liberties ; Warr, and that most deadly, if thou deny it them.*"

These men of Kent bearing green branches might well have suggested to Shakespeare the scene in Macbeth near Birnam Wood, when Malcolm says :—

" Let every soldier hew him down a bough
And hear't before him ; thereby shall we shadow
The numbers of our host and make discovery
Err in report of us."

The men of Kent seemed to have gained their ends, if the pleasant story of the old monk be true, no less surely and less strenuously than did the Scottish soldiers who fulfilled the baneful witches' prophecy to Macbeth.

Of some of the many historic incidents which have taken place within the confines of our county, of some of the great

Between Yalding and Wateringbury

number of great men who were natives of or dwelt in Kent we shall learn as we touch at the towns and villages, castles and fields where they were enacted or where they lived, but a few words may fittingly be said as to the origin of those broad hop-fields, those May-rich stretches of cherry orchards which remain in the memory of so many who know Kent intimately, as of those who know it but casually, as characteristic features of the land.

" Hops and pickerel, carp and beer
Came into England all in a year."

So runs one of the many versions of an old rhyme. The date was some time in the sixteenth century, and since then the hop has become so much acclimatised that it is to be found wild in many parts. Of the half-dozen counties in which the plant is grown extensively for commercial purposes Kent has easily the first place, with between thirty and forty thousand acres devoted to its cultivation. Of the appearance of a hop-field in its various seasons, from the bareness of the winter, the sticking and stringing of the bines to the growing crop, to the fulness of growth when the whole fields are masses of more or

Kentish Orchard.

less orderly tangled bines with their clusters of hanging blooms, to the time when those clustered blooms are gathered by an army of "hoppers," we shall see something again and again along the highways and byways of our county and more especially about the Maidstone district and in the valley of the Medway. Yet the hop is so characteristic that we find fields of it on hillsides and in valleys in all parts, its cultivation being well distributed; and the railway traveller passing through the county, though there may be no hop-fields within sight of the line, may know that where he sees round brick buildings with coned tops and small pointed cowls there is a hop drying place, or oast-house, and that hop-fields are not far away. The name of these oast-houses, it has been said, was introduced with hops from Flanders in the sixteenth century, being an adaptation of the Flemish " buys," but the suggestion, though ingenious, is incorrect, as old records testify that the word " oast " stood for a kiln in Kent long before the hop had been introduced—" lime-oasts " are referred to nearly a couple of centuries before hop-oasts could have been wanted, and the word probably survives in such place-names as Limehouse.

The same may be said of the Kentish orchards of cherry and apple, which we meet with in all parts, though except in spring, when under their light load of indescribable beauty, their extent is not easily recognised. Strawberries, too, are grown over wide tracts of hillside at Orpington, about Cudham, and in other places, while great fields of gooseberries and currants form further extensive plots in this great garden of England.

Rarely, however, has the division into hop-fields and fruit-fields been so extensive as to do more than diversify the scenery ; the " garden " has not become a formal one. It is saved from the curious patchwork effect which we get between Calais and Dunkirk, and in other tracts immediately across the Channel, by its many hedges, and even where there are not broad stretches of woodland or rich parklands, by the many spinneys and coppices, by bold clumps of trees, by the young woodland growths known as springs and springshaws, which are to be seen in all parts. The preservation of game has no doubt been responsible for the conservation of the beauty of much of our scenery, a fact which may be worth remembering when we inveigh against closed woods. So well-wooded does much of our county appear that its richness as agricultural land might almost be overlooked. Its fame, however, in this regard has been long-lived, for, as the old rhyme has it,—

> " A Knight of Cales,
>   A gentleman of Wales
>   And a Laird of the North Countree,
>   A Yeoman of Kent,
>   With his yearly rent,
>   Will buy them out all three.'

Though the yeoman of Kent flourished thus his eldest son was scarcely a man of means, if " The Wooing Song of a

Yeoman of Kent's Sonne " is to be believed. It was a case of
" the son to the plough "—duly given him by his godfather—
and in the song we see how with his house and land and small
beginning of livestock he set more or less peremptorily about
getting a wife. There is an easy pride about the wooing,
which suggests that the youthful farmer knew his value in the
matrimonial market, and if the lady did not choose to have
him—there were others who would.

> " Ich have house and land in Kent,
>   And if you'll love me, love me now ;
> Two-pence half-penny is my rent,—
>   Ich cannot come every day to woo.
> (*Chorus.*) Two-pence half-penny is his rent
>   And he cannot come every day to woo.
>
> Ich am my vather's eldest zonne,
>   My mouther eke doth love me well !
> For Ich can bravely clout my shoone
>   And Ich full well can ring a bell.
> (*Chorus.*) For he can bravely clout his shoone,
>   And he full well can ring a bell.
>
> My vather he gave me a hogge,
>   My mouther she gave me a zow ;
> Ich have a god-vather dwells there by
>   And he on me bestowed a plow.
> (*Chorus.*) He has a god-vather dwells there by
>   And he on him bestowed a plow.
>
> One time Ich gave thee a paper of pins,
>   Anoder time a taudry lace ;
> And if thou wilt not grant me love
>   In truth Ich die bevore thy vace.
> (*Chorus.*) And if thou wilt not grant his love
>   In truth he'll die bevore thy vace.
>
> Ich have been twice our Whitson Lord,
>   Ich have had ladies many vare ;
> And eke thou hast my heart in hold,
>   And in my minde zeemes passing rare.
> (*Chorus.*) And eke thou hast his heart in hold,
>   And in his minde zeemes passing rare.
>
> Ich will put on my best white sloppe
>   And Ich will wear my yellow hose ;
> And on my head a good gray hat
>   And in't Ich sticke a lovely rose.
> (*Chorus.*) And on his head a good gray hat
>   And in't he'll sticke a lovely rose.

Wherefore cease off, make no delay,
　　And if you'll love me. love me now ;
　　Or els Ich zeeke zome oder where, —
　　For Ich cannot come every day to woo.
(*Chorus.*) 　Or els he'll zeeke zome oder where,
　　For he cannot come every day to woo."

The dialect of the song is curiously unlike that of the Kent of to-day, but it may be that it has changed since the verses were written, and also, it is probable that the spelling has been conventionalised by some old-time copyist. The song is said to date back to Tudor times, and to be the original on which was founded the popular Scottish one—" I hae laid a herring in saut."

Before proceeding to wander about our county, it may be well to touch upon a subject on which non-Kentish folk are for ever jarring their more fortunate fellows : What is the difference between "a man of Kent" and a " Kentish man "? This is not a conundrum, nor is the difference merely one of words. It is a question, however, with several answers, and perhaps— unlike the ways of singing tribal lays—not a single one of them is right. One authority tells us that the " men of Kent " are those born within the limits of the diocese of Canterbury, while " Kentish men " are those born within the limits of the diocese of Rochester. The more commonly accepted explanation is, however, that the " men of Kent " are those born east and south of the Medway, while " Kentish men " are those born to the left bank of that river, which cuts the county into two very unequal portions. This explanation may be historical as well as geographical, for, according to some records, the eastern part of Kent was settled by Gothic and the western by Frisian tribes, so that the jealousy may be a survival of ancient rivalry. That it is jealousy may be found by calling an East Kent friend a " Kentish man," or, within the same friend's hearing, referring to one from Sevenoaks as a " man of Kent."

Man of Kent, or Kentish man—under whichever of these banners he is enrolled—the native of the county is proud of his birthplace,—is proud of all that it has stood for in history, of the part which has been played by sons of Kent in all spheres of action ; he is proud not only of the traditions of his county, of the way in which Kent has stood for freedom from the time of William the Norman, but he also likes to recall that it was Kent which led the forlorn Royalist hope against the triumphant Parliamentarians, that it was Kent which—with unpleasant results to the petitioners—petitioned the Government of King William III. to be true to its trust. He also likes to recall that, if his county has won honour in the highways of history, it has also won for the White Horse a proud place in those byways of history which are devoted to sport, and especially in the national game of cricket. The saying that "the Battle of Waterloo was won on the playing-fields of Eton" was true in a wider sense, for the spirit cultivated on cricket field and bowling green has been no small factor in the growth of the British Empire, and it will be a sad day when the tendency to watch games rather than play them shall have struck a blow at the national character. In the games of a country's youth can be read that country's destiny.

CHAPTER II

In Canterbury Cathedral we have something of a natural centre from which to begin our wanderings about Kent—a centre that draws, and has drawn for many centuries, visitors from all parts of the world. In this magnificent pile is summed up in stone the whole history of Christianity from its first coming to England, and here took place one of the most dramatic tragedies in our tragic records, an episode which, though it arose, perhaps, out of the petulance of a monarch impatient of ecclesiastical control, yet had the effect in the long run of welding more closely together Church and State.

There are many ways of approaching the beautiful Cathedral, perhaps the least impressive being that followed by those who arrive in the city by rail It is true that glimpses of the edifice may be had from the train, but they are glimpses not comparable with those views which meet the visitor who approaches by some one or other of the highways or byways, which afford something of a bird's-eye view of the "metropolitical" city, with the Cathedral magnificently dominating the whole. As Erasmus said, the sight is one to strike even those who only see it from a distance with awe.

Perhaps the best approaches—for those who can choose their routes—are the ones from the west to the north-east. From the hill just below the scattered hamlet of Broad Oak, and again from the road at the foot of the hill, near the river Stour, we see the Cathedral stand with bold dignity from amidst the surrounding buildings, its form clearly defined against the distant hills, above the skyline of which is seen the beautiful

Perpendicular Tower—"Angel Steeple" as it was, "Bell Harry" as it is now called.   From the hill above Hackington, on the road leading north to Herne Bay, another fine view of the city as a

Norman Porch, Canterbury.

whole with the Cathedral as the centre is to be had, and another similar one from just below the brow of the hill on the road to Blean where the left side of the road is fringed with a row of old pines through which the Cathedral appears, finely framed.

Another impressive view is that from the road which approaches from the south-west, parallel with the course of the Stour and at a half mile or so from its right bank. Yet another view, and in some regards perhaps the best, is that to be had from the west, above Harbledown, and this is the more interesting in that here we are on the old Pilgrims' Road, and get such a view of the City and Shrine as rewarded pious

Canterbury.

pilgrims from London, or others after their long journeying from Southampton and Winchester, along the middle heights of the northern downs of Surrey and Kent. It was here that such pilgrims as had ridden dismounted, as soon as the Angel Steeple came in view, to complete the journey to the Shrine on foot. The early tower was surmounted by a steeple crowned with a gilt angel. Yet another and a more intimate view, though marred by the prison in the foreground, is to be had from the little hill on which St. Martin's Church stands, half a

The Stour from High Street

mile to the east of the Cathedral. This view aroused the
enthusiasm of Arthur Penrhyn Stanley, when, as Dean of
Canterbury, he wrote those " Historical Memorials of Canterbury," which must be read by all who would know, with any
fulness, the great story of the great building, and his account
may well be borrowed here :

" Let any one sit on the little hill of the little church of St. Martin and
look on the view which is there spread before his eyes. Immediately
below are the towers of the great Abbey of St. Augustine, where Christian
learning and civilisation first struck root in the Anglo-Saxon race, and
within which now, after a lapse of many centuries, a new institution has
arisen, intended to carry far and wide to countries of which Gregory and
Augustine never heard the blessings which they gave to us. Carry your
view on, and there rises high above all the magnificent pile of our Cathedral,
equal in splendour and state to any the noblest temple or church that
Augustine could have seen in ancient Rome, rising on the very ground
which derives its consecration from him. And still more than the grandeur
of the outward buildings that rose from the little church of Augustine and
the little palace of Ethelbert, have been the institutions of all kinds, of
which these were the earliest cradle. From Canterbury, the first English
Christian city ; from Kent, the first English Christian kingdom, has, by
degrees, arisen the whole constitution of Church and State in England
which now binds together the whole British Empire. And from the
Christianity here established in England has flowed, by direct consequence,
first, the Christianity of Germany—then, after a long interval, of North
America—and lastly, we may trust, in time, of all India, and all Austra-
lasia. The view from St Martin's Church is indeed one of the most
inspiriting that can be found in the world ; there is none to which I would
more willingly take any one, who doubted whether a small beginning
could lead to a great and lasting good—none which carries us more
vividly back into the past, or more hopefully forward to the future."

After considering the Cathedral from a distance, we may
well make our way to its precincts and see the beautiful building from near at hand. Entering by the richly sculptured
Christ Church Gate we find ourselves at once within those
precincts with the Cathedral immediately in front of us.
Details of all that is to be seen within and about it must be
sought in a guide-book, which this is not ; such guide-books,
large and small, may be bought at a hundred shops of the city,
or of the old man who stands ready to take charge of bicycles
beneath the ancient gateway of Christ Church, giving on
to the Cathedral. The lofty nave, the beautiful choir, the
various chapels, each with its point of interest, its ancient
tradition, in succession claim our attention as we go to
the pilgrims' steps, by the tomb of that national hero, the

Black Prince, with his helmet and gauntlets, his sword scabbard and surcoat, on which the royal leopards and the *fleur de lys* still show plainly after hanging for over five centuries above the dust of their wearer. We may trace through the ancient cloisters, in which the present seems to fall from us and be

The Cathedral from Christ Church Gate.

one with the past, the way which Thomas à Becket went on that fateful day when hurried from his palace by his devoted monks and pursued by the irate knights. The whole story of the tragedy has been pieced together with graphic fulness from the ancient records in Dean Stanley's work. The four knights of King Henry, "spurred to outrage by a passionate outburst of their master's wrath," had followed the Archbishop

from France to England, and after forcing themselves into his
presence and demanding certain things in the King's name,
went out, armed and returned to find the Churchman had gone
to the Cathedral; following they came up with him as he was
mounting the steps from the transept to the choir. It was
about five o'clock in the afternoon of December 29th, and in the
dim Cathedral the pursuers could not see their prey. " Where
is the traitor Thomas Becket," cried Fitzurse. The Primate
descended the steps again, saying, " Here I am, no traitor, but
a Priest of God." The knights sought to drag him from the
sanctuary of the Cathedral but the Archbishop firmly with-
stood them ; " all the bravery and violence of his old knightly
life seemed to revive in Thomas as he tossed back the threats
and demands of his assailants." Then the blows fell sharp
and sudden, and the whole of Christendom was soon ringing
with the story of the brutal murder of a prince of the Church
in the sacred edifice. A small stone let into the floor is pointed
out for the gratification of those who can realise the scene the
better for that detail, as marking the spot on which the Archbishop fell. The Cathedral has had its burnings and rebuildings
since that momentous day in 1170, but still it is the memory
of à Becket that has left its most enduring mark on Canterbury. His martyrdom and canonisation led to the place
becoming one of the most frequented shrines of Christendom,
and indirectly gave to us our first great national poem in
Chaucer's " Canterbury Tales."

The position of the actual " shrine," which was not that of
the martyrdom, but of the burial place—of which a drawing
is to be seen in the Cottonian MSS.—is pointed out to all
visitors, and the very dints in the stone worn by generations of
devout pilgrims are shown, for " the bricks are alive at this day
to testify, and therefore deny it not " ; but the shrine itself has
long since passed away, though there is, as Dean Stanley pointed
out, still sufficient interest around its ancient site " to require a
full narrative of its rise, its progress, and its fall, in any historical
records of the great Cathedral of which in the eyes of England
it successively formed the support, the glory, and the disgrace.
Such a narrative, worthily told, would be far more than a mere
investigation of local antiquities. It would be a page in one
of the most curious chapters of the history of the human
mind—it would give us a strange insight into the interior

The spot where Becket fell is indicated by the small square stone of the pavement.

working of the ancient monastic and ecclesiastical system, in one of the aspects in which it least resembles anything which we now see around us, either for good or for evil; it would enable us to be present at some of the most gorgeous spectacles, and to meet some of the most remarkable characters of mediæval times : it would help us to appreciate more comprehensively and more clearly some of the main causes and effects of the Reformation."

To the tomb of Becket Richard Cœur de Lion walked all the way, after landing at Sandwich, that he might render thanks "to God and St. Thomas" for his deliverance from his enemies and his success at the siege of Acre ; it was at the same tomb that Louis VII., the first King of France to set foot in England (1179), offered thanks (and jewels) in gratitude for his son's recovery from a dangerous illness.

It was fifty years after the murder that there took place the translation of St. Thomas of Canterbury, which made the shrine become more widely popular. Fire had largely destroyed the edifice shortly after the great tragedy, but the rebuilding had proceeded apace, and for just upon half a century the body of the murdered Primate had lain in the crypt. Two years' notice of the approaching translation was given that people from all parts of the Christian world might attend, and the consequence was that Canterbury witnessed such a sight as, the various chroniclers agree, had never been seen in England before.

The Archbishop Stephen Langton "through the range of his episcopal dominions had issued orders for maintenance to be provided for the vast multitude, not only in the city of Canterbury itself, but on the various roads by which they would approach. During the whole celebration, along the whole way from London to Canterbury, hay and provender were given to all who asked, and at each gate of Canterbury, in the four quarters of the city, in the four licensed cellars, were placed tuns of wine, to be distributed gratis, and on the day of the festival wine ran freely through the gutters of the streets." They did things in a generous fashion in those days, though the debt incurred was such that it took four of Langton's successors to wipe it off. But Canterbury has witnessed many events since then, some of which vied in splendour with the celebration of the translation of the Saint's body to the shrine. Such for example was the enthronisation in 1295 of Archbishop Winchelsey, who, as a boy of humble parentage, had some years before sought a gratuitous education at the school of the city over which he was to rule.

Of the pilgrimages to the Shrine of St. Thomas we have the most lasting and most fascinating account in Chaucer's great work, where we see a representative company setting out from

A Glimpse of Detling on Pilgrim's Road.

Southwark and proceeding in leisurely fashion along the highway to the great centre of attraction on which pilgrims from the east were converging from Sandwich, from the south by the Dover Road and from the west by that Pilgrim's Road which we shall touch again and again on our Kentish byways. The route of London pilgrims undyingly portrayed by the

father of our poesy is indicated by widely separated lines in his
poem :—

> " Lo, Depèford, and it is half wey pryme ;
> Lo, Grenèwych, ther many a shrewe is inne . . .
> Lo ! Rouchestre stant heer faste by ! . . .
> Before I come to Sidenbourne."

At " Boghton-under-Blee " the pilgrims were overtaken by
the Canon's Yeoman and then later comes a reference which

Harbledown Hill.

has greatly puzzled Chaucerian commentators.   Introducing the
Manciple's Tale the poet begins.

> " Woot ye nat where ther stant a litel toun,
> Which that y-cleped is Bobbe-up-and-doun,
> Under the Blee in Caunterbury wey ? "

This has sometimes been taken as meaning Harbledown, and
sometimes, on the strength of there being a field known as
" Up-and-down " in the parish, as meaning Thanington.   In
either case it would seem as though the pilgrims would be so
near the end of their journey as to have been more likely to be
thinking of getting accommodation for the night than having
time for two further stories, yet the description applies so well

to Harbledown that the village is likely to remain identified with the place " ycleped Bobbe-up-and-doun."

Chaucer's " Tales " were written, presumably, about an ordinary company of pilgrims setting out in the springtime of (probably) 1387, possibly spending in leisurely fashion four days on the journey, which now is an easy day's ride for a cyclist, and a mere mouthful of miles to a motor.

> " Whàn that Aprillè with his shourès soote
> The droghte of March hath percèd to the roote,
> And bathèd every veyne in swich licòur
> Of which vertù engendred is the flour ;
> When Zephirus eek with his swetè breeth
> Inspirèd hath in every holt and heeth
> The tendrè croppès, and the yongè sonne
> Hath in the Ram his halfè coursy-ronne,
> And smalè fowelès maken melodye,
> That slepen al the nyght with open eye,—
> So priketh hem Natùre in hir coráges
> Thanne longen folk to goon on pilgrimages,
> And palmeres for to seken straungè strondes,
> To fernè halwès, kowthe in sondry londes ;
> And specially, from every shirès ende
> Of Engèlond, to Caunturbury they wende,
> The hooly blisful martir for to seke,
> That hem hath holpen whan that they were seeke."

Though the poet tells us that in the spring the English folks' fancy lightly turned to thoughts of pilgrimage, Canterbury was a well-honoured shrine all the year round.   More especially was this so in December and July, the anniversaries of the martyrdom and translation.   Then, too, at every fiftieth anniversary, or jubilee of the translation, the celebration was far more numerously attended ; then indulgences were granted to all pilgrims and the festival lasted for a long July fortnight.

Of the many great pilgrimages that took place there are particulars in various chronicles and in the city records.   It was during the fifteenth century that the fame of St. Thomas was at its height, that the old city saw the whole year long a stream of pilgrims reaching flood proportions in July and December.   At the first jubilee after Chaucer's company had visited the shrine, that of 1420—two centuries after the translation—the festival lasted for fifteen days, from noon on St. Thomas's day, and the ancient record tells us that the Bailiffs of the city—William Bailey and William Ickham —

arranged with the townsfolk to make suitable provision for the many expected visitors, in the preparing of lodgings, beds and food in and around the city. The coming of the pilgrims on this occasion meant the crowding into the city of about one hundred thousand men and women, English and foreigners, in addition to the ordinary inhabitants. The "foreigners" included Irish, Welsh, and Scots, and it is interesting in this connection to recall that in Kent a foreigner at the present day signifies anyone who is unlucky enough to belong to the shires, or anywhere other than Kent. When Canterbury was thus invaded by a pious army of a hundred thousand pilgrims we may be sure that it was a merry place during the week of jubilee, for having performed their duties at the Shrine our forefathers turned readily to amusement. So amply were preparations made that the victuallers were enabled to sell Gascony wine and white wine for eightpence a gallon, while they asked but a penny for two loaves. Then must the narrow lanes and streets, the wider "markets" and the suburbs without the walls have been like one great fair.

There were, however, but half a dozen such jubilees, for before 1570 came round Henry VIII. and the "Hammer of the Monasteries" had established the Reformation and done that work of destruction in which the jewelled Shrine of St. Thomas passed from the sight of men. In 1538 it is said that Henry VIII. addressed a summons to "Thomas Becket, some time Archbishop of Canterbury," charging the dead Prelate with treason, contumacy and rebellion, and this summons having been duly read before the Shrine and thirty days having elapsed without the 368-years-dead Churchman having put in an appearance, the case against him was formally argued at Westminster—with the inevitable result. Sentence was duly pronounced that the bones of the contumacious one should be burnt and that the offerings made at the Shrine should be forfeited to the crown.

Great was the change that had come over men in a couple of centuries, for that which was so readily violated in the reign of the eighth Henry had been so guarded in the reign of the second Edward that when a powerful baron, Lord Badlesmere, visited the Shrine in arms, and with armed companions, the outraged citizens informed the King and the nobleman was tried and decapitated for insulting the Shrine by the presence of accoutrements of war. Between the time of Becket's murder and translation came the unhappy rule of King John, whose uneasy conscience made him a frequent visitor to the Shrine. Scarcely a year passed but that monarch came to Canterbury, and from his sojournings there came a romantic tradition showing how

> " Unlearned men hard matters out can find
> When learned bishops princes eyes do blind."

The story as set forth in an olden ballad in the Percy " Reliques " has the novelty of showing us the darkling King John in a pleasant guise.

> " Ile tell you a story, a story so merrye
> Concerning the Abbot of Canterburye."

The Abbot kept up such state that King John sent for him, said that he suspected treason, and that except he could answer three questions his head should be smitten off his body. The hard questions were duly asked and the Abbot craved three weeks in which to find the answers. The King allowed the time limit and the ecclesiastic went off

> "all sad at that word,
> And he rode to Cambridge, and Oxenford ;
> But never a doctor there was so wise,
> That could with his learning an answer devise."

Sadly he rode back to Canterbury with but three days of the three weeks' grace to run ! He met his shepherd, who inquired the news, and on learning his master's sad case said,

> " ' Now cheare up, sire abbot, did you never hear yet,
> That a fool he may learn a wise man witt ?
> Lend me horse, and serving men, and your apparel,
> And I'll ride to London to answere your quarrel.
>
> ' Nay, frowne not, if it hath bin told unto mee,
> I am like your lordship, as ever may bee ;
> And if you will but lend me your gowne,
> There is none shall know us at fair London towne.'
>
> ' Now horses and serving men thou shalt have,
> With sumptuous array most gallant and brave,
> With crozier, and miter, and rochet, and cope,
> Fit to appeare 'fore our fader the pope.'

'Now, welcome, sire abbot,' the king he did say,
'' 'Tis well thou'rt come back to keepe thy day :
For and if thou canst answer my questions three,
Thy life and thy living both saved shall bee.

' And first, when thou see'st me here in this stead,
With my crown of golde so fair on my head,
With all my liege-men so noble of birthe,
Tell me to one penny what I am worth.'

' For thirty pence our Saviour was sold
Amonge the false Jewes, as I have bin told :
And twenty-nine is the worth of thee,
For I thinke thou art one penny worser than hee.'

The king he laughed, and swore by St. Bittel,
' I did not think I had been worth so littel !
—Now secondly tell mee, without any doubt,
How soone I may ride this whole world about?

' You must rise with the sun, and ride with the same
Until the next morning he riseth again ;
And then your grace need not make any doubt
But in twenty-four hours you'll ride it about.'

The king he laughed and swore by St. Jone,
' I did not think it could be gone so soone !
—Now from the third question thou must not shrinke,
But tell me here truly what I do thinke.'

' Yea, that shall I do, and make your grace merry ;
You think I'm the Abbot of Canterbury ;
But I'm his poor shepheard, as plain you may see,
That am come to beg pardon for him and for mee.'

The king he laughed, and swore by the masse,
' He make thee lord abbot this day in his place !'
' Now naye, my liege, be not in such speede,
For alacke I can neither write ne read.'

' Four nobles a weeke, then I will give thee,
For this merry jest thou hast showne unto mee ;
And tell the old abbot when thou comest home,
Thou hast brought him a pardon from good King John.' "

This pleasant story showing that Canterbury had its legends
centuries before that diverting son of the city, Richard Harris
Barham, set about inventing new ones, must not keep us from
the storied stones of the Cathedral. The beauty of the
building to be properly enjoyed should be allowed to sink in

quietly, and that alas is not easy except so far as the nave is concerned. To visit the Shrine, the various chapels and tombs, to penetrate the crypt, to go to the " martyrdom " it is not only necessary to pay, but having paid one is led round by an iterating cicerone who confuses where he would enlighten, who gabbles certain archæological, architectural or other data, and hurries his little flock on to the next view point. The magnificent Cathedral is converted into a mere show-place, to be " done " as quickly as the cicerone can take his party round ; though it may be said that visitors who wish to go round unaccompanied and peacefully can obtain the privilege—by due notice and further payment. The uninteresting way in which all too often the guides who show people over places of interest drone forth their lore was noted by Byron when describing Don Juan's journey from Dover to London—

> " They saw at Canterbury the cathedral ;
>   Black Edward's helm, and Becket's bloody stone,
>   Were pointed out as usual by the bedral,
>   In the same quaint uninteresting tone :—
>   There's glory again for you, gentle reader !   All
>   Ends in a rusty casque and dubious bone,
>   Half solved into these sodas and magnesias,
>   Which form that bitter draught, the human species. "

It is by repeated visits that the magnificence of the structure grows upon us, and we learn to appreciate the beauty and nobility of the whole, the interest of the details. The study of its varied workmanship from Norman times onward needs such repeated visits, the mere enumeration of its attractive features, the events connected with its growth would occupy far more than a chapter of this volume. The more notable tombs include those of the Black Prince and King Henry IV. and his queen, besides a large number of ecclesiastical dignitaries. Among those of the latter something of a morbid interest attaches to that in the eastern transept of Abbot Chichele (1449), giving as it does two effigies of the Abbot, the one as alive in his canonicals and the other as in death ; and to that of Dean Fotherby (1619) with its sculptured mass of skulls and bones. Most curious perhaps of all the tombs is that of Stephen Langton, the Archbishop of Canterbury to whom England owed King John's submission to the terms of Magna Charta—curious not for its form but from

D

its position, half of it being in the Warriors' Chapel, and half of it projecting through the wall.

Among the things which one would like to forget are the gimcrack pulpit in the nave, and the monument to

The West Gate.

Archbishop Temple in " Becket's Crown," where the bronze figure of the kneeling man is set against a toy wall that looks as if it had been designed in children's bricks, or built up of modelling clay ; a striking contrast with another modern monument — the dignified recumbent marble figure of Archbishop Tait.

The cool, low-pitched Norman crypt with its sculptured pillars and its painted crowns of thorns still showing in the roof, has various points of interest, one being the ancient holy-water well which was discovered about five years ago at the eastern end near the Virgin Mary's chapel. Water from this well—with, it was supposed, some of the martyr's blood—was carried away as a precious souvenir by the pilgrims who sought the shrine of St. Thomas, and it is recorded that after Henry II. had performed penance at the temporary grave of à Becket, he carried off with him one of the usual phials. These little bottles, made of lead and worn suspended round the neck, became the " hall mark " of one who had performed the pilgrimage to Canterbury. Another feature of the crypt worthy of more than passing mention is the little chapel built by the Black Prince to commemorate his marriage with Joan, "the Fair Maid of Kent." A quaint stone head in the roof above the organ is pointed out as a " portrait " of the fair Joan.

This chapel in the crypt was later given by Queen Elizabeth to the use of Huguenot refugees—and there every Sunday afternoon a French Huguenot service is still held. An old tradition said that the whole crypt was given over to the foreign weavers, but the tradition is unsupported by any evidence and seems to have no foundation beyond the fact that their religious services were held here. The Black Prince has left his name at a well on the Harbledown Road which he passed on his pilgrimage to the shrine of St. Thomas, and it was at his own desire that he was buried here, though the wish that he should be laid in the crypt was not fulfilled.

There is beautiful stained glass, some of it very old, for not all was destroyed in the days when our Puritan fathers lost their heads and continued the work of destruction begun a century earlier by the burly Defender of the Faith. Richard Culmer —" Blue Dick," as he is nicknamed—parson successively of Goodnestone, Chartham, St. Stephen's, Harbledown, and Minster, all in the Canterbury district, distinguished himself at the time that Laud was a prisoner in the Tower of London, by breaking some of the Cathedral's glass windows, "standing on the top of the city ladder, near sixty steps

high, with a whole pike in his hand, when others would
not venture so high." This feat of vandalism, says Barham

The Nave, Canterbury Cathedral.

in recording it, " the cœrulean worthy called ' rattling down
proud Becket's bones.' " High in the lofty roof above the
place where stood the ancient Shrine is to be seen a golden

crescent, which cannot fail to excite the curiosity of the visitor whose attention is drawn to it. A pretty, but wholly unwarranted, legend accounts for it as a souvenir of the Saracen maid, who, knowing but the words "Gilbert" and "London," found her way from the East to her English lover, and became the mother of Thomas à Becket. A more likely account says that it was the centre from which radiated a number of banners captured in the East, which were hung above the Shrine because St. Thomas was credited with having achieved victory for Richard Cœur de Lion at Acre.

It is a vision of lofty nave, of quaint side chapels, of rich glass old and new, of monuments ranging from the dignity of the fourteenth century to the "taste" of the nineteenth, of a magnificent crypt with quaintly carven pillars, of beautiful cloisters, of a great simple Chapter House with its record of cathedral dignitaries, that we take out with us as we leave the Cathedral to wander about the precincts. Before doing so we may recall portions of Mr. Henry Newbolt's fine poem, "The Building of the Temple (an Anthem heard in Canterbury Cathedral)" [1] :—

The Organ. O Lord our God, we are strangers before Thee, and sojourners, as were all our fathers : our days on the earth are as a shadow, and there is none abiding.

O Lord God of our fathers, keep this for ever in the imagination of the thoughts of Thy people, and prepare their hearts unto Thee.

And give unto Solomon my son a perfect heart to keep Thy commandments, and to build the palace for the which I have made provision.

Boys' voices.   O come to the Palace of Life,
      Let us build it again.
      It was founded on terror and strife,
      It was laid in the curse of the womb,
      And pillared on toil and pain,
      And hung with veils of doom,
      And vaulted with the darkness of the tomb.

Men's voices.   O Lord our God, we are sojourners here for a day,
      Strangers and sojourners, as all our fathers were :
      Our years on the earth are a shadow that fadeth away ;
      Grant us light for our labour, and a time for prayer.

Boys.   But now with endless song,
      And joy fulfilling the Law ;
      Of passion as pure as strong . . .
      Let us build the Palace of Life anew.

---

[1] *The Island Race*, by Henry Newbolt, 1907, p. 121.

Men.	Let us build for the years we shall not see.
Boys.	Lofty of line and glorious of hue
	With gold and pearl and with the cedar tree,
Men.	With silence due
	And with service free,
Boys.	Let us build it for ever in splendour new,
Men.	Let us build in hope and sorrow, and rest in Thee

The quiet lawns about the Cathedral have that air of dignity and peace which we are wont to associate with the precincts of a cathedral or with the quadrangles of an old University. The houses or gardens of the various dignitaries give on to this pleasant space, from which we may contemplate the spacious and beautifully proportioned building, the Bell Harry Tower, still half hidden by the scaffolding of the workmen who have long been engaged in its repair. Passing round the east we come to scraps of ruined walls and noble arches—the remains of part of the old monastery buildings which extended along this side of the Cathedral. Passing through here we come to the " Dark Entry," celebrated by the "legend" which Barham invented to fit the name. The story forms one of the " Ingoldsby Legends," and tells how a merry Canon and his "niece" were poisoned by the Canon's servant, jealous Nell Cook, and how they were buried in one grave by the scandalised monks ; how the cook was put into a vault beneath the paving of the " Dark Entry " ; and furthermore how every Friday night Nell Cook's ghost haunts the place of her interment with fatal effect to those who encounter it.

" A hundred years were gone and past since last Nell Cook was seen,
    When, worn by use that stone got loose, and they went and told the
        Dean.—
    —Says the Dean, says he, ' My Masons three ! now haste and fix it tight ; '
    And the Masons three peep'd down to see, and they saw a fearsome
        sight.

Beneath that heavy paving-stone a shocking hole they found—
It was not more than twelve feet deep, and barely twelve feet round ;
—A fleshless, sapless skeleton lay in that horrid well !
But who the deuce 'twas put it there those Masons could not tell.

And near this fleshless skeleton a pitcher small did lie,
And a mouldy piece of ' kissing crust,' as from a warden-pie !
And Doctor Jones declared the bones were female bones and, ' Zooks !
I should not be surprised,' said he, ' if these were Nelly Cook's.'

It was in good Dean Bargrave's days, if I remember right,
Those fleshless bones beneath the stones these Masons brought to light ;
And you may well in the ' Dean's Chapelle ' Dean Bargrave's portrait
    view,
' Who died one night,' says old Tom Wright, ' in sixteen forty-two !'

And so two hundred years have passed since that these Masons three,
With curious looks, did set Nell Cook's unquiet spirit free ;
That granite stone had kept her down till then—so some suppose,—
—Some spread their fingers out, and put their thumb unto their nose.

But one thing's clear—that all the year on every Friday night,
Throughout that Entry dark doth roam Nell Cook's unquiet Sprite :
On Friday was that Warden-pie all by that Canon tried ;
On Friday died he, and that tidy Lady by his side !

And though two hundred years have flown, Nell Cook doth still pursue
Her weary walk, and they who cross her path the deed may rue ;
Her fatal breath is fell as death ! the Simoom's blast is not
More dire—(a wind in Africa that blows uncommon hot).

But all unlike the Simoom's blast, her breath is deadly cold,
Delivering quivering, shivering shocks unto both young and old,
And whoso in that Entry dark doth feel that fatal breath,
He ever dies within the year some dire, untimely death !"

The "legend" was of course nothing but an ingenious fiction of the humorous "Ingoldsby," but it has probably sent a shiver down the backs of many pedestrians who have had to pass through the Dark Entry on Friday nights, and it has met with severe reprobation at the hands of some dignified writers on the Cathedral who resented the "most unsavoury fashion" in which the clerical humorist wrote his story about the Canterbury precincts.

Now there are but ruined portions of the great Benedictine Monastery of which the Cathedral Church was at one time the neighbour. This monastery, dating as it did from the time of Augustine, grew to a place of great importance with the growing importance of the Archbishops of Canterbury— for those dignitaries dwelt with the monks—and among the ruins remaining are some fine Norman arches, and portions of walls, but scarcely sufficient for the ordinary visitor to reconstruct in imagination the great building where hospitality was given by the monks to distinguished pilgrims visiting the Shrine. To the student of ecclesiastical architecture and lore every foot of the Precincts, as of the building itself, is charged with interest ; but to the ordinary sojourner it is an impression of the whole that remains—of neatly-kept ruins and comfortable looking houses set back in comfortable gardens, all around the warm-grey stone cathedral, every detail of which contributes to the impressive and beautiful dignity of the whole.

Oast House (formerly a Chapel), at Horton, near Canterbury

CHAPTER III

THOUGH, as we approach it, Canterbury is dominated by its Cathedral, and though the story of that Cathedral dominates the story of the city as a whole, yet has that city a very interesting story to tell, a story which is to a very great extent written in stone about its ancient buildings, in its narrow, tortuous streets, its many survivals of mediævalism in architecture, in its old lanes, and their names. That the city stood on the Roman highway which ran from Dover to London, is told to the postman every time he delivers a letter in Watling Street, though there was a town here, it is believed, long before the coming of the conquering legions of Cæsar.

In the old abbey of St. Augustine, in a score of churches, the ecclesiastical history of the place is found recorded with a fulness which affords abundant opportunity of much study to the curious, which shows that even though we ignored the Cathedral we should find this the first centre of Christian influence in England. Indeed, the Abbey of St. Augustine would claim attention first had not the Cathedral overshadowed it, for here we are brought more directly into touch with the bringer of Christianity to England. In the Chronicles of Bede we are told that, when the chronicler wrote, the inscription still to be read on St. Augustine's tomb ran :

" Here resteth the Lord Augustine, the first Archbishop of Canterbury,
Who erewhile was sent hither by blessed Gregory Bishop of the City
of Rome, and being helped by God to work miracles, drew over King

Ethelbert and his race from the worship of idols to the faith of Christ. Having ended in peace the days of his ministry, he departed

Bell Harry Tower from the Dark Entry.

hence seven days before the Calend of June in the reign of the same king, A. D. 605."

After the Dissolution the old abbey was partly used as a royal palace, and later it fell into such a ruinous state that by 1836 it had degenerated into a sort of provincial Vauxhall, as may be seen from the following advertisement :—

OLD PALACE GARDENS, CANTERBURY.

Mr. STANMORE,
(Late of Canterbury Theatre),
Begs most respectfully to inform the inhabitants of Canterbury and its Vicinity that the above Gardens will open under his direction
ON TUESDAY, JULY 31ST, 1836,
and will continue open every
TUESDAY AND THURSDAY EVENING,
during the season upon the principle of
THE ROYAL GARDENS, VAUXHALL,
And trusts these entertainments will give satisfaction and meet with the support it will be his study to deserve. The beauty of the Gardens are known to all, and their appearance will be highly imposing when
ILLUMINATED
with nearly
TWO THOUSAND VARIEGATED LAMPS.
The Concert
will take place in the spacious Orchestra erected in the Gardens, for which
Miss MEARS,
of the Theatre Royal, Covent Garden, and Drury Lane, and
Mr. WARREN,
Late of Royal Gardens, Vauxhall, and several other professional persons are engaged.

A part of the gardens will be appropriated to
DANCING,
And will be open to the Public without any extra charge and for which
A FULL QUADRILLE BAND IS ENGAGED.
Mr. Stanmore is making arrangements with numerous performers for
SINGING and DANCING,
SLACK and TIGHT-ROPE DANCING,
GYMNASTIC EXERCISES,

And every kind of amusement suitable for Gardens also
with
Mr. Fenwick the celebrated artist in fireworks, who will
have the honor of firing during the season of which due
notice will be given.

ADMISSION :

One Shilling each Person.   Children under twelve years
of age half-price.

Gardens open at Half-past Seven.   Performance to com-
mence at Eight.

This hand-bill—eloquent testimony to the taste of the nineteenth century at its worst—is preserved at the fine Missionary
College which a dozen years later was opened on the site, the
old building being preserved and restored with reverent care.
Some of the ruins are still to be seen at the back of the college,
but the place is changed beyond all recognition since a certain
picnic party came from Tappington Everard to inspect the
ruins.   On this occasion such talk took place as all too
often does take place when those who think they should be
interested in antiquities pretend that they are.   Ingoldsby
records the visit in an admirable bit of fooling.   For " Bolsover " of course we should read St. Augustine.

"To souls so congenial, what a sight was the magnificent ruin of
Bolsover ! its broken arches, its mouldering pinnacles, and the airy tracery
of its half-demolished windows.   The party were in raptures ; Mr.
Simpkinson began to meditate an essay, and his daughter an ode ; even
Seaforth, as he gazed on these lonely relics of the olden time, was betrayed
into a momentary forgetfulness of his love and losses ; the widow's eye-
glass turned from her *cicisbeo's* whiskers to the mantling ivy ; Mrs. Peters
wiped her spectacles ; and ' her P.' supposed the central tower ' had once
been the county jail.'   The squire was a philosopher, and had been there
often before, so he ordered out the cold tongue and chickens.

' Bolsover Priory,' said Mr. Simpkinson, with the air of a connoisseur,
—' Bolsover Priory was founded in the reign of Henry the Sixth, about the
beginning of the eleventh century.   Hugh de Bolsover had accompanied
that monarch to the Holy Land, in the expedition undertaken by way of
penance for the murder of his young nephews in the Tower.   Upon the
dissolution of the monasteries, the veteran was enfeoffed in the lands and
manor, to which he gave his own name of Bowlsover, or Bee-owls-over (by
corruption Bolsover),—a Bee in chief, over three Owls, all proper, being the
armorial ensigns borne by this distinguished crusader at the siege of Acre.'

' Ah ! that was Sir Sidney Smith,' said Mr. Peters ; ' I've heard tell of
him, and all about Mrs. Partington, and——'

' P., be quiet, and don't expose yourself !' sharply interrupted his lady.
P. was silenced, and betook himself to the bottled stout.

'These lands,' continued the antiquary, 'were held in grand serjeantry by the presentation of three white owls and a pot of honey——'

'Lassy me ! how nice,' said Miss Julia.   Mr. Peters licked his lips.

'Pray give me leave, my dear—owls and honey, whenever the king should come a rat-catching into this part of the country.'

'Rat-catching !' ejaculated the squire, pausing abruptly in the mastication of a drumstick.

'To be sure, my dear sir : don't you remember that rats once came under the forest laws—a minor species of venison?   "Rats and mice and such small deer," eh?—Shakspeare, you know.   Our ancestors ate rats ("The nasty fellows !" shuddered Miss Julia in a parenthesis) ; and owls, you know, are capital mousers——'

'I've seen a howl,' said Mr. Peters ; 'there's one in the Sohological Gardens,—a little hook-nosed chap in a wig,—only its feathers and——'

Poor P. was destined never to finish a speech.

'*Do* be quiet !' cried the authoritative voice, and the would-be naturalist shrank into his shell, like a snail in the 'Sohological Gardens.'

'You should read Blount's *Jocular Tenures*, Mr. Ingoldsby,' pursued Simpkinson.   'A learned man was Blount.   Why, sir, his Royal Highness the Duke of York once paid a silver horse-shoe to Lord Ferrers——'

'I've heard of him,' broke in the incorrigible Peters ; 'he was hanged at the old Bailey in a silk rope for shooting Dr. Johnson.' "

The veritable gatherings from history and the comments thereon were continued further, and may be read in the no less veritable record of the doings of " The Spectre of Tappington."

A little to the east of St. Augustine's stands on its eminence St. Martin's Church, originally built during the Roman occupatiou, the church in which Queen Bertha, the Christian wife of Ethelbert, worshipped, and in which it is probable that the King was baptized after the coming of Augustine.   The feelings of those with a sense of antiquity may well be deeper here than at the neighbouring Abbey and Cathedral, for here we are in touch with Christianity as it had reached this country before the coming of the great missioner.   On this hill stood many of the Roman villas in the days when the City of the men of Kent was the *Durovernum* of the invaders, and much Roman material is utilised in the older parts of the building, which has many features of interest to the archæologist and ecclesiologist, though it is by its ancient traditions that the building appeals first to most visitors, and then by the beauty and quiet of it, as we walk about the trim graveyard with its ancient yews and its wealth of blossoms among the crowded gravestones, its neat paths like a garden.   At the east side is a raised terrace where we can sit and muse and, recalling Dean Stanley's words already quoted, admire the distant view over St. Augustine's to the Cathedral, somewhat spoiled in the foreground by modern houses and the ugly severity of the county gaol.

Mr. Wombwell, the great menagerie man, must have known how Mr. Stanmore had been allowed to treat the ruined abbey outside the eastern-walls of the city in 1836, when he in 1859 proposed to visit Canterbury and finding the ancient West Gate not quite high enough to allow the passing through it of his elephant-drawn cars, had the impudent assurance to petition

The West Gate, Canterbury.

the Mayor and Corporation, to be allowed to pull it down. That the confidence with which such a request could be preferred was not over-extravagant in the mid-nineteenth century is shown by the fact that the Corporation gravely debated this petition and that on a division the gate was only saved from destruction by the casting vote of the mayor. This old gate—now well looked after, though it is not many years since it stood a picture of piteously neglected age — is the only one remaining of the seven gates which gave admittance to the well-walled city. Just without it runs the main stream of the Stour with patient disciples of old Izaak frequently angling from the parapet of the bridge ; and not always unsuccessfully, for I have watched an excited youth play and land, to the admiration of his fellows, a plump trout of about a foot in length.   Up to the eighteenth century all the gates and most of the wall were standing ; now there remain but portions of the wall to the east of the Cathedral and by the Dane-John—with close-grown lawns where the old ditch was,

The West Gate from Within.

and fruit trees growing up the ancient flint walls.   Enough remains however to show that Canterbury must have been a notable stronghold in mediæval times, but the city's " expatiations," as old Fuller puts it, beyond the walls, and the changed temper of the times, long since made the walls nothing but an interesting survival.

Intramural Canterbury was but little more than half a mile across from east to west and north to south, and rather less than half a mile at its narrowest from the West Gate to

where St. George's Gate stood. Within this square half mile
or so of city are gathered buildings so many and so charged
with ancient tradition that the visitor making a stay of
some time in the neighbourhood should take as guide some
volume such as that by Dr. J. Charles Cox. For the more
hurried passer-by there is but a general impression of irregular
streets with shops and houses with quaint gables, with strange
bowed, rounded and square projecting windows, with upper
floors bulging over the lower in the old Tudor style. It
may be doubted whether any other square half mile of the
country can show so great a variety of ecclesiastical and
domestic architecture and can awaken such varied traditions.
We may see little (unless we visit the Museum) of the remains of
the Roman occupation, the early Christian period is only pointed
out in bits of walls and portions of old buildings, but the Norman
flinty Keep of the Castle gives us some idea of the aspect of the
place about eight centuries ago ; though the way in which it
is neighboured by small houses and by the harmful, necessary
gas-works has gone far to debase it. According to Leland
" the most anncyent building of the towne appeareth yn the
castel," but the nineteenth century not only allowed the gas-
works to be erected close to that same castle, but even gave
over the great keep to the Gas Company by way of " coal shed."
The reproach dates back to the time of Thomas Ingoldsby—
from whom there is no escaping in East Kent—for in the
legends of that worthy we read :—

> " The keep, I find, 's been sadly alter'd lately,
>   And, 'stead of mail-clad knights, of honour jealous,
> In martial panoply so grand and stately,
>   Its walls are filled with money-making fellows,
> And stuff'd, unless I'm misinformed greatly,
>   With leaden pipes, and coke, and coals and bellows ;
> In short, so great a change has come to pass,
> 'Tis now a manufactory of Gas."

Well might visitors to the metropolitical city despair of citizens
who could turn the ancient abbey into a dancing saloon, could
contemplate pulling down an ancient monument for the con-
venience of a travelling showman, and make of a fine Norman
Keep a coal shed. As, however, better feelings prevailed in the
case of St. Augustine's and the West Gate, so have they done
in that of the Castle. Coal, I understand, has been given notice

to quit, and the ancient edifice is, it is hoped, before long to be
added to the public monuments of the city as a fitting neighbour
to the Dane-John, that curious conical mound of supposed pre-
historic origin which rises just within the walls near the southern
railway station, and in the shadow of which is raised Canterbury's
latest monument, that to the soldiers of East Kent who fell in

Old House in St. Dunstan's Street.

the South African War—the oldest and newest of Canterbury's
memorials thus closely neighbouring each other.

Canterbury might almost be described as a city of byways.
It is true that it has a High Street, and that St. Dunstan's Street,
Wincheap Street, Longport Street, some of the ways by which
we approach, are broad, but once within the old city the highways have dwindled into more interesting byways, the very High
Street itself, with its plate-glass shopfronts beneath overhanging
upper storeys and quaint gables, has more of the old than the

E

new about it ; while in the rambling side streets and lanes is endless variety of attraction.   Here we may visit the birthplace of
Christopher Marlowe, the residence of Richard Lovelace (the
beautiful thirteenth century Greyfriars' House bridging a
branch of the Stour), the birthplace of Thomas Sidney Cooper (in
St. Peter's Street), which the veteran artist gave to the city when
founding the Sidney Cooper School of Art ; we may visit in
St. Mildred's Church the place where Izaak Walton—whom
it is pleasant to meet more than once in our Kentish wanderings
—was married in 1620 to Rachael Floud.   Another Canterbury
worthy to be recalled is Stephen Gosson, the poet, player, and
playwright, who turned and rended the playhouse, players, and
plays.   The memory of Marlowe's association is perpetuated
by a monument close to the Christ Church Gate—a graceful
monument which does not harmonise with the massy stone
gateway, a monument still wanting statuettes in three of its
four niches, and a monument made hideous by the gimcrackery
lamps which stand at its four corners.   Here of old stood the
Butter Market, and when it was decided to demolish the edifice
as "unsafe," the oak beams by which the roof was supported
could not be removed until dragged down by teams of horses !
as old inhabitants who regret the march of improvement are
delighted to tell.

Leaving fact for fiction scarcely less real, we may follow the
way that little David Copperfield went, first on the penniless
tramp at the end of which he made himself known to his aunt,
and later when the worthy Betsy Trotwood drove the grey
pony and chaise from Dover to take the rehabilitated David,
re-named Trotwood, to school.   It was many years ago, but
the hand of "improvement" has happily lain but lightly on
Canterbury, and Dickensians may well seek to identify Mr.
Wickfield's house described by Boz with such minute faith-
fulness.

" I asked for no more information about Mr. Wickfield, as she offered
none, and we conversed on other subjects until we came to Canterbury,
where, as it was market-day my aunt had a great opportunity of insinuating
the grey pony among carts, baskets, vegetables and hucksters' goods.   The
hair-breadth turns and twists we made, drew down upon us a variety of
speeches from the people standing about, which were not always com-
plimentary ; but my aunt drove on with perfect indifference, and I dare
say would have taken her own way with as much coolness through an
enemy's country.

" At length we stopped before a very old house bulging out over the road ; a house with long, low lattice windows bulging out still farther, and beams with carved heads on the ends bulging out too, so that I fancied the whole house was leaning forward, trying to see who was passing on the narrow pavement below.   It was quite spotless in its cleanliness.   The old-fashioned brass knocker on the old-fashioned door, ornamented with carved garlands of fruit and flowers, twinkled like a star ; the two stone steps descending to the door were as white as if they had been covered with fair linen ; and all the angles and corners, and carvings and mouldings, and quaint little panes of glass, and quainter little windows, though as old as the hills, were as pure as any snow that ever fell upon the hills.

" When the pony-chaise stopped at the door, and my eyes were intent upon the house, I saw a cadaverous face appear at a small window on the ground floor (in a little round tower that formed one side of the house) and quickly disappear.   The low arched door then opened and the face came out."

If Dickens made a composite picture for his house he might well have taken "the beams with carved heads on the ends bulging out" from the beautiful old house at the corner of Broad Street and Lady Wotton's Green.   Canon Benham unhesitatingly identifies the place : " I avow that I have no doubt as to Mr. Wickfield's house.   There it is, halfway up the High Street."   The makers of picture postcards represent another residence without the West Gate.

The face that came out to admit Miss Trotwood and her nephew was, of course, that of the "humblest person going"— Uriah Heep—and having sought to identify the house with the carved beam outside so uncommonly like Uriah, the follower in the steps of Copperfield may look among other houses for "a humble abode" such as that in which David had tea with the Heeps, mother and son, and may then seek the little inn —by some identified as the "Sun"—where Mr. and Mrs. Micawber put up after they had come to see if there might be an opening for a man of Wilkins Micawber's talents in the Medway coal trade.   They found that the coal trade on that river might require talent, but it certainly required capital—a thing very shy of turning up where Mr. Micawber was about.

To return again from the fascinations of fiction to fact, mention must be made of the old house in which we have a relic of the Continental weavers who came hither in Elizabeth's time, and made Canterbury flourish anew by its manufacture of various woven stuffs.   It is true that of the Walloons from the Spanish Netherlands, who first settled here, there were said to be only eighteen householders besides children and servants, but "the Queen, as a further mark of her favour, in 1568 granted to them *the undercroft of the cathedral church*, as a place of worship for themselves and their successors. After which, the persecution for religion still continuing abroad, the number of these refugees multiplied so exceedingly that in 1634 the number of communicants in the *Walloon* Church was increased to 900 ; and there was calculated to be of these

Where Mr. Micawber stayed in Canterbury.

refugees in the whole kingdom 5,213, who were employed in instructing the *English* in weaving silk, cotton, and woollen goods ; in combing, spinning and making different kinds of yarns, worsted, crewels, etc., etc. At the beginning of King Charles II.'s reign, anno 1665, there were in Canterbury 126 master weavers, their whole number here amounting to near 1,300, and they employed 759 *English* ; so that the King thought proper to grant them a charter in 1676, by which it appears that their number here was then but little short of 2,500." Twenty years later came the Revocation of the Edict of Nantes, and some 5,000 French Protestants are said to have come to this country. "Great numbers of these came to *Canterbury*, and joined themselves to the *Walloon* Church, and by their industry the wealth of this place increased considerably; it became more populous; the poor, even to their children, found a constant employment, and the owners of houses finding sufficient tenants for them, and their rents increased. were induced to rebuild or to add great improvements to them, much to their own emolument and the public welfare of the city." By the end of the eighteenth century silk-weaving had largely moved to Spitalfields, and the industry had been so much affected by the improved making of printed muslins and chintzes in other places that the number of those engaged in weaving here had been greatly reduced. As weaving declined, however, an old county historian tells us, the cultivation of hops increased, and the hops from the Canterbury district, he adds, were highly esteemed by the London brewers for their great strength, "doing more execution in the copper than those of any other district." To-day the old weaving industry is represented by the many-gabled building overhanging one branch of the Stour, where visitors may see something of the old home-weaving still carried on, and may see a delightful old house, one of the most picturesque of its kind remaining, but so neat and well looked after with its flower-grown window-boxes as to suggest the sham mediævalism of the "Old London" of some years ago. The window-boxes give a pleasant bit of colour to the view of those who pause on the bridge and look down the stream, but they are something of an anachronism. Tudor folk did not indulge in such decorative "hints that nature lives." Opposite the Canterbury Weavers is a house bridging the stream, and here we have one of the many ancient hospital foundations in which the city is rich, though they have mostly been rebuilt.

Wandering about the many lanes and streets of Canterbury, with its numerous churches, its quaint irregular houses, "bulging," as Dickens has it, and gabled, it is not difficult to realise something of its past when the ways were thronged with pilgrims, when friars and monks were to be met with everywhere in the miry and unpaved thoroughfares. It was near the end of the fifteenth century that the King kindly empowered the Mayor and Corporation to pave the streets *at*

Mercery Lane.

the charge of the inhabitants thereof.   On the dissolution of St. Augustine's Monastery, about half a century later, say the city records of 1542, "the city was supplied with building and paving stones from its ruins on paying a trifle to the gatekeeper."

The memories of the old place are many and varied. Hither, when the burly Henry VIII. was contemplating marriage with Anne Boleyn, was ·brought Elizabeth Barton, the Holy Maid of Kent, to set men, lay and cleric, marvelling, later at Tyburn to pay the penalty of her "visions" and of the folly of the credulous who would have employed her as tool to their own ends.   She was a maid-servant from Aldington who saw visions, and professed to be divinely inspired in her utterances against the King's projected marriage.   Examined by ecclesiastical authorities, she was at first made much of, but her seeings and sayings were not to the temper of Henry and Cromwell, and she and some of her supporters were duly executed.

On February 19th, 1623, there set out from Dover across the narrow seas a notable party of five adventurers, consisting of "Thomas and John Smith" (*i.e.* Charles, Prince of Wales, and the Marquess—after Duke—of Buckingham), Sir Richard Graham, Sir Francis Cottington, Secretary, and Mr. Endymion Porter, "Bed-chamber servant of Confidence to his Highness," though the trouble met with in passing through Canterbury bid fair to stop the little expedition.   The Prince was going off on a secret adventure that he might see the Spanish Infanta, with whom there was some idea of his marrying.   With the whole escapade we have here little concern, but the adventurous journey across Kent may be cited as a pleasant bit of county lore pieced together after much research by that good man of Kent, Sir Henry Wotton.   Cottington and Porter having been sent ahead to provide a vessel at Dover, the others, "with disguised beards and with borrowed names," set out from Buckingham's Essex seat on February 18th.

"When they passed the River against *Gravesend*, for lack of Silver, they were fain to give the Ferry Man a piece of two and twenty shillings, which struck the poor fellow into such a melting tenderness, that so good Gentlemen should be going (for so he suspected) about some quarrel beyond Sea, as he could not forbear to acquaint the Officers of the Town with what had befallen him, who sent presently Post for their stay at *Rochester*, through which they were passed before any intelligence could arrive.   On the brow of the Hill beyond that City, they were somewhat perplexed by espying the

French Ambassador, with the King's Coach and other attending him, which made them baulk the beaten road, and teach Post-Hackneys to leap Hedges. At *Canterbury*, whither some voice (as it should seem) was run on before, the Mayor of the Town came himself to seize on them, as they were taking fresh Horses, in a blunt manner, alleadging first a Warrant to stop them, from the Councel, next from Sir *Lewis Lewkner* Master of the Ceremonies, and lastly from Sir *Henry Manwaring*, then Lieutenant of *Dover-Castle*. At all which confused fiction, the Marquess had no leisure to laugh, but thought best to dismask his Beard, and so told him, that he was going covertly with such slight company, to take a secret view (being Admiral) of the forwardness of his Majesties Fleet, which was then in preparation on the narrow Seas : This, with much ado, did somewhat handsomely heal the disguisement. On the way afterwards, the Baggage Post-Boy, who had been at Court, got (I know not how) a glimmering who they were ; but his mouth was easily shut. To *Dover*, through bad Horses, and those petty impediments, they came not before six at night."

That the disguised Prince and his companions got through to Dover with no further trouble was probably owing to the fact that news of their escapade was little likely to get ahead of them in days when communication was necessarily slow. Indeed, in 1637, as we learn from that maker of many books, John Taylor the Water Poet, Canterbury had regular communication with London but twice a week : "The Foot Post of Canterbury doth come every Wednesday and Saturday to the sign of the Two-Necked Swan at Summers Key, near Billingsgate."

A quarter of a century after his escapade, when the Prince, become King, had nearly reached the tragic close of his struggle with his people, it was Canterbury that made the last attempt on behalf of the old order against the new, though it must be said that it was not altogether devotion to the monarch which gave rise to the Petition of Kent and the subsequent insurrection. The good people of Canterbury were greatly annoyed at the Puritan ordinances, which forbade the celebrating of Christmas, and determined to do as they had done before, and duly arranged for a service on Christmas Day, 1647, "a heinous offence in those times of reformation," says the contemporary historian "of that Honorable though Unfortunate Expedition," who was himself a participator. The service was duly held at St. Andrew's Church, "where the Reverend Mr. Allday, then resident minister of the parish, preached a sermon suitable to the day, a thing then so much out of use that the people began to forget that Christ was ever born, as well as the celebration of His birth." The "new saints" tried by external disturbance to drown the speaking within. The mayor sought to persuade the people to open their shops, and on one tradesman expostulating with him, struck the first blow. Tumult followed, until a certain barber, " a man swelled as full of ungodly schismatical principles of rebellion as a toad with poison," shot some one, and the tumult was only stayed by agreement between the leaders of the two parties.

In a " Perfect Diurnal " of Parliament under the date of December 30th, 1647, it is recorded that a letter had been received that day out of Kent, from some of the committee of the said county, acquainting the House with "the great riot that was at Canterbury on Saturday last." A week later the trouble had abated, only to be aroused afresh by the arrival of an armed body of troops, and later by the special commission sent by Parliament to try the offenders. The Grand Jury not only ignored the bill but " composed upon the spot a petition to Parliament, which, to my mind, was worthy of ' unconquered Kent,' and of a people whose ancestors always claimed the right to march in the van of the English army."[1]

Out of this disturbance thus rose the Petition of the Men of Kent, which was forbidden to be presented, and thus led to the petitioners forming a resolution that it should be presented if necessary with sword in hand, and so to the military expedition, which was finally crushed at Colchester, in Essex. The men of Kent claimed the right to petition Parliament, but had less success than when they parleyed sword in hand with William of Normandy. The "Petition" was simple in expression, but for the time was marked by a boldness which could but irritate those who had grown tired of " treating " with their Sovereign. It ran :—

"To the Right Honorable the Lords and Commons assembled in Parliament at Westminster.

The Humble PETITION of the Knights, Gentry, Clergy, and Commonalty of the County of KENT subscribed by the Grand Jury on the 11th of May, 1648, at the Sessions of the Judges, upon a Special Commission of Oyer and Terminer, held at the Castle of Canterbury, for the said County.
SHEWETH
That the deep sense of our own miseries, with a fellow-feeling of the dis-

---

[1] Colonel Colomb, F.S.A., *Arch. Cantiana*, xi.31–49.

contents of other Counties exposed to the like sufferings, prevaileth with us, thus humbly to present to your Honors these our ardent desires.

I. That our most Gracious Sovereign Lord ᛕing CHARLES, may with all speed be admitted in safety and honor, to treat with his two Houses of Parliament, for the perfect settling of the peace, both of Church and Common Wealth, as also of his own just Rights together with those of the Parliament.

II. That for prevention and removal of the manifold Inconveniences, occasioned by the continuance of the present Army, under the command of the Lord Fairfax, their Arrears may be forthwith audited, and they disbanded.

III. That according to the fundamental Constitution of this Common Wealth, we may for the future be governed and judged by the English Subjects undoubted birth-right, the known and established Laws of the ᛕingdom, and not otherwise.

IV. That, according to the Petition of our Right, our Property may not be invaded by any Taxes or Impositions whatsoever; and particularly, that the heavy burthen of Excise may no longer be continued, or hereafter imposed upon us.

All which our earnest desires, we humbly recommend to your serious considerations, not doubting of that speedy satisfaction therein which the case requires, and we humbly expect. Whereby we may hope to see (what otherwise we cannot but despair of) a speedy and happy end of those Pressures and Distempers, whose continuance will inevitably ruin both ourselves and posterities. Your timely prevention whereof, by a mutual agreement to what we here propose, in order thereunto, shall oblige us ever to pray."

The men of Kent struggled unavailingly for their petition in 1648, and again half a century later, as we learn at Maidstone.

Of the rioting at Canterbury some fun was made in Hudibrastic verse by a partisan of Parliament, who affected to believe that it was for the good cheer of Christmas rather than for the King and their rights as freemen that the men of Kent rose. The verses appeared in a quaint contemporary news-sheet.

"Verses by Mr. Egerton on certain men of Canterbury, declaring themselves for God, ᛕing Charles, and ᛕent, January, 1648.

"The roast-meat men of Canterbury,
Counting it no small injury
To lose their spiced broth, and their pies,
Their wassails and their fooleries,
Resolved ere Christmas went away
They would some uncouth gambol play;
For now debar'd of their good cheer,
They took the double size in beer:
And now so long they sit and fuddle,
'Till each agreed to broach his noddle
Then one saith this, another that,

And the third he talks he knows not what.
'Till one upstart, whose nose to handle
Had often saved them fire and candle,
And he in broken sense relates
The wrong to be debar'd their cates ;
And tells them if they do not rise
To right plum-pottage, and mince-pies,
Hereafter may things never whittle,
And the plum-pottage burn the kettle,
And may each bak'd meat (heaven forbid)
Lose both the bottom and the lid.
At this each swain lift up his snout
And wrath incensed all the rout :
And now away the clowns do reel,
And out of doors each one doth wheel ;
He gets a mattock or a rake,
A third will need his coulter take,
And all with an inspired rage,
Set forth in martial equipage.
Fear now upon the townsmen falls,
To see these frantic bachannals ;
They lock their doors, but to no end,
The madmen do them open rend,
And he that hath not broth or pie,
Within his lard or buttery,
Was surely bangèd, back and head,
And all his chattels forfeited.
But to prohibit this wild course
Out comes the Mayor on his horse ;
But they of him stand in no awe,
His crown is crack't, he doth withdraw ;
And thus, elated with success,
They needs will further yet transgress.
For God, and for King Charles, they cry,
Plum-pottage and sweet Christmas pie ;
But out, alas ! this did no good.
Their language was not understood.
And now these birds in cages sing,
Wee'l no more Christmas revelling."

Though largely a place of old traditions, Canterbury has so much to show within its limits that makes those traditions real that to the visitor with a sense of antiquity its every street has something of interest, from whichever side the city is approached. Its air is one of comfortable prosperity allied with age. It is true that some of the outlying thoroughfares, some of the poorer districts, may be dingy, but these are small portions of the whole ; it is true that we carry away impressions of ugly barracks as well as of quaint streets, of irregular-sized, many·

St. John's Hospital.

gabled, and bow- and bay-windowed houses, but they are by no
means dominating features. He is unfortunate who first

approaches the city by the Northgate leading out to Thanet, for it is the most uninteresting way, lined on the one hand by military barracks and on the other by a dull river-side suburb. It is true that as a military station Canterbury first comes into history in the time of the Roman occupation, but the barracks of to-day are wanting in beauty themselves, and have not about them the glamour of the old and but half known.

It is a city of many churches, of many " hospitals " and alms-houses, of narrow byways, of quaint houses and of illimitable traditions ; a city set amid hills, amid woodlands and hopfields ; a city in which past and present join hands without anything jarring in the alliance. It is true that Canterbury's latest historian has suggested that motors—"those throbbing, noisy, evil-smelling machines "—should be left outside the city, as their presence is "a vulgar and irreverent anachronism." But the view is that of the zealous antiquarian, who forgets that a city is not only a kind of object for a national museum, but a living entity, and that it is in the freshness of life, in its adaptation to, and recon-ciliation with, the spirit of the time that a place like Canterbury at once excites our reverent admiration and compels our affection.

In the days of the Pilgrims few folk reached the confines of the city unless on foot—if they rode thither they dismounted when the Angel Steeple of the Cathedral came in sight, and so, no doubt, it might be thought that chaises, carriers' waggons and coaches successively were "anachronisms," to say nothing of the railway, but that, it is true, is without the limits of the ancient walls, yet these various improvements in locomotion have not harmed the city. When motorists, remembering the showman's nearness to success in his desire to demolish the West Gate, wish the old streets widened and straightened, it will be time enough to protest against vulgarity and irreverence. To object to their admission to the ancient thoroughfares is worse than objecting to the illumination by gas and electric light of the venerable buildings that were anciently lighted by torches and candles.

Kent has long been famous as a cricketing county, and " Canterbury week," at the beginning of August, is so notable a feature of the season that it cannot but be amusing to some readers to recall a great contest that once took place here. About a hundred and fifty years ago one James Love, whose enthusiasm for the game was greater than his genius as a poet, wrote "An Heroic Poem" on cricket, which he concluded prophetically with

"And now the Sons of Kent compleat the Game,
And firmly fix their everlasting Fame,"

showing clearly enough that he knew the county would, in 1906, establish its position as champion. In July, 1773, however, it was the noblemen and gentlemen of Kent and Surrey who met in the neighbourhood of Canterbury in friendly rivalry, and the three days' match roused considerable interest, though Kent, it must be confessed, made but a bad second, as we see from the account given in the *Kentish Gazette*:

"The following is a List of the Noblemen and Gentlemen Cricketers, who played on Monday, Tuesday, and Wednesday last in Bourn-Paddock, Surry against Kent, for Two Thousand Pounds :

Those marked thus B were bowled out ; C catched out.

SURRY.

Names.	Out by whom.	1st.	Out by whom.	2d.
Lord Tankerville	B. out by May	o	C. out by Mr Davis	3
Mr Bartholomew	C. out by Simmons	3	B. out by Miller	10
Mr Lewis	B. out by the Duke	o	Last Man in	21
Mr Stone	B. out by the Duke	12	B. out by Miller	24
Stevens alias Lumpey	B. out by Miller	6	B. out by Miller	8
John Woods	C. out by Sir H. Mann	6	C. out by R. May	6
Palmer	C. out by Mr Davis	22	C. out by the Duke	38
Thomas White	B. out by the Duke	5	C. out by Mr Hussey	60
Valdin	Last Man in	17	B. out by the Duke	1
Childs	B. out by May	o	B. out by the Duke	3
Francis	B. out by the Duke	5	C. out by Wood	36
	Byes	1	Byes	7
		77		217

KENT.

Names.	Out by whom.	1st.	Out by whom.	2d.
Duke of Dorset	B. out by Woods	25	B. out by Woods	1
Sir Horace Mann	B. out by Woods	3	C. out by L. Tankerville	22
Mr Davis	B. out by Woods	4	C. out by Mr. Lewis	o
Mr Hussey	Last Man in	o	B. out by Woods	o
Miller	C. out by Valdin	13	Run out	10
Simmons	B. out by Lumpey	5	C. out by Yaldin	4
R. May	B. out by Woods	o	Last Man in	o
Thomas May	B out by Lumpey	4	C. out by Childs	5
Louch	C. out by Mr Stone	5	B. out by Lumpey	26
Pattenden	C. out by Mr Lewis	o	B. out by Lumpey	1
Wood of Seale	C. out by Woods	1	C. out by Mr Bartholomew	9
	Byes	3	Byes	o
		63		78

The third Duke of Dorset, who did yeoman service on behalf of the county which, as plain Mr. Sackville, he had represented in the House of Commons and of which he was Lord Lieutenant, is remembered in the cricketing field as a member of the Hambledon Club, and as one of the committee that drew up the original laws of the M.C.C. Sir Horace Mann was Sir Horatio Mann, of Bishopsbourne, "the King of Cricket," who did not succeed his more distinguished uncle, the British Envoy at Florence, in the baronetcy until 1786. The match moved a contemporary rhymester, J. Duncombe, to tell the story of "Surrey Triumphant, or the Kentish Men's Defeat," in a lengthy ballad parodying "Chevy Chase." The poet ascribed the defeat of the Men of Kent to their playing the match in harvest time :—

> "God prosper long our harvest-work,
>   Our rakes and hay-carts all !
> An ill-tim'd cricket match there did
>   At Bishopsbourn befall.
>
> To bat and bowl with might and main
>   Two Nobles took their way ;
> The hay may rue, that is unhous'd
>   The batting of that day.
>
> The active Earl of Tankerville
>   An even bet did make,
> That in Bourn paddock he would cause,
>   Kent's chiefest hands to quake ;
>
> To see the Surry cricketers
>   Out-bat them and out-bowl.
> To Dorset's Duke the tidings came,
>   All in the park of Knowle :
>
> Who sent his Lordship present word,
>   He would prevent his sport.
> The Surry Earl, not fearing this,
>   Did to East Kent resort. . . .
>
> This game did last from Monday morn
>   Till Wednesday afternoon,
> For when Bell Harry rung to prayers,
>   The batting scarce was done. . . .
>
> Their husband's woful case that night
>   Did many wives bewail,
> Their labour, time, and money lost,
>   But all would not prevail.

Their sun-burnt cheeks, though bath'd in sweat,
    They kiss'd, and wash'd them clean,
And to that fatal paddock begg'd
    They ne'er would go again.

To Sevenoak town this news was brought
    Where Dorset has his seat,
That, on the Nalebourn's banks, his Grace
    Had met with a defeat.

' O heavy news !' the Rector said,
    ' The Vine can witness be,
We have not any cricketer,
    Of such account as he.'

Like tidings in a shorter space,
    To Barham's Rector came,
That in Bourn-paddock knightly Mann
    Had fairly lost the game.

' Now rest his bat,' the Doctor said,
    ' Sith 'twill no better be ;
I trust we have, in Bishopsbourn,
    Five hands as good as he.

Yet Surry-men shall never say,
    But Kent return will make,
And catch or bowl them out at length,
    For her Lieutenant's sake.'

This vow, 'tis hoped, will be perform'd
    Next year, on Laleham down ;
When, if the Kentish hearts of oak
    Recover their renown,

From grey goose-wing some bard, I trust,
    Will pluck a stouter quill :
Thus ended the fam'd match of Bourn,
    Won by Earl Tankerville.

God save the King, and bless the land
    With plenty and increase ;
And grant henceforth that idle games
    In harvest time may cease !"

Fordwich Town Hall.

CHAPTER IV

ROUND ABOUT CANTERBURY

NOT only is the metropolitical city the most obvious centre of interest in Kent, but it is also a centre from which radiate highways and byways full of beauty and crowded with interest. Within a few miles we may visit scenery of the most varied character, from the quiet woods of the north and west to the clayey "cliffs" of the Thames estuary, from the wide marsh-lands where the Stour once met an inlet of the sea east of Fordwich to the bare stretches of chalk downs where the ancient Watling Street crosses the heights that lie between here and Dover. Starting in Canterbury it will be found that the highways which, roughly speaking, bisect the city from north to south, and again from west to east, are the London to Dover and Maidstone to Margate roads, and any one of these four main routes out of the city offers its attractions to the lover of country life and scenery no less than to the seeker after old-time lore. A few miles from Canterbury in any direction by these roads, or by that which leads to Sandwich, or by the ancient Stone Street which goes due south, and has (on the map) all the apparent straightness which we are taught to associate with the old Roman ways, but which seems to the pedestrian or cyclist like a switchback on a grand scale, takes us amid varied hilly and well-wooded scenery, broad stretches of hop-lands and of farmfields. All around are small villages each dominated by its grey stone or flinty

F

church, sometimes spired but more often square towered, generally rising from amid trees. Most of the villages, too, have in their neighbourhood twin-pointed oast-houses, the old ones of red brick with lichened roofs looking pleasantly picturesque, the new ones slate-roofed and ugly. The villages by the Stour or Little Stour are further marked by their tall, white-painted mills, like toy copies of the grain elevators that line the great highway across the Canadian prairies. Go which way we may it is through a country of pleasant prosperity, of nestling villages and of wide prospects, with broad stretches of woodland starred in spring with wood-

Sandwich from the Ramsgate Road.

anemones and primroses, and clouded in May with the wonderful blue of the wild hyacinths massed in their millions. These " bluebells " of the spring—in the summer and autumn many people give the name to the more delicate and shyer hare-bell—form indeed a noticeable feature in many parts of Kent even to within fifteen miles or so of London. In almost any direction we shall find them within a short journey of our cathedral centre—most plentifully perhaps by the pleasant by-road which goes by the top of the Scotland Hills— so called presumably on account of their gorse-dotted bareness— and then passes through the quietude of the Trenleypark Woods, the varied slopes of which show indigo beneath the under-growth with myriad blooms.

In setting out from Canterbury we are confronted by so
many attractive alternatives that the visitor whose time is
limited may almost be reduced to the condition of the donkey
in the fable who died of starvation between two equally
attractive bundles of hay. We, having time, may choose
that one which must in the past have been one of the best
trodden ways, that which takes us by the level eastern road
parallel with the Stour to Canterbury's ancient port of
Fordwich. Time was, at the close of the sixteenth century,

A Mill on the Stour.

when the Canterbury folk objected to having their port two
miles away, and so set about considering the advisability of
making the river navigable for goodly vessels right up to the
city, but the scheme did not get much further than consideration and the spending of money, and in the course of time
instead of bringing it up to Canterbury it became necessary to
retire the shipping to Sandwich, and little Fordwich was left
a quiet place of memories. Two miles of straight road, with
the character of canal country, but with pleasant hills rising
away, on either hand, bring us to Sturry, a straggling village,
probably owing its name to its original situation on an ey or

island of the Stour, and turning to the right we come in about
quarter of a mile to as pretty an approach to a quiet village as
the keenest Syntax in search of the picturesque could wish—a
narrow rising bridge over the river amid trees backed by
cottages. Although a one-time port, and "limb" of the
Cinque Ports—"there are five of 'em" as a Sandwich cicerone
sagely informs those who see the lions of the place under his

On the Stour at Fordwich.

guidance—Fordwich to-day has little of interest to show
beyond its small, square town-hall or court-house and its small
church, both of them standing—separated only by an inn—on
the right bank of the Stour. In the compact little town-hall
the visitor may see the actual ducking-stool in which Fordwich
scolds were lowered from a kind of crane at the quayside
into the river in accordance with an old custom which sought
to cure by indignity ; and he is furthermore shown a little loft
or attic in the court chamber in which, it is said, the drenched

scold was shut up to dry herself and reflect on her unpleasant
ways (and possibly to vow vengeance on all and sundry who
had taken part in or witnessed her ducking).   In the fine old
timbered hall is an ancient deed-chest and a couple of drums
which, according to the attendant, were used by the press-
gangs of a century ago.   Most people would think that the
work of a press-gang could have been performed in silence and
suddenness better than by giving advertisement of its approach

Sturry

with the banging of drums.   Here, too, is to be seen a list of
the mayors of Fordwich from 1292 to 1884 when the town
ceased to have a corporate existence, while below on the
ground floor the visitor may go into the tiny gaol, or lock-up,
the last prisoner in which was—close upon a century ago—a
man who was imprisoned for a year because he could not pay
a debt of thirty shillings.   After falling into desuetude for
some time the hall, one of the most perfect of its kind remaining, was furbished up, its lath and plaster removed, its
revealed timbers newly polished and it took its rank as a show

place, speaking to the present of a widely different past.   A
little to the east of the hall is the church, a quaint old building
with many features of interest, including old box pews and
inward leaning pillars between the nave and north aisle
which may well make nervous the worshippers who sit near.

Of the days when seaworthy craft came up to Fordwich

Fordwich Church

there are now but few memorials ; where the vessels came
laden with goods for the monks of St. Augustine's and the
citizens of Canterbury, are now but a few pleasure boats
floating for the use of visitors.   A relic of the navigability of
the water is to be seen in the towing-path, by which the sinu-
osities of the stream may be followed by leisurely walkers from
here to Sandwich through scenery marked by so much of same-

ness that most people will rest satisfied by seeing it from the windows of the railway train between Sturry and Minster, or by sampling it at this Fordwich end, at pleasant Grove Ferry, some miles further east, or in the neighbourhood of Minster.

Camden quotes "old *Robert* of Glocester in the time of King *Henrie* 3" as saying: "In the countray of Canterbury, most plenty of Fish is," and the Stour may well attract anglers who have had their curiosity excited by references to "Fordwich trout." According to Fuller, "Kent affording trouts, at a town called Fordwich, nigh Canterbury, differing

Interior of the Town Hall, Fordwich.

from all others in many considerables," notably in largeness, in its cunning, and in the whiteness of its flesh. Izaak Walton does not refer to any attempts of his own after the cunning fish, but he devotes a pleasant passage in the "Compleat Angler" to its history. "There is also in Kent, near to Canterbury, a trout called there a Fordidge trout, a trout that bears the name of the town where it is usually caught, that is accounted the rarest of fish; many of them near the bigness of salmon, but known by their different colour; and in their best season they cut very white, and none of these have been known to be caught with an angle, unless it were one that was caught by Sir George Hastings, an excellent angler, and now with God; and he hath told me he thought that trout bit not for hunger but wantonness, and it is rather to be believed, because both he, then, and many others before him, have been curious to search into their bellies, what the food was by which they lived, and hath found out nothing by which they might satisfy their curiosity." Old Walton's theory that the Fordwich trout fed not in fresh water would lead us into the bitter discussion which agitates anglers who study the Salmonidæ, and may therefore be dismissed. Returning to the place that gave the fish its name, we may follow footpaths up the hill-side into Trenleypark Wood, towards Elbridge, past a well in which, says tradition, thieves were drowned, or following the southerly road, may pass up a lane between flowery banks—a floral red, white and blue, as I recall it in May, with campion, greater stitch-wort, and wild hyacinths—and turning to the right at the top pass on to the Canterbury-Sandwich road, with a glimpse of the Cathedral as we look down over the Scotland Hills. On the left we pass the polo ground of the Canterbury Cavalry Depot, partly fenced by an old brick wall which an Earl Cowper intended building round the hill-top estate, on which he contemplated erecting a mansion. Local folk tell a tale of this wall, that the nobleman introduced " foreign " labour, and Canterbury objected so emphatically that the wall was never completed and the projected mansion abandoned. Stretches of the wall—part hidden by the grove of trees and shrubs—and a red brick gateway on the Sandwich road are all that remain of the scheme. By shady up-and-down byways, through Trenleypark Woods, or the varied Sandwich road, we may visit a cluster of pleasant villages. On the main road, scattered along the left bank of the Little Stour, is Littlebourne, with picturesque old oast-houses and pretty, if sophisticated, glimpses of the stream from the bridge. Eastward a mile, keeping to the river, on which at various points trout fishers may be seen patiently luring the fish to their hooks, we come to Wickhambreux—variously spelt and locally known as Wickham—another little Stour village, with its church at the corner of the small green which looks like a trim village lawn pleasantly shaded by limes and chestnuts. North-west of both these villages are pleasant byways and footpaths through broad stretching unhedged meadows on the hill-side ; north-eastward the open road leads down to the Stour marshes, and so to Grove Ferry and the Great Stour, with which our smaller

stream runs irregularly parallel until they join at East Stourmouth. In this little village and its western neighbour we have
places the names of which have become misnomers, the mouth
of the Stour being now, as the crow flies, some miles to the
east, and, as the river flows, twice as far.

Returning to Wickhambreux—one of the several Frenchified
names in this district—we find ourselves scarcely out of it
before we reach its immediate neighbour, Ickham, consisting
mainly of a long, straggling village street, with the church
standing back from it, a church worth recalling as having been
the living of Meric Casaubon, the sixteenth-century classical
scholar, son of one more famous, Isaac. The conjunction of
the names Ickham and Wickham suggests an old counting-out
rhyme which may well have originated in this neighbourhood :—

> " Ickham, pickham,
> Penny Wickham,
> Cockalorum jay,
> Eggs, butter, cheese, bread,
> Hick, stick, stone dead ! "

From Ickham a footpath may be followed across the fields
to Wingham, reaching the centre of the village near the large
church, but in the month of May it is well to go by road, for
on leaving the village the hopfields on our left are protected
from the wind by a hawthorn hedge of unusual height and
trimness. For probably a third of a mile we follow this thin,
flat hedge of about twelve feet high, and with great stretches
of it in bloom it makes a highly pleasing guard to the
growing hops. Wingham, too, is perhaps seen at its best as
approached from the western high road ; it stands on the
further bank of a small tributary of the Little Stour, its houses
well set among trees amid which some large copper beeches
make a notable bit of colour. Following the Z-shaped road,
we pass the church and several timbered houses—some
obviously old and some all too trimly planned. Here was
anciently an ecclesiastical college, and here a memorable
marriage took place on Michaelmas Day, 1360, when Elizabeth
Plantagenet, widow of the Earl of Kent, eight years after
having taken the vows at Waverley Abbey, in Surrey, married
Sir Eustace Dabrieschescourt. The eloping nun and her
young husband were " personally convened before the Archbishop of Canterbury for the said transgression, at his manor

house of Haghfield, upon the seventh ides of April," his Grace
enjoining a series of penances which the lady lived to practise
for over half a century, so that she must have been but a young
widow when she entered Waverley. The story is told with
eighteenth-century innuendo by Horace Walpole in one of his
papers in the *World*. From this place, too, set out "Best's
son, the tanner of Wingham," to join the forces of the rebellious
Cade at Blackheath.

Southward hence lies Goodnestone with its splendid park,
a footpath through which marks the olden track of the
eastern Pilgrims' Way. The village, which is set in the
park, will have pleasant memories for lovers of Jane Austen,

Ploughing near Wingham.   Ash Church in the distance

who visited her brother Edward Austen Knight at the neighbouring Rowling House, and engagingly wrote of the social life
and "formal dances" of the neighbourhood. Writing from
Godmersham—also her brother's house—in 1813, she says, " I
am mistress and miss altogether here, Fanny being gone to
Goodnestone for a day or two, to attend the famous fair, which
makes its yearly distribution of gold paper and coloured persian
through all the family connections."

Following the Pilgrims' Way from Goodnestone we may go
to scattered Adisham, chiefly notable for its church, considerably restored, which was founded as long ago as the seventh
century. From here many roads will take us up over the

broad and swelling chalk downs with distant windmills, and great stretches of sheep-dotted pasture and of unhedged arable land, giving us broad views in many directions, or, following the line of the railway, we may go to Nonington, and for the sake of its magnificent trees to Fredville Park, bisected by a delightful foot-path way.   Hence by Wollage Green, or Womenswold, are beautiful ways to the southern end of Barham Downs ; the first takes us up through Woolwich Wood and the second through the parkland of Denne Hill.   Before going Canterburywards along Barham Downs, with their many

Wingham.

historical associations, we may cross the main Down to the twin villages of Wootton and Denton.   The first of these was the birthplace of Sir Egerton Brydges, poor poet, indifferent novelist and admirable bookman, whose bibliographical works, which he belittled, are remembered with gratitude, while his verses and fiction, which he belauded, are forgotten.   A winding mile—and steep descent—takes us to Denton, set on the Folkestone high road, but looking from above like a neat village in an extensive park.   Here Brydges resided for some years, but Denton is chiefly memorable because Tappington in this parish, the residence of Richard Harris Barham's father,

was the original of the Tappington Everard of the " Ingoldsby
Legends." Thomas Gray stayed at Denton in the summer of
1766, writing of it to a friend : " My residence was eight miles
east of Canterbury in a little quiet valley on the skirts of
Barham Down. In these parts the whole soil is chalk, and
whenever it holds up, in half an hour it is dry enough to walk
out."

Denton.

Going from the small village to Tappington we pass the
church beautifully set among woodland on the left. The old
manor house of the Barhams has its chief interest to-day as
the—of course wholly imaginary—scene of various of the
legends so ingeniously devised by the humorous clergyman.
When the " Ingoldsby Legends " were published some critics
objected firstly that there was no such person as Thomas
Ingoldsby and—with the duplicity of legal wording—if there
were such a person then there was no Tappington Everard.
In a preface to the second edition of his strange fictions the
author said :

" In order utterly to squabash and demolish every gainsayer, I had thought at one time of asking my old and esteemed friend, Richard Lane, to crush them at once with his magic pencil, and to transmit my features to posterity, where all his works are sure to be ' delivered according to the direction ' : but somehow the noble-looking profiles which he has recently executed of the Kemble family put me a little out of conceit with my own, while the undisguised amusement which my ' Mephistopheles Eyebrow,' as he termed it, afforded him, in the ' full face,' induced me to lay aside the

Tappington.

design. Besides, my dear sir, since, as has well been observed, ' there never was a married man yet who had not somebody remarkably like him walking about town,' it is a thousand to one but my lineaments might, after all, out of sheer perverseness, be ascribed to anybody rather than to the real owner. I have, therefore, sent you, instead thereof, a very fair sketch of Tappington, taken from the Folkestone road (I tore it, last night, out of Julia Simpkinson's *album*) ; get Gilke's to make a woodcut of it. And now, if any miscreant (I use the word only in its primary and ' Pickwickian ' sense of ' Unbeliever ') ventures to throw any further doubt upon the matter, why, as Jack Cade's friend says in the play, ' there are the chimneys in my father's house, and the bricks are alive at this day to testify it ! ' "

Which shows that Ingoldsby did not trouble to verify his quotation.

The legends are written at large in the works of Thomas Ingoldsby and must not detain us in the neighbourhood of the house which Barham made the home of the family which he founded by the name of Ingoldsby. It is, however, difficult to get away from these fictional "legends" in eastern Kent. Returning from Denton, we pass by the noble extent of Broome Park, with its grand beeches—there are delightful foot-path ways through it—and reach the Dover Road on the Canterbury side of the "half-way house." Here, going towards the city, we pass along the broad highway of an old Roman road crossing the downs near their summit, along which are tumuli and earthworks, pointing to the antique use of the high ridge. As we go towards Canterbury we have the summit of the down to the right with delightful open roads and field-paths for those who can appreciate the beauty of lonely ways in a windswept country with glimpses now of a windmill, and now of a high perched water tower. To the left we get glimpses into the Elham Valley—along which a railway runs for the use of those who prefer the lazier way of seeing the country—with pleasant villages at which we shall peep presently. Barham Downs, or that tract of the old road to which the name is generally applied, extends roughly from the eighth to the twelfth milestone from Dover—for the inexorable and awful statement of Mr. F.'s aunt is still true : "There's mile-stones on the Dover road." The district is particularly rich in ancient barrows which have afforded many interesting relics for the better reading of the otherwise unrecorded past.

Here it is supposed that Cæsar, having penetrated thus far from Deal, fought and overcame his island enemies and here he formed huge camps, the remaining earthworks being regarded as some of those thrown up by his legions. Here, in 1213, King John collected an army of 60,000 men when excommunicated by the Pope and threatened by invasion from France. Here, half a century later, on further threats of invasion from over channel, Simon de Montfort assembled a general muster of the national forces ; here the Cavaliers mustered in 1642 and here only a century ago was formed a great camp at the time that Napoleon was collecting an army on the heights above Boulogne and the whole of the southern coast of England, from Essex to Cornwall, was alert with anticipations of a descent on the part of the great military bogey of the Continent. Two years before invasion by Napoleon seemed imminent, on the outbreak of the war, Wordsworth had addressed a spirited sonnet " To the Men of Kent " :—

> " Vanguard of Liberty, ye men of Kent,
> Ye children of a soil that doth advance
> Her haughty brow against the coast of France,
> Now is the time to prove your hardiment !
> To France be words of invitation sent !
> They from their fields can see the countenance
> Of your fierce war, may ken the glittering lance,
> And hear you shouting forth your brave intent.
> Left single, in bold parley, ye, of yore,
> Did from the Norman win a gallant wreath ;
> Confirmed the charters that were yours before ;—
> No parleying now ! In Britain is one breath ;
> We all are with you now from shore to shore :
> Ye men of Kent, 'Tis victory or death ! "

Not always has it taken war or threat of war to cause the gathering of great numbers of folk on these heights.

Here Charles I. rode out on a beautiful day in May, 1625, to welcome the coming of his Queen Henrietta Maria after the " rough passage in her transfretation to Dover "—and to recall, it may be, that escapade of little more than two years earlier, when he had ridden this way, as we have seen, on his journey incognito to spy out a possible bride in the Spanish Infanta. Then he had ridden in secret with a couple of companions, now he came attended by his brilliant Court, for, as James Howell puts it in his " Epistolæ Ho-Elianæ," " there was a goodly train of choice ladies attended her coming upon the bowling green on Barham Downs, upon the way, who divided themselves into two rows, and they appeared like so many constellations ; but methought that the country ladies outshined the courtiers." The women of Kent might well feel gratified at the commendation of the epistler. No one who loiters about the downs here but will recognise—climatic conditions affording Queen's weather—that it was a splendid meeting-place for the royal consorts whose life together was so early to be dashed by trouble. Now, we have no bowling green up here, but Howell was perhaps describing the close turf of the downs rather than an actual place on which bowling was played. Now that " bowling green " affords one of the most picturesquely situated of golf links, with a beautiful view across the narrow Elham valley in which may be seen, just below the links, almost hidden in varied foliage and reached by a quarter of a mile avenue of pines and beech, the village of Bishopsbourne. A mile further down the valley is Kingstone (Kingston in the Ordnance Survey) also prettily grouped in trees, whilst a further mile along, well nigh hidden by valley foliage, is the village of Barham, from which the downs

Elham.

derive their name. It seems curious that the high Canterbury and Dover road should for so many miles be free of villages or even hamlets, while to the west, and roughly parallel with it, is a long series of villages, more especially as according to the authorities the present highway is the ancient Roman Watling Street. Water is, however, more necessary to man than highways, and the villages named are planted along the Little Stour, certainly one of our county streams which, though it has no large town, offers the most pleasing variety in these small centres of rural activity.

Barham and Kingston are villages typical of this district but neither need detain us. It is at Bishopsbourne, quiet, rustic little place as it is to the eye, that we come in touch with an interesting bit of history. Its massive square-towered flint church, with tiled roof, set in a small, tree-surrounded God's acre, seems a fitting place to have memories of the great churchman who gave up preferment and London life that in rural retirement he might devote himself to the writing of a great work. The fine sombre yews and copper beech, the graceful birches and the magnificent chestnuts, humming in blossom time with myriad bees, make an unforgetable setting for the village church, and the church itself attracts us the more in that it was to this humble living that Richard Hooker was preferred by Queen Elizabeth in 1595, and hither he came to write the later books of his treatise, "Of the Laws of Ecclesiastical Polity." Hooker's history has been told in one of Izaak Walton's "Lives," those masterpieces of biography in brief, and from the angler's beautiful book a few passages may well be recalled in the place where Hooker worked during the last six years of his life and where he lies buried. As his epitaph runs—

> " Though nothing can be spoke worthy his fame,
> Or the remembrance of that precious name,
> Judicious Hooker ; though this cost be spent
> On him that hath a lasting monument
> In his own Books, yet ought we to express,
> If not his worth, yet our respectfulness."

And our respectfulness shall be expressed for us by two of the most diverse men—Izaak Walton and John Keble—

" This parsonage of Bourne is from Canterbury three miles, and near to the common road that leads from that city to Dover ; in which parsonage Mr. Hooker had not been twelve months, but his books, and the innocency and sanctity of his life, became so remarkable, that many turned out of the road, and others, scholars especially, went purposely to see the man whose life and learning were so much admired : and alas ! as our Saviour said of St. John Baptist, 'What went they out to see? a man clothed in purple and fine linen ?' No, indeed : but an obscure, harmless man : a man in poor clothes, his loins usually girt in a coarse gown, or canonical coat ; of a mean stature, and stooping, and yet more lowly in the thoughts of his soul ; his body worn out, not with age, but study and holy mortifications ;

G

his face full of heat-pimples, begot by his unactivity and sedentary life. And to this true character of his person let me add this of his disposition and behaviour : God and Nature blessed him with so blessed a bashfulness that as in his younger days his pupils might easily look him out of countenance ; so neither then, nor in his age, did he willingly ever look any man in the face, and was of so mild and humble a nature that his poor parish-clerk and he did never talk but with both their hats on, or both off at the same time."

A man of a disposition scarce less retiring, the author of the " Christian Year," visiting Hooker's tomb just ninety years ago, wrote the following Wordsworthian lines.

> " The grey-eyed morn was sadden'd with a shower,
> A silent shower, that trickled down so still,
> Scarce droop'd beneath its weight the tenderest flower,
> Scarce could you trace it on the twinkling rill,
> Or moss-stone bathed in dew.   It was an hour
> Most meet for prayer beside thy lowly grave,
> Most for thanksgiving meet, that Heaven such power
> To thy serene and humble spirit gave.
> ' Who sow good seed with tears shall reap in joy.'
> So thought I as I watch'd the gracious rain,
> And deem'd it like that silent sad employ
> Whence sprung thy glory's harvest, to remain
> For ever.   God hath sworn to lift on high
> Who sinks himself by true humility."

It was at the rectory nearby that Hooker died, and there he had his many talks with Hadrian à Saravia, a prebendary of Canterbury Cathedral, a notable divine of mixed Spanish and Flemish parentage and of wide experience, who became one of the translators of the authorised version of the Scriptures, and with whom we shall meet again in our Kentish wanderings. Within the church here the most notable thing is the monument to Hooker, but in pre-Reformation days the place boasted a remarkable "relic" purporting, according to its donor, to be a bit of the stone on which the Archangel Gabriel descended when he saluted the Virgin Mary.

About a mile or so from Bishopsbourne, towards Canterbury, is one of the largest of the Little Stour villages—Bridge, which probably owes its name to the fact that it was here that the Watling Street crossed the stream.   The pleasantest way to Bridge is through Bourne Park—with a glimpse of the tower of Hooker's church— in which the river widens into a lake before the mansion.   It is believed to have been in Bourne Park, in

a hollow known as "Old England's Hole," that Cæsar completed his first great victory over the Britons and established
himself firmly on Barham Downs, and, to present something in
the nature of anti-climax, it was here that the notable cricket match

Bishopsbourne Church.

referred to in the previous chapter took place. From Bridge to
Patrixbourne extends the estate of Bifrons, which may be skirted
by road, still following the course of the Little Stour, but through
which the more leisurely visitor may go by footpath—and park-

land footpaths are among the most pleasing of byways.   Patrixbourne is chiefly noticeable for its small Norman-spired church,
with many features of interest.   Its beautifully carved external
stonework and windows are only excelled in Kent by those at
Barfreston.   Some of the scattered "Tudor" cottages cannot
fail to arrest the attention of passers by.   The most notable,

Patrixbourne Church

inquiry elicits, were timbered and carved only about forty years
ago by an early appreciator of the old-time timbered dwellings
which we have all now come to admire.   Some of the carvings
seem modelled on those of the old house at the corner of
Lady Wotton's Green in Canterbury.   Almost opposite these
cottages may be had a glimpse of grounds in which the curious
but scarcely lovely art of the topiarian is shown in many

examples. Where the road forks right and left for Beakes-bourne and Canterbury there stands on the little triangle a splendid pine, which should afford a hint to other places with such deltas, where the tiniest no-man's land may be handsomely beautified for every man's benefit.

Due south from Canterbury runs another of those roads which are the most enduring marks of the Roman occupation, but where the Watling Street remains a well-used highway, its neighbour the Stone Street has, so far as considerable traffic is concerned, fallen into desuetude. Farm fields, fringed with flowering hedgerows, with hopfields nearer the city, and with occasional stretches of woodland, remain in the memory after a journey along this ancient highway. Here during a ten-minutes' rest I have seen a dozen different kinds of birds, and a hare loping across the road as though human traffic were but an occasional incident disturbing the peace of

> " Things
> That glide in grasses and rubble of woody wreck ;
> Or change their perch on a beat of quivering wings
> From branch to branch, only restful to pipe and peck ;
> Or, bristled, curl at a touch their snouts in a ball ;
> Or cast their web between bramble and thorny hook."

Again it is noticeable that the villages lie away from the thoroughfare, and again the keeper to the highway, though he may have pleasant prospects over the country, misses the infinite variety of the byways. Beautiful are the lanes and roads, the many woodland ways and field-paths that are open to us here, to be reached by any of the turnings off the Stone Street, east or west. The villages and hamlets are widely scattered, and many miles may be covered without the pedestrian seeing anything but old-time farmsteads and occasional cottages, old and new. The villages east of our road, Nackington, Lower and Upper Hardres, and Stelling, have little to tell of history, though at Upper Hardres it is remembered that Henry VIII. left his hunting-knife at the neighbouring mansion in gratitude for hospitality received on one of his journeys to or from France, and that the Hardres of that day brought back and fixed in his wall the gates of Boulogne as a trophy, after being at the siege of that town. The bricks are not alive at this day to testify.

To the west of Stone Street, within the arbitrary radius of a few miles of the Cathedral City which we are here following, are the villages of Petham and Waltham, neither of which has anything of special note to tell us, except that tradition points in the neighbourhood of the former to ancient entrenchments as marking the place to which the Britons retreated after the Roman soldiers had defeated them in the neighbourhood of Barham Downs. Not far from Waltham is a hamlet named Sole Street—one of the several instances of duplicated names in our county, for another place with the same name will be found near Cobham. Sole signifies a dirty pond of standing water, and "Street" is a common place-name in this immediate neighbourhood, for it will be recognised, especially by the sojourner in the smaller places, that such names have a way of grouping themselves. We have noticed that on the Little Stour, out of a succession of five villages, Bishopsbourne, Bridge, Patrixbourne, Beakesbourne, Littlebourne, four of them have the same termination, pointing, it may be, to the time when men moved within but a small radius, when places were differentiated as persons were by a mere change in the prefix. A mile or so west of Sole Street, neighbouring Waltham, is Crundale, to the rectory of which is attached a theological library left by will nearly two centuries ago, while a beautiful and diversified footpath walk of three or four miles, with charming views, may be taken to Wye.

Returning up Stone Street, or branching off from Petham by Garlinge Green, we may cross by Chartham Downs to the next great road from Canterbury, that leading to Ashford. Here we reach the lovely valley of the Great Stour, a valley in which have developed such large centres as Ashford and Canterbury and many places of minor historical or commercial importance, but more attractive to the seeker after rural quiet and beauty. Leaving part of the road along this portion of the Stour Valley to be dealt with when we take Ashford as our centre, we may follow it in leisurely fashion from Chilham, situated six miles from Canterbury, at the northern end of Chilham Park—itself like an extension of the larger Godmersham Park, and notable for its populous heronry. It is a lovely bit of country, offering walks of varied character up the hills on either side of the valley, and especially for those who like woods by footpaths and byways through the Denge Woods, which stretch in an irregular fashion most of the way from Chilham to Petham. From a dozen points in the immediate neighbourhood good views are to be had.

Chilham, with its timbered houses, its very picturesque village "square," its church and the entrance to the park, all brought into one charming *coup d'œil*, is itself interesting in that here are the remains of an old Norman castle, successor of a Roman building ; for the tradition that this was the place where the Romans and Britons fought is strengthened by the finding of many remains.

Chilham.

Here the Romans had a camp, and a mound on the right bank of the river is not only attractive as affording a grand view of the valley, but also because its name—variously rendered—is said to be corrupted from that of one of Cæsar's tribunes killed in the neighbourhood. The mound is known as Julaber's or Julliberrie Grave, but examinations which have been made have not revealed any remains to indicate that it was a burial place.

The valley road from Chilham follows the winding Stour, taking an almost abrupt turn about a mile before we reach Chartham, where the student of tumuli and entrenchments finds further materials awaiting him.   Near Chartham is the hamlet of Horton, the one-time church of which has been converted into an oast-house !   Beyond Horton, keeping to the Stour, we reach one of Kent's three Miltons, the tiny Milton-next-Canterbury, with a population of probably less than a score of persons.   A mile or so further, at Thanington, we reach almost to the suburbs of the city.   Here took place a Tudor tragedy.   Judge James Hales, born in Canterbury, had much to do with his native county, being among those who received Anne of Cleves at Dover, and among those most active against Kentish Nonconformists, and when, after Queen Mary's accession, he got into disgrace, he ended by going mad and drowning himself in a shallow stream hereabouts.   A case in which his widow sued for trespass done to a leasehold estate which had belonged to him gave rise to much legal quibbling, amusing to the non-legal mind.   In Plowden's " Report " may be read :

" Sir James Hales was dead, and how came he to his death ?   It may be answered by drowning ; and who drowned him?   Sir James Hales ; and when did he drown him ?   In his life-time.   So that Sir James Hales being alive caused Sir James Hales to die ; and the act of a living man was the act of a dead man.   And then after this offence it is reasonable to punish the living man who committed the offence and not the dead man."

A more attractive way of returning to Canterbury is by crossing the Stour a mile or so beyond the Chilham turning, going through Shalmsford Street, past the great County Asylum and keeping to the higher ground, with wide outlook over the valley and towards the City.   Another pleasant way is by Chartham Hatch, which lies up the hill to the north, and so through Howfield Wood by the old Pilgrims' Way from the west, nearby the tiny hamlet of Petty France. As we emerge from the wood looking downward to the Stour we see the old Tonford or Tuniford Farm, with remains of an ancient mansion, inviting to the curious in old domestic architecture.   One of Thomas Sidney Cooper's early pictures painted here, " Banks of the Stour, Tonford, with Cattle," moved one of the artist's Canterbury admirers to a sonnet :

" A Summer's noon—a cool, translucent stream,
     Shallow, rush-fring'd, tempting the vagrant cows,
     White, brinded, black, with smooth or hornèd brows—
Gracefully grouped, the placid creatures seem

In mute enjoyment's ruminating dream ;
   A withered trunk spreads to entrasted boughs
   Over the scene where freshest verdure glows—
Whilst far away the Christ Church turrets gleam.
Beautiful work ! in art and feeling true—
   A lovelier transcript of the face divine
   Of nature backing in the sunny shine,
The gifted hand of Genius never drew ;
   Heart-felt, home-breathing—here all charms combine
Till wonder smiles at the familiar view."

Harbledown may almost be visited as part of Canterbury, a
small village set on a hill-side, with the roadway between two

The Cathedral from Harbledown Hill.

high banks at the top, and on either bank a church—the parish
one to the north—affording especially fine views. The old
Hospital fronting the southerly church was built originally by
Lanfranc for lepers, and here was a regular stopping place for
Canterbury Pilgrims, Harbledown being the Bobbe-up-and-
doun of Chaucer, and though the Hospital has been rebuilt,
it still contains links with the past, but it can no longer
boast of having Becket's shoe, from which holy water was
sprinkled on passing pilgrims. Near by the Black Prince's
Well, which that noble warrior visited, may be seen. At
Harbledown lived the painter on whose canvases are fixed so

many scenes from the neighbourhood, that celebrated son of
Canterbury, Thomas Sidney Cooper.

Passing from Harbledown up the main London Road, we rise
with wide woodlands stretching on either hand to the "ville,"
as it was once called, of Dunkirk, but a pleasanter way for the
pedestrian is by a zig-zagging road and then by a footpath
through the woods, reaching Dunkirk at its high-perched church.
The name is so strange a one for an English village that it is
said to be not very long since letters addressed here arrived
occasionally *viâ* the French Dunkerque. The story runs
that the "ville" received that name — one less surprising
when we have visited the "ville de Sarre," the Scotland

Boughton Church and Boughton Street from near Selling Station.

Hills and Petty France, all within a few miles of Becket's
shrine—from smugglers who made their hiding places in
the extensive woods which still stretch for miles to the north-
east and south.   From Dunkirk a straight, steep hill, from the
summit of which is afforded one of the many magnificent views
which break upon us in wandering about this well favoured
county, descends to Boughton Street--the Boughton-under-
Blean of the "Canterbury Tales," in one of the most fertile
bits of the country. The small village of Blean lies away to
the north-east, but the extensive woods, though sub-divided
under various local names, are known collectively as the Blean
Woods. Little more than a mile to the north of Boughton,

prettily situated on the hillside overlooking the Graveney Marshes, is the village of Hernehill.

It was in this district that the latest Kentish "rising" took place when a Cornishman, John Nichols Tom, who had settled in Canterbury some years earlier, set up as a new Messiah and gathered a number of credulous country folk about him. At the end of 1832 Tom, having assumed the style and name of Sir William Percy Honeywood Courtenay, stood for Parliament as candidate for Canterbury and actually

Hernehill.

polled 375 votes, though a few days later, as candidate for East Kent, he had again to retire with only four. Having been convicted of perjury as witness in a trial of smugglers he was found insane and kept in an asylum for four years. In August, 1837, he was released and shortly afterwards began preaching communistic doctrines and declaring that he was the Messiah. He was described as a man of fine presence with a remarkable resemblance to the traditional representations of Christ, injudicious comment on which fact may have led his disordered wits on the way of imposture. A number of "disciples" gathered around him and he armed them in primitive fashion

and mounted on a white horse with a flag bearing a lion led
them about the neighbourhood.   All was at first but harmless
if distressing mania.   Then came a charge of enticing farm
labourers from their service, and the shooting by the fanatic of
one of the constables who sought to serve the warrant.   The
same day—May 31st, 1838—soldiers were marched out from
Canterbury and the rioters were found in the woods between
Dunkirk and Hernehill.   Tom ran forward and shot an
officer, while one of his followers killed the wounded man.
The soldiers were ordered to fire and charge with the bayonet,
and "Courtenay" and eight of his mad band were killed on

Low Tide at Whitstable.

the spot, the place where he fell being henceforward known as
"Mad Tom's Corner."

These extensive Blean Woods afford endless variety of walks
and of views where they are intersected by roads and footpaths
—though it is not always easy to recognise the difference
between a public footpath and a gamekeeper's track, and
warnings to trespassers are to be met with over the whole
tract of scattered woods and densely planted game covers of
oak, pine, sweet chestnut and other trees.   Without ignoring
the warnings the pedestrian may do many miles of exploring
woodland ways between Dunkirk and Herne.   From Canterbury
two main roads run over this hilly rise north, touching the woods
at various points, the one through Blean to Whitstable, the

other *via* Sturry to old Herne and so to the newer Herne Bay. Both Whitstable and Herne Bay have fallen into the hands of developers of sea-side resorts and flourish as holiday places within easy reach of London.   The first of these places was used in Elizabeth's time by those journeying from London to Canterbury and Dover.   Paul Hentzner, in 1597, records that he came thither by water (*via* Queenborough) and walked hence to Canterbury.

Whitstable, just beyond the mouth of the Swale which cuts Sheppey from the mainland, is the more venerably picturesque with its small, old irregular dwellings along the front, its boat-building yards and its fleet of oyster dredging boats.   It is of oysters that one thinks as soon as the place is mentioned and it is out here, in the wide estuary of the Thames, that the famous oyster beds are situated—famous since the time of the Romans, though some of their bivalves were taken from the neighbourhood of Richborough.   There is yet the appearance of something of the unsophisticated fishing village about parts of Whitstable but villadom is invading it and on either side the cliffs are marked out for future roads—roads only known as such by the name-posts marking their limits.   An anonymous writer in the "Gentleman's Magazine" half a century ago recovered an amusing legend as to the origin of Whitstable which may well be given as he set it forth :

"While strolling on the Kentish coast last summer I halted at a roadside inn, in what I found was styled 'West end of Herne.'   I inquired, among other matters, the distance to Whitstable, and received the desired information from the portly, goodnatured-looking mistress, with the addition, ' Ah, sir, that's a queer place ; you'll see all the houses stuck up and down the hill, just as the devil dropped 'em, as folk say here.'   I naturally asked the particulars of this diabolical feat, and in answer was favoured with the following tale, which I do not give in the good lady's own words, lest I should wound the *amour propre* of the respected citizens of Durovernum, for, according to her, ' it was all along of the wickedness of the Canterbury people,' of which some instances were supplied.

Canterbury, as all the world of Kent knows, is ' no mean city ' now ; but six centuries ago, when it was the resort of thousands of pilgrims, it was so glorious that it excited the wrath of the foul fiend, and its inhabitants being as bad as Jerome describes the people of Jerusalem to have been when that city too was famous for pilgrimages he sought and obtained permission to cast it into the sea, if the service of prayer and praise usually performed by night and by day at the tomb of St. Thomas the Martyr should be once suspended.   Long and eagerly did Satan watch ; but though the people grew worse and worse daily, the religious were faithful to their duties, and

A Jotting in Whitstable.

he almost gave up the hope of submerging the proud city. At length, however, his time came. A great festival had been held at which the chaplains at the saint's tomb had of course borne a prominent part, and when night came, utterly exhausted, they slept—all, and every one.

The glory of Canterbury was now gone for ever. Down pounced the fiend and endeavoured to grasp the city in his arms ; but though provided with claws proverbially long, he was unable to embrace one half, so vast was its size. A portion, however, he seized, and having with a few strokes of his wings reached the open sea, he cast in his evil burden ; thrice he repeated his journey, portion after portion was sunk, and the city was all but annihilated, when the prayers of the neglected St. Thomas prevailed, and an angelic vision was sent to Brother Hubert the Sacristan, which roused and directed him what to do. He rushed into the church, and seizing the bell-rope, he pulled vigorously. The great bell, Harry, which gives its name to the centre tower of the minster, ordinarily required the exertions of ten men to set it in motion, but it now yielded to the touch of one, and a loud boom from its consecrated metal scared the fiend just as he reached the verge of the sea : in despair he dropped his prey and fled, and Canterbury has never since excited his envy by its splendour.

There was a remarkable difference in the fate of the different parts of Satan's last armful, from which a great moral lesson was justly drawn by my informant. Those very few houses in which more good than bad were found were preserved from destruction by falling on the hill-side, and they thus gave rise to the thriving port of Whitstable ; while the majority, where the proportions were reversed, dropped into the sea a mile off, and there their remains are still to be seen ; but antiquaries, if ignorant of the facts of the case, have mistaken them for the ruins of Roman edifices submerged by the encroaching ocean."

Little more than four miles of cliff walk brings us to Herne Bay. The "cliffs" are mostly of clay and of but insignificant height after leaving the Tankerton suburb of Whitstable, where at low tide a long spit of land runs northward, and is known as Street Stones, marking, according to some conjectures, part of the village swallowed by the sea, or marking, if we accept the veritable history just quoted, part of the devil's armful of Canterbury so unceremoniously dumped in the sea. Herne Bay is a modern resort with a pier nearly three-quarters of a mile in length—successor to one on which sail-propelled tram-trucks ran. The stone balustrading at the pier entrance formed part of the parapet of the old London Bridge, demolished in 1832. "Canterbury ys V myles fro the se flat north agaynst Heron," says Leland, but it is an underestimate even for the flying crow, and must have been less so in Leland's time, thanks to the subsequent erosion of the coast. For as recently as 1818 Herne Bay hamlet was described as being on a jutting point of land.   Now there is no such point. Leland referred to the inland village of Herne.

From Herne Bay we have an admirable view of the four mile distant twin towers of Reculver, and beyond dimly may be seen the coast of Thanet and its terminal point at Margate Pier.   Over the higher cliffs—the clay as we near Reculver giving place to sandstone—it is a pleasant walk, though coastal erosion has made it necessary to take a goodly detour inland, the footpath at one place having disappeared within the past four or five years.

To-day at Reculver there is little to be seen but the towers of the old church, towers from the summit of which

Herne Bay.

magnificent views are to be had, extending from the Essex coast and the isle of Sheppey in one direction and in the other over the green marshes with swaying reeds where once ships sailed between the mainland and Thanet to that isle and Margate. Many centuries have passed since this was the Roman station of Reculbium, since Ethelbert had a palace here to which he retired on giving up that at Canterbury to the monks who had won him over to Chris'.anity.   Of the Roman station but an ancient bit of wall remains ; Saxon palace, monastery, and surrounding town have all gone to the destroying sea, which but a few miles south has retreated, leav- ing miles of land fronting the one-time port of Fordwich and leaving Reculbium's "twin" station Rutupiæ far inland. Little more than half a century ago, before the old ruins were more fully protected by the Brethren of the Trinity House, many ghastly relics were washed out of the crumbling church-yard. Quite recently acorns—one with its cap still adhering—ebon with age were brought up from the bottom some distance from the shore, but the graves are no longer rifled by the sea, as they were when Douglas Jerrold, sojourner at the ancient village of Herne, wrote his essay, " A Gossip at Reculvers " :

The Reculver.

" One day, wandering near this open graveyard, we met a boy, carrying away, with exulting looks, a skull in very perfect preservation. He was a London boy, and looked rich indeed with his treasure.

'What have you there ?' we asked.

'A man's head—a skull,' was the answer.

'And what can you possibly do with a skull ?'

'Take it to London.'

'And when you have it in London, what then will you do with it ?'

'I know.'

'No doubt. But what will you do with it ?'

nd to this thrice repeated question, the boy three times answered, 'I know.'

H

'Come, here's sixpence. Now, what will you do with it?'

The boy took the coin—grinned—hugged himself, hugging the skull the closer, and said very briskly—'Make a money-box of it.'

A strange thought for a child. And yet, mused we as we strolled along, how many of us, with nature beneficent and smiling on all sides, how many of us think of nothing so much as hoarding sixpences—yea, hoarding them even in the very jaws of desolate Death."

It is not quite a hundred years (1809) since the church at Reculver was demolished, the materials being partly utilised for Hillborough church a couple of miles away and partly acquired by various people who could put in any claim. The epitaph of the church was quaintly entered in his books by the

Herne Bay.

parish clerk—"the last tax that Mr. Nailor (vicar) took was these words, ' Let your ways be the ways of rightness and your path the path of peace,' and down come the church, and whot was is thoats about is flock that day no one knows." The very year following this wanton destruction the Trinity House began protecting the ancient towers against the sea, as they were recognised as a valuable landmark for sailors. They were something more than landmarks in the middle ages, for then it is said that the sails of vessels were reverently dipped in passing.

To the original twin towers built here attaches the legend that they were erected by the survivor of twin sisters during

the Wars of the Roses.   These sisters, one abbess of a convent
near Faversham, were going by sea to make an offering at the
shrine of the Virgin at Broadstairs, when their vessel was
wrecked off Reculver and one of the sisters died.   The
survivor, to perpetuate the memory of her sister and as a
warning to mariners, caused the ancient church to be repaired
and the two towers to be erected.   So says tradition.   Those who
prefer an alternative story may turn to the " Ingoldsby Legends "
and read it at length in " The Brothers of Birchington."
    Directly inland from Herne Bay something short of two

Approach to Reculver from Herne.

miles lies the " beautiful village of Herne " : " this demure, this
ancient, village.   It seems a very nest—warm and snug, and
green—for human life ; with the twilight haze of time about it,
almost consecrating it from the aching hopes and feverish
expectations of the present.   Who would think that the bray
and roar of multitudinous London sounded but some sixty
miles away ?   The church stands peacefully, reverently, like
some shy visionary monk, his feet on earth—his thoughts with
God.   And the graves are all about ; and things of peace
and gentleness, like folded sheep are gathered round it."
The church, about which the main road makes a curious
detour, is worthy of more than passing mention, for it was here

that Nicholas Ridley, bishop and martyr, held his first cure, and here, for the first time in English it is said, he caused the "Te Deum" to be sung. When nearly twenty years later under sentence of death during the Marian persecutions the Bishop remembered his first cure and wrote :—

"From Cambridge I was called into Kent by the Archbishop of Canterbury, Thomas Cranmer, that most reverent Father and man of God, and of him, by and by, sent to be vicar of Herne, in East Kent. Wherefore, farewell Herne, thou worshipful and wealthy parish, the first cure whereunto I was called to minister to God's word. Thou hast heard of my mouth oft-times the word of God preached, not after the Popish trade, but after Christ's Gospel. Oh ! that the fruit had answered to the seed. And yet I must acknowledge me to be thy debtor for the doctrine of the Lord's Supper, which at that time God had not revealed unto me ; but I bless God in all that godly virtue and zeal of God's word, which the Lord, by preaching of His Word did kindle manifestly both in the heart and life of that godly woman Lady Fiennes ; the Lord grant that His Word took effect there in many more."

A mile and a half due west of Herne we come again upon traces of another bishop and martyr, for it was at the Archiepiscopal palace of Ford that Cranmer was arrested to enter upon that troublous imprisonment which ended at the stake. Of the palace, long the residence of Canterbury's archbishops, there are but scanty remains to be seen, but the many byways lying between the coast about Herne Bay and the Sturry and Thanet road offer beautiful views, now in quiet lanes and now over wider stretches of unhedged fields. As we near Chislet the broad marsh country towards Thanet affords an extensive view, without hedges but dotted here and there with trees, and now and again showing amid larger clumps the roofs and chimneys of small cottages and farmsteads. Here in these marshlands may be heard the pathetic "ewe-ewe" cry of the curlew, or the "seven whistlers," as it is termed by Kentish fishermen. From Chislet, with its striking church with central tower, we may join the main road at Upstreet and so return to Sturry near Fordwich, whence we began this zig-zagging around the Canterbury district, or turning east we may shortly reach Thanet. Here, as in other places in this district, some of the dispossessed French religious seminaries have made a settlement—and their black-coated students are to be met with on many of the roads around Canterbury.

CHAPTER V

WILLIAM CAXTON—one of the sons of whom Kent may well be proudest—wrote in 1480 of the Isle of Thanet, " Thanatos, that is Tenet, is a ylonde besydes Kent and hath the name Thanatos, of deth of serpentes, for ther ben none. And the earth thereof sleeth serpentes yborn in other londes. Ther is a noble corn lond and fruytful. Hit is supposed that this Llonde was haalowed and blessed by St. Austyn, the first Doctour of Englishmen, ffor ther he arrived first." The legend that there are no snakes in Thanet, and that such reptiles, if imported, promptly died long persisted, and is referred to by several old writers. It looks as though St. Augustine's arrival had driven them hence as St. Patrick's ban cleared them out of Ireland.

To-day the Isle of Thanet suggests to most people little beyond the fact that its shores are occupied by popular holiday resorts, and certainly its coast is so much marked by such places that it well may be in the course of a few generations that they will have merged the one in the other, until from the marshes west of Birchington to the marshes west of Ramsgate will be one " endless meal of brick." Birchington, Westgate, Margate, Broadstairs, Ramsgate—town follows town with extraordinary closeness, with "expatiations" into inland villages until the whole district has become a veritable playground for London's holiday makers. Those who are ready to dismiss the Isle as this and this alone do an injustice to it and to the varied interests that it has to offer. To one who has wandered much about the few miles of inland Thanet, the most memorable things are the wide stretches of green or golden corn, the incessant singing of innumerable larks.   In picturesqueness and variety Thanet may not vie with some other parts of the county, but there are magnificent wide views from the high ground in the middle of the Isle, where we see the boat-dotted sea to the north and a wide stretch of marshland, tree-and-farm dotted, extending south and west for miles, backed by the chalk downs of the Dover and Folkestone district.   To the west on a clear day may be seen the tower of Canterbury Cathedral, so that in one view we may get the ground where St. Augustine landed and the great centre for over a thousand years of those who have occupied his chair.   For those who like the bracing winds that come in from the North Sea there is a delight in Thanet's chalk cliffs which rise at the North Foreland to their greatest height between the two most populous towns.

Where wide and well-dyked marshes spread between Reculver and Birchington, was a few centuries ago the inlet of the sea which cut Thanet off from the mainland, so broad and deep that in the sixteenth century folk were still living who had seen goodly vessels pass.   Then the only crossings were by St. Nicholas Wade and at Sarre, where now the roads diverge for Margate and Ramsgate.   Following the first of these we come to the small scattered village of St. Nicholas-at-Wade, with across the fields a couple of miles or so to the east the village of Acol.   The Ordnance Survey map shows an unfenced and unmetalled road from St. Nicholas to Acol, passing near the Beacon—a tall, square, pointed column, which is a familiar landmark from all sides, standing in the midst of open fields; but the unlucky pedestrian or cyclist who follows it after journeying for about a mile finds the rough roadway end abruptly in a cornfield, with the alternative of returning to St. Nicholas and journeying round by a main road, of following the "lynch" dividing the crops, or of boldly pushing through the growing corn towards a road, indicated a quarter of a mile away by the finger-post showing above the sea of grain.

In the neighbourhood of Acol, on the way south to Minster, on the top of the hill is an extensive old chalk-pit, which we may imagine to be the scene of "The Smuggler's Leap," on

which Ingoldsby made his story, showing how Exciseman Gill was willing to give his soul for a horse that would allow of his overtaking Smuggler Bill. The smuggler was overtaken as he took his fatal leap, and the demon horse vanished. The legendist adds a variety of impeccable morals :—

> " Another sound maxim I'd wish you to keep,
> To mind what you're after, and—' Look ere you Leap.'
> Above all, to my last gravest caution attend—
> *Never borrow a horse you don't know of a friend!!!*"

Ramsgate from the Pier.

The inch of story out of which Barham made his ell of legend, runs —:

> " Near this hamlet (Acol) is a long, disused chalk-pit of formidable depth known by the name of ' The Smuggler's Leap.' The tradition of the parish runs, that a riding officer from Sandwich, called Anthony Gill, lost his life here in the early part of the present (eighteenth) century, while in pursuit of a smuggler. A fog coming on, both parties went over the precipice. The smuggler's horse only, it is said, was found crushed beneath its rider. The spot has, of course, been haunted ever since."

Another tradition is associated with this great disused chalk-pit, the bottom of which now makes a goodly ploughed field, and the road-edge of which is so deeply grown with ivy that it might almost be passed unrecognised. When Egbert had had his cousins murdered and had taken the Kingship, a mysterious light showed where the bodies were buried under his very throne in his palace at Eastry. The King was alarmed, and, having consulted the Archbishop as to what he had best do, sent to ask forgiveness of the sister of the murdered men, and to offer what restitution he might. The Princess Domneva

Dec 06

Eastry.

demanded as much land for a monastery as a hind, at one course, could cover. Egbert was willing to be let off thus easily, and the hind was released near Westgate, and ran by Woodchurch and near Acol, across Thanet. Thunor, one of the King's men who had murdered his rivals, sought to stop the hind by riding across its course, "but whilst he was thus acting, the wrath of Heaven came upon him, the earth opened, swallowed him up, and he went down with Dathan and Abiron alive into hell, leaving the name of Tunorsleap, or Thunor-Hyslepe, to the fields and place where he fell to perpetuate the memory of his punishment."

The ground thus miraculously bounded was granted to Domneva, who founded on it the Monastery of Minster. The way that the deer went, now only to be vaguely guessed at, was long known as St. Mildred's Lynch; St. Mildred, the daughter of Domneva, being a Thanet person, second only in importance to Augustine.

Lynch, or linch it may be said, is a local word for a raised way, generally the grassy ridge separating fields in a hedgeless district, such as is the greater part of this Isle of Thanet. The legend was recorded in monkish Latin verses, which have been Englished as :—

> " Domneva's monk distinguished Thanet bears
> The deer's famed course the holy island wears,
> Cursed be the man who violates the bound,
> Another Thunor's leap shall the vile wretch confound."

As we approach Birchington, whether from St. Nicholas or from visiting the neighbourhood of Acol in quest of ancient ghosts, to the right above the trees of Quex Park is to be seen a tall tower, one of the two erected by former owners of this ancient estate. The old family of Quekes, or Quex, "ended in the sixteenth century in a daughter," who married a Mr. Crispe, who so well adapted himself to his new Thanet estate, that he not only became sheriff of the county but in the Isle itself was known as " Regulus Insulae Thaneti." A later owner of the estate of the same family had a lively experience, when an energetic Royalist, "the brave Captain Golding," a Thanet man, it is said, suddenly descended on the coast near Birchington, landed a party of Englishmen and others, hurried them up to Quex Park, took Mr. Henry Crispe out of his bed, hurried him to the shore and carried him off to Flanders, refusing to release him until three thousand pounds ransom had been paid. Crispe's family sought to raise this sum but could not get the necessary licence to pay it, for Cromwell had his suspicions that Mr. Crispe was in collusion with his captors, and that the whole scheme was an elaborate way of raising money on behalf of Prince Charles. If these suspicions had been justified, Crispe would no doubt have returned quietly when the affair had blown over, whereas he was kept for eight months a prisoner at Bruges, and was then only released on the money being raised by the sale of part of his lands.

We have an account of the event in a letter from the nephew of the " prisoner," which was printed in a contemporary pamphlet, amply entitled "Sad News From Kent, shewing how forty armed men, desparate fellows, plundered Sir Nicholas Crispe's house, after which they set a watch over his servants at twelve o'clock at night, July 18th, 1657, and carried them to the waterside to be transported to Dunkirk. With Sir Nicholas Crispe his escape from them upon terms. Sent in a letter by young Mr. Crispe, of Dover, to his kinsman in London, Mr. Kathern, who desired the truth might be published to prevent mis-informations." Mr. Crispe tells the story of the raid in a straightforward fashion, as though the experience of preceding years had thoroughly accustomed folk to romantic adventures :—

"Cousin Kathern,—My kind love remembered unto you and my cousin your good wife. I know you have heard of that sad news from Queax. There came about forty men well armed with carbine, pistol and sword, and poleax every man there, it is thought they came from Dunkirke, thus coming to the house they quickly broke the lock of the outward gate, so entering into the outward court, they secured all the servants lay without the doors, then came to the dwelling-house, and knocked very loud, one asking who was there, being about 12 o'clock at night, they told him they must come in, and the party that spake to them but being newly laid down in his cloathes, before he could come down, with four blows at the hall-door with a two-handed sledge the door gave way and entered the hall before him, secured him and the rest of the servants immediately that lay within the house, then caused the maid to show them my uncle's chamber and Sir Nicholases, when they were entered there they told them they wanted money and that they well could supply their wants, which was done after 3 hours' time in the plundering the house, and what they could get, they then told my uncle and Sir Nicholas that they must go along with them, and to that purpose carried the coachman to put horses in the coach to carry their plunder and uncle and Sir Nicholas to the waterside, and on their way they had a parlie with Sir Nicholas about leaving him behind ; it was agreed immediately that him engaging to pay them 1000 pounds in 28 days' time at Bridgs to one they named : that he should be free to come home again ; which was done. So Sir Nicholas returned home again, but my old uncle they have inhumanely carried away in his old age, and as yet we hear not any word of the least there of how he doth or where he is. Thomas Smith the butcher went voluntarily along with him. I could not well sooner give you this account, for we knew not the certaine truth of things till my father came home about the middle of last week. My father, wife, and self

present our kind love unto you. I am sure if he return not speedily we
shall want him dearly for he is very good towards my aged parents. In
haste with thanks for all your favour, I remain,
                    Your affectionate Kinsman to command,
                                        HENRY CRISPE.
I pray at your leisure convey this letter to my father-in-law's Lodging."

It is a story of kidnapping made to the hand of some writer
of romance. The Captain Golding who performed the act of
brigandage was a man who feared no risks in his loyalty to the
exiled Prince, for, being in command of a valuable merchant
ship, he scorned to remain under the rule of the Commonwealth, so ran away and sold the ship and cargo—the fact that
they did not belong to him weighing nothing, of course—and
handed the proceeds over to Charles. Here, at Quex Park,
the scene of Golding's bold raid, William of Orange was wont
to stay when *en route* for Holland.

Birchington is just a pleasant holiday resort—still in the
making—where from this side we first touch at the chalk
" cliffs," to dignify them with a big name. Many of the breaks
and caves in these cliffs are said to have been utilised by the
smuggling fraternity in the good old days. Of its eastern
neighbour, the neatly-planned Westgate, it may also be said that
it is simply a pleasant, trim, holiday resort. Both places have
sprung into popular favour within the last twenty or thirty
years, and bear the stamp of their modernity. Birchington
is a place of pilgrimage for all admirers of the dual genius
of Dante Gabriel Rossetti—thither he went early in 1882,
broken in health, and there he died and is buried, and his
memory perpetuated in stained-glass windows in the church.
Inland from Westgate lies the old manor of Daundelyon,
Daundelion, or Dent-de-Lion—the family of which name was,
centuries since, extinct, and the mansion destroyed. It was
one of these Daundelyons who gave one of its bells to St. John's
Church, Margate :

> "John de Daundelyon with his great Dog
> Brought over this bell on a mill cog."

It is explained that " the Dog " was probably the name of
the vessel, but the jingle suggests rather that John was com-
panioned by a canine friend, for a cog seems to have been the
kind of boat in which the bell was brought from Flanders.

The Daundelyon estate was for a time the property of Charles James Fox, and later, before the close of the eighteenth century, became much frequented by visitors to Margate : " Alcoves, shrubs, flowers, a bowling green, a platform for dancing, an orchestra, and other accommodations are erected here for the entertainment of company, who often drink tea at this delightful spot, and during the season have a public breakfast on Wednesdays and Saturdays, with dancing and other amusements, under the superintendence of the master of the ceremonies." Later, Margate's visitors found their pleasures on the "front" rather than inland, and the old place was happily allowed to fall back into quietude.

It was in the mid-eighteenth century, when the virtues of sea bathing had recently been discovered, that Margate began to come into popularity as a resort for holiday-makers from London. Towards the end of that century a Margate Quaker, by name Benjamin Beale, introduced bathing-machines—not, as is sometimes said, for the first time in England—and the popularity of the place has so gone on increasing that it would be idle to attempt a description of the town, scattered upon the cliffs and running far inland. In olden times it afforded a place of debarkation for the Continent, but it is, as a holiday resort, a place where thousands of people can go and have all the miscellaneous entertainment which is associated with the general idea of a holiday by the sea. In the eighteenth century it was a place to which the cit went, pretending to be a gentleman—" haughtily bending the head backwards, through the dread of being thought to have contracted a sneaking stoop behind the counter "; while the impecunious nobleman went there to economise. Already, when Thomas Gray visited it in the spring of 1766, he could describe it as " Bartholomew Fair by the Seaside." We get glimpses of the place, of the extortions practised on London visitors, in " An Excursion to Margate in the month of June, 1786." Hardwicke Lewis, Esq., as the title-page of the brochure informs us, was the author of this imitation of Sterne's " Sentimental Journey " and he describes, without any softening, the state of the passengers who journeyed to Thanet by the hoy, and of their arrival :—

"After tumbling and rumbling, tacking and retacking. we reached Margate, to the great joy of Neptune's patients, who were as tired of his prescription as if fees had been paid for it ; the few who were not affected by the tow'ring motion experienced from hunger pains that need not be described ; their stores being in the cabin, partook of scents that 'all the perfumes of Arabia could not sweeten' : For my part, I fasted from food to glut on affliction, and ' wished no other relish.' It was impossible to land at the Pier, through the lowness of the tide ; boats put off therefore to our relief—for, to say truth, the Margatians are a friendly sort of people, when-ever they can use a WRECKING-HOOK, or make demands upon the purse."

Another and far better writer journeyed to Margate in the old hoys which did duty for nearly two centuries, as we learn from the Water Poet, who tells us that in 1637 "A Hoy from Rochester, Margate in Kent, or Feversham and Maidstone doth come to St. Katherine's Dock." These about the year of Waterloo gave place to the steam packet. That later writer was Charles Lamb, who has left us an account of the voyage in a delightful essay, telling how Elia and his cousin Bridget journeyed from London, of some characters they met on board, and of how one of the company pointing out Reculver was therefore considered "no ordinary seaman."

"Can I forget thee, thou old Margate Hoy, with thy weather-beaten, sun-burnt captain, and his rough accommodations—ill-exchanged for the foppery and fresh-water niceness of the modern steam packet? To the winds and the waves thou committedst thy goodly freightage, and didst ask no aid of magic fumes, and spells, and boiling cauldrons. With the gales of heaven thou wentest swimmingly ; or, when it was their pleasure, stoodest still with sailor-like patience. Thy course was natural, not forced, as in a hot-bed ; nor didst thou go poisoning the breath of ocean with sulphureous smoke—a great sea chimæra, chimneying and furnacing the deep ; or liker to that fire-god parching up Scamander.

Can I forget thy honest, yet slender crew, with their coy reluctant responses (yet to the suppression of anything like contempt) to the raw questions, which we of the great city would be ever and anon putting to them, as to the uses of this or that strange naval implement ? 'Specially can I forget thee, thou happy medium, thou shade of refuge between us and them, conciliating interpreter of their skill to our simplicity, comfortable ambassador between sea and land !—whose sailor-trowsers did not more con-vincingly assure thee to be an adopted denizen of the former, than thy white cap, and whiter apron over them, with thy neat-fingered practice in thy culinary vocation, bespoke thee to have been of inland nurture heretofore— a master cook of Eastcheap ? How busily didst thou ply thy multifarious occupation, cook, mariner, attendant, chamberlain : here, there, like another Ariel, flaming at once about all parts of the deck, yet with kindlier minis-trations, not to assist the tempest, but, as if touched with a kindred sense of our infirmities, to soothe the qualms which that untried motion might haply raise in our crude land-fancies. And when the o'er-washing billows drove us below deck (for it was far gone in October, and we had stiff and blowing weather) how did thy officious ministerings, still catering for our comfort, with cards, and cordials, and thy more cordial conversation, alleviate the closeness and the confinement of thy else (truth to say) not very savoury, nor very inviting, little cabin ?

With these additaments to boot, we had on board a fellow-passenger, whose discourse in verity might have beguiled a longer voyage than we meditated, and have made mirth and wonder abound as far as the Azores. He was a dark, Spanish-complexioned young man, remarkably handsome, with an officer-like assurance, and an insuppressible volubility of assertion. He was, in fact, the greatest liar I had met with then, or since. He was none of your hesitating half story-tellers (a most painful description of mortals) who go on sounding your belief, and only giving you as much as they see you can swallow at a time—the nibbling pickpockets of your patience—but one who committed downright daylight depredations upon his neighbour's faith. He did not stand shivering upon the brink, but was a hearty, thorough-paced liar, and plunged at once into the depths of your credulity. I partly believe, he made pretty sure of his company. Not many rich, not many wise, or learned, composed at that time the common stowage of a Margate packet. We were, I am afraid, a set of as un-seasoned Londoners (let our enemies give it a worse name) as Alderman-bury or Watling Street, at that time of day could have supplied."

The old Margate Hoy—journeying immortal in the pages of Charles Lamb—was replaced in the Thames and its estuary by the "great sea chimera" of the steam packet and in the early "forties" of the nineteeth century many are the references to the Red Rover commanded by Captain Large—it is referred to by Barham in the "Ingoldsby Legends" and in the twenty-fourth of "Mrs. Caudle's Curtain Lectures" we learn how Job and Margaret Caudle took the dear children to Margate by the Red Rover ; how Job—a good sailor—behaved "like a brute" to his wife—who was a bad sailor—and how that good lady's ire was aroused by a rencontre with Miss Prettyman on the jetty.

It has been shown that the sentimentalist visiting Margate drew attention to the Margatian's fondness for the "wrecking hook" and for making demands on the purses of visitors, but the place was then in a transition stage towards its position as a mere holiday resort. The old inhabitants of Thanet are said to have been amphibious creatures, making a couple of fishing voyages and returning home for harvesting operations in their fruitful isle.

The old-time inscription round the chancel of one of the

Thanet churches—that of Monkton—

> " Insula rotunda Thanatos quam circuit unda
> Fertilis et munda nulli est in orbe secunda."

has been thus roughly rendered by an eighteenth century visitor—

> " Round is rich Thanet's sea-encircled isle
> Whose happy fields with richest verdure smile."

But tradition says that, besides being fishermen and farmers the men of Thanet had no objection to doing a bit of smuggling when occasion offered, and a century-old Margate adver-

Margate in December.

tisement of an ass-hirer whose donkeys were alternately employed by ladies and smugglers ran—

> " Asses here to be let ! for all purposes right—
> To bear angels by day and spirits by night."

Margate faces north, and leaving it by the chalk cliffs which rise to upwards of fifty feet from the shore we come to Kingsgate hamlet by the North Foreland, a place which, known originally as St. Bartholomew's Gate, gained its present name because King Charles II. landed here in 1683. Here was long since an old portcullis and gate inscribed " God Bless Bart'lem's Gate," followed by the distich

> " Olim Porta fui Patroni Bartholomaei,
> Nunc Regis Jussu regia Porta vocor,"

which our eighteenth century sentimentalist Englished thus,

> " Kings-Gate's my name, to Royal Mandate true,
> Yclep'd in former Times *Bartholomew*."

The sentimentalist continued,

" So charming is this scite, which afforded *Maria* a short respite from sorrow, that we were loth to quit it. Before we ordered the carriage, I presented her with a few lines, said to have been written by GRAY on the spot : If they were so, it will afford some idea of his being a sort of poet ; for they have sense and meaning as well as jingle—His other works are too *sublime* for *human* comprehension, and are vastly, like SWIFT's song, by a *person* of *quality ;* which seems to mean prodigious things, but is errant *nonsense*—let me except a few pretticisms in the favorite Elegy."

The half dozen stanzas thus praised refer to the sham ruins which Lord Holland raised here in accordance with the queer taste of his time, and are marked by little beyond savage satire,

> " Old and abandoned by each venal friend
>   Here Holland took the pious resolution,
> To smuggle a few years, and strive to mend
>   A broken character and constitution.
>
> On this congenial spot he fixt his choice,
>   Earl Godwin trembled for his native land,
> Here sea-gulls scream, and cormorants rejoice,
>   And mariners, tho' shipwreck'd, dread to land.
>
> Here reigns the blust'ring north and blighting east,
>   No tree is heard to whisper, bird to sing ;
> But nature cannot furnish out the feast,
>   Art is invok'd new horrors still to bring :
>
> Lo ! mould'ring towers and battlements arise,
>   Arches and turrets nodding to their fall,
> Unpeopled palaces delude the eyes
>   And mimic desolation covers all.
>
> Oh ! cried the sighing peer, had Bute been true,
>   Or Mansfield's promise not bestow'd in vain,
> Far other scenes had bless'd our happier view,
>   And realiz'd the ruins which we feign—
>
> Purg'd by the sword, and purified by fire,
>   Then had we seen proud London's hated walls
> Owls would have hooted in St. Peter's choir,
>   And foxes stunk and litter'd in St. Paul's."

To the south of Kingsgate is the famous North Foreland, the high chalk cliff surmounted by a lofty lighthouse—successor of an olden beacon for warning shipmen off the dangers of the Goodwin Sands—the light of which is said to be visible thirty miles away. It was here off the Foreland and north of the Goodwins, in May, 1666, that Admiral Blake, supported by Prince Rupert, engaged in a fight, "the longest and most stubborn that the seas have ever seen," against the Dutch under De Ruyter, a fight which necessitated the remnant of the English fleet seeking the harbourage of the Thames, and caused De Witt to declare "that English sailors might be killed and English ships burned, but that there was no conquering Englishmen." Six weeks later the fleets encountered again within sight of the Foreland, and by gaining a signal victory the English went far to justify De Witt's tribute. At an old house in Sandwich many years ago were discovered some old panel pictures—now hanging in the Guild Hall of that ancient Cinque Port—showing a fight between the English and Dutch fleets which may well have been the encounter which took place here.

To the south of the Foreland we come to another of the pleasant summer resorts that line the Thanet cliffs, Broadstairs, a quieter place than its more populous neighbours, and one that is remembered as another of those with Dickensian associations, for Boz was as enthusiastic about the county of his adoption as the most enthusiastic of those who pride themselves on their technical title to being Men of Kent. At Broadstairs, "one of the freshest and freest little places in the world," after having occupied earlier lodgings in the High Street, Dickens rented the quaintly-shaped Fort House, later named Bleak House from one of his stories, though it was not the original from which that novel took its title.

Many are the references to Broadstairs in Dickens's correspondence : "The general character of Broadstairs as to size and accommodation was happily expressed by Miss Eden, when she wrote to the Duke of Devonshire (as he told me) saying how grateful she felt to a certain sailor, who asked leave to see her garden, for not plucking it bodily up and sticking it in his button hole. You will have for a night-light in the room we shall give you, the North Foreland lighthouse. That and the sea and air are our only lions." The shallow shore which makes of the Thanet coast so admirable a bathing-ground is well indicated in the summary description of Broadstairs embodied in an article Dickens wrote on "Our Watering Places" :—

"The ocean lies winking in the sunlight like a drowsy lion ; its glassy waters scarcely curve upon the shore ; the fishing boats in the busy harbour are all stranded in the mud. Our two colliers . . . have not an inch of water within a quarter of a mile of them and turn exhausted on their sides, like faint fish of an antediluvian species ; rusty cables and chains, ropes and rings, undermost parts of posts and piles, and confused timber defences against the waves lie strewn about in a brown litter of tangled seaweed and fallen cliff. . . . The tide has risen ; the boats are dancing on the bubbling water ; the colliers are afloat again ; the white bordered waves rush in. . . .

Broadstairs.

The radiant sails are gliding past the shore and shining on the far horizon ; all the sea is sparkling, heaving, swelling up with life and beauty this bright morning."

Broadstairs is said to have had its name from the broad way down to the shore, once defended by a strong gate and port-cullis, but it is also said to have been anciently Bradstow. Inland is the pleasant village of St. Peters' with its stories of smugglers, and underground hiding-places, and southwards we come over the open down to Ramsgate, occupying the south-eastern corner of Thanet. The ancient British name of Thanet, we are told, was Ruim, and hence Ramsgate, which suggests that in this tripper paradise we have, perhaps, the first settled place on the one-time island. Here, again, we are in a populous pleasure place familiar to many thousands of visitors. In the time of Eliza- beth there were but five-and-twenty houses, but to-day it almost rivals Canterbury in size, having developed very rapidly in the eighteenth and nineteenth centuries, especially since the im- proved service by rail and sea placed the sands and bracing air of this easternmost part of Kent within easy reach of London.

The ancient Christmas custom of "hodening," here, the carrying round of the head of a dead horse, by a bell-ringing and carol-singing company, was supposed to be the survival of a festival commemorating the landing of the Saxons under Hengist and Horsa, the head presumably being an example of the pun made obvious. The term hodening or hoodening is still used in some parts of the isle to denote Christmas Eve carol-singing. A Thanet clergyman, thirty years ago, noted the old custom thus : " I made enquiry of an old retired farmer in my parish (Monkton) as to the custom called *Hoodning.* He tells me that formerly the farmer used to send annually round the neighbourhood the best horse under the charge of the wagoner, and that afterwards, instead, a man used to represent the horse, being supplied with a tail, and with a wooden (pronounced ooden or hooden) figure of a horse's head, and plenty of horse-hair for a mane. The horse's head was fitted with hobnails for teeth ; the mouth being made to open by means of a string, and in closing made a loud crack. The custom has long since ceased."

From Ramsgate we look south-westward over Pegwell Bay, where, through the silted-up sand, the Stour, after innumerable twistings during the finish of its course, finds its way to the sea. Pegwell itself—famous for its shrimps—forms now but a western extension of Ramsgate. At the back of it is Ozengell Hill, the highest point in Thanet, and one affording a magnificent view, with the village of Manston on its western slope. The railway is cut through the southern side of this hill, and when it was made a number of Saxon graves, dating from the fifth and sixth centuries, were found in the chalk, and also some Roman graves, showing that the two races lived here simultaneously. Keeping inland from the Bay we approach, with a wide view over the marshes of the Stour valley, a place crowded with memories, if the conjectures of the historians be correct.   Here, along this southernmost part of the Isle of Thanet, we come to Ebbsfleet—the point at which Hengist and Horsa are said to have landed with their Saxons in A.D. 449, five centuries after Cæsar had landed with his legionaries a few miles further to the south, the point at which, as John Richard Green has put it, " English history begins." And not only the Saxons, but here also, in 597, landed after their long journey from Rome the tall Augustine and his forty monks.   Pleasant marsh-meadows dotted with trees and fed over by innumerable sheep, a few scattered cottages with the distant sea, the line of Ramsgate's chalk cliffs, and nearer and whiter the low buildings of a coastguard station by the sea-wall beyond the reclaimed meadows with, a little inland off the road, a farm in which the name still survives—such is Ebbsfleet ; a place over which the mind may ponder, but which has nothing to show the eye directly associated with the memorable past. However, as Green, the first of picturesque historians, puts it, "a higher sense than that of beauty draws us to the landing-place of our fathers."   Even the country immediately surrounding must have changed greatly since the coming of Augustine, for centuries later the sea covered much of these marshes so that ships bound for the estuary of the Thames passed over them and up between Thanet and the mainland to the open water again, while ships of some size could go up the now narrow Stour to Fordwich, if not to Canterbury itself.   Doubts have been thrown on the statement that Hengist and Horsa landed at this place, but, as Green has pointed out, everything in the character of the ground confirms the tradition which fixes this spot at Ebbsfleet.   The Jutes who came in three " keels " under the leaders whose names are ever twinned in our memory, would be wise in landing on Thanet, divided as it was by the inlet of the sea from the mainland, for, securing the island they had, in modern military language, a safer base from which to conduct their campaign than they might have found on the mainland of Kent, for though they came first as allies to aid in driving off the Picts, they soon came in such numbers that they may well have been looking forward to the quarrel with those who had invoked their aid which was to help them to a permanent footing.

The Jutes had been in the country for nearly a century and a half, had made of the country England, when the second

notable landing took place, and the missionary Augustine came
to win the country for the religion of Christ. The coming of
Augustine was—the story is summarised in all the history books
—the result of Gregory, then Deacon, and afterwards Bishop of
Rome, seeing English slaves offered for sale in the Roman
market-place, and having an opportunity of happy pun-
making. "From what country do these slaves come?"
Gregory asked. The slave dealer answered, "They are
Angles." "Not Angles but Angels, with faces so angel-like,"
said the Deacon, adding, "From what country do they come?"
"They come," was the reply, "from Deira." "De ira, ay,
plucked from God's ire and called to Christ's mercy," com-
mented Gregory, "and what is the name of their king?"
"Aella," said the slave merchant; and again Gregory found it
a word of good omen, "Alleluia shall be sung in Aella's land,"
he said. It was more than ten years after Aella's death that
Gregory's promise was fulfilled, and he as Bishop sent
Augustine to the land of the Angles with interpreters from
Gaul. Ethelbert, then King, was married to Bertha, a Christian
Princess from Gaul, and he gave the missionary monks a
hearing, in the open air it is recorded for fear of magic. The
place of meeting, where Augustine preached his first sermon,
is supposed to have been on the chalk downs, above what is now
Minster—near, perhaps, to the place where later Domneva's
hind was to mark out Minster's limits. The King, surrounded
by his wild soldiers, sat on the bare ground, and in front
was the devoted band of monks dominated by Augustine, "a
man of almost gigantic stature, head and shoulders taller than
anyone else," with, as their insignia, a silver cross and large
board, on which was painted a figure of Christ. Augustine
preached and Gaulish interpreters translated for the benefit of
the English, but Ethelbert, though no doubt partly prepared
for the new faith by his wife and her attendant bishop, was
not immediately converted. He gave the new comers permission to exercise their religion in his town of Canterbury,
and later, on his conversion, gave them his palace there, and
removed to Reculver.

It is the Jutish chieftains, Hengist and Horsa, and the
Christian missionary, Augustine, who are chiefly remembered
when we visit this quiet stretch of marshland meadows between
the modern gaiety of Ramsgate and the ancient dignity of

Sandwich. In old days, when Christianity ruled mainly through the personalities of the saints, a well-remembered celebrity was St. Mildred—at Westgate there is St. Mildred's Bay, at Acol the little church is dedicated to St. Mildred—a woman "endued with such God-like vertue," as the old chronicler declares, that she lay "in a hot oven three hours together" without suffering any inconvenience, and one whose name was remembered, as we have seen, in St. Mildred's Lynch, and who left more than her name at Ebbsfleet, for a stone was long since pointed out as that on which she had placed her foot at landing, and this stone was said to have the power, if ever removed from its site, of miraculously flying back to its place. It was also sometimes said to be the stone on which St. Augustine set his foot. But the stone has long passed into mere tradition. When the Saints went out of favour in England then miracles ceased—as though by a further miracle.

From Ebbsfleet a straight road goes to Sandwich, with the Stour running south past Richborough on the right, and running north on the left, for the road passes up a great loop which the river takes before turning north by Sandwich, to take its final convolutions before reaching Pegwell Bay. Here was the old Roman Stonar, and here was salt-making carried on, where now are made the concrete blocks for use in the great naval harbour at Dover. Before crossing the Stour again into Kent proper, we may turn to the right off the Ramsgate and Sandwich road, just beyond the coastguard station, and, passing Ebbsfleet Farm on our left, go over the level crossing—with a most ingenious stile for the passage of bicycles—and by shady roads and a hop-field—there are but few of the typical Kentish bines in Thanet—reach the scattered village of Minster, once a famous ecclesiastical centre, now a place to which Ramsgate and Margate holiday-makers journey in brakes for an afternoon's jaunt. Not that there is much to be seen there, beyond the fine old church, the trumpery spire of which, surmounting a square tower, is a familiar landmark. The church, which is happily one of those left open daily for the inspection of visitors, has a number of flat Roman bricks in its tower, and though much restored has many features of interest. Here Meric Casaubon, the scholar-son of a great scholar, held the living for a time. On his ejection, in 1644, he had a notorious successor in Richard Culmer, the divine who broke the glass of Canterbury

Cathedral. His new parishioners greatly resented Culmer's appointment, and when he went to read himself in they had locked the church door and hidden the key. Culmer broke a window, and got in thus. After the ceremony the irate Minster folk opened the door, dragged him out, and beat him unmercifully, jeering at him as a thief and a robber. On his seeking a parish servant, he was refused any girl who was not illegitimate. He broke the stained glass of the church, and looking on the wooden and iron crosses which surmounted the spire as " monuments of superstition and idolatry," he himself, by moonlight, fixed ladders for a couple of workmen to remove the symbols. His parishioners pointed out that he was only doing his work by halves, as the church itself was built in the form of a cross, and he himself was the greatest cross in the parish. So bitter was the struggle against " Blueskin Dick "— so named because he wore a blue gown, having an objection to black—that the parishioners spent £300 in trying to get him removed ; they even offered him the income of the living for life, and to pay for another minister themselves, if he would go away, but he refused, and remained until the Restoration. It must have been a lively sixteen years in the experience of the village !

An ancient monastery flourished long until the Danes under Sweyn destroyed it and its inmates, when the body of its patroness, St. Mildred—which had escaped destruction—was carried off to St. Augustine's at Canterbury. The story runs that—even as the stone on which she had set foot at Ebbsfleet —the body refused to be removed until it at length yielded to the prayers of the Abbot of St. Augustine, who made off with the precious relic by night for fear of the opposition of the good folks of the island which had so long been St. Mildred's particular province. In this instance the prized relics had been given to St. Augustine's by Knut, the son of that very Sweyn who had destroyed Minster and burned the Abbess and her nuns in their buildings ; but it is curious to find that in the days when miracles were wrought by the remains of saints the dignitaries of one church or monastery were not above purloining relics from each other's keeping ; if the thing could be managed it not only brought new honour to the enriched shrine but sometimes meant new dignity for the purloiner.

It is only in tradition, and in tradition hidden in many

books rather than revealed on the tongues of men, that Minster now suggests anything of its old-time importance ; of the days when it was a port on the arm of the sea which ran up to that other ancient town, of which but the twin towers stand at Reculver ; of the days when Romans and Saxons successively occupied the neighbourhood ; of the days when the island to which it was the principal gate became a stronghold of the newly-come religion ; or of the days when the Danes descended, destroying all before them. Now, Minster is a quiet little village, with occasional bustle at its railway station—junction of

Sarre Wall

the Ramsgate and Deal lines—situated with a wonderful view over the marsh-land, and with animation in its narrow streets and about its church when the brakes drive in from Ramsgate. Up from the town, past the high-perched workhouse and its *vis-à-vis* cemetery, runs the road over St. Mildred's Lynch and past the chalk pit of gruesome memories, to Birchington, through broad stretches of farm crops divided by lynches, no longer visible when the crops are growing—for it is still partly true of Thanet as it was when an ancient writer described the Isle as " all cornfields and very little enclosure." Leftwards the roads lead to the pleasant village of Monkton, and so to Sarre and out of Thanet. Sarre, as the westerly gate of

Thanet, was at one time a place of some importance.   To the ford here came the monks from Canterbury to visit their churches and estates in the fertile island, and here, probably, crossed many of those pilgrims from the Continent who had landed at Minster.   Now Sarre is a pleasant village of old, red-brick houses, at the foot of the rising ground of Thanet, with its straight road or " wall " crossing the marsh-lands to the next gradual hill rising to Upstreet and so to Canterbury.   Perhaps the most notable things about the village to-day are the inscriptions at either end, French fashion, on pieces of wood on house-walls—on the east " Ville de Sarre," on the west " Ville of Sarre "—and the fact that the sojourner here can, within two or three miles, enjoy such great diversity of country as is to be had in the cattle-dotted marshes, the hedgeless fields of Thanet, or the hilly and hedged lanes to the west of the marshes.

At some unnamed spot in Thanet was born Thomas Charnock, a sixteenth-century experimentalist, who had the misfortune to be pressed for a soldier when he was within but a short month of discovering the elusive secret of the philosopher's stone.   It must have been an insult added to injury to have to fire lead that, had he been left to his peaceful avocations, might have been converted into a metal more precious !

CHAPTER VI

SANDWICH, DEAL, AND THE GOODWINS

LEAVING Thanet near the point where its oldest associations are clustered about the quiet neighbourhood of Ebbsfleet Farm we may follow the main road along the narrow peninsula which the Stour convolutions make of the southern portion of the isle and so reach Sandwich, but by doing so we should miss a place which was of importance centuries before Ebbsfleet saw the landing of the Christian missionaries or the Saxon ally-invaders. Where we find the south-flowing Stour on our right and the north-flowing Stour on our left we are in the neighbourhood of some of the most interesting ruins which our country has to show, ruins which have yielded up treasures to many museums and about which volumes have been written. The old remains lie half a mile or so away from us at this point to our right, on the rising ground immediately beyond the river and the railway, here running parallel. The massy walls remaining are mostly hidden from railway passengers carried within a few yards of them and may not seem much to the uninitiated, but they represent one of the great strongholds built along the Saxon shore by the Romans, and not only that but they form the most extensive remains of the Roman occupation of England which the country has to show. The ruins are all there is now of the important Roman station of Rutupiæ. From that station, guarding the southern entrance to the channel which cuts off the Isle of Thanet from the mainland, was visible the station of Reculbium at the northern end.

Rutupiæ, nearer to the coast of the Continent and guarding the shore between Thanet and the high chalk cliffs to the south was the more important. Its story, as rendered up to excavators and archæologists is written at length in the transactions of the *Archæologia Cantiana*, and in Roach Smith's earlier volume dealing with old Roman stations in Kent and other works. Here have been recovered many ancient relics and **an** extraordinarily large number of coins throwing much light on the Roman rule, which have taken their places in various museums. Of such coins there is practically a sequence illustrating the whole period of the Roman occupation.

Some massive ruined walls as much as thirty feet high, rising from cultivated fields on an eminence on the right bank of the Stour, are all that the visitor sees. It needs the knowledge of the past, the realisation of the change which has been occasioned by the retiring of the sea, to form any idea of the time when these walls formed but portions of a great frontier fortress, when the Roman triremes were brought close to the place and when the oysters taken in the immediate neighbourhood were delicacies for the Roman epicure. Then the hill on which the ruins now stand overlooked the waters of the sea where now it looks eastward to sandy flats and westward to the diversified marshland of Ash Level. Within the massive walls of Richborough it is probable lived the Count of the Saxon Shore—the " Comes Limitis Saxonici per Britanniam " —whose duty it was to see after the safeguarding of the coast from the Wash to Southampton. Though primarily a fortress there can be little doubt that there was an ancient town at Rutupiæ, for not only was the site one of great military strength, but near to the immediate south we may trace the amphitheatre in which the legionaries of the Count of the Saxon Shore probably indulged in their games.

More than half a century ago, a Deal versifier, by name G. R. Carter—perhaps a relative of the eighteenth century Elizabeth Carter—wrote several sonnets to Richborough Castle, one of which may be cited as an example of local talent though its closing couplet is somewhat suggestive of the art of sinking in poetry.

> " Throned on the bosom of a sunny hill,
>   Behold the wreck of Rome's imperial sway !

The ivy to its walls is clinging still,
　　A gloomy mourner o'er its latest day ;
　　But sweetest summer-birds attune their lay
Around the Stour that flows beneath its brow,
　　And flowers are kissed to slumber by the ray
Which tints the clouds with crimson glory now ;
And consecrated are the dreamless brave
　　O'er whom this castle lifts its mouldering pride,
Their dirge seems uttered by the rippling wave,
　　Their requiem by the plaintive winds is sighed.
Oh ! thus, when death relieves me from my cares,
I fain would have a tomb sublime as theirs."

Possibly the first stronghold erected by the Romans in
England, Richborough, was a place of importance during the
four hundred years of their stay and remains one of the most
eloquent witnesses to a distant and interesting past   An old
writer describing the site of the Roman city said that time
had devoured every trace of it " and to teach us that cities are
as perishable as men, it is now a cornfield, when the corn is
grown up, one may see traces of the streets intersecting each
other, for wherever the streets have run, the corn grows thin."
I cannot substantiate the pretty story, not having been able to
recognise any such thin lines through the flourishing crops.
Wide stretches of peas, potatoes and corn reach almost to the
walls on three sides, while on the fourth the steep bank masked
by many trees dips down to the level marsh.   A stout fencing
has been erected where the wall has crumbled— or been taken
away for road making.   On payment of a small fee permission
may be had to enter the great enclosure where sheep are
pastured, to visit the strange subterranean way, and to examine
the great walls twelve feet thick, so stoutly built of flint and
stone with courses of red tile that when some of the materials
were being removed the vandals responsible found it too
strong for working.   These grand ruins can be visited by
field-paths from Ash or Sandwich, or from the hamlet of Salt
Pans on the Ramsgate Road where a ferry takes us across the
Stour and following the marsh dykes brings us to the level
crossing on the railway and to the path leading up the steeper
side of the height on which the ruins stand.   The last is
perhaps the most impressive approach.

Sandwich, quaint old Cinque Port of tortuous streets and
ancient houses, suggestive by its very name of a dim, historic
past, and of modern golf links, lies on the right bank of the

Stour at its extreme southerly bend. As we approach it, the town, dominated by the curiously topped tower of St. Peter's Church, has the look of a foreign city. Over the

The Barbican, Sandwich.

river is a toll bridge and a quaint (restored) barbican spans the road, upon the wall of it being set out an elaborate scale of tolls, providing for payment from drivers of " Berlin chaises," " chairs," and " calashes." As the scale is dated 1905 these vehicles of the past seem to belong to the present. Long gone are the days when Swift penned his warning to writers—

> " Beware of Latin, authors all
> Nor think your verses sterling,
> Though with a golden pen you scrawl,
> And scribble in a berlin."

Now the author passes untolled on a bicycle, wondering whether the tollman would be able to differentiate a calash from a berlin. Motors are ignored on the scale, ranking presumably as " locomotives."

North, Sandwich looks over the flats by ancient Stonar and more ancient Richborough to Ebbsfleet and Thanet ; east it looks over sandy levels to where the retreating sea has gone, and all about these level river and shore meadows is now played the royal and ancient game of golf. On approaching Sandwich as we are now doing from the north the way in which all sorts and conditions of people play the great game is at once made strikingly manifest. Girls not yet in their 'teens are playing here ; there is a burly drayman—it is the dinner hour—refreshing himself, with his leathern apron tucked up cornerwise to show he is off duty, handling his iron with vigour and precision. We might be in the town of St. Andrews, patron saint of golf, by the way in which all ages and all classes follow the game. Out towards the sea are the more notable links. Probably few of those who come hither to indulge in the game are aware that in the sand dunes between here and Deal it was anciently the pleasant custom to bury thieves alive. Women criminals were drowned in the Guestling stream. The Cinque Ports had their own courts and were allowed seemingly to devise their own methods of punishing offenders.

It is said to be a good test of a man's bump of locality if once having visited Sandwich he can find his way through it— say from the Canterbury to the Deal roads—without making a misturning. The thing has been done. Dotted about the town are old houses of Tudor and earlier times, while a portion of worked flint wall—level as bricks—where the old guildhall once stood shows the wonderful way in which some earlier craftsmen did their work. Bits of carved decoration and old doorways and windows are to be seen in many of the streets, while some plain and unsuggestive exteriors hide olden and interesting bits. A one-time wayside inn (now dislicensed) has a fine stone arched room like a bit of an old crypt, and here tradition tells was one of the sleeping places for pilgrims bound for Canterbury. (The curious who go upstairs will find such a contrast between the now and then as may shock them.) On one of the pillars is a rudely incised shield with marks that might be meant for two crescents and a cross.

The chief "lion" of Sandwich is its plain, modern Guildhall the outside of which scarcely suggests that the inside is well worth a visit. Here is to be seen the ancient woodwork from the older town hall, and here the visitor has an object-lesson in the legal phrase "empanelling" a jury, for the removal of a panel reveals the jury box literally set in the wall. In the upper rooms are portraits of civic worthies and a very interesting series of pictures illustrating a great seventeenth century sea-fight between the Dutch and English, probably that of 1666, referred to in the preceding chapter. These pictures were only discovered in a house in the town in 1839. Other old pictures recovered at the same time show the entrance of a Stuart King and his Queen into Sandwich. On the beams are pikes which were of old carried before the judges at the time of the Assizes, reminding us of the fasces used in external decoration here and at the Canterbury Court House. Now Sandwich has fallen from something of its old estate, and the Assizes are no longer held there, though it is the seat of a Petty Sessions. It was here early in April—it should have been on the first of that month—in 1845 on a man who had been tried for some offence being found not guilty; the jury in its wisdom added a recommendation to mercy! Sandwich, raised but a few feet from the surrounding level, was at one time walled partly with stone and partly with high banks of earth—as Gravelines on the French coast is to-day. Now these old defences are formed into pleasant promenades. Once the most famous port in the kingdom, then for a time the seat of baize manufacture and market gardening, thanks to the influx of Flemish folk in Elizabeth's time, the town had fallen into a condition of neglect and is said only to have "wakened up" during the past quarter of a century or so since the great golf revival. Market gardening is still carried

on and the name Polders, or Poulders, applied to the
country lying between here and Woodnesborough, is a survival
of a Dutch word brought in in the sixteenth century, while
other names of persons and places found in the district—
Felderland, Flemings, etc.— are doubtless traceable to the
same influence.

It was at Sandwich that there dwelt, according to the
pleasant old ballad, "A beautiful lady whose name it
was Ruth" who was beloved by a young seaman of Dover.
The lady's parents would have nothing to do with the sailor and
locked the fair Ruth away from him, until at length in despair he
went off to Spain that his love might once more be given her
freedom. In Spain a lovely lady

> "with jewels untold,
> Besides in possession a million of gold,"

fell in love with and married him. Ruth ran away from home
to follow her lover to Spain—only to meet him with his
gorgeous wife "in Cadiz as she walked along the street." Ruth
decided to remain in his neighbourhood and opportunely the
wife died and the reunited lovers returned to her forgiving
parents. It is a whole romantic novel in a couple of hundred
lines, at the close the seemingly humble mariner inviting Ruth's
parents—still sorrowing over her disappearance—to his wedding,
when they find in the bride their long lost daughter!

> "'Dear parents,' said she, 'many hazards I run,
> To fetch home my love and your dutiful son;
> Receive him with joy, for 'tis very well known,
> He seeks not your wealth, he's enough of his own.'
>
> Her father replied, and he merrily smiled,
> 'He's brought home enough, as he's brought home my child;
> A thousand times welcome you are I declare,
> Whose presence disperses both sorrow and care.'"

Sentimental visitors to the old Cinque Port may well spare a
thought for the true lovers who went through so much—but
had their way in the end in despite of parental opposition,
while readers of modern novels may find amusement in seeing
how old is the convention which dictates the removal of a
husband or wife who is *de trop* so as to round off a story with
a happy ending.

K

Inland from Sandwich lie many clustering villages but a mile or two apart, approached by roads and lanes largely through unfenced fields, most of them having much to interest the student of history as it is written in the parish churches and their monuments, with rich hints of Saxon and Roman times. One of the most interesting is the nearest, Woodnesborough, with its suggestion of Saxon origin in its name. Here was a colony of the Flemish baizemakers, of whom we are reminded by the appearance of several of the old red-brick houses and cottages. Woodnesborough, set upon a little hill with pleasant outlook over the marsh to Ramsgate, is a

Woodnesborough.

village amid cherry orchards, hopfields and gardens. Here we reach the ground that, varied with bill and hollow, rises gradually to the Barham Downs. Ash to the north-west on the Canterbury road, or Staple-next-Wingham to the west, Chillenden—which gave one of its most notable priors to Canterbury Cathedral—to the south-west, may be taken on the byways to the Downs and so into the country referred to in the Canterbury district, or a pleasant rising road from Chillenden may be followed round Knowlton Park and thence by an open road with extensive views to the straggling village of Eastry, a couple of miles south of Woodnesborough on an old Roman road that ran from here to Dover. At Eastry King

Ethelbert had a palace, and here it is said that King Egbert had his cousins murdered and buried under his throne as the least likely place in which the bodies should be discovered. The palace at Eastry was frequently visited by Thomas à Becket, and here he hid on the eve of his flight to the continent, before the reconciliation which led to his return and the great tragedy of Canterbury. With little to show beyond some old cottages made more attractive by the near neighbourhood of certain newer ones, Eastry is pleasantly situated on a hill. To the south on the next hill is Betteshanger with its beautiful park set amid beautiful country. Once a week the park is thrown open to visitors, but at all times the roads alongside afford many glimpses of lovely woodland and turf. The roads, indeed, are like drives through a park, bordered as they are with great variety of trees and shrubs and sloping banks grown thickly with Rose of Sharon—long stretches of greenery thickly starred with gold in flowering time. From Little Betteshanger windmill is to be seen a magnificent view backwards to Thanet and eastwards over Deal to the sea : all round us are wide stretching fields of corn, of peas, of beans and of the sainfoin which gives to so many of our summer scenes in East Kent a touch of unaccustomed colour, the red patches showing markedly among the varied greens and contrasting strongly with picturesque patches of yellow where the persistent charlock has defied the farmer. The open roads wind up and down hill, southerly to join the Dover road and easterly to Deal and the sea, with the squat church tower of Northbourne village, from which the lordly owner of Betteshanger takes his title—showing prettily grouped in trees. South-west of us is the retired village of Tilmanstone near the pleasant Dover to Sandwich Road, passing further to the west than the old Roman way which takes a straighter course at more unequal heights by Studdal, or Studdle, for the signposts offer diversity of spelling. Coming shorewards by Northbourne, we reach Mongeham and Sholden, which run together and on into Deal with but little interval.

Deal to-day is a curious mixture of the old and the new, of the fisherman's and sailor's town devoted to the sea, and of the holiday resort depending upon the attractions of the shore ; for there are many people like the young man in the comedy, who only " dote upon the sea—from the beach." When the Stour

K 2

channel silted up and the old Roman Rutupiæ became no longer of service as a port, Sandwich rose into prominence, then when the sea retreated further to the east, to Deal fell much of that sea business for which Sandwich had become unfitted. When Thomas à Becket returned from exile, when Richard of the Lion Heart came home from Palestine, they landed at Sandwich, but when Anne of Cleves came to wed with Henry VIII., when Queen Adelaide first came to England, it was at Deal they landed. Perhaps in some distant century Deal will have become an inland town and its place be taken by some as yet undreamed-of town on the Goodwins. Mean-

Deal.

while, however, the Deal of the holiday maker enjoys a pleasantly diversified life along its sea front, old, or Upper Deal, being left stranded inland. Originally a "limb" of the neighbouring Cinque Port of Sandwich, Deal duly succeeded to much of the maritime importance of the older place and to that has now added the attractions of a pleasant front, a good beach and one of the most interesting of outlooks over the water, for the attraction of holiday making visitors.

It was somewhere in the neighbourhood of Deal that Cæsar brought his troops from the French coast in the year 55 B.C. when the bellicose attitude of the islanders on the heights above Dover made him seek a landing-place less favourable

to the defenders. This place was—the story is told at length
by Napoleon III. in his *History of Julius Cæsar* and by the
Rev. Frances T. Vine in his *Cæsar in Kent*—somewhere
between the ending of the chalk cliffs at Walmer and the mouth
of the Stour. Cæsar's own description of his landing-place
is shown to tally with Deal and according to Camden, writing
in 1586, there anciently hung in the Castle of Dover a chart
showing that the Roman leader did land at Deal and later
defeated the Britons on Barham Down. Even in Camden's time
that chart was only known by a transcription and tradition so
that it may well be accepted as evidence honorable on account

High Street, Deal.

of its age, while for the archæologist there is to be found
further evidence in the earth all round the neighbourhood.

> " And lofty Dele's proud towers are shown
> Where Cæsar's trophies grace the town,"

said Camden, Englishing Leland, and though the "trophies"
are not obvious to the visitor now they will be found in plenty
by the student. In the *Commentaries* it is recorded how
stubborn a fight the barbarians, possessing all the advantages of
knowing where the shallows were, made against the landing of
the legionaries, driving their armed chariots at full speed into
the water, and hurling stones and arrows at the foe. A
standard-bearer of the Tenth Legion seems to have borne a

notable part in changing the fortunes of the day: calling upon the gods for the success of his venture, he cried out "leap down, soldiers, unless you wish to betray the eagle to the enemy ; I, at any rate, shall have performed my duty to the state and my general." With this he jumped into the water, bearing the eagle standard towards the enemy. His fellows at once plunged after him, though they had long hesitated as it had not been possible to bring the vessels close in shore. Other deeds of heroism are recorded, and before sundown the invader had won his footing on the land and driven the natives to the shelter of the woods and hills to the West. Later came the Roman advance, the capture of the Barham ridge, and further defeats of the Britons—driven ever westwards.

It is difficult to-day, standing on the front and watching a crowd of sun-burned children gazing with rapt attention at a Punch and Judy show, to realise the old days when Deal, as a town, was not ; when extensive woodlands came probably far nearer to the coast ; to realise those days, nearly twenty centuries ago, when Rome, as though prophetically, reached out after this small island destined to an empire greater than her own. We must investigate the sand-hills — supposed to be artificially formed—to the north, pursue our investigations north to Richborough, and south to Dover, before we can grasp anything like an idea, both of the landing of those troops from Europe's further extreme, and of the manner in which they made their way through the country and consolidated their power. Many centuries later Deal saw the *reductio ad absurdum* of invasion when, in 1495, that persistent pretender, Perkin Warbeck, made one of his ineffectual descents on the coast as " Richard IV." The men of Deal and Sandwich sufficed to beat off the invader, inflicting on him heavy losses in slain and prisoners.

In the "good old days "—in time as in space, "'tis distance lends enchantment to the view," and if we may believe our elders, " man never is but always has been blessed "—in those days which are, by courtesy, called good, the whole of the coast along here was famous as a smuggling resort, and Deal was a particularly notorious centre. We have seen that the Thanet folk were ready to do a bit of smuggling when occasion offered, but from Deal, all round the coast until our Kentish story merges in that of Sussex, the coast has its traditions of smugglers and their cuteness in running their wares inland ; of their bravery in fighting the preventive officers ; of the way in which gentry and squires, aye, and even those who dwelt within the shadow of the old church towers, profited by the illicit transactions of those who spent their lives in support of the saying that stolen fruit are sweetest (and most profitable). The old Admiralty House, little more than a hundred years ago, is said to have had a room where, within a few feet of the seat of authority, smuggled goods were housed, and here it is said on one occasion the wife of the chief official kept a wounded smuggler *perdu* until he was nursed back to a state of health in which he could make good his escape. There is a curious kink in the nature of a large number of people by which they glory in doing mild illegalities—evading the income-tax which they themselves have imposed through their representatives ; in smuggling small things from abroad that they may have them the cheaper, or in buying things that someone else has smuggled for the same reason. In the palmy days of smuggling those who ran the risks of running a cargo generally did so as much to the benefit of ostensibly law-abiding receivers of smuggled goods as to their own. The old point of view was taken down a few years ago from a Deal man of eighty-eight : "Good times them, when a brave man might smuggle honest. Ah ! them were grand times ; when a man didn't go a-stealin' wi' his gloves on, an' weren't afraid to die for his principles." His "principles," of course, being those of the folk who found how profitable Free Trade was in Protectionist days. The "cut-throat town of Deal," as a seventeenth-century lady who could have but unhappy memories of the place wrote, has long ceased to be a smugglers' centre. But though traditions of the smuggling days are to be picked up now and again, it is mostly in the pages of the writers of eighteenth-century fiction that those days are made to live.

One smuggling story may be given from that storehouse of local lore *The Kentish Garland*.

"During the French War an eminent banking firm of Hebraic origin carried on a flourishing connexion between the rival interests of France and England : needless to state that each belligerent was totally unaware of the services rendered to the opposing nation. A large swift vessel, propelled by sails and the oars of hardy Deal boatmen, carried to the former country despatches from the English Government for their French spies, and to the French Government a cargo of English guineas, which at that time fetched thirty shillings ; and having safely disposed of this freight, the ship was laden in return with silk, brandy, lace, and tobacco, also letters from the spies : the latter were duly delivered to our authorities, and the former disposed of in and out of our county at a considerable profit. The captain was much trusted by his employers, and on one voyage he was informed his cargo was the largest he had carried—from ten to thirty thousand guineas. The head of the honourable firm anxiously awaited the return of his faithful servant, who appeared with a very rueful countenance, and informed him that, being chased by a government vessel, and fearful of being overhauled, they had cut the throats of the bags, and the yellow-boys were at the bottom of the sea ! The banker raved, and demanded the spot where the catastrophe had occurred ; the information rather reluctantly given, specified a spot close to the French coast, and the honest Hebrew, instinctively feeling that he had been ' done,' communicated with his French agents. Divers descended and brought back the bags, not, however, with their throats cut, but intact, save that, in place of their original contents, a stone was in each of them ! All parties being engaged in an illegal transaction the only revenge the banker could take was by dismissing the captain from his employment, who laughed in his face, when he literally danced and swore with rage. The crew, who shared in their chief's disgrace, seemed rather ' flush ' of money for some time, while the captain first bought a piece of ground and built himself a house ; in a short time he got a few more houses, land followed, and . . . . in the second generation his descendants were squires, and parsons, and justices of the peace."

At the north end of what is now the Marina—for Deal is stretching out to the sand-hills on the north and to Walmer on the south—used to stand Sandown Castle, one of the series built along the coast in the time of Henry VIII., when the condition of affairs on the Continent was such as to bring invasion of England within the range of probabilities. Sandown, now a thing of the past, is mainly memorable as having been the final scene of incarceration and of the death of Colonel John Hutchinson, that one of the heroic band of regicides who lives immortal in the biography written by his wife. Hutchinson's principal achievement was his stubborn defence of Nottingham against the Royalists. Though he had made submission to the restored Charles II. he was soon imprisoned on a specious pretext and about four months before his death (Sept. 11, 1664) was removed to the ruinous and unhealthy castle on this shore. Lucy Hutchinson, who had sought permission unavailingly to share her husband's imprisonment, took lodgings in " the cut-throat town of Deal," as she stigmatised it, and had to walk daily to and from the castle, but she was

away at the Nottinghamshire home when he died, leaving as
his last message to the wife who had shared his fortunes : " Let
her, as she is above other women, show herself in this occasion
a good Christian, and above the pitch of ordinary women."
Of the biblical monument which she raised to her husband's
memory—not published until nearly a century and a half
after his death—Green neatly says " the figure of Colonel
Hutchinson stands out from his wife's canvas with the grace
and tenderness of a portrait by Van Dyck."

Hutchinson had something of the taste of the virtuoso and
we learn from his wife that while imprisoned here at Sandown,
" When no other diversions were left him he diverted himself
with sorting and shadowing cockle-shells, which his wife and
his daughter gathered for him, with as much delight as he used
to take in the richest agates and onyxes he could compass,
with the most artificial engravings."   There is something
pathetic in the man of action in the prime of life—Hutchinson
was not fifty at his death—thus having to occupy himself with
the childish occupation of sorting shells.

At Deal was born in 1717 Elizabeth Carter, a notable worthy
in eighteenth century literary circles, a lady who did two
remarkable things in that she gained commendation of her
learning from Samuel Johnson and in that she made a sum of
one thousand pounds through a translation of Epictetus.   By
extraordinary perseverance she is said to have mastered Latin,
Greek, Hebrew, French, Italian, Spanish, German, Portuguese
and Arabic, and besides such linguistic attainments " she took
a great interest in astronomy, ancient and modern history, and
ancient geography, played both the spinnet and German flute,
and worked with her needle to the last days of her life " !   That
Mrs. Carter—the eighteenth century gave the courtesy title to
spinsters of mature years—was no mere blue-stocking we learn
from a famous remark of Johnson's : " My old friend Mrs. Carter
could make a pudding as well as translate Epictetus from the
Greek and work a handkerchief as well as compose a poem."
The greater part of the good lady's long life was spent in her
native town—with excursions to London and the Continent—
but her house has long since gone.   Though she died in her
eighty-ninth year while on a visit to London and was buried
there, a monument was duly erected to her memory in Deal
Chapel, of which her father had been perpetual curate.

A mile south of Sandown, but well within the town, is Deal Castle itself, another of the Tudor defences, which have been described as glorified blockhouses, and one still in use as a residence, set in a hollow near the shore and looking now rather like a superior piece of castle building erected by some giant children at play and left untouched by any tide but that of time, than a place for preventing the landing of an enemy. Deal Castle lacks the associations of the passed Sandown or of its neighbour at Walmer, another survivor from the times of Tudor panic or prevention policy.

When some two centuries ago a great storm swept the country and did more damage than the great fire of London of a few years earlier, the townspeople of Deal gained an unenviable notoriety. Hundreds of shipwrecked mariners—a thousand according to Defoe—had reached the temporary safety of the Goodwin Sands but the Deal boatmen would not put off to their rescue, contenting themselves with gathering from the waters floating valuables and leaving the men to drown with the next tide. Well might Defoe, the historian of the Great Storm, write

"If I had any Satire left to write,
    Could I with suited spleen indite,
My verse should blast that fatal town,
And drown'd sailors' widows pull it down ;
    No footsteps of it should appear,
And ships no more cast anchor there.
The barbarous hated name of Deal shou'd die,
    Or be a term of infamy ;
And till that's done, the town will stand
    A just reproach to all the land."

The charge of inhumanity has long since lost any point, and the men of Deal, picturesque loungers about the old capstans along the shore as they seem on a sunny afternoon, are when roused by storm ready and daring in their efforts to succour unhappy vessels driven on the Goodwins.

"Full many lives he saved with his undaunted crew,
    He put his trust in Providence, and cared not how it blew."

This epitaph on a Deal worthy might be applied to many of his fellows, ever ready to launch their boat to the rescue of those in peril on the sea.

Walmer has become a kind of southern suburb of Deal, and

Walmer Castle, partly hidden by trees and climbing ivy so that it seems a massive bower of greenery fronting the sea, is a few hundred yards from the shore at the point where the chalk cliff runs down to the level ground. A range of massive, squat buildings, trimly ivy-clad to the tops of their castellations and masked on either side by trees, such is the old-time seat of the Lord Warden of the Cinque Ports, the ornamental representative of that Count of the Saxon Shore on whom in past times so much depended. Within a century the sinecure office of Lord Warden was held by William Pitt, the great Duke of Wellington, W. H. Smith, M.P., and the present Lord Curzon. Now it is held by the Prince of Wales, and the Castle is not occupied but has become a show place where may be seen many things recalling to memory the notable Wardens, and especially those most notable of them all, William Pitt and the great Duke of Wellington. It was while Pitt was residing at Walmer Castle in 1802 that his birthday was celebrated by a dinner for which occasion Canning wrote his song " The Pilot that weathered the Storm." In the following year the " pilot " was accompanied to Walmer by his niece the eccentric Lady Hester Stanhope, and it was perhaps here that she retorted on one of the minister's supporters who had made an unfortunate remark upon a broken spoon being on the table, " Have you not yet discovered that Mr. Pitt sometimes uses very slight and weak instruments to effect his ends ? " It was only during the last three years of his life that Lady Hester Stanhope lived with her illustrious uncle, but she should be gratefully remembered by visitors for having planned the gardens. Pitt himself had the protecting plantation of beech and other trees formed, while about the grounds are pointed out various notable individual trees—the willow, originally a branch from the tree by Napoleon's grave in St. Helena, the lime under which Napoleon's conqueror was wont to sit in the evening of his days, an acacia said to have been planted by Queen Elizabeth and various others with similar personal association with departed greatness.

Pitt was the last Warden of the Cinque Ports on whom it fell to make preparations to repel a possible invader. When the massing of " Napoleon's banners at Boulogne " made it appear likely that the long-continued warfare was to cross the Channel Pitt organised and reviewed a large body of volunteers drawn from the Cinque Ports and their "limbs" and busied himself in promoting works of coast defence generally; his Martello Towers along the southern part of our county will be visited later on.   Here, too, when Nelson's fleet lay in the Downs, it is said that the great seaman came to confer with Pitt in a room that is one of those pointed out as marked by historic associations.

Wellington became Lord Warden of the Cinque Ports in 1829 and frequently resided at Walmer Castle thenceforward until his death on September 14, 1852.   The great soldier is indeed the Warden who has left the stamp of his personality most strongly on the place, who is best remembered in anecdote.   "The gaunt figure of the old Field-Marshal" had been familiarised by over twenty years' residence when

> " In the night, unseen, a single warrior,
>   In sombre harness mailed,
> Dreaded of man, and surnamed the Destroyer,
>   The rampart wall had scaled.
> He did not pause to parley or dissemble,
>   But smote the Warden hoar ;
> Ah ! what a blow, that made all England tremble,
>   And groan from shore to shore."

Longfellow's tribute to *The Lord Warden of the Cinque Ports* is a literary failure when contrasted with Tennyson's noble *Ode on the Death of the Duke of Wellington*, one stanza at least of which we may recall when visiting the place with which the story of his old age is indissolubly associated.   For years he had been here—most appropriately appointed of all the long line of Wardens—within sight of the country of that sinister " World-Victor " whom he had conquered :

> " Mourn, for to us he seems the last,
> Remembering all his greatness in the Past.
> No more in soldier fashion will he greet
> With lifted hand the gazer in the street.
> O friends, our chief state-oracle is mute :
> Mourn for the man of long enduring blood,
> The statesman-warrior, moderate, resolute,
> Whole in himself, a common good.
> Mourn for the man of amplest influence,
> Yet clearest of ambitious crime,
> Our greatest yet with least pretence,   .
> Great in council and great in war,
> Foremost captain of his time,

Rich in saving common-sense,
And, as the greatest only are,
In his simplicity sublime.
O good gray head which all men knew,
O voice from which their omens all men drew,
O iron nerve to true occasion true,
O fall'n at length that tower of strength
Which stood four-square to all the winds that blew !
Such was he whom we deplore.
The long self-sacrifice of life is o'er.
The great World-victor's victor will be seen no more."

St. Margaret's Bay.

Inland and southwards from Walmer the chalk cliffs rise
with some suddenness, and the whole aspect of the shore has
changed when we reach the small village of Kingsdown, partly
built upon the beach and partly up a narrow lane through the
hills—steep almost as the main street of Cornish Clovelly.
Beyond Kingsdown is the bold precipitous chalk cliff leading
to Hope Point, beyond which again nestles St. Margaret's Bay.
From the chalk heights here we see inland the rolling hills,
beautiful with corn, and northwards the whole tract of low

country to Thanet—the tract from which the Roman legions, the Saxon invaders, and then the Christian missionaries successively found their way into the country. Seawards we are looking across the Downs—the Piccadilly of the sea, as it has not very happily been named—to the Goodwin Sands : the Downs famous in our annals as a naval rendezvous, the Sands notorious for centuries for their heavy toll of wreckage and lost life.

"All in the Downs the fleet lay moored"

sang the poet who told of the romantic attachment of Black-eyed Susan for her William, and this roadstead has long been famous for its comparative safety in time of storm, the force of the waters being broken by the great stretch of the Goodwin Sands. Roughly speaking, the Downs extend from the North Foreland in Thanet to the South Foreland in the neighbourhood of Dover, and afford an anchorage extending about eight miles by six. In the great storm of November 26, 1703, the shipping in the Downs suffered terribly—as might be gathered from the fact already recorded of the barbarity of the Deal folk at that time. The great south-western gale swept men-of-war and merchantmen from their anchorage on to the Goodwins, and the loss could not be properly computed. According to Defoe thirteen ships of the Navy, and probably nearly two thousand men, were among the lost. The following letter, " coarse and sailor-like," was written by a sailor of H.M.S. *Shrewsbury*, and suggests something of the horror of the scene :—

Sir,—These lines I hope in God will find you in good health ; we are all left here in a dismal condition, expecting every moment to be all drowned : for here is a great storm, and is very likely to continue ; we have here the real admiral of the blew in the ship call'd the *Mary*, a third rate, the very next ship to ours, sunk. with Admiral Beaumont, and above 500 men drowned : the ship call'd the *Northumberland*, a third rate, about 500 men all sunk and drowned : the ship call'd the *Sterling Castle*, a third rate, all sunk and drowned above 500 souls : and the ship call'd the *Restoration*, a third rate, all sunk and drowned : these ships were all close by us which I saw ; these ships fired their guns all night and day long, poor souls, for help, but the storm being so fierce and raging, could have none to save them : the ship call'd the *Shrewsberry*, that we are in, broke two anchors, and did run mighty fierce backwards, with 60 or 80 yards of the sands, and as God Almighty would have it, we flung our sheet anchor down, which is the biggest, and so stopt : here we all pray'd to God to forgive us our sins, and to save us, or else to receive us into his heavenly kingdom. If our sheet anchor had given way, we had been all drown'd : but I humbly thank God, it was his gracious mercy that saved us.   There's one, Captain Fanel's ship, three hospital ships, all split, some sunk, and most of the men drown'd.

There are above 40 merchant ships cast away and sunk : to see Admiral Beaumont, that was next us, and all the rest of his men, how they climbed up the main mast, hundreds at a time crying out for help, and thinking to save their lives and in the twinkling of an eye, were drown'd : I can give you no account, but of these four men-of-war aforesaid, which I saw with my own eyes, and those hospital ships, at present, by reason the storm hath drove us far distant from one another : Captain Crow, of our ship, believes we have lost several more ships of war, by reason we see so few ; we lye here in great danger, and waiting for a north-easterly wind to bring us to Portsmouth, and it is our prayers to God for it ; for we know not how soon this storm may arise, and cut us all off, for it is a dismal place to anchor in. I have not had my cloaths off, nor a wink of sleep these four nights, and have got my death with cold almost.

Yours to command,
MILES NORCLIFFE.

Fortunately the terrible incident stands alone, and though there have been many wrecks on the Goodwins since, and many disastrous storms, there has been nothing nearly so calamitous to record as the great storm of 1703.   Most of us visiting this bit of the coast know the Downs as a brilliant strip of sea with an ever-passing procession of shipping, from grey war vessels and swift ocean-going liners to white or red sailed yachts and brown-sailed fishing boats, but when out at sea the stormy winds do blow, and much shipping has sought the shelter of the Downs, it is a memorable sight.

On the Goodwins at low tide it is possible to land on parts of the long extent of sands ; indeed, cricket has been indulged in on them by some zealous folk ; other parts are quicksand, in which, it is said, wrecked vessels rapidly disappear. It has been suggested that where the sands now extend was at one time an island, such as Thanet, and that this has been worn away by the sea, but it would be curious if at the same time that the sea was retiring from the Stour Valley it should have been eroding the coast so markedly in the immediate neighbourhood. The legend associating Tenterden Steeple with the swallowing up of certain lands of Earl Godwin, and thus with the forming of the God-win or Goodwin Sands may be better considered at the western town.   An old tradition declared that beneath the waters in the neighbourhood of the sands could be seen remains of Earl Godwin's castles and towns.   But such tradition is not uncommon on various coasts ; it is to be met with off Chichester, in the neighbouring county.

The quaint old versifier, John Taylor, known as the Water Poet, who had, it must be admitted, but a pennyworth of poetry to an unconscionable quantity of water, made *A Discovery by Sea from London to Salisbury*, and early in his tremendous voyage he had the unpleasant experience of grounding on the Goodwins. A single shrimper, however, sufficed to do the work of a lifeboat crew :—

> " Till near unto the haven where Sandwich stands,
> We were enclosèd with most dangerous sands ;
> There were we sous'd and slabber'd, washed and dashed,
> And gravel'd that it made us half abash'd :
> We look'd, and pry'd, and starèd round about,
> From our apparent perils to get out ;
> For with a staff as we the depth did sound,
> Four miles from land, we almost were on ground,
> At last, unlook'd for, on our larboard side
> A thing turmoiling in the sea we spy'd,
> Like to a merman : wading as he did,
> All in the sea his nether parts were hid,
> Whose brawny limbs, and rough, neglected beard,
> And grim aspect made half of us afeard ;
> And as he unto us his course did make,
> I courage took, and thus to him I spake :
> ' Man, monster, fiend or fish, whate'er thou be,
> That travelest here in Neptune's monarchy,
> I charge thee by his dreadful three-tined mace
> Thou hurt not me or mine in any case ;
> And if thou be'st produced of mortal kind,
> Show us the course how we some way may find
> To deeper water from these sands so shallow
> In which thou seest our ship thus wash and wallow.'
> With that, he (shrugging up his shoulders strong)
> Spake (like a Christian) in the Kentish tongue.
> Quoth he, ' Kind sir, I am a fisherman,
> Who many years my living thus have won
> By wading in these sandy troublous waters
> For shrimps, whelks, cockles, and such useful matters,
> And I will lead you (with a course I'll keep)
> From out these dangerous shallows to the deep.'
> Then (by the nose) along he led our boat,
> Till (past the flats) our bark did bravely float.
> Our sea horse, that had drawn us thus at large
> I gave two groats unto, and did discharge."

Which cannot be regarded as extravagant salvage.

CHAPTER VII

FOLLOWING our coast on from the point at which we looked back over the low land and out over the Downs and the Goodwin Sands, we have a choice of routes. At low tide the venturesome can easily get round Hope Point by the shore, a way I have not tried : pedestrians who prefer grand views over land and sea may follow the cliff roads and footpath over the short turf of the chalk heights, with some steep climbing well repaid by the extensive views, by the beautiful air and by the ever-singing larks, which accompany us unceasingly all round the coast, and perhaps by a glimpse of some of the sea-birds that make their home here. Cyclists will do well to follow the main road by Ringwold, and from the neighbourhood of its church, with a singular minaret-shaped turret, to look back over the sloping valley to the sea. From Ringwold there is a beautiful footpath over the Lynch and the Free Downs—about the parish rights over which there has recently been some trouble—to the village of St. Margaret's, or St. Margaret's at Cliff as it is sometimes named. If the main road is followed—an up and down hill course through a well-wooded tract—we turn to the left in the neighbourhood of Martin Mill to reach the most retired of our seaside places.

St. Margaret's, the village from which the justly celebrated little bay takes its name, is perched high on the downs a mile or so from the sea, but the exploiting of the beauties of the bay will perhaps at no very distant date link the two villages together. At present St. Margaret's is the 'church town,' as they say in Cornwall, of St. Margaret's Bay. At the foot of the hills, on a scanty plot of ground is a group of houses, on the top are large hotels and a coastguard, while away over the swelling uplands are to be seen—the shadows of coming events—notices as to eligible building sites, markings as of roads in posse. The possible St. Margaret's Bay is, however, a thing of speculation, and probably not of the near future ; the actual St. Margaret's Bay is one of the pleasantest and most retired spots on our coast, over two miles from its

Norman Church, St. Margaret's.

railway station at Martin Mill. It has indeed no parallel in Kent. A long flight of broad, shallow steps, a wide steep road and a steeper " zig-zag " provide means of getting from the height to the shore where a few houses and cottages clustered among trees nestle in almost subtropical warmth. As after coming from the windswept headland of Hartland Point we find flowering Clovelly almost too warm, so coming from the windy open, chalk downs above we find St. Margaret's in a summer heat. The precipitous face of the cliff where it trends inward to form the small bay is grown with many trees and shrubs nearly to the water, giving a luxuriant air to the whole and contrasting strongly with the bold chalk cliffs standing, sheerly precipitous, at either horn of the bay. Cliff paths in either direction pass up over the short turf of the chalk to Hope Point from which we have come, or to the South Foreland, the twin light-houses of which show plainly a mile or so away. Unspoiled as yet it bids fair to become popular with those who seek a quiet holiday resort, and so perhaps to get its character changed by the very enthusiasm of the people who like it as it is.

The South Foreland lighthouses should be visited not only by those interested in those twinkling points of fire by which the seaman steers his course, but by all who would appreciate the more extended view which is to be had from them, with the endless procession of shipping passing to and from the Channel. The Foreland cliffs are nearly four hundred feet above the shore, so that the lights are seen at a great distance —nearly thirty miles, it is said. The grand cliff footpath walk which may be followed all the way to Dover is far preferable to the road. The shore route is not to be recommended unless to those who like a spice of danger, for it can only be taken at low water and the precipitous cliffs offer no footing to any-one who should be caught by the tide. About the chalk cliffs here may be seen any number of gulls and guillemots, and occasionally rare sea birds are noted in the neighbourhood.

At Dover, the door or key of England according to the con-fused similitudinising of one of the translators of Matthew Paris, we are in a place of mixed memories, a place which probably fifty people pass through for every one who pauses there sufficiently long to know much about it. To the traveller journeying to or from the Continent Dover is but a place for changing from train to steamer, or steamer to train, and it will not even be that if the projectors of the new " Ferry " have their way, for then railway carriages will run straight on board —it will be but a pausing place while changing from land travel to sea faring. To such travellers Dover is just a town of call dominated by cliffside barracks and a castle, a town scattered about the hollow at the foot of the hills flanked by great cliffs and rounded downs on either side. The sojourner in Dover

finds that it is something more than that, finds that it is at once
a place of many memories worth recalling and a centre from
which in various directions interesting journeys may be made
by footpath, road or rail.   It was to Dover, it will be remembered, that Mr. Jarvis Lorry and Miss Manette came on their
way to meet the varied experiences which are set forth in
the *Tale of Two Cities*, and Dover was the place at which, after
his long tramp, little David Copperfield made himself known
to his aunt.   It is to Dover that a large proportion of travellers
to and from the Continent come that they may cross the inter-
vening water at its narrowest ; it was Dover that was the port
of connection with Gaul before the coming of the Romans ;

Dover.

and it was at Dover that Cæsar would have landed if the
Britons had permitted.   In those distant days the sea penetrated
some distance inland along the small valley of the stream, the
Dour, from which the town takes its name but now the creek
has got silted up, what level ground there is having been utilised
for building houses and docks.   Now the town is protected by
the great naval harbour works still in construction.   Beyond
Sandwich we might have seen the huge concrete blocks made
for these works, each single block the size of the railway truck
on which it was borne ; as many miles west of Dover may be
observed the gathering of the shingle used for the same purpose.
The great stretch of the harbour needs to be looked at from

above for the proper appreciation of the magnitude of the under-
taking—from either the Castle Hill or from the western heights
towards Shakespeare's Cliff. From any of these bold eminences,
too, we have a fine view of the town, and a glimpse of the
French coast opposite.

Most sojourners in Dover are first drawn to the Castle, as
they have been for several centuries, for, as in 1597 the young
German lawyer named Paul Hentzner wrote, "upon a hill, or
rather rock, which on its right side is almost everywhere a
precipice, a very extensive castle rises to a surprising height,

Dover Castle, Town and Harbour from the Railway.

in size like a little city, extremely well fortified, and thickset
with towers, and seems to threaten the sea beneath." Though
the Romans had an important station here, the only obvious
link with them is in the pharos still standing at the end of St.
Mary's Church in the Castle precincts—companion to one
which probably stood on the opposite hill. Of the Roman
Castle patient archæologists are hard put to it to trace out
the design, but in the existing edifice with its various towers,
its underground passages, its armouries we have a very fine
specimen of the Norman Castle, with however, of course,
many modifications during modern times. From the top of

the Keep we may get yet another splendid view, embracing a goodly stretch of the French coast as well as of the British cliffs to the north and west ; may see the coasts-linking steamers reduced to toy dimensions in perspective cutting their way across the Channel, and the trailing smoke of other vessels showing where the narrow seas lead onward to the ocean.

From the earliest times, from the days when the Romans erected the pharos to guide their vessels to the nearest point of land from Gaul, Dover has been the scene of momentous arrivals and departures innumerable. Here for many centuries England has welcomed the coming and speeded the parting guest. Sometimes there has been a dramatic touch in the welcome, as when in 1416 the good Duke Humphrey of Gloucester, warden of the Cinque Ports and constable of Dover Castle, welcomed the Emperor Sigismund. According to the story, he rode into the water with a naked sword in his hand and obtained from the powerful visitor a promise that if permitted to land he would neither exercise nor claim any jurisdiction in England. The scene is illustrated, with other incidents in the history of Dover, in the windows of the new Town Hall. The reception reminds us of the way in which the men of Kent dictated their terms to the Conqueror. Sometimes there is a touch of humour rather than of purpose about the stories told of these royal and imperial visits, for it runs that when Queen Elizabeth came to Dover the worshipful Mayor, standing on a stool, began a loyal address with "Most gracious Queen, welcome —— " He was allowed to proceed no further for her imperious Majesty unceremoniously broke in with :—

> "Most gracious fool
> Get off that stool.'

According to tradition good Queen Bess must have had a Silas Wegg-like tendency to drop into poetry on the slightest provocation and to have been particularly fond of dubbing her loyal lieges fools—the jingle which she is supposed to have improvised on visiting Coventry ends in the same tenour. Her judgment as to the capacities of her subjects seems to have been much the same as that which Carlyle had of his contemporaries, though in her time it was something less than forty millions who were "mostly fools." Another traditional association of Queen Elizabeth is to be had where in the neighbourhood of the Castle the visitor is shown a highly decorated brass cannon twenty-three feet long popularly known as "Queen Elizabeth's pocket pistol." The gun, really a present from the Emperor Charles V. to King Henry VIII., was cast at Utrecht and bears the inscription

> " Brecck sevret al mure endewal
>   Bin ic gebeten
> Doer Berch en dal boert minenbal
>   Van mi gesmeten."

which has been Englished :

> " O'er hill and dale I throw my ball
> Breaker my name of mound and wall."

Dover has had to suffer in olden war-time from its nearness to the Continent ; indeed, according to Camden, King Arthur held his Court in the Castle here, and after an absence in France had to fight the usurping Mordred for his throne. The tradition is sufficiently strong to account for the names of Arthur and Guinevere being attached to rooms and towers in the Castle. Hengist and Horsa are said to have held it, too, at one time. In the thirteenth century Dover was the scene and centre of much fighting : when King John did his best to allow his country to lie at the proud foot of a conqueror, the Dauphin, in 1216, with the aid of the barons, tired of the vacillations of their king, secured the whole of Kent, except Dover, only to be told by his father that "unless he had taken Dover Castle, he had not gained a foot of land in England." Piqued, as we may believe by the parental reproof, the Dauphin returned from London to besiege Dover. He had to raise the siege and return to it again with reinforcements from France ; but Hubert de Burgh, the Constable, met the coming fleet and won a notable naval victory within sight of his stubbornly brave garrison at the Castle. Towards the close of the same century Dover was more than once ravaged by the French at a time when the Cinque Ports' fleet was away, and later the King established a mint at Dover for the benefit of the ill-used townspeople; while later still, to hasten the return of their prosperity, it was enacted that all merchants, travellers and pilgrims bound for the Continent should embark at the port of Dover only.

Four centuries later watchers on the cliff about Dover might have seen something of another naval engagement, when the Invincible Armada came up the Channel, followed by Drake and his sea-dogs. "Never," says Motley, "since England was England, had such a sight been seen as now revealed itself in those narrow straits between Dover and Calais. Along that low, sandy shore, and quite within the range of the Calais fortifications, one hundred and thirty Spanish ships— the greater number of them the largest and most heavily-armed in the

Ewell from Kearsney Station.

world—lay face to face, and scarcely out of cannon-shot, with one hundred and fifty English sloops and frigates, the strongest and swiftest that the Island could furnish, and commanded by men whose exploits had rung through the world." Of the result of that memorable encounter it is not necessary here to speak, but it is well that Dover should remember that the two great fleets—the one to be destroyed, the other to triumph in signal fashion—were drawn up in battle array within sight of these high cliffs.

In the town itself we have a comfortable, prosperous-looking place, rich in story, but without any special features of interest

to show.   In the graveyard of the old St. Martin's Church was
buried the satiric poet, Charles Churchill, who had died in
Boulogne at the early age of thirty-three.   A brave line from
his poem, " The Candidate," served as his epitaph :—

> "Life to the last enjoyed, here Churchill lies."

The whole passage may be taken as curiously prophetic of
his burial in a place through which so many thousand persons,
" travel-bound," should pass—

> " Let one poor sprig of Bay around my head
>   Bloom whilst I live, and point me out when dead
> Let it (may Heav'n indulgent grant that pray'r)
> Be planted on my grave, nor wither there ;
> And when, on travel bound, some rhiming guest
> Roams thro' the Church-yard, whilst his Dinner's dress'd,
> Let it hold up this Comment to his eyes :
> Life to the last enjoy'd, here Churchill lies ;
> Whilst (O, what joy that pleasing flatt'ry gives)
> Reading my Works, he cries—*here* Churchill lives."

Little more than half a century after the satirist had been
buried his grave was visited by a notable " rhiming guest," a
keener satirist and a far greater poet—Lord Byron—who wrote
commemorative lines entitled " Churchill's Grave ; a Fact
Literally Rendered " :—

> " I stood beside the grave of him who blazed
>   The comet of a season, and I saw
> The humblest of all sepulchres, and gazed
>   With not the less of sorrow and of awe
> On that neglected turf and quiet stone,
> With name no clearer than the names unknown,
> Which lay unread around it ; and I ask'd
>   The Gardener of that ground, why it might be
> That for this plant strangers his memory task'd,
>   Through the thick deaths of half a century ?
>
> .   .   .   .
>
> Thus spoke he,—' I believe the man of whom
> You wot, who lies in this selected tomb,
> Was a most famous writer in his day,
> And therefore travellers step from out their way
> To pay him honour,—and myself whate'er
>   Your honour pleases : '—then most pleased I shook
> From out my pocket's avaricious nook

Some certain coins of silver, which as 'twere
Perforce I gave this man, though I could spare
So much but inconveniently :-- Ye smile,
I see ye, ye profane ones, all the while,
Because my homely phrase the truth would tell.
You are the fools, not I—for I did dwell
With a deep thought and with a soften'd eye
On that Old Sexton's natural homily,
In which there was Obscurity and Fame—
The Glory and the Nothing of a name."

The barracks, batteries and military works with which many
parts of the heights about the town are covered and honey-
combed need neither detain us nor move us to the con-
temptuous indignation of a Cobbett, but it is not possible to be
long in or about Dover without being made aware that it is a
garrison town.

To the south-west rises a height which, from some
unknown date, has been called Shakespeare's Cliff, on the
assumption that it is the "horrible steep" referred to in that
wonderful scene in *King Lear*, in which the blinded Gloucester
seeks to destroy himself, and is pathetically deceived by his
son Edgar. It has been disputed whether the cliff to which
Shakespeare's name is attached was ever seen by him and
whether the description applies to it, but the disputation is
idle in that Edgar is describing a precipice as seen in the
mind's eye and is doing so with intended exaggeration. From
the same spot a few minutes later he pretends to be gazing
upwards—

" Look up a-height ; the shrill-gorged lark so far
Cannot be seen or heard."

The scene is laid in " fields near Dover," and the description is
sufficiently near to satisfy any but the most literal. Whoever
it may be that first identified this cliff with Shakespeare's
scene, the identification has appealed to popular sentiment,
and Shakespeare's Cliff it is likely to remain as long as a
Shakespeare-reading civilization endures. It is a steep climb
up past the coastguard station to the "dread summit of this
chalky bourn "—the top of the cliff is 350 feet above the
sea level—and, despite the quidnuncs, most devout Shakes-
peareans' will wish to recall the opening passage of the
memorable scene :—

Glou.   When shall we come to the top of that same hill ?
Edg.   You do climb up it now : look, how we labour.
Glou.   Methinks the ground is even.
Edg.   Horrible steep.
Hark, do you hear the sea ?
Glou.   No, truly.
Edg.   Why, then your other senses grow imperfect
By your eyes' anguish.

Shakespeare's Cliff.

Glou.   So may it be, indeed :
Methinks thy voice is alter'd, and thou speak'st
In better phrase and matter than thou didst.
Edg.   You're much deceived ; in nothing am I changed
But in my garments.
Glou.   Methinks you're better spoken.
Edg.   Come on, sir ; here's the place : stand still. How fearful
And dizzy 'tis to cast one's eyes so low !
The crows and choughs that wing the midway air
Show scarce so gross as beetles : half way down
Hangs one that gathers samphire, dreadful trade !
Methinks he seems no bigger than his head :

The fishermen that walk upon the beach
Appear like mice ; and yond tall anchoring bark
Diminished to her cock ; her cock, a buoy
Almost too small for sight : the murmuring surge
That on the unnumber'd idle pebbles chafes
Cannot be heard so high. I'll look no more,
Lest my brain turn and the deficient sight
Topple down headlong.
Glou.   Set me where you stand.
Edg.   Give me your hand : you are now within a foot
Of the extreme verge : for all beneath the moon
Would I not leap upright.
Glou.   Let go my hand.
Here, friend, 's another purse ; in it a jewel
Well worth a poor man's taking : fairies and gods
Prosper it with thee ! Go thou further off :
Bid me farewell, and let me hear thee going.
Edg.   Now fare you well, good sir.
Glou.   With all my heart.
Edg.   Why I do trifle thus with his despair
Is done to cure it."

The cliff which Edgar is supposed to have been describing has
three practical interests attaching to it besides its sentimental
association with the name of Shakespeare—through it runs a
railway tunnel three-quarters of a mile long, and through it
(when the English people, as a gallant Admiral has twitted them,
have thrown off fear) will be run the loop tunnel which will take
trains down to the Channel Tube and so to France. Long
talked about, often delayed, the "Tunnel" seems an inevitable
coming event as soon as timid opposition shall have been worn
away, and as at present designed it will start from England in
a great loop beneath this cliff and the neighbouring heights.
The third utilitarian interest attaching to Shakespeare's Cliff is
that at the southern end of the present tunnel may be seen
evidence of the borings that have been made to prove Kentish
coal a matter of consideration.   Some of us would find no gratification in the converting of this corner of Kent into a new Black
Country and look with equanimity on the but qualified success
that has been attained. The promoters of the scheme have done
their best to prove that old Lambarde was wrong, for speaking
of Kent he says, "There is no Minerall or other profit digged out
of the belly of the earth here."   He had apparently forgotten
that the "minerall" known as Kentish ragstone was largely used
in building Kent's many churches, and that when Westminster

Abbey was a-building the King commanded that Kentish stone was not to be used for any other purpose until the Abbey was completed.

The road from Dover to Folkestone is variedly beautiful, passing as it does between sloping chalk hills. Another steeper and more attractive way takes us up over the cliffs—Shakespeare's Cliff, Abbot's Cliff—attaining a height of 524 feet before the sharp descent into Folkestone begins, and yet another way for those who like the fascinations of shore walking is round by the foot of the cliffs, one of the most delightful and varied journeys of the kind to be taken. It is a rough walk of about ten miles but the views of the successive cliffs, the fallen portions on the shore, and, as we get nearer to Folkestone, the floriferous Undercliff and Warren, amply repay the stout walker for the roughness of the journey. There are, too, several opportunities of leaving the shore and attaining the heights by steps and zig-zag paths, should the pedestrian wish for surer footing than the beach affords, but this stretch is quite unlike any other shore walk which our county has to offer and is one in which those with a taste for geology and botany may find much delight. For those to whom the whole distance is over much a portion of the shore may be examined, say, from near Shakespeare's Cliff to the steps known as Peter Becker's Stairs, and the Warren may be visited from Folkestone.

Inland from Dover lie many pleasant places to be reached by those in search of open hilly fields, pleasant footpaths and rustic lanes. Northwards by the Castle Hill we may go on, passing near the place where the extensive buildings of the transplanted Duke of York's School are being erected on a grand and healthy height, and so to Guston, Whitfield and East and West Langdon, villages situated on high ground which boast of being so healthy that they have long been celebrated as places inhabitants of which have attained great longevity. From West Langdon a pleasant up and down road through corn and clover takes us by a small place rejoicing in the name of Little America, and really the small homestead set in a clearing backed by trees and fronting the "rolling" farmlands so suggests the new world that it is easy to believe American visitors driving out here from Dover find the place "just cunning." Beyond is the broad extent of Waldershare Park with an old-fashioned Belvidere from the summit of which is to be obtained a mag-

nificent view.   An early nineteenth century writer put it thus :
" here might pleasure roam in sylvan scenes, or contemplation
muse on Nature's fairest features ; or thence expand the enrap-
tured thought to worlds of brighter glory, beyond the verge of
this terrestrial orb."   Several private roads and footpaths cross
the beautiful park with its grand and varied trees, but the
cyclist finds himself refused admission and if he would see more
than the fringe of the park and would avail himself of the
privilege of climbing the Belvidere he had best leave his cycle
at Eythorne, at the northern corner, near which a footpath gives
access to the park.   Malmains Farm in the neighbourhood
perpetuates the Norman family who held Waldershare for the
first three centuries after the Conquest.   By the roadside along
the west of the park, by a pleasant strip of beech-trees may
be seen in June many flowers of the beautiful and not very
common white helleborine—one of perhaps a dozen different
kinds of rare and common orchises which may be found about
this Dover district by the patient botaniser.   The Undercliff
towards Folkestone is particularly rich in different species of
these fascinating plants.

Reaching the south-western corner of Waldershare Park we
come to one of the most interesting of our churches at Coldred.
The small edifice, dedicated to St. Pancras, is placed within
entrenchments supposed to have been thrown up by the
Romans—several of the churches in this part of Kent are thus
situated—and but for a neighbouring farmhouse stands alone
at some distance from the village, which, according to tradition,
owes its name to Ceoldred, King of Mercia, who came hither
in the eighth century to help the Men of Kent against the
West Saxons.

A couple of miles north of Coldred, past Sibertswold—which
has become corrupted into Shepherds Well—lies the small
village of Barfreston, with a church which will well repay the
visitor, whether he approach it from Canterbury or Dover.   It
si equally accessible from either of these places, being something less than a couple of miles from Shepherds Well station.
According to Sir Francis Burnand, in his amusing *Zig-zag
Guide Round and About the Bold and Beautiful Kentish Coast*,
I should perhaps say that it is equally inaccessible from both,
for the humorist makes much fun about the difficulty of
reaching Barfreston.   That, however, is but the way of the

humorist, for any walker equal to a journey of three miles or so can go to and from the quaint church by a pleasant road partly through open fields, passing on the way some fine old yew trees, suggesting that this was one of the pilgrim routes converging on Canterbury.

Detail of South Door of Barfreston Church.

Standing on a knoll projecting from the hillside, the tiny church of Barfreston is a rare specimen of Norman architecture which must appeal even to those least susceptible to such. Its beautifully carved doorway, its rose window, its numerous carved heads and grotesques take the eye at once, and inside there are matters no less interesting—wreathed pillars and

remains of frescoes.   Though restored nearly seventy years ago
the little church is not one of those spoiled in restoration.   It
is a place about which to linger, for it shows us more than any
other existing church of the kind the loving work which our
forefathers devoted to their places of worship, even where these
were in but sparsely populated centres, for it does not seem
likely that the village of Barfreston was ever a large one.   Now
the little hillside church, in its small God's acre, tells us much
of the distant days—probably the twelfth century—when it was
erected.   As Sir Francis Burnand—dropping into seriousness
—says, " To all to whom the tranquil delight of an ancient
church is dear, to all who revel in a daydream, to all who love
to be silent, to ponder, and, undisturbed by verger, by professional explainer, or by any other sort of bore, to sit, to rest,
and to be thankful, Barfreston Church on a warm, sunny day
in August offers the very haven where they would be :

' I have been there and still would go.' "

In a quiet, retired church like this, bearing in its every stone
evidence of the deep faith in which it was wrought, set amid
fields on a hillside with nothing but a few quiet dwellings near,
religion seems to wear another aspect than that which it bears
even in an antique pile like Canterbury Cathedral.   There it is
the traditions of which we think, of the princes of the church,
of the great tragedy, and of many splendid scenes of which the
edifice has been the centre or background.   Here it is as
though the men had built the church as an expression of the
religion which was in them, rather than with any idea of
splendour.   There we are made to feel at every turn that we
are in a show place.   Here we seem to get nearer to the spirit
which first animated man in the building of churches.

From Barfreston we may return to the Dover and Canterbury
road in the neighbourhood of Sibertswold, and so get back to
Lydden at the head of the short valley of the Dour.   It was
perhaps in this neighbourhood, coming from Barham Downs,
that the German traveller, Hentzner, had an unpleasant experience in a narrow escape from thieves—or ghosts !   He and his
companions had set out on post horses, presumably at night,
for it was two or three o'clock in the morning when they reached
Dover.

"In our way to it, which was rough and dangerous enough, the following accident happened to us : our guide, or postillion, a youth, was before with two of our company, about the distance of a musket shot ; we, by not following quick enough, had lost sight of our friends ; we came afterwards to where the road divided ; on the right it was downhill and marshy, on the left was a small hill : whilst we stopped here in doubt, and consulted which of the roads we should take, we saw all on a sudden on our right hand some horsemen, their stature, dress and horses exactly resembling those of our friends ; glad of having found them again, we determined to set on after them ; but it happened, through God's mercy, that though we called to them, they did not answer us, but kept on down the marshy road at such a rate, that their horses' feet struck fire at every stretch, which made us, with reason, begin to suspect they were thieves, having had warning of such ; or rather, that they were nocturnal spectres, who, as we were afterwards told, are frequently seen in those places : there were likewise a great many Jack-a-lanterns, so that we were quite seized with horror and amazement. But fortunately for us our guide soon after sounded his horn, and we, following the noise, turned down the left-hand road, and arrived safe to our companions ; who, when we had asked them if they had not seen the horsemen who had gone by us, answered, not a soul. Our opinions, according to custom, were various upon this matter ; but whatever the thing was, we were, without doubt, in imminent danger, from which that we escaped, the glory is to be ascribed to God alone."

I have not seen Hentzner's "spectres" in the neighbourhood on day-time visits,—perhaps those interested in psychical research might have better luck at night, for man is a more timid creature in the dark and spooks are mostly born of darkness and timidity.

Lydden, scattered along the roadside in a hollow of the chalk hills, is between the fourth and fifth milestones from Dover. Those who like the highway may follow the course of the Dour to its outlet at the town to which it gives a name. Doing so we pass through Ewell where King John retired from Dover after disgracefully resigning his crown into the hands of the Papal Legate, and where the Knights Templars had a residence. Those who prefer the more alluring byways and heights have choice of the hills north and south. North, by a steeply rising unfenced road fringed with the pale yellow rock-rose— with a glimpse into the deep railway cutting and the mouth of the tunnel—leads to Coldred ; while south-westerly a pleasant lanes goes to Alkham, pleasant, that is, for those who like the varied ups and downs of the chalk hill country. Enquiring the way on my first visit to this retired village I was told at Lydden "it is about two miles—it will take you half an hour." " But I have my bicycle," I objected. " Oh, yes, I know," came the retort, " but it'll take you quarter of an hour to push it up, and another quarter to get it down." This was fairly accurate, though there is a short level stretch at the top. The descent into Alkham is by a beautiful, steep, partly grassy and overshaded lane, and arrival in the village reminds one of arrival in some Swiss hamlet. Indeed, if Alkham were not so near to home it would surely attract many visitors. It is a small place, the houses scattered about the hillsides in a little Happy Valley with lovely country meadows, woodlands and lanes on every side ; with some of the cottages so perched on the hillside that the gardens are laid out terrace-wise. For those who like a quiet country village Alkham will be found one of the most fascinating that our county, despite its richness in such, can offer ; it needs no old associations, no traditions, its beauty is all-sufficient and is such as to draw us again and again, to live in our memory as a haunt of ancient peace. About midway between Alkham and Dover and visitable from either are the remains of St. Radigunds Abbey (sometimes called Bradsole Abbey) a twelfth century establishment. The fine gateway has unfortunately suffered from " restoration " but the ruins, largely incorporated in farm buildings, will well repay the visitor not only on account of their extent but as showing how in days when men are not supposed to have studied the picturesque in scenery the monks yet frequently fixed the sites of their places where beautiful country lay before their eyes. A pleasant footpath may be followed from the Abbey to Copt Hill and thence the open road be taken back to Dover, " inhaling great draughts of space " as the poet of the open road has put it.

CHAPTER VIII

THOUGH the older streets of Folkestone possess yet some of the attractiveness of the old-time fishing village, and though the town is advertised as one of the " beauty spots " of England, its attractiveness to some of us lies less in itself than in its being a centre whence may be made many excursions to places of interest and of most varied beauty. Yet there is a beauty about the panorama of the town approached by road either from the summit of the hill as we reach the declivity down which the way from Dover twists, or from the north, where the road through the opening between the conical Sugar-Loaf Hill and Cæsar's Camp gives a wide view of the valley on the sea side of which the red-brick town is clustered. Approached thus, Folkestone is really beautiful, the more sudden entry between the bare downs made by the railway gives quite another impression. So steep are the sides of the conical hill and of the broader Cæsar's Camp that the small boys butterfly hunting on them look as though their footing must be most precarious, and the nervous observer expects momently to see them roll over and over until stopped by the hedges below. The cattle seem to be emulating the surer-footed goats as they walk along narrow paths which they have made to and fro along the side of the hill until the whole front of Cæsar's Camp looks as though cut into a series of tiny grassy terraces.

The view from Cæsar's Camp—which is by some authorities believed not to have been a camp of Julius Cæsar's, though admitted that it may have been formed by one of his successors —is a magnificent one across the downs east and west and

M 2

over green fields, and the pleasant orchards of Cherry Garden
Valley to Folkestone and Sandgate and the hills about Hythe,

Fishermen's Quarter, Folkestone.

with a mile and a half in front of us the waters of the Channel.
On this high point it is suggested that the Romans probably had
another pharos for the guidance of their vessels crossing the

narrow seas trom Gaul. The road which keeps along the
high ground at the back of Cæsar's Camp and its companion

High Street, Folkestone.

hill offers an ever changing panorama as we go on past the
Folkestone Water Works to Paddlesworth or to where the
Elham Valley begins.

Reaching Folkestone we find that its appearance of flatness as seen from the heights was only appearance, for it is disposed about irregular cliffs at the shore side and is not without variety. It is a pleasant, prosperous seaside town so favoured by its situation, facing south and enringed by hills, that it has won repute as a mild health resort in our unpleasanter seasons and as a holiday place in summer time ; its streets, its front and its Lees—or cliff walk—all bear witness at once to its popularity and to its prosperity, while down at the harbour with the coming and going of the Boulogne steamers— the French town is dimly visible in favourable weather —there is always matter to attract the lounging idler. Up on the Lees—to be attained by a lift from the beach—is a memorial to Folkestone's most famous son, William Harvey, the discoverer of the circulation of the blood. Harvey, quaintly described by Fuller as the eldest of "a week of sons," was born April 1st, 1578, and the memorial was erected to commemorate the tercentenary of his birth. The Lees, rough shrub-grown cliff offering breezy views from the top and sheltered nooks below, is a favourite promenade to the west, while to the east round the cliff point to Eastwear Bay are the greater stretches of the cliff-side Warren, happy hunting grounds for the botanist, entomologist, fossil

An Alley in Folkestone.

hunter, **and** geologist—where the botanist may depend upon finding various specimens of the orchis family.

Folkestone from the Harbour.

An ancient place with Cæsarean and Saxon traditions and a "limb" of the Cinque Port of Dover, Folkestone as we see it to-day is quite modern. Though the building of "pleasant houses" was noted in the early part of the nine-teenth century, though somewhat later it was described as a place "which its maligners call a fishing town, and its well-wishers a watering-place," it was not until the opening of the railway, in 1844, that the town began to gain its modern repute and the patronage of holiday-makers to any extent. It had been an important fishery village for a long time, and in the days when Free Trade had not attained the dignity of capital letters was a notorious centre for smuggling enterprise. The old church has many interesting features, including a window placed there by medical men as a memorial to Harvey, who used to call his native place the "Montpellier of England."

It is believed that some human remains found about twenty years ago were actually those of St. Eanswith, a grand-daughter of Ethelbert, to whom the church is dedicated. Eanswith had a nunnery here, but Danish ravages and the encroaching sea played havoc with the oldest Folkestone, over the history of which historians fumble and theorise. Near St. Eanswith's Church stood Folkestone Castle, supposed to have been founded by Ethelbert's son Eadbald, a reactionary prince who reverted from Christianity to heathenism "and in the old heathen fashion took his father's wife for his own." The Kentish men, according to Green, followed Eadbald to the altar of Woden as readily as they had followed Ethelbert to the altar of Christ, but Eadbald's daughter Eanswith was to found a nunnery here—the first religious house for women in England—gain canonisation and become a kind of patron saint of Folkestone. A small church dedicated to her will also be found in the marshland to the west.

Folkestone has given its name—in some parts of our county —to heavy rain-clouds, which are known variously as "Folke-stone girls," "Folkestone lasses," and "Folkestone washer-women"; why the womenfolk of the place should have come to be specially identified with the rain-clouds driving in from the sea is not recorded. The way in which the phrase is used would make plain to the hearer what was meant, but "Folkestone-beef" might puzzle many people. It is dried dog-fish. These congeners of the shark—minus their sinister heads and betray-ing tails—are sometimes sold under plausible aliases to inland housewives. The dog-fish is a good food-fish, though prejudice

is against its general use honestly under its own name.   Frank
Buckland wrote :—

" Most of the fishermen's houses in Folkestone Harbour are adorned
with festoons of fish hung out to dry ; some of these look like gigantic
whiting.   There was no head, tail, or fins to them, and I could not make
out their nature without close examination.   The rough skin on their
reverse side told me at once that they were a species of dog-fish.   I asked

The Old Town, Folkestone

what they were?   ' Folkestone-beef,' was the reply.   ' What sort of fish
is this ? '   ' That's a Rig.'   ' And this? '   ' That's a Huss.'   ' And this other ? '
' That's a Bull Huss.'   ' This bit of fin ? '   ' That's a Fiddler.'   ' And this
bone ? '   ' That's the jaw of Uncle Owl,' etc., etc.
     Here, then, was a new nomenclature ; but I determined to clear up
the matter, so, day after day, when waiting in the harbour for the trawl
boats to arrive, I took down my two volumes of ' Yarrell's British Fishes.'
A class was soon assembled, and turning over the pages one by one, I asked
the name of the fish.   In this way I got a curious collection of local

names. I give now only the dog-fish kind. A 'rig' is the 'common tope,' Yarrell ; a 'bastard rig' is the 'smooth round,' Yarrell ; the 'huss or robin huss' is the small spotted dog-fish ; the 'bull huss' the large spotted dog-fish ; the 'fiddler' is the angel, or shark ray ; 'Uncle Owl's jaw' belongs to a species of skate.

I must here bear testimony to the excessive civility and really gentleman-like conduct of the Folkestone fishermen ; at first they were shy of me, and tried to cram me with impossible stories, etc. ; but we soon became the best of friends, and I really believe I have made some true friends among these rude but most honest and sterling men."

We have seen that at Deal King Henry VIII. built certain castles with the object of repelling the advances of would-be invaders. At Folkestone we come to the first of the martello towers which Pitt designed for the same purpose when Napoleon seemed inclined to bring his conquering eagles across the straits. In the *Monthly Mirror* of September, 1805, we find : "The martello towers are at length begun to be adopted by Government in the neighbourhood of Folkestone. Four of them are in great forwardness, within a quarter of a mile of the town, just at the bottom of the hill, where they command the beach, and cross each other at right angles, so as to produce great havoc on an invading army." Much fun was poked at these ugly defences, but they never had to withstand any more serious enemy. With the great change that has taken place in matters of warfare, the improvements in gunnery, the towers, of course, have become useless from a military point of view. Most of those remaining dotted along the southern coast here —ugly memorials of something approaching national panic— are now utilised as holiday residences, not, it is easy to believe, without certain drawbacks.

Sandgate—or Sangate as it was termed of old, thus approximating to the Sangatte of the opposite coast—a little to the west of Folkestone, is another and smaller pleasant holiday resort, one that has special attractions in that it lies at the foot of the hills, along which delightful walks may be had inland, and from which beautiful views are obtainable. Sandgate Castle, another of the eighth Henry's buildings, has been so transmogrified as to have " very little of the masterpiece left." To the north-west of Sandgate lies the extensive Shorncliffe Camp, formed first during the Napoleonic scare, and now one of the most important places of the kind in the kingdom. On this coast the military are in evidence all along ; from Dover

Sandgate from the Lees, Folkestone.

garrison we reach the famous Shorncliffe Camp ; at Shorncliffe
we are but a short distance from Hythe, with its School of
Musketry and busy rifle ranges by the shore, while towards the
other side of the marsh country we reach Lydd, not only
notable for its Artillery and Engineers' camp, but as having
added a new word to the language in the name of a certain
high explosive.   At Sandgate, some years ago, there occurred
a serious landslip, the results of which were for a long time
visible in the broken road and fissured houses.

At Hythe, still further west, we reach the last place in our
county where the hills come down near the coast—westward is
the ever widening stretch of marshland which continues into
Sussex, and, broken only by the small eminence on which Rye
stands, extends onward to the spur dominated by Winchelsea.
Hythe, another of the Cinque Ports, has had its harbour so
silted up that the old hillside town is some distance from the
beach.   It is itself successor of the Roman Lemanis—now
Lympne—a port which the retiring sea has left considerably
inland, about three miles to the westward.   The " neat and
cheerful appearance " of Hythe, which an old chronicler noted,
is still remarkable.   The visitor, either making a stay here or
passing through in leisurely fashion, has several things to attract
his attention.   The streets run along the foot and up the slope
of Quarry Hill, the connection of street with street being sometimes by long gradients and sometimes by steps.   The old church,
high perched, draws many sightseers to its gruesome " crypt,"
in which are stacked and arranged on shelves the remains—
skulls and a medley of bones—of thousands of people.   " They
are supposed to have been the remains of the Britons, slain in
a bloody battle fought on the shore between this place and
Folkestone with the retreating Saxons in the year 456 ; and to
have attained their whiteness by lying for some length of time
exposed on the seashore.   Several of the skulls have deep
cuts in them, as if made by some heavy weapon, most likely of
the Saxons."   This is but one theory.   Anyway, the visitor not
unwilling to look upon things with

> " an eye
> That hath kept watch on man's mortality,"

may see here such an assembly of " poor Yoricks " as has not
many parallels.   The squeamish had best stay away.   And
yet the very number of the skulls, the very size of the piled-up

miscellany of bones, seems to impart a less painful feeling than the consideration of a single skull.   Hamlet himself would have felt less moved to moralising by a multitude of skulls than by the famous one turned up at the burial of Ophelia.   The attractiveness of the morbid might inspire a Hervey or a Zimmermann with an essay—let us into the open again. Before leaving the church, however, it would be well to visit

Hythe from the Canal.

the grave of an Essex worthy buried here—a worthy whose name is associated with the hopeful rather than the depressing. Here is buried Lionel Lukin, a man whose name may not be widely familiar, but who deserves to be remembered as the first inventor of the " unsubmergible " lifeboat.

Lionel Lukin who was born at Dunmow—famous for its porcine rewards for marital forbearance—was a fashionable coachmaker in London in the latter part of the eighteenth century. He is described as a man of fertile mechanical genius, who, after various experiments, took out a patent in 1785 for an "improved method of construction of boats and small vessels, for either sailing or rowing, which will neither overset in violent gales or sudden bursts of wind, nor sink if by any accident filled with water." The specification goes on to show that this is done by fitting "to the outside of vessels, of the common or any form, projecting gunnells sloping from the top of the common gunnell in a faint curve towards the water, so as not to interfere with the oars in rowing, and from the extreme projection (which may be greater or less, according to the size and the use which the boat or vessel is intended for) returning to the side in a faint curve at a suitable height above the water-line. These projecting gunnells may be solid, of any light material that will not absorb water, or hollow and watertight, or of cork and covered with thin wood, canvas, tin, or other light metals, mixture, or composition. The projections are very small at the stem and stern, and increase gradually to the dimensions required." Inside, at stem and stern, and under the seats, cork or other water-repelling material was also to be used. Lukin interested the Prince of Wales and various admirals in his plan, but none of them could be induced to take official steps to test its utility, so he lent his boat, the *Experiment*, to a Ramsgate pilot that it might be tested in rough seas. She crossed the Channel several times in weather in which other boats would not venture out, and then disappeared—it being suggested that she had been confiscated in a foreign port as a smuggler! A few years after Lukin had sought to establish his lifeboat, another inventor built one substantially on Lukin's lines—and was rewarded with a Parliamentary grant. Lukin died, and was buried at Hythe in 1834, at the great age of ninety-two. Besides his tomb in the churchyard, there is a memorial window in the church.

West and north of Hythe rise well-wooded hills with roads and lanes leading to many pleasant retired villages set on the heights and in the hollows of the downs. To the south-west is the beginning of Romney Marsh, the portion nearest the town, being given up to rifle-butts, has warning War Office notices and red flags indicating the danger of walking on it at practice time. About the flat, shrub-dotted ground may be found an

abundance of the cheerful blossoms of the thrift, and along
here rather later, as indeed along most parts of the Kentish
coast, though in some less plentifully, may be found, too, the
striking yellow-horned poppy, the long seed-pod "horn" being
something like that of the plant's Californian cousin, the
eschscholtzia of our gardens.   Along the coast, towards Dymchurch, are to be seen a number of the ugly martello towers.

Just north of Hythe is Saltwood, with its picturesque castle,
in which, according to tradition, there met the four knights—
Reginald Fitzurse, Hugh de Moreville, William de Tracy and
Richard le Bret—who had stolen privily away from the Court
of King Henry in Normandy to act upon his hasty words : " In

Dymchurch.

the darkness of the night—the long winter night of the 28th of
December—it was believed that, with candles extinguished,
and not even seeing each other's faces, the scheme was concerted."   Early next day they mounted their chargers and rode
along the Stone Street due north to Canterbury and the
achievement of their murderous resolve.

Though Saltwood Castle dates from the eleventh century,
its fine gate-house was built in the fourteenth by Archbishop
Courtenay.   There have been many alterations, some of which
were occasioned during the reign of Queen Elizabeth owing to
that rare visitant in these parts—a destructive earthquake. The
Castle is open to the public once a week and is well worth
visiting for, among other things, the fine view obtainable.

Beautiful byways may be followed hence to Postling, lying on the slope against the downs, with—immediately in front of us as we approach—the noble cluster of trees surmounting Tolsford Hill, a landmark plainly visible from the platform of Hythe railway station and from other points for miles around.   On our way to the small village of Postling, with its interesting old church, we come to the cross roads known as Postling Vents—"vent" or "went" is a not uncommon Kentish word signifying ways.

To the west of Postling on the hillside is the finely situated Horton Park or Monks Horton.   It was at Monks Horton (sometimes named Mount Morris) that that "handsome, fat, and merry" creature Elizabeth Robinson, afterwards Mrs.

Postling.

"Blue-Stocking" Montagu, lived with her parents, and whence she wrote many of her entertaining letters.   Here, at the age of fourteen, she was party to a "summons" issued to a neighbouring old bachelor who was "very much our humble servant, and would die, but not dance, for us."

"*Kent.*

"To J. B., Esq.

"WHEREAS, complaint has been made to us Commissioners of Her Majesty's Balls, Hops, Assemblies, &c., for the county aforesaid, that several able and expert men, brought up and instructed in the art or mystery of dancing, have and daily do refuse, though often thereunto requested, to be retained and exercised in the aforesaid art or mystery, to the occasion of great scarcity of good dancers in these parts, and contrary to the laws of gallantry and good manners, in that case made and provided : and whereas, we are likewise credibly informed that you, J. B., Esq., though educated in the said art by that celebrated master — Lally, senior, are one of the most notorious offenders in this point, these are therefore in the name of the Fair Sex, to require you, the said J. B. Esq., personally to be and to appear before us at our meeting holden this day at the sign of the Golden Ball, in the parish of Horton, in the county aforesaid, between the hours of twelve and one in the forenoon, to answer to such matters as shall be objected against you, concerning the aforesaid refusal, and contempt of our jurisdiction and authority; and to bring with you your dancing shoes, laced waistcoat and white gloves. And hereof fail not, under peril of our frown, and of being from henceforth deemed and accounted an old batchelor. Given under our hands and seals this eighth day of October, 1734, to which we all set our hands."

It may be wondered if the "all" comprised Mr. Matthew Robinson's whole dozen of sons and daughters.

Two years later the sprightly Elizabeth had to tell of adventures when Lady T—— had bespoke a play at a town eight miles away (Ashford or Folkestone). After the play there was supper at an inn and at two in the morning they set out for their respective homes and "before I had gone two miles I had the pleasure of being overturned, at which I squalled for joy, and to complete my felicity, I was obliged to stand half an hour in the most refreshing rain, and the coolest north breeze I ever felt; for the coach braces breaking were the occasion of our overturn and there was no moving till they were mended. You may suppose we did not lose so favourable an opportunity of catching cold; we all came croaking down to breakfast the next morning and said we had caught no cold, as one always says when one has been scheming, but I think I have scarce recovered my treble tones yet." Her letters afford very lively reading, for though she preferred London to Horton, "Handel and Gaffarelli to woodlarks and nightingales" (in December!), she found time in the country for keeping up correspondence with various friends: "here we sleep with our forefathers and all the acts that we do, which are to eat, drink, sleep, and die, are they not written in the Book of the Chronicles?"

A couple of miles beyond Postling we reach one of the pleasantest villages among these chalk hills at Lyminge, though the activity of the modern builder is not improving the interesting old place. The church, and the monastic remains without it, are full of interest, for Ethelburga who had married the King of Northumbria and won him to Christianity, returned after his death to the kingdom of her brother, Eadbald, and founded her nunnery and built a basilical church here at Lyminge.

N

Ethelburga it is believed utilised in her buildings much of the material left by the Romans, who appear to have had a noble villa here, about a mile east of the Stone Street which runs from Lympne to Canterbury. The church was built by St. Dunstan in the tenth century and he in turn utilised much of the material of St. Eadburg's (or Ethelburga's) earlier edifice. Roman bricks and herring-bone masonry are among the notable features of a particularly interesting church. The charters relating to Lyminge which are preserved in the British Museum are among the earliest and most important that remain relating to ecclesiastical matters in Saxon times. The church is happily—as fortunately so many of our old Kentish churches are, and as all should be—open to visitors every day.

At Lyminge we are in the Elham Vale, and Elham itself lies a couple of miles further to the north-east. Anciently a market town Elham has no special attractiveness though it has given its name to a beautiful valley which breaks through the chalk here in a southerly direction to Folkestone, and northerly at the western foot of the Barham Downs towards Canterbury. In the church is a library bequeathed a century ago by one Dr. Warley, of Canterbury—a library peculiarly rich in seventeenth century biblical rarities, and one which no student of the Civil War period can afford to overlook. Following the valley southward we come, less than two miles from Lyminge, to Etchinghill scattered along the roadside. Here the chalk hills rise rapidly on the east and we have a choice of ways. Eastward, by about two miles, rising two hundred feet, through beautiful lanes is Paddlesworth, but southward, too, there are attractions, for the road goes through Beach-borough Park, and on an eminence here is a summer-house— no one journeying to Folkestone by rail can fail to have seen it—whence a magnificent and extensive view over the country and sea may be had. Visitors are allowed the privilege of climbing to the summer-house that they may enjoy the wide prospect. Beachborough has remained in one family for over three centuries and in the time of the Civil War the then head of the family, Sir William Brockman, was one of the Men of Kent who signed the Petition which led to the Kentish struggle of 1648, and one of the defenders of Maidstone in its short contest with Fairfax.

Point after point here might be cited as offering views over the country of hills and woodland, with the sea beyond, views that might have suggested some of Mr. A. C. Swinburne's wonderful descriptive passages.

" Hills and valleys where April rallies his radiant squadron of flowers
and birds,
Steep strange beaches and lustrous reaches of fluctuant sea that the
land engirds,

Lyminge.

Fields and downs that the sunset crowns with life diviner than lives
in words. . . .
Higher and higher to the north aspire the green smooth-swelling un-
ending downs ;
East and west on the brave earth's breast glow girdle-jewels of
gleaming towns ;
Southward-shining, the lands declining subside in peace that the
sea's light crowns."

Through Newington, with its lofty towered church, and
Cheriton Street, we may follow the valley to Folkestone—with
Cæsar's Camp and Sugar-loaf Hill rising boldly on our left,
or taking the second turning to our right after leaving
Newington may go by Cheriton Church along a beautiful
winding road to the sea at Seabrook between Hythe and
Sandgate.

Other villages lie northwards of the strip of coast from
Eastwear Bay to Romney Marsh that we have been sauntering
about in this chapter.   There is Paddlesworth, with its Norman
church perched over six hundred feet above the level of the
sea and surrounded by narrow, winding, tree-shaded lanes,
leading in any direction the wanderer listeth.   North of
Paddlesworth a couple of miles or so is beautiful little
Acrise and so by a narrow, unfrequented road through
delightful country of farmland and woodland we may go on
to the Tappington and Denton of our Canterbury district.
Rejoining the main road near Denton Church and turning to
the right we may come back Folkestonewards over Swingfield
Minnis, or taking the turning beyond the tenth milestone
from Canterbury may go to Swingfield itself and visit the farm
of St. John's with its remains of an ancient chapel.   With
respect to the name Swingfield Minnis, it may be pointed out
that Minnis is a Kentish word with various meanings.   It is
defined in Parish and Shaw's invaluable *Dictionary of the
Kentish Dialect* as " A wide tract of ground, partly copse and
partly moor ; a high common ; a waste piece of rising ground."
Swingfield Minnis is no longer common.

Beautiful winding ways through much woodland take us
from Swingfield village to the fascinating little Alkham
described in the previous chapter.   From Swingfield, too,
other devious byroads may be taken,—by those who prefer
them to the generally less attractive high roads—through
characteristic chalk down country by Hawkinge—the lonely
church of which was rifled by King John—and by Capel
(Capel le Ferne as it is prettily named) to the high Dover and
Folkestone road.

Twilight on the Stour.

CHAPTER IX

ROMNEY MARSH

THE flat tract of land stretching from Sandgate on the east to the Sussex border on the west and practically converted into an island by the thirty-mile long military canal which begins by the former place and joins the Rother little more than two miles to the north-east of Rye, is a place of peculiar fascination. Of the narrowest between Sandgate and Hythe this tract broadens out to nearly a dozen miles at its widest and is nearly half as long again at its longest. Commonly spoken of as Romney Marsh, it is really divided up under various names— Romney Marsh, Walland Marsh and Denge Marsh, and on it will be found some interesting towns and villages, many old parish churches, some with but very few parishioners, and on it also is the well-known point of Dungeness. To most people visiting Dungeness for the first time unprepared there is a surprise in store—knowing or knowing by repute the chalk headlands of the North and South Forelands, Shakespeare's Cliff and Beachy Head, they mostly regard the cape that comes between the two last named as being of a similar nature. They find instead a spit of shingle beach running out into the sea— and growing, they are told, at the rate of a yard or so every year—flat loose shingle sparsely grown with foot-high shrubs, spotted in June with golden dabs of flowering broom and singularly spired over with beautiful foxgloves. The Ness lies

Romney Marsh and the Church at Lympne.

nearly four miles from Lydd, the most southerly town of **our** county, and is best approached by the railway which runs from that town past Lloyd's Signalling Station to the near neigh-

bourhood of the massy Dungeness Lighthouse, twenty miles
from the cross-channel light on Cap Grisnez, of the relations
of which lights Mr. George Meredith has sung —

> " Where Grisnez winks at Dungeness
> Across the ruffled strip of salt."

Lambarde describes Dungeness as " Neshe, called in Saxon
nesse, which seemeth to be derived of the Latine Nasus, and
signifieth a Nebbe or Nose of the land extended into the Sea,"
and he goes on to say " before this Neshe lieth a flat into the
Sea, threatening great danger to unadvised Sailers." It has
always been a notoriously dangerous point for shipping.

Those who prefer pedestrianism will find the walking over the
loose stones more than a little tiring, for the " roads " of the
map are but tracks across the beach. " Backstays," broad
pieces of wood attached snowshoewise to the soles of their
boots, are used by some of the people of the district. Whether
reached afoot or by rail the spot well repays the visitor. It is
quite unlike anything else that our county has to offer
and, whether approached from the woodlands north of the
Marsh or by the road that runs near the sea-front from Hythe,
offers a great contrast to the scenery through which we have
been passing. Near to Lydd large tracts of turnips in full
bloom appear a veritable Field of Gold. But soon the cultivated
fields give place to rough grass and this in turn to the gorse,
broom, foxgloves and other flowers that find sustenance and
flourish amid the stones. Some dotted coastguard stations,
some batteries and two or three isolated houses, along the south
and eastern sides of the Ness are all the buildings besides
those of the signalling station and lighthouse. The railway
station is little more than a shed and tickets taken at Lydd are
collected before we set out upon the brief journey. West of
the station about a couple of miles is an inn, and north-east of
it about a mile is another, so that the visitor spending some
time in this comparative solitude may find refreshment without
having to wait for an infrequent train back to Lydd, or without
having a lengthy walk to the next coastal town—Rye, about ten
miles west, or New Romney, about six miles and a half north.
To the lover of quiet with wind and waves, where his solitude
is little likely to be broken in upon by his fellows, anywhere on

these miles of Denge or Dunge beach may be cordially
recommended. The appearance of the beach is of a level, its
highest point is but twenty feet above the sea. There was at

Lydd.

one time a project for establishing a harbour near Dungeness
but it has not been proceeded with. Should the scheme ever
be carried out and roads make the district accessible it may
well be believed that a bracing holiday resort would spring up

about it ; even on summer nights the air here is described as
" hand-cold."   The whole of this tract is said to abound in
hares, and is a popular coursing ground, though the loose stones
make poor running for the dogs.

Returning from Dungeness over the beach and marsh to
Lydd we may visit our county's limit by the Holmstone tract,
conspicuous for its holly trees, about a mile and a half from
the town, and thence join the road which runs from Lydd to
the first of the Sussex coastguard stations, and so reach the
former place.   Lydd, a pleasant marsh town, is a member of
the Cinque Port of Romney and though the sea has left it two
and a half miles inland it may still be regarded as a fishing
place.   The Ripes, or Rypes, pasture-lands running southward
to the stony beach are occupied by a military camp, where
artillery practice is carried on.   Indeed the town has given its
name to " Lyddite," the high-power explosive first made here
and the composition of which as now employed in the British
Army is an official secret.   Recent experiments with a new
highly powerful explosive are described as " having produced
all the effects of an earthquake for several miles around '—which
suggests that a further deadly "peacemaker" is being perfected
at Lydd.

The handsome church which stands in the middle of the
town, and shows its embattled tower from far off amid trees
as we approach, is interesting not only for its brasses but
because when Thomas Wolsey was ascending his honorous
estate, to use the words of the faithful Cavendish, he was vicar
here, and his ambition might be said to be typified in the way
in which he raised the tower of the church from more
modest dimensions to its present height.   In Wolsey's time the
church belonged to Tintern Abbey.

About three miles from Lydd by a winding road, or nearly
a mile less if we take the footpath that leaves the road to the
right little more than half a mile beyond the railway bridge
and crosses the marsh fields, we come to New Romney, a
place the name of which has become something of a misnomer
by the passing of centuries—as the oldest existing roadway
over the river Thames still rejoices in the name of Newbridge.

Where old and New Romney stand—a couple of miles
apart—once ran the River Rother which now reaches the sea

to the south of Rye, finishing its course wholly through Sussex
instead of through Kent.   Its mouth was so silted up at
the close of the eleventh century that New Romney was
established nearer the sea.   The change in the Rother's
course is said to have followed a great storm in the time of
Edward I., the road from Romney to Appledore—known as the
Rhee wall—marking the ancient course.   Romney or Old Romney was at one time an important seaport with a goodly harbour,
the resort of much shipping ; but first came the silting up of the

Lydd from Romney Marsh.

Rother Estuary, and then the deflecting of the river's course
to the west and the old Cinque Port fell from its proud
position.   It appears to have been a notable place for storms
too for Thomas à Becket when seeking to escape secretly out
of England set sail from this port and could not get away
owing to the great storm raging and (saith Lambarde) "both
the town of Rumney and the Marsh received great harme in
the 8th year of the reign of King Edward the third, by an
hydeous tempest that threw down many Steeples and Trees,

and above 300 Mills and Housings here." Now the small place sleeping quietly inland on the Marsh suggests nothing of its important past.

This bit of country was compared by Bishop Parry to the Roman Campagna. In his address in 1879 to the Kent Archæological Society, as we read in that rich storehouse of Kent facts and fancies the *Archæologia Cantiana*, the then Bishop of Dover said :

"But take our Roman-ey this Roman Marsh of ours, in one of its calmer, brighter, happier moods. The sun, let me say, is hasting to his setting over Fair Light, and the shadows are lengthening out Hythe-wards. A gentle evening breeze rustles peacefully among the flags along the dyke side. The blue sky overhead was never more blue. Where are we? Is this Kent? Are we in England at all? Or have we dropped down somewhere upon the Campagna, outside the walls of Rome? For lack of a ruined aqueduct your eye rests on the grey wall of Hope or Eastbridge, or on the solitary arch of Midley. On the one side rises a tall landmark across the plain, the Campanile of Lydd ; on the other stretches far away the long ridge of the Alban and Sabine Hills, which folk here-about call Lympne and Aldington. But I know better, for while my friend the Marsh Rector and I are still arguing the point, there comes creeping along the road to Ostia (New Romney, he calls it), a heavy waggon drawn by the wide-horned, mild-eyed, melancholy oxen, which every Roman artist knows so well."

There is an olden saying which describes the world as being divided into "Europe, Asia, Africa, America and Romney Marsh." Why the Marsh, as it is commonly called in South Kent, was given this position it is difficult to determine, unless it was meant to suggest its inaccessibility ; if so, *nous avons change tout cela.* For even the railway has invaded the district, with its line from Appledore to Brookland, Lydd, Dungeness and New Romney (or Littlestone-on-Sea). The embanking of the Marsh by Dymchurch Wall was done at some early unknown period, but it has meant the preservation of a con-siderable tract of valuable corn and grazing land. Cobbett the agricultural enthusiast said that he had never before seen such corn as he saw on Romney Marsh, and went on to ask derisively how long it would be after the end of the world before the American prairies had anything to show like it. If his spirit revisits the glimpses of the moon in some miles' square tract of wheat in Manitoba or Minnesota he must regret that derision. There is rich, deep earth on which crops flourish exceedingly so that Romney Marsh, having the usual drawbacks of marshland as a place for human habitation, has come to be described as that part of Kent conspicuous for wealth without health. As Lambarde puts it, "the place hath in it sundry villages, although

Parish Church, Dymchurch.

not thick set, nor much inhabited, because it is *Hyeme malus, Æstate molestus, Nunquam bonus,* Evill in winter, grievious in sommer, and never good; as *Hesiodus* (the old poet) sometimes said of the Country where his father dwelt." Here, says the same topographer, anyone shall find good grass underfoot rather than wholesome air above the head. That the resident may find. The visitor staying by the shore and going about the small, scattered hamlets, the tree-embowered old churches and farmsteads, finds the summer air wholesome enough. In the reign of Edward IV., partly, it is suggested, owing to the unwholesomeness of the country, partly owing to the fact that it lay so exposed to attacks from the sea, Romney Marsh was so suffering from want of inhabitants, that to allure men to inhabit it the King granted many privileges.

"That the Inhabitants of all the Towns within the limits of *Rumney* Marsh should be incorporated by the name of Bayliff, twenty-four Jurates and Commonaltie of *Rumney* Marsh in the Countie of *Kent*, having a Court from three weeks to three weeks, in which they hold plea of all causes and actions, reall and personal, civil and criminal; having power to choose four Justices of the Peace yearly amongst themselves, besides the Bayliffe, who is armed with the like Authoritie; having moreover return of all the Prince's Writs, the benefit of all fines, forfeits and amerciaments, the privileges of Leet, lawday and tourne, and exemption from tolle and tare, scot and lot, fifteen and subsidie, and from so many other charges as I suppose no one place within the Realm hath."

However much this Charter with its fascinating legal terminology may have had an effect in the fifteenth century, in the twentieth it cannot be said that Romney Marsh—it is still pronounced Rumney—is in any danger of being over-populated, some of its twenty parishes having less than a score of parishioners, while in some, such as Orgarswick, Blackmanstone and others, the church has lapsed from use. The winding roads across the marsh from hamlet to hamlet or village have much of interest for those who can find pleasure in flat scenery, diversified, however, by many trees, by plentiful wild flowers both in the fields and along the dykes—variously known as dicks, deeks and waterings—by which the whole marsh is so criss-crossed, that unless with someone who knows the path it is often better to keep to the quiet road than try the footpath way. As Tom Shoesmith says in Mr. Kipling's story of *Dymchurch Flit* :

"The Marsh is just riddled with diks an' sluices, an' tide-gates, an' water-lets. You can hear 'em bubblin' an' grummelin' when the tide works in 'em, an' then you hear the sea rangin' left an' right-handed all up along the wall. You've seen how flat she is—the Marsh? You'd think nothin' easier than to walk cend-on across her? Ah, but the diks an' the water-lets, they twists the roads about as ravelly as witch-yarn on the spindles. So ye get all turned round in broad day-light."

How it was that the Pharisees—or Farisies, or fairies—were all shipped from the Marsh across Channel is told in the same delightful story in Mr. Kipling's *Puck of Pook's Hill.* The Marsh was seemingly at one time favoured by supernatural beings for we have it on the word of Thomas Ingoldsby that

"a Witch may still be occasionally discovered in favourable *i.e.* stormy seasons, weathering Dungeness Point in an eggshell, or careering on her broomstick over Dymchurch wall. A cow may yet be sometimes seen galloping like mad, with tail erect, and an old pair of breeches on her horns an unerring guide to the door of the crone whose magic arts have drained her udder."

The dykes by which the marsh is drained, with their rich yellow irises, their reeds and sedges and various other aquatic plants, offer many attractions to the field naturalist and botanist. The extensive pastures are fed over by large numbers of sheep—said to be a particularly hardy breed—indeed the district is said to feed more sheep than any other in the country of the same extent. There are, too, a goodly number of cattle dotted about, though fewer, perhaps, than on the Stour marshes. Says old Fuller, pointing out how the goodness of the soil of the county generally may be guessed from the greatness of the Kentish breed where both the cattle and the poultry are as he puts it allowed the largest of the land : " A giant ox, fed in Romney Marsh, was some six years since to be seen in London, so high that one of ordinary stature could hardly reach to the top of his back." This was probably the same beast noted by John Evelyn in his "Diary" on April 29, 1649 : " I saw in London a huge ox bred in Kent, 17 feet in length, and much higher than I could reach." That some of the farm horses are particularly fine I have seen, remembering especially a magnificent team of four which had taken a prize early this summer at the Ashford show. Drawing one of the long old-fashioned wains, and glossily groomed, their tinkling approach advertised their merit, for the proud carter had decorated his splendid charges with red cloth tasselled trappings and tinkling bells. An old marsh man who was near me as they passed said, "Well, I never. Time was when all the horses about used to be like that, but it's many years since I've heard the bells, or seen 'em decked this way."

A Mill on Romney Marsh.

It is a quiet place, for the most part, this small fifth of the world, even at its largest centres—the points of the greatest liveliness being the musketry and artillery grounds at either end. The sleepy inland hamlets, the restful looking farms, the old churches showing among their groups of trees suggest quietude, and it is pleasant to know from the old proverb, and to gather from the appearance of the populous pasture, the rich looking farm lands, that it is associated with comfortable wealth. Following the road from Appledore to Romney we may visit some of the villages on or near the road—Brookland, on what is technically Walland Marsh, is worth visiting on account of its Early English Church with its curiously engraved leaden Norman font and its massive timber bell-tower, octagonal in shape and detached from the main building. To this church belongs a curious story accounting for the detachment of the bell-tower. It is recorded that considerable laxity was shown in regard to the marriage tie, and the marriage of maidens was so rare that on one occasion a maid coming to be married at Brookland the spire leapt down from the building in surprise at such an unusual spectacle!

Snargate—where "Ingoldsby" Barham was once Rector—and Brenzett are both on the Rhee Wall road, and where other roads go right and left shortly beyond the latter place, to the right we come to Brookland in about a mile and a half, and to the left (in about the same distance) to Ivychurch, the high turreted tower of which is a landmark for some distance round.

In Dymchurch on the shore, roughly speaking in the middle of the Marsh front—with martello towers on either side—we have a place which has some repute as a quiet holiday resort, though it is being challenged by the new Littlestone-on-Sea, a seaward expatiation of New Romney, which has the advantage (or disadvantage, so much depends upon point of view) of a railway station. Dymchurch, a quiet, scattered village by the protecting sea-wall—Dymchurch-under-the-Wall as it is sometimes named—is supposed to have been a Roman station owing to a number of remains found here over half a century ago and pointing to the early settlement of parts of the Marsh. Indeed the great earth Wall which preserves the whole valuable tract of Romney Marsh, and inside which the Hythe road runs, is by some theorists said to have been thrown up during the Roman occupation. Through the wall, which has occasionally suffered during severe storms in recent years, are the large sluices by which the Marsh is drained. The quiet village, which with its open aspect and its broad sands finds favour as a resort with those people who like a restful rather than a strenuous holiday, is threatened with a colony of railway-carriage bungalows made out of the discarded rolling stock of the Metropolitan Railway ! In bright sunshine Dymchurch, with its wide sea outlook from the wall, is a delightful place, far from the madding crowd, and from it as a centre the whole extent of the marsh can easily be explored from Hythe to Dungeness by a pedestrian of ordinary endurance; winding roads and (once mastered) more direct footpaths go in all directions while inland four or five miles lie the hills which form an always pleasant background to the Marsh; hills on which various landmarks are visible—here the massy church of Lympne and there the obelisk at Bilsington.

Along the foot of these hills—cutting the marshland from the mainland—runs the long Military Canal from east of Hythe to its junction with the Rother in the neighbourhood of Rye. This canal, with its pleasant elm-shaded road alongside, has a quiet charm and much picturesqueness to offer and the walk along it is one full of attraction to the lover of solitude. From Hythe to Appledore the pedestrian touches no village or hamlet, but for rest or refreshment pleasant villages are always accessible within a short distance on the higher ground. The canal was formed a century ago for defensive purposes and owes its existence to the same provocation as that which brought about the building of the martello towers.

All round our southern and eastern coasts—as we have seen —we are reminded of the "good old days" of smuggling and in those days Romney Marsh was especially famous as a law-defying district. And smuggling, as we saw at Sandwich, was a "trade" profitable both on the outgoings and the incomings, there were export as well as import duties to evade, and the most notable product of the country hereabouts, wool, was one of the most valuable to the smuggler. As early as the reign of Edward I. wool was excepted from the "merchandises" which might be exported, and again and again proclamations were issued to prevent the passing abroad of this valuable commodity. Rich flocks fed on the Marsh, yet but small

O

proportion of the wool found its way to the home market.
Indeed it is said that the bold men of this part of the county
not only exported their own wool but actually went into the
neighbouring districts and bought up Wealden wool for their
illicit trade.   Within two years, at one time, forty thousand

Old Romney.

packs of Kent and Sussex wool were landed at Calais.   This
smuggling had to be carried on in a bold fashion, for wool-
packs were not things which could be easily secreted, but the
men of the Marsh held together—and even found powerful
supporters—so that the revenue officers did not have an easy
time of it.   Indeed in 1688 when one of these officers with

a posse of men had captured eight or ten "owlers," as they were termed, with horses laden with wool, and had taken them for committal to the Mayor of Romney, that worthy refused to do more than admit them to bail. As a consequence, when the revenue officers sought rest at Lydd they were harried hence by the smugglers and their friends and had to flee pursued by half a hundred supporters of the illegal traffic, and were we may be sure mightily glad to reach Rye with whole skins. Smugglers, many stories show the truth of it, were far more popular with the majority of people than were the excise officers. Much has been written about the "free trading" as carried on in the Marsh and the adjacent districts, the romance of the theme having appealed to several story writers. The churches it is said were even used as storehouses for the smuggled goods, horses were borrowed at night from farmyards—and returned in the early morning with mysterious presents from the free traders. We can well believe that the sentiment so admirably put into *A Smuggler's Song* by Mr. Rudyard Kipling was a century or two ago that of hundreds of coast dwellers who could not have put it into words—

> " If you wake at midnight and hear a horse's feet,
> Don't go drawing back the blind or looking in the street,
> Them that asks no questions isn't told a lie.
> Watch the wall, my darling, while the gentlemen go by.
>   Five and twenty ponies
>   Trotting through the dark—
>   Brandy for the Parson,
>   'Baccy for the clerk ;
>   Laces for a lady ; letters for a spy,
> And watch the wall, my darling, while the gentlemen go by." [1]

Fairfield Church, in a lonely part of the marsh country between Brookland and Appledore, is said to have been one of the sacred edifices of which the smugglers made a temporary warehouse for their goods. This church is dedicated to St. Thomas of Canterbury from whom Becket's Barn in the parish presumably derives its name. Snargate Church was another storehouse for illicit traders. The stories of the coast smugglers and of the efforts to prevent them would easily fill a volume, but space may be found to give a portion of an Act of Parliament passed in the reign of William III. in which it is ordained that :—

[1] " Puck of Pook's Hill."

" Whereas it is a common practise in Romney Marsh and other places adjacent for evil disposed persons to sheer their sheep and lodge wooll near the sea-side and sometimes to bring wooll out of the country more remote and lodge it as aforesaid where by fraud and force in the night time the said persons do cause the same to be transported to France to the increase of the trade of that kingdom and the destruction of the trade of England. To prevent these practices for the future be it further enacted by the authority aforesaid that all and every owner and owners of wool shorn or housed laid upp or lodged within ten miles of the sea-side within the counties of Kent and Sussex shall be obliged to give an exact account in writing within three days after the sheering thereof of his, her, or their number of fleeces, and where lodged or housed to the next adjacent port or officer of His Majesties Customs or the like notice before he, she, or they shall presume to remove any part or parcel thereof of the said number of fleeces and weight and the name of the person or persons to whom it is disposed and the place to which it is intended to be carried and take a certificate from the officer who first entered the same upon penalty of forfeiting all such wooll as shall not be so entred or otherwise disposed of and the owner or owners also to be liable to the further penalties of three shillings for every pound weight of all such wooll."

Despite all ordinances against it, wool smuggling out of the country went on for long as merrily as did spirit smuggling in, and the general liking for a bargain made the smuggling fraternity as has been said far more popular than the revenue officers.

Turning from law to romance we may recall an olden ballad telling the tragical story of the " Smuggler's Bride "

" Attention give, and a tale I'll tell,
Of a damsel fair that in Kent did dwell,
On the Kentish coast when the tempest rolled
She fell deep in love with a smuggler so bold.

Upon her pillow she could not sleep,
When her valliant smuggler was on the deep,
While the winds did whistle she would complain,
For her valliant smuggler that ploughed the main.

When Will arrived on his native coast,
He would fly to her that he valued most—
He would fly to Nancy, his lover true,
And forget all hardships he'd lately been through.

One bright May morning the sun did shine,
And lads and lasses, all gay and fine,
Along the coast they did trip along,
To behold their wedding and sing a cheerful song.

Young Nancy then bid her friends adieu,
And to sea she went with her lover true ;
In storms and tempests all hardships braves,
With her valliant smuggler upon the foaming waves.

One stormy night, when the winds did rise,
And dark and dismal appeared the skies,
The tempest rolled, and the waves did roar,
And the valliant smuggler was driven from the shore.

' Cheer up,' cries William, ' my valliant wife.'
Says Nancy, ' I never valued life,
I'll brave the storms and tempests through,
And fight for William with a sword and pistol too.'

At length a cutter did on them drive ;
The cutter on them soon did arrive : ·
' Don't be daunted. Though we're but two
We'll not surrender, but fight like Britons true.'

' Cheer up,' says Nancy with courage true,
' I will fight, dear William, and stand by you."
They like Britons fought, Nancy stood by the gun,
They beat their enemies and quickly made them run.

Another cutter now hove in sight
And join'd to chase them with all their might ;
They were overpowered, and soon disarmed,
It was then young Nancy and William were alarmed.

A shot that moment made Nancy start,
Another struck William to the heart ;
This shock distressed lovely Nancy's charms,
When down she fell and expired in William's arms.

Now Will and Nancy love bid adieu,
They lived and died like two lovers true.
\oung men and maidens now faithful prove,
Like Will and Nancy who lived and died in love."

The ballad writer it will be observed is not troubled by the
illegality of the occupation in which the faithful couple were
engaged—love and the fact that they died together justified all.
Now leaving the Marsh—the picturesqueness and charms of
which grow upon us the better we become acquainted with them
—and setting out for the villages among the hills we may repeat
some appropriate lines, *The Pedlar leaves the Bar Parlour at
Dymchurch*, by Mr. Ford Madox Hueffer, a poet who has lived
in the district, learned it intimately and sung of it hauntingly.

" Good-night, we'd best be jogging on,
The moon's been up a while,
We've got to get to Bonnington,
Nigh seven mile.

But the marsh ain'd so lone if you'v beeted a good song,
And you bum it aloud as you cater along,
Nor the stiles half so high, nor the pack so like lead,
If you've heard a good tale and it runs in your head.

So, come, we'd best be jogging on,
The moon will give us light
We've got to get to Bonnington
To sleep to-night."

Rawlinson Farm, back view.

Half-timbered House, Rawlinson Farm, Rolvenden

CHAPTER X

LYMPNE TO THE "DENS.

IF Romney Marsh has charms that grow upon us, there is perhaps even more that is attractive—greater variety of immediate surroundings and the added views—from the hills that lie close inland from the neighbourhood of Hythe to near Appledore at the further end of the demi-lune. It is a district of open fields, of flowery edges, of woodland hollows, and strips of shaws along the fields, of dipping and rising lanes and small but pleasant villages, with occasional magnificent views over the wide extent of Romney Marsh. Leaving the narrow main street of Hythe by a broad and rapidly rising high road trending inland we may come to this district, or following the low road by the canal we may reach West Hythe, the earliest successor as port, it is believed, to its once important neighbour Lympne, now but a small village. Inland a short distance from West Hythe there used anciently to stand Shepway Cross, at which "our Limenarcha" or Lord Warden of the Cinque Ports was sworn in; here, too, the Cinque Port Courts were held in early times. Rather more than a mile further along are the scattered remains of Stutfall or Studfall Castle, the Roman castrum of the port of Lemanis, in a wild and lonely bit of country suited to the ancient memories it conjures up. The Roman ruins broken and overgrown as seen here and at Richborough are far more impressive than where such remains are neighboured by modern buildings.

The hills rise somewhat sharply along this part of our journey, and before visiting the ruins it is well to see them from below and to recall that this was in Roman times a port, either a bay or, as some suppose, the estuary of the Rother which it is thought may have flowed out here before it took to erratic ways. Archæologists have discussed the matter with various theories, and readers who would learn further details of these Roman remains—Reculver, Richborough, and Lympne —should read the book on the subject, published in 1850 by

Lympne Castle.

Charles Roach Smith, referring for later researches to the rich volumes of the *Archæologia Cantiana.* Here we must be satisfied with a glimpse at the ruins, greatly changed it must be remembered by landslips during the many centuries that have elapsed since the last of the Romans left this outpost of their empire. Now high and dry some miles inland it is difficult to realise that Lympne was one of the great keys of Britain, equal in importance to Dover and Richborough. It is curious that a corruption of the Roman "Portus Lemanis" should remain in Lympne on the heights above, but that the castrum itself should have taken on the new name of Stutfall or Studfall.

Lympne Castle, nowadays, means not the older Roman castrum, but the comparatively new place close to the church on the brow of the hill above, forming with the church a remarkable pile which serves as a notable landmark miles away in the marshes. This castle—long degenerated into a farmhouse—was built in the reign of Henry V., and may have succeeded a Norman watch-tower. Now it is being largely added to by a new owner, and though the additions bid fair to be in keeping with the rest, they will sadly destroy the land-side view of the grand old church, which is, as has been said, a fine landmark. Its massive central tower is supposed to be the work of Lanfranc, who employed in its building much stone from the ancient castrum below. From the God's acre—with sheep nibbling among the tombs, a high stemmed sundial near its entrance gate—may be had a wonderful view seawards over the marshland, and away to Dungeness.

Inland from Lympne a couple of miles is its nearest railway station at Westenhanger (once Ostenhanger), near to which are the remains of an ancient mansion where, says a wholly unsupported tradition, Rosamond Clifford lived before she went to Woodstock. According to an old writer, the house was "moated all round, and had a drawbridge, a gatehouse and portal with a portcullis, and the walls all embattled and fortified with nine towers, one of which was called Fair Rosamond's Tower." That tower, the sentimental visitor may like to know, is one of those remaining. The house is said to have had one hundred and twenty-six rooms, and as many windows as there are days in the year. A worthy place for the housing of a king's love. When Queen Elizabeth made one of her magnificent progresses—costly outings as they proved to her loyal entertainers—she stayed "at her own house at Westenhanger." Here for a time after the fighting at Maidstone in 1648 the Royalists kept some of their Parliamentarian prisoners. At the beginning of the eighteenth century the greater part of the mansion was pulled down, and a hundred years later that which remained had become a farmhouse. At Westenhanger we are on the Stone Street which runs straightly, through Stanford

Westenhanger Castle.

about a mile beyond, north to Canterbury, but for a strange bit of wriggling up the downs by Horton Park, the formation of which probably led to the alteration of the way. Between two and three miles out of Stanford is Sellinge, which may be reached by pleasant footpaths and from which the southerly road will take us back to the hills fronting the marsh at Court-at-Street—only a mile and a half by direct road from Lympne. Along that direct road new residences being built show that the hills with their magnificent southerly views are attracting twentieth century summer residents, as two thousand years ago they attracted the Romans. Here we are on the road which connected Lemanis (Lympne) with Anderida (Pevensey) and all along here it is recorded that remains of Roman settlements have been discovered so plentifully as to suggest that the road was "bordered with villas."

Court-at-Street is described by Lambarde as " Courtofstrete, commonly Court of Strete, truly, and Bellirica (or rather) Belcaire, anciently, that is, Bello-castrum, the Faire Castle." Its early history can only be guessed at, now it is but a small hamlet with memories of a remarkable imposture belonging to the transition period when England was passing from her allegiance to Rome to the consolidation of the Protestant Church. The imposture may be introduced in words written less than forty years after.

" The enemy of mankinde, and Prince of darknesse, Sathan the Devill, perceiving that the glorious and bright shining beams of God's holy truth and gladsome Gospell had pearced the misty thick clouds of ignorance, and shewed (not only to the people of *Germanie*, but to the inhabitants of this Island also) the true way of their deliverance from damnable error, Idolatory, and Popish superstition : And fearing, that if he did not now bestirre him busily, he was in perill to lose infinite numbers of his Subjects, and consequently no small part of that his spirituall Kingdome : he practiced most carefully in all places, with Monks, Friars, Priests, Nunns, and the whole rablement of his religious army, for the holding of simple souls in wonted obedience, and the upholding of his usurped Empire in the accustomed glory, opinion, and reverence.

" And for this purpose (amongst sundry sleights, set to shew

in sundry places, about the latter end and declination of that
his reign) one was wrought by the Holy Maid of *Kent*, in a
Chappell at this town, in devise as malicious, indeed as
mischievous, and in discovery as notorious, as any whatsoever. But because the midst, and end of this Pageant, is yet
fresh in the knowledge of many on live, and manifested to all
men in books abroad : and for that the beginning thereof is
known to very few, and likely in time to be hid from all, if it

Small Hythe.

be not by some way or other continued in minde : I will
labour only to bewray the same, and that in such sort, as the
maintainers thereof themselves have committed it to the
world in writing."

This Holy Maid of Kent, or Nun of Kent, who demonstrated
at Court-at-Street was one Elizabeth Barton, in 1525 a domestic
servant, about twenty years of age, at near-by Aldington.
Having suffered from fits, in which she was given to strange
utterances, she came to be looked upon as a prophetess, and in

the hands of some would-be miracle-workers proved a ready tool. She professed to be divinely inspired and her sayings were widely believed. She was removed to Canterbury and later to London ; churchmen and nobles listening to her with respect. Then in an unhappy hour she declared against the divorce of the King and his marriage with Anne Boleyn, and this in the long run led to her undoing. From divine prophecy she went on to treasonable utterances, declaring that the re-married monarch had ceased to be King in the eyes of God. After repeated examinations by Cranmer in 1533, Elizabeth Barton confessed to the fraud which she had been carrying on to gain applause, and at the instigation of certain monks and other people, and in the following spring, she and five of her abettors were hanged at Tyburn. The chapel with which the " Holy Maid " was associated stood on the seaward slopes from the present hamlet on Aldington Frith, or " Fright." Later, if Thomas Ingoldsby is to be believed, the place came to be looked upon as the resort of evil spirits : " warlocks, and other unholy subjects of Satan, were reported to make its wild recesses their favourite rendezvous, and that to an extent which eventually attracted the notice of no less a personage than the sagacious Matthew Hopkins himself, Witchfinder General to the British Government." The murderous witchfinder's association with Kent does not seem to be true ; his hideous work was mainly carried out in East Anglia, and in East Anglia he himself suffered as he had made others suffer, and on the same charge.

The seaward slope affords again beautiful and wide views over the marshes diversified with woodland, and here before turning to the right where the road forks we may pause to repeat another of Mr. Hueffer's poems inspired by this locality, " Aldington Knoll, The Old Smuggler Speaks " :

> " Al'ington Knoll it stands up high,
> Guidin' the sailors sailin' by,
> Stands up high fer all to see
> Cater the marsh and crost the sea.
>
> Al'ington Knoll's a mound a top,
> With a dick all round and it's bound to stop,
> For them as made it in them old days
> Sees to it well that theer it stays.

For that ol' ⟨noll is watched so well
By drownded men let outen Hell ;
They watches well and keeps it whole
For a sailor's mark—the goodly ⟨noll.

Farmer Finn as farms the ground
Tried to level that goodly mound,
But not a chap from Lydd to Lym'
Thought *that* job were meant for him.

Finn 'e fetched a chap fro' th' Sheeres,
One o' yer spunky devil-may-keeres,
Giv' him a shovel and pick and spade,
Promised him double what we was paid.

He digged till ten, and he muddled on
Till he'd digged up a sword and an skillington—
A grit old sword as long as me,
An' grit ol' bones as you could see.

He digged and digged the livelong day,
Till the sun went down in Fairlight Bay ;
He digged and digged, and behind his back
The lamps shone out and the marsh went black.

And the sky in the west went black from red,
And the wood went black—an' the man *was dead.*
But wheer he'd digged the chark shone white
Out to sea like Calais light.

Al'ington ⟨noll it stands up high,
Guldin' the sailors sailin' by,
Stands up high for all to see
Cater the marsh and crost the sea."

From the forked roads—the left continuing our westerly
journey, the right leading shortly to the village—we have
a delightful view across the field of a cluster of grey stone, red-
roofed cottages, oast-houses and a church which forms for
some distance round an admirable landmark.   This is Aldington.   Here in 1511—when the " Holy Maid " was a child of
six running about some cottage garden in the neighbourhood—
came one who was a sworn foe to all miracle workers.   This
was the great Dutch scholar Desiderius Erasmus, presented
to the living of Aldington by Archbishop Warham.   Never,
says one of the biographers of Erasmus, was there a more
flagrant abuse of church funds.   The scholar only held the
living for about sixteen months when he resigned it in con-

sideration of a pension of twenty pounds a year. And the archbishop who had conferred the benefice naively thought it was as well, seeing that Erasmus "could not preach the word of God to his parishioners or hold any communication with them in their own tongue, of which he is entirely ignorant." Northward a short distance from Aldington are Smeeth and Brabourne reserved for visiting when we take Ashford as a centre.

Returning to the road from which we have our picturesque glimpse of the church which Erasmus must so inadequately have served, we look over the churchless parish of Hurst. Several places have this wealden name as termination here— Goldenhurst (an old building with secret passages), Falcon-hurst, &c. The name may be taken as indicative of the well wooded nature of the country round ; for miles to the west we pass through scattered woodland on the right as our road trends nearer to the Marsh on our left. Terminations of place-names have a way of grouping themselves in districts, and here after Aldington we come to scattered Bonnington and then on a hill-top to Bilsington with memories of a thirteenth century Priory of Austin Canons, the remains of which—as is so often the case—now form part of a farmhouse, nearly a mile inland. Though Bilsington is scattered about four cross-roads on a hill-top it is but a low hill, for we have descended considerably since leaving Aldington and our road has brought us within less than half a mile of the Military Canal and the Marsh. On a high, open field on the marsh side of the village stands a tall obelisk which is a distinguishing landmark from below. This was raised to the memory of Sir William Cosway, Lord of the Manor here, who was killed by falling off a coach in pre-railway days. The Manor is said to have carried with it the office of Cupbearer to the Crown.

From Bilsington pleasant wooded roads go north past small retired hamlets and farmhouses to the valley of the East Stour and Ashford, but keeping roughly parallel with the canal, we pass where we come nearest to that waterway, through Ruckinge and a couple of miles beyond reach the railway (Ashford and Hastings Branch of the S.E.R.) at Ham Street. From here our road loops in again past Warehorne and Kenardington— both showing picturesquely grouped in trees — on by-roads towards the Marsh. Warehorne was at one time the scene of a fair of some importance in the district. At Kenardington, which is now a small village, but when the Rother came nearer may well have been of greater importance, the Saxons are said to have raised earthworks against the Danish invaders. The journey from Ham Street to Appledore may be made almost entirely by footpaths, giving more intimate knowledge of this country where the wealden woodlands are merging into the marsh levels.

At Appledore, which is described as the eastern point of the

Appledore.

great Andredsweald of Sussex, Surrey, and Kent, we have come down near the banks of the canal again—the railway station is, indeed, over a mile away on the marsh itself—to a large and straggling village with a wide main street. All about, except to the north-east, by which we have approached, extend marsh-land levels. Over the canal is Walland Marsh extending downwards to Lydd and Dungeness, to the south-west is the Isle of Oxney, made by the Rother and its branches, backed by Rye, whilst west and north is the upper Rother level with, beyond, the wooded rising ground about Tenterden. Apple-dore Church is an interesting old edifice near the canal. Towards the close of the ninth century, when the Rother still flowed out by Romney, this was presumably a place of some importance, for here the Danish leader, Hasting, brought his ships and established himself, building, it is said, a fort or castle on the slope overlooking the marsh where now the church stands. It was then that the folk of Kenardington threw up their earthworks to keep off the harrying seamen.

The Isle of Oxney—about five and a half miles long by three broad—is surrounded by the Rother, a branch of it known as the Reading Sewer, and the Royal Military Canal, so that it retains its insular character despite the changes in the channel of the Rother. The isle is really a delightful spot with its high, well wooded ground—over two hundred feet in the centre—rising from the surrounding marshes; especially abruptly from the southern side where the main stream of the Rother flows. As we approach from the Marsh, one of its eastern hills shows plainly with two trees on it. The actual county boundary there, however, is the Kent Ditch, the Rother having become a purely Sussex river, though to the east of the isle it flows for a short distance wholly in Kent. The name Oxney, it is suggested, may owe its derivation to oxen-ey, or island, that is the island on which oxen are pastured. It has long been celebrated for its pastures, and that it maintains its reputation may be readily believed as we wander about it, though its sheep far outnumber its kine. The isle is divided into two parishes, Stone cum Ebony and Wittersham. Stone, about two miles from Appledore, was long remarkable as having in its church, "time out of mind," an old altar, sup-posed Roman or Brito-Roman, with oxen figured on it. This was removed from the church to the vicarage garden by the Rev. William Gostling, the author of a *Walk in and About Canterbury*, who was appointed Vicar of Stone in 1753. Gostling's father, a minor Canon of Canterbury, was a celebrated chorister for whom Purcell wrote the anthem "They that go down to the sea in ships," and of him Charles II. is reported to have said "You may talk as you please of your Nightin-gales; but I have a Gostling who excels them all." Royal puns are granted a long lease of life. Writing of the altar about a century ago a Kentish topographer declared "the

P

bason or hollow at top retains a blackness, as if burnt by the fire occasioned by the sacrifices made on it."

Wittersham, towards the western end of the island ridge, has an effective landmark in its church. It is the largest village in the isle, and from it we may go down across the Rother valley by Peasmarsh to Rye. Stone and Wittersham are about three miles apart by a delightful road affording excellent views ; midway between the two, at the Stocks, we come to four cross-roads with oast-houses, a mill, and one of the most beautiful of timbered cottages ; following the left turning we may go by Iden and Playden to Rye, but keeping to our own county we turn to the right and by a winding road descend to the northern stream which we cross at Reading Street, of old named Ebony,

Between Appledore and Tenterden.

and thence in about three miles, climbing upward from the Level, reach Tenterden. From Wittersham we may more easily and no less pleasantly reach Tenterden by way of Small Hythe, a place the name of which reminds us that it was in olden times on the Rother estuary. Small Hythe with picturesque old cottages is at the foot of the hills about three miles south of Tenterden for which it was the one-time landing-place. At Small Hythe and at Stone ferry are toll gates where everything has to pay—"there's only one thing we let in or out free, and that's a dog."

At Tenterden we reach a very attractive old town which long rested on the dignity of its fame as a member of the Cinque Port of Rye, and as one of the first places in which the woollen manufacture was established, in the reign of Edward III.

It is not many years since that Tenterden remained untouched by the railway, the nearest station being several miles off. Now the Kent and East Sussex Railway runs hither from Headcorn and then along the Rother valley to Robertsbridge Junction. At Tenterden, too, we are in the Wealden district with the terminal " den "—signifying, we are told, " a wooded valley affording pasturage "—familiar in numerous place names within the area of a few miles : Rolvenden, Newenden, Benenden, Biddenden, Halden, Bethersden,' and a score

High Street, Tenterden.

of others. With its broad green-margined street, its well-kept appearance, the town is one to impress the visitor favourably, and it has considerable value as the centre from which may be explored some of the most delightful out-of-the-way wealden hamlets and villages, woodlands, parks and lanes ; we may go along some beautiful valleys, we may follow the course of the Rother to old Bodiam, we may explore the isle of Oxney and we may easily reach the marshlands which extend east and west of Dungeness, in Kent and Sussex.

P 2

"Tenterden Steeple is the cause of the breach in Goodwin Sands," so runs an old saying arising out of the apocryphal story which tells that when Tenterden church was built the Abbot of St. Augustine's at Canterbury (to which it belonged), used for the purpose stones which had been brought together to repair the sea wall protecting Earl Godwin's now submerged estate to the east of Deal. Fuller, after pointing out how people laughed at the unlogical reason of the man who declared that as the sands were firm land before the steeple was built, and were after overflowed, and that therefore Tenterden Steeple caused Goodwin Sands, goes on to accept the tradition :

"But one story is good till another is heard. Though this be all whereon this proverb is generally grounded, I met since with a supplement thereunto. It is this. Time out of mind money was constantly collected out of this county to fence the east banks thereof against the eruption of the seas ; and such sums were deposited in the hands of the Bishop of Rochester. But, because the sea had been very quiet for many years, without any encroachings, the Bishop commuted that money to the building of a steeple and endowing of a church in Tenterden. By this diversion of the collection for the maintenance of the banks, the sea afterwards brake in upon Goodwin Sands. And now the old man had told a rational tale, had he found but the due favour to finish it. And thus, sometimes, that is causelessly accounted ignorance in the speaker which is nothing but impatience in the auditors, unwilling to attend the end of the discourse."

The story thus gravely accepted by the author of "'The History of the Worthies of England'" is of course nothing but a myth, but before dismissing it we may see the goodly use of the story which was made " by the Reverend Father Master Hugh Latimer" in the last of his eight sermons preached before King Edward VI. and his Council at Westminster.

" Here was preaching against covetousness all the last year in Lent, and the next summer followed rebellion; ergo, preaching against covetousness was the cause of the rebellion. A goodly argument. Here now I remember an argument of Master More's which he bringeth in a book that he made against Bilney : and here by the way I will tell you a merry toy. Master More was once sent in commission into Kent, to help

to try out, if it might be, what was the cause of Goodwin Sands,
and the shelf that stopped up Sandwich Haven.   Thither

Tenterden Steeple.

cometh Master More, and calleth the country afore him, such
as were thought to be men of experience, and men that could
of likelihood best certify him of that matter concerning the

stopping of Sandwich Haven. Among others came in before
him an old man, with a white head, and one that was thought
to be little less than an hundred years old. When Master
More saw this aged man, he thought it expedient to hear him
say his mind in this matter; for, being so old a man, it was
likely that he knew most of any man in that presence and
company. So Master More called this old aged man unto
him, and said ' Father,' said he, ' tell me, if ye can, what is the
cause of this great arising of the sands and shelves hereabout
this haven, the which stop it up that no ships can arrive here?

Tenterden from the Rolvenden Road.

Ye are the eldest man that I can espy in all this company, so
that if any man can tell any cause of it, ye of likelihood can
say most in it ; or at leastwise more than any other man here
assembled.' ' Yea, forsooth, good master,' quoth this old man,
' for I am well-nigh an hundred years old, and no man here in
this company anything near unto my age.' ' Well, then,' quoth
Master More, ' how say you in this matter? What think ye to
be the cause of these shelves and flats that stop up Sandwich
Haven?' ' Forsooth, sir,' quoth he, ' I am an old man ; I think
that Tenterton Steeple is the cause of Goodwin Sands. For I
am an old man, sir,' quoth he, 'and I may remember the
building of Tenterton Steeple; and I may remember when

there was no steeple at all there. And before that Tenterton Steeple was in building, there was no manner of speaking of any flats or sands that stopped the haven ; and therefore I think that Tenterton Steeple is the cause of the destroying and decay of Sandwich Haven.' And even so, to my purpose, is preaching of God's word the cause of rebellion, as Tenterton Steeple was cause Sandwich Haven is decayed. And is not this a gay matter, that such should be taken for great wise men that will thus reason against the preacher of God's Word?"

A hundred years or so ago there still hung out from the tower

Rolvenden.

of Tenterden church, at the end of a piece of timber about eight feet long, a beacon, "a sort of iron kettle, holding about a gallon, with a ring or hoop of the same metal, round the upper part of it, to hold still more coals, rosin, &c." Maybe this was one of the very beacons fired to signal the approach of the Invincible Armada when

" Far on the deep the Spaniard saw, along each southern shire,
Cape beyond cape, in endless range, those twinkling points of fire."

At Tenterden it may be recalled, John Hoole the translator of Tasso and Ariosto lived during his later years. Hoole—

" the great boast and ornament of the India House " according
to Charles Lamb in ironical mood—is probably very little read
nowadays and chiefly remembered by certain anecdotes in
Boswell's " Life of Johnson."

All round Tenterden as has been said are picturesquely
attractive walks by up-and-down roads, the deviousness of which
suggests that they were formed while still the Weald was covered by forest.   The road to Rolvenden offers wide views over
the Rother Valley from high ground and descending to where
the Hexden Channel runs through a bit of the Level we reach

Benenden.

Newenden by the Rother where that river is the boundary cutting us off from Sussex.   Newenden is said by Camden to be
the Anderida of the Romans.   Its position suggests that it may
well have been an important place in the days when the Rother
estuary penetrated into the Weald, but later authorities than
Camden refuse to give it the honour of being considered Anderida, identifying that place with Pevensey in the neighbouring
county.   To the west of Newenden is Sandhurst, worth visiting
for its interesting old church perched upon a hill overlooking
the Kent Ditch (sometimes named the Kennett) which here
divides us from Sussex and on the other side of which is Bodiam.
From Sandhurst church turning back we may go north by road

round curiously named Megrim's Hill; we can return the way
we came, through the village, or may cross the fields by footpaths on our way to the Benenden Road. Benenden itself is
a pleasant village on high ground and beyond it Hemsted
Park claims the highest point in the Weald. The church
here is said at one time to have had a detached belfry like that
of Brookland in the Marsh—and like it to have been a smugglers' church. Fine tracts of woodland lie all about stretch-

Biddenden.

ing north a great part of the way to Biddenden, a village the
most notable attraction of which is the tradition of the
" Biddenden Maids."

An old account of the Biddenden Maids was sent by a
Tenterden correspondent to worthy William Hone and was by
him duly incorporated in his " Every Day Book." This
account had been printed on a broadside by local printers for
the edification of visitors drawn by the Easter custom at
Biddenden Church and is still to be purchased in the village

in that form.   That custom was the giving to strangers by the Churchwardens of about one thousand rolls with an impression upon them of the two " Maids " referred to in the legend, which in the fuller account of Hone is as follows :

"In the year 1100, at Biddenden, in Kent, were born Elizabeth and Mary Chulkhurst, *Joined together by the Hips and Shoulders, and who lived in that state, Thirty-Four Years !!* At the expiration of which time one of them was taken ill and after a short period died ; the surviving one was advised to be separated from the corpse which she absolutely refused by saying these words, '*as we came together, we will also go together,*' and about six hours after her sister's decease, she was taken ill and died also.   *A stone near the Rector's Pew marked with a diagonal line is shown as the place of their interment.*

> " ' The moon on the east oriel shone,
> Through slender shafts of shapely stone,
> The silver light so pale and faint,
> Shewed the twin sisters and many a saint,
> Whose images on the glass were dyed ;
> Mysterious maidens side by side
> The moonbeam kissed the holy pane,
> And threw on the pavement a mystic stain.'

" It is further stated that by their will they bequeathed to the Churchwardens of the Parish of Biddenden, and their successors, churchwardens for ever, certain pieces or parcels of land in the parish, containing abt twenty acres, which is hired at forty guineas per annum, and that in commemoration of this wonderful Phenomenon of Nature, the Rolls and about 300 quartern Loaves and Cheese in proportion, shd be given to the Poor Inhabitants of the Parish.

" This   account   is   entirely   traditionary,   the   Learned Antiquarian Hasted, in his account of the Charities of the Parish, states the Land was the gift of two Maidens, of the name of *Preston* : and that the print of the women on the cakes has only been used within these eighty years, and was made to represent two poor widows, as the general object of a charitable benefaction.   It is possible that the investigation of the learned Antiquary brought to light some record of the name of the Ladies for in the year 1656 the Rev. W. Horner, then Rector of the parish, claimed the land as having been given to augment his glebe, but was non-suited in the

Court of Exchequer. In the pleadings preserved in the Church, the names of the Ladies are not stated, not being known."

At the time when Hasted wrote his *History of Kent* and threw doubts upon the quaint, local tradition the annual value of " the Bread and Cheese Land " as it was called was about £31 10s. and the number of cakes distributed was six hundred. The legend is now at least two hundred years old and the idea that it may be historical cannot be scouted by those of us who remember "The Siamese Twins," the "Two Headed Nightingale," and other much-talked-of monstrosities. In the twelfth century the Biddenden Maids won long fame as benefactors, in the twentieth such an unhappily associated couple would win large salaries as music-hall or show "freaks." The present day broad-sheet gives the sisters names as Eliza and Mary, and the portrait-stamped cakes are still to be bought by curious visitors.

Between Biddenden and Tenterden, reached down a steep and grassy lane, is the broad expanse of Breeches Pond, starred in summer with many lilies, yellow and white. A perfect spot for a hot weather swim.

The sojourner in the rural parts of our county must often be struck by the curious names attached to farms and small hamlets. In this district round and about Tenterden we pass Puddingcake, Rats Castle (another near Tonbridge), Castweazel, Arcadia, and—both near High Halden—a Children's Farm and a Bachelor's Farm ; near Benenden may be found a Great Nineveh and a Little Nineveh, while a Frog's Hill near Newenden is balanced by a Frog's Hole near Biddenden.

CHAPTER XI

ROUND ABOUT ASHFORD

IF Ashford, a town—thanks to railway works and various industries—of upwards of ten thousand inhabitants, has not in itself much to attract attention it is a centre from which may be reached a large number of beautiful and interesting spots. Its position by the confluence of the East Stour with the Great Stour makes their differing valleys, and the adjacent hills, and the narrow valley through which together they flow towards Canterbury, all easily accessible, while the town's position too at the junction of railways from Canterbury, Folkestone, Romney and Maidstone makes it a centre for those who depend upon trains, no less good than it is for those who walk or cycle. Within a radius, roughly speaking, of eight miles— and no one is worthy of the name of pedestrian who cannot manage sixteen miles a day—any one making Ashford his headquarters may enjoy scenery of the most diverse character and visit places of the most varied interest. The marshlands about the East Stour, the chalk downs stretching from Wye, the parks and woodlands to the north, the valley of the Great Stour, "the dim blue goodness of the Weald" towards Tenterden are all before him where to choose. The town itself is a clean and comfortable looking place on rising ground with a manufacturing extension over the river to the south-east where the railway works are established. In the broad High Street is the Market Hall, and near it the large, handsome church of Kentish stone, with its fine central tower, having four corner turrets ; this tower was built by one, Sir John Fogge

A Corner in Ashford.

in the reign of Edward IV., and over his tomb is hung his helmet, as that of the Black Prince is hung at Canterbury.

According to Shakespeare, that "headstrong Kentishman, John Cade"—whom pedantical authorities have made into an Irishman—hailed from Ashford and thence set out to reform the little world of England—"I tell thee, Jack Cade the clothier means to dress the Commonwealth, and turn it, and set a new nap upon it," and furthermore "Dick, the butcher of Ashford," went with that force which the messenger to the King so scornfully described–

> "His army is a ragged multitude
> Of hinds and peasants, rude and merciless."

Jack Cade and his rabblement we shall meet again at Blackheath. After the ringleader had fled he was killed we are told in the garden of Alexander Iden, a Kentish esquire of Ripley Court, Westwell, and near Benenden is an Iden Green which might have disputed the title to be considered the scene of Cade's capture with another place by Hothfield if Cade Street over in Sussex had not already claimed the distinction.[1]

If the poor honour of including Jack Cade among Ashford's worthies be questioned there is no doubt that in this town was born John Wallis, one of the greatest precursors of Sir Isaac Newton in the field of mathematics,—a man, too, who so mastered the art of reading ciphers that he was at once feared and admired by both royalists and republicans in the time of trouble. He was born here in the year that Shakespeare died. When Wallis was fifty Samuel Pepys recorded meeting "Dr. Wallis, the famous scholar and mathematician ; but he promises little." When he was eighty-five the vigorous old man wrote to the diarist, "Till I was four-score years of age, I could pretty well bear up under the weight of those years ; but since that time, it hath been too late to dissemble my being an old man. My sight, my hearing, my strength, are not as they were wont to be."

To the north of Ashford along the high land to the left of the River Stour we have magnificent stretches of parkland

[1] See Mr. E. V. Lucas's " Highways and Byways in Sussex," p. 308.

A Byway in Ashford.

and woods, with small and interesting villages but a mile or two apart. The first great park is Eastwell, to reach which we pass the scattered village of Kennington which is partly on the road that runs along the lovely Stour valley to Canterbury, but mainly occupies the rising road towards Eastwell, and appears to be growing into a kind of villa suburb of Ashford. Where the road forks beyond,—the right branch that which continues up through the hills to Faversham, and the left a winding lane towards Westwell,—there stands a striking somewhat ornate turreted gatehouse of squared black flints and stonework. This is the entrance to Eastwell Park and is well worth a visit ; corkscrew stairs lead upwards to the roof from which an extensive view may be had, and a peep taken into the grandly timbered park. The lodge-keeper explains that the gateway came from " the Exhibition," and tells with bated breath that each little flint in the building cost twopence halfpenny and that they were brought from Rome. In the room over the gateway is a huge wall-painting on tiles showing the battle between Alexander and Darius. This is presumably a restored copy of an ancient work and was prepared at Naples. On the opposite wall is a slab dated " Maidstone 1845 " on which are five uninspired verses dealing with the picture, the first and last stanzas of which will give a sufficient taste of their quality.

> " Listen, Gentles, every one,
> This is Philip's mighty son
> Alexander valliant ⟨night
> Bearing him in mortal fight
> 'Gainst the Persian ⟨ing his foe.
> ⟨nightly deed and ⟨nightly blow. . . .
>
> Haply great Apelles' hand
> Limned me in Grecian land
> Buried long beneath the ground
> In Pompei (*sic*) was I found
> O'er these gay fantastic stones
> Lay my wretched master's bones."

The closing lines are as cryptic as the attendant's remark that the gate came from " the Exhibition."

Defoe described Eastwell Park as the finest that he had ever

seen, and many of his successors from the glimpses allowed
them may feel inclined to echo his words.   Long the seat of
the Earls of Winchilsea and at one time that of His Royal
Highness the Duke of Edinburgh, the park is rich in
warnings against trespass.   Where ancient use—dating probably from the days of the Canterbury Pilgrims—has given
us the right of crossing the park from the church we are
warned that bicycles must not enter, and that dogs whether
accompanied by their owner or not will be incontinently
shot[1] while all the rigours of the " Law "—the quotation
marks are not mine—will be brought to bear upon those
people who leave the defined footpath.   It is reasonable to
suppose that a dog has as much right to be on a public
footpath as a man.

One of the Earls of Winchilsea and Nottingham distinguished himself in the first half of the nineteenth century as
an uncompromising opponent of all measures of political
reform and was especially bitter over the matter of Catholic
Emancipation, to oppose which on October 10th, 1828, he
presided at a huge meeting on Penenden Heath.   A few
months later he wrote of the Duke of Wellington that he
" under the cloak of some coloured show of zeal for the
Protestant religion, carried on an insidious design for the
infringement of our liberties and the introduction of Popery
into every department of the state."   The Iron Duke replied
with a challenge and the two noblemen fought a duel in
Battersea Fields.   The Duke fired and missed, and his opponent then fired in the air and apologised for the language of
his letter.   " And may all other duels have that upshot in
the end."

Leaving the gate by the Westwell lane we follow the park
wall and after a short distance come to a break in the privacy
of the domain where a short road into it takes us to Eastwell
Church standing against the timbered hillside at the very edge
of the magnificent sheet of water which is about half a mile in
length and a quarter in breadth and is beautifully surrounded
by the greenery of park turf and groups of fine trees.   Pausing

---

[1] And this though the law says that a dog may not be shot unless actually
engaged in chasing deer, game or sheep.

on the bridge which crosses the narrow neck of the mere we shall generally see a number of various wild fowl. Eastwell Church, of rough flints and stone with old grotesque heads above the top windows of its embattled tower, is chiefly interesting as the burial-place of a supposed romantic figure. Here was laid in 1550 one "Richard Plantagenet," the reputed natural son of Richard Crookback. The story runs that this Richard as a lad of sixteen was at the fatal Battle of Bosworth, and on hearing the cry of "The King is dead, long live the King!" fled hither and lived in a mean manner until his identity was discovered by the owner of Eastwell who gave him permission to build for himself a small house on the estate. This he did and here Richard Plantagenet lived for over sixty years. A nameless tomb in the chancel is pointed out as that in which he was buried. Here is a subject that might well inspire a writer of historical romance.

West of the noble park is prettily situated Westwell with an old creeper-clad spired church that has some interesting Early English stained glass. Here in 1574 was a case of "satanic possession," in which a servant girl, gifted with ventriloquism horrified the credulous, until examination before magistrates led to her confessing the cheat and the recording of it ten years later in Reginald Scot's "Discoverie of Witchcraft." Here in 1814 Barham was curate, to be followed six years after by another writer who was very popular with our grandparents, G. R. Gleig, author of "The Subaltern" and other novels. Gleig served as an officer at Waterloo, later took Holy Orders, and after a year at Westwell, was presented to the perpetual Curacy of Ash and then to the Rectory of Ivychurch, both in Kent, and later came to be Chaplain General of the Forces. At the north of Eastwell Park is Challock Church with a prominent castellated tower, and north of this, a mile or so on the Maidstone Road, is the village of Challock Lees to be approached by a lovely winding lane—up hill and down dale—zig-zagging between leafy, and flower-grown hedges, festooned with wild clematis. The four cross-roads beyond will take us one to the village of Moldash and so to Canterbury, one to Leaveland, Badlesmere, Sheldwich and Throwley and so to Faversham; Badlesmere gave his title to the rich nobleman who paid with his life for desecrating the shrine of St. Thomas at Canterbury by appearing before it in arms.

Turning southwards from Challock we follow a lovely route through wonderful scenery by the Challock and King's Woods over White Hill by Soakham Down to Wye at the further side

Boughton Aluph.

of the Stour. Where the road forks nearly at its highest the left branch is the more direct, but the right skirting the east part of Eastwell Park is perhaps the more beautiful and takes us to Boughton Aluph with its fine decorated church to be seen well from the White Hill descent. This is but one of

several Boughtons in Kent, the most famous of all—thanks to
the Wotton family—lying some miles to the west of this.   As
we descend White Hill, above a chalk pit on the other side of
the valley is seen a great conventional crown outline cut in
the turf of the down ; inquiry elicits that this was done by
Wye folk to commemorate the Coronation of King Edward VII.

Before crossing the River Stour, the valley may be followed
a little way northwards to Godmersham with its magnificent
park, part of the beautiful stretch of diversified woodland that
reaches from Eastwell to Chilham Castle.   Godmersham is
interesting to Jane Austen's admirers as it was one of the
noble estates inherited by her brother Edward Knight and one
which she frequently visited, as her correspondence shows.   In
1813 she made a two months' stay and wrote whimsically to
one of her sailor brothers then stationed in the Baltic, " I
wonder whether you and the King of Sweden knew that I was
come to Godmersham with my brother.   Yes, I suppose you
have received due notice of it by some means or other.   I
have not been here these four years, so I am sure the event
deserves to be talked of before and behind, as well as in the
middle."   Lord Brabourne, who was grandson of Edward
(Austen) Knight, has described the place admirably.

" Godmersham Park is situated in one of the most beautiful parts of
Kent, namely, in the valley of the Stour, which lies between Ashford and
Canterbury.   Soon after you pass the Wye station of the railway from the
former to the latter place, you see Godmersham Church on your left hand,
and just beyond it, comes into view the wall which shuts off the shrubberies
and pleasure grounds of the great house from the road ; close to the church
nestles the home farm, and beyond it the Rectory, with lawns sloping
down to the River Stour which for a distance of nearly a mile runs through
the east side end of the park.   A little beyond the church you see the
mansion, between which and the railroad lies the village. divided by the
old high road from Ashford to Canterbury, nearly opposite Godmersham.
The valley of the Stour makes a break in that ridge of chalk hills, the
proper name of which is the Backbone of Kent
" So that Godmersham Park, beyond the house, is upon the chalk downs,
and on its further side is bounded by King's Wood, a large tract of woodland containing many hundred acres, and possessed by several different
owners "

This is the grand wood which links Godmersham with Eastwell, and its plantations of Spanish chestnut and silver birch

are especially noticeable. The chestnuts are periodically cut down for hop-poles, and a couple of seasons' growth where a number of birches have been left standing is particularly striking. On the banks about here the viper's buglos makes a splendid show with its tall spikes of cymed blossoms, blue almost as the borage, and where six or eight spikes rise

Godmersham.

together challenging comparison with the larkspurs of our gardens.

Wye, lying at the foot of the chalk downs which rise to the east of the Stour, with its dismantled windmill and its old timbered houses, with quaintly carven heads, is a quiet enough place to-day, though it is believed to have been an important one centuries agone. Its liveliest times now are when race meetings are held, for Wye is one of our Kentish centres familiar to the horse-racing fraternity. The chief worthies of the small town are Aphra Behn, the seventeenth century dramatist and novelist, John Sawbridge, Lord Mayor of London, and zealous upholder of Wilkes, and Sawbridge's sister, Mrs. Catherine Macaulay, the historian. Canterbury was long regarded as having the distinction of being the birthplace of Aphra Behn, "the first female writer who lived by her pen in England." But Mr. Edmund Gosse some years ago ascertained that she was born at Wye, for there she was baptized on July 10th, 1640. The daughter of a local barber named Johnson, she came to be one of the most noted authors and wits of her time, "she was the George Sand of the Restoration, the *chere maître* to such men as Dryden, Otway, and Southerne, who all honoured her with their friendship"; she is to be remembered as the introducer of milk punch into England, and as one of the few women whose talents in life gained for them in death burial in Westminster Abbey. Lord Mayor Sawbridge, who takes us from literature to politics, was born at Olantigh—the park of which occupies much of the hillside from here to Godmersham—where also had been born the fifteenth century Archbishop Kempe, who rebuilt Wye Church. Sawbridge's name is familiar to those who have followed the story of Wilkes's life at all closely. As Sheriff of London he five times returned Wilkes as duly elected for Middlesex in defiance of the House of Commons, and, to balance his townswoman's introduction of milk punch, was said to be the greatest proficient at whist of his time. He is buried in Wye Church.

The name of Mrs. Catherine Macaulay may not be very familiar to readers of the present generation, but little more than a hundred years ago she was an important personage in the writing and controversial worlds. Like her brother, the Lord Mayor, she was an intense enthusiast for "liberty," and her "history" was at one time known as "the Republican history," so that she was as extravagantly belauded by one set of people as she was extravagantly belittled by others. When another and a greater Macaulay was making his name as historian, Croker wrote "Catherine, though now forgotten by an ungrateful public, made quite as much noise in her day as

Thomas does in ours." At about the same time Hallam declared that Catherine Macaulay was read "not at all." Isaac Disraeli a few years earlier had said of her "history" that "combining Roman admiration with English faction she violated truth in her English characters and exaggerated romance in her Roman." A partial critic on the other hand wrote, " Mrs. Macaulay's history is honestly written, and with considerable ability and spirit, and is full of the freest, noblest sentiments of liberty," while Mary Wollstone-craft wrote of the historian as "the woman of the greatest abilities that this country has ever produced." Walpole and Gray praised her, Pitt "made a panegyric" of her work in the House of Commons, Lecky described her as "the ablest writer of the new Radical school," but posterity has well-nigh forgotten her. Still, in Wye she should be remembered, and before parting with her it may be recalled that Dr. Johnson was one of her sturdiest opponents.

"Sir, I would no more deprive a nobleman of his respect, than of his money. I consider myself as acting a part in the great system of society, and I do to others as I would have them to do to me. I would behave to a nobleman as I should expect he would behave to me, were I a nobleman and he Sam Johnson. Sir, there is one Mrs. Macaulay in this town a great Republican. One day when I was at her house, I put on a very grave countenance, and said to her, 'Madam, I am now become a convert to your way of thinking. I am convinced that all mankind are upon an equal footing ; and to give you an unquestionable proof, Madam, that I am in earnest, here is a very sensible, civil, well-behaved fellow-citizen, your footman ; I desire that he may be allowed to sit down and dine with us.' I thus, sir, showed her the absurdity of the levelling doctrine. She has never liked me since. Sir, your levellers wish to level down as far as themselves ; but they cannot bear levelling up to themselves. They would all have some people under them ; why not then have some people above them?"

When the author of the " Dixonary " so disliked by the pupils of Miss Pinkerton's Academy for young ladies on Chiswick Mall, was at Cambridge a couple of years later, he made merry over the lady again : " Several persons got into his company the last evening at Trinity, where, about twelve, he began to be very great ; stripped poor Mrs. Macaulay to the very skin, then gave her for his toast and drank her in two bumpers."

All about Wye towards the east roll the chalk downs—"fit

emblem of the deluge ebb "—and the climbing of them is rewarded by extensive views. Trimworth, Crundale, Wye and Broad Downs, the different tracts are named, and by footpaths over the turf and almost deserted lanes we may climb among them, seeing of human habitations only an occasional farmhouse and buildings, or tiny hamlet in a hollow of the hills. At Trimworth and in other parts of these downs, many ancient remains have been recovered. Just east of Wye is the bluff of the downs with its chalk pit and crown, near to which the mounting road to Hastingleigh and Brabourne runs. From this road with the down rising on our left and a row of windblown beeches on our right, we get glimpses into the fertile valley of chequered fields, now pasture white-dotted with sheep, now a deeper green, or gold, where the corn is growing, or ripening to the reaper.

To the south of Wye over this lower ground we may go by road and field paths to the small village of Brook at the foot of the hill, passing on our way at Withersdane St. Eustace's Well which in the days of miracles was famous for its curative properties, thanks to an abbot—afterwards St. Eustace—who came from Normandy to preach the better observance of Sunday. The story of how it got its name may best be given in the words of the monkish chronicler, Roger of Wendover, who tells us that the abbot

"landed near the city of Dover, and commenced the duty of his preaching at a town called Wi. In the neighbourhood of that place he bestowed his blessing on a certain spring, which by his merits was so endowed with the Lord's favour that, from the taste of it alone, the blind recovered sight, the lame their power of walking, the dumb their speech, and the deaf their hearing ; and whatever sick person drank of it in faith, at once enjoyed renewed health. A certain woman who was attacked by devils, and swollen up as it were by dropsy, came to him there, seeking to be restored to health by him ; he said to her, 'have confidence, my daughter, go to the spring at Wi, which the Lord hath blessed, drink of it, and there you will recover health.' The woman departed, and, according to the advice of the man of God, drank, and she immediately broke out into a fit of vomiting ; and, in the sight of all who were at the fountain for the recovery of their health, there came from her two large black toads, which, in order to show that they were devils, were immediately transformed to great black dogs, and after a short time took the forms of asses. The woman stood astonished, but shortly ran after them in a rage, wishing to catch them ; but a man who had been appointed to take charge of the spring, sprinkled some of the water between the woman and the monsters, on which they flew up into the air and vanished, leaving behind them traces of their foulness."

A manifestation of another sort is recalled at Hinxhill, near Willesborough, for here it is said for nearly six weeks in 1727 a field " of a marshy, peat-like texture " burned until about three acres of ground had been consumed to ashes yielding smoke "and strong smell like a brick-kiln." At Willesborough, nearing Ashford again, there was in the eighteenth century a hundred year old tombstone the inscription on which began " Here lyeth entombed the Body of William Master the second son of Michael Master Esquier. After a batchelor lyfe he came to an untimely Abel's death at the age of twenty-six years." The old tradition ran that William Master was killed by his brother as they sat at dinner, because they had both been paying court to the same lady, and William had proved successful. It is further said that it was this tragic event which gave Thomas Otway the theme on which he founded his gruesome tragedy of " The Orphan."

Brabourne, situated in the lower part of the downs, is a pleasant village with a handsome church near to which about a century ago in place of the present yew there stood a venerable one, measuring within an inch of fifty-nine feet in circumference, and conjecturally said to be three thousand years old. John Evelyn that tree-enthusiast has more than one reference to it. Visiting Brabourne on August 2nd, 1663, he wrote, " In the churchyard of the parish church I measured an overgrown yew tree that was eighteen of my paces in compass, out of some branches of which, torn off by the winds, were sawed divers goodly planks." Kent is so particularly rich in grand old churchyard yews that it has to suffice to point them out but here and there.

Among the most interesting features of this church are some ancient monuments, curious brasses to the Scott family of Scotts or Scots Hall—long since gone—in the neighbouring parish of Smeeth, several members of which won to prominence from the fourteenth to the sixteenth century. At the time of the Armada the Sir Thomas Scott of that day within twenty-four hours of receiving his orders from the Privy Council equipped four thousand men and took them to the rendezvous for the Men of Kent on Northbourne down. His great

grandfather Sir William had been a prominent figure on the
Field of the Cloth of Gold and had rebuilt Scots Hall so
that it rivalled the most splendid houses in Kent. This Sir
Thomas was in his day "a man of note, intelligence and
action"; he was one of the commissioners for reporting
on the methods of improving the breed of horses in this
country; he was one of the commissioners for draining and
improving Romney Marsh, and he was superintendent of the
improvement of Dover harbour—one of the many energetic
and capable men who did so much to make the Elizabethan
period an age of extraordinary national development. Here it
must suffice to recall him in some curious elegiac verses, written
it is surmised by his better remembered kinsman Reginald :

> " Here lyes Sir Thomas Scott by name ;
>   Oh happie Kempe that bore him.
> Sir Raynold, with four knights of fame,
>   Lyv'd lyneally before him.
>
> His wieves were Baker, Heyman, Beere,
>   His love to them unfayned.
> He lyved nyne and fifty yeare,
>   And seventeen soules he gayned.
>
> His first wief bore them every one ;
>   The world might not have myst her.
> She was a very paragon
>   The Lady Buckherst's syster.
>
> His widow lyves in sober sort,
>   No matron more discreeter ;
> She still reteiynes a good report,
>   And is a great housekeeper.
>
> He (being called to special place)
>   Did what might best behove him.
> The Queen of England gave him grace
>   The King of Heav'n did love him.
>
> His men and tenants wail'd the daye,
>   His kinne and countrie cryed ;
> Both young and old in Kent may saye
>   Woe work the day he dyed.
>
> He made his porter shut his gate
>   To sycophants and briebors,
> And ope it wide to great estates,
>   And also to his neighbours.

His House was rightly termed Hall
   Whose bred and beefe was redie ;
It was a very hospitall
   And refuge for the needie.

From whence he never stepped aside,
   In winter nor in summer ;
In Christmas time he did provide
   Good cheer for every comer.

When any service should be doun,
   He lyked not to lyngar ;
The rich would ride the poor wold runn,
   If he held up his fingar.

He kept tall men, he rydd great hors,
   He did write most finely ;
He used fewe words, but cold discours
   Both wysely and dyvinely.

His lyving meane, his charges greate,
   His daughters well bestowed ;
Although that he were left in debt,
   In fine he nothing owed.

But dyed in rich and happie state,
   Beloved of man and woman
And (what is yeate much more than that)
   He was envied of no man.

In justice he did much excell,
   In law he never wrangled :
He loved rellygion wondrous well,
   But he was not new-fangled.

Let Romney Marsh and Dover saye ;
   Ask Norborne camp at leyseur ;
If he were woont to make delaye
   To doe his countrie pleasure.

But Ashford's proffer passeth all—
   It was both rare and gentle ;
They would have pay'd his funerall
   T' have toomb'd him in their temple."

Another of Sir William's great grandsons was Reginald Scot,
whose " Discouerie of Witchcraft " is a famous book, for he

with an insight far in advance of his age sought to stay the hideous persecution which, especially in rural districts, made any lonely aged person (and many others) liable to a charge of witchcraft with but the rarest opportunity of escape from consequent barbarities. The title-page text which Scot employed was happily chosen, " Beleeue not euerie spirit, but trie the spirits, whether they are of God ; for manie false prophets are gone out into the world." The full title, too, is worth citing as a delightful example of the alluring art which was employed in the devising of .such in the days when the making and reading of books were more leisurely undertakings than they now are.

The discoueri
of Witchcraft,
Wherein the lewde dealing of witches
and witchmongers is notablie detected, the
knauerie of coniurors, the impietie of inchan-
tors, the follie of soothsaiers, the impudent fals-
hood of cousenors, the infidelitie of atheists,
the pestilent practices of Pythonists, the
curiosity of figurecasters, the va-
nitie of dreamers, the begger-
lie art of Alcu-
mystrie.
The abhomination of idolatrye, the hor-
rible art of poisoning, the vertue and power of
naturall magike, and all the conueiances
of Legierdemaine and iuggling are deciphered :
and many other things opened, which
haue long lien hidden, howbeit
verie necessarye to
be knowne.
Heerevnto is added a treatise vpon the
nature and substance of spirits and diuels,
&c : all latelie written
by Reginald Scot
Esquire.

Many of Scot's contemporaries hailed his reasonable exposure of unreasonable superstition with joy, for, as one of them put it, he " dismasketh sundry egregious impostures, and in certaine principall chapters, and speciall passages hitteth the nayle on the head with a witnesse." James VI. of Scotland described the work as " damnable," and on becoming James I. of England the same bigoted and pedantical monarch ordered all copies of the " Discouerie" to be burnt. Though Scot, who spent most of his life in his native district, probably learned much witch lore from the Kentish folk of the time, he has a further claim on our consideration here as being the author of the first practical treatise on hop cultivation in England, the " Perfect Platform of a Hop-Garden, and necessary instructions for the making and maintaining thereof, with Notes and Rules for Reformation of all Abuses." (1573.)

Another and far different writer who hailed, and took his title, from this district was the late Lord Brabourne, who on the maternal side was as we have seen a great nephew of Jane Austen, and who won wide popularity a generation ago with his stories for children, stories marked by that combination of fancy with simplicity which is one of the surest appeals to the juvenile imagination. Many of his stories too, notably those in " Higgledy Piggledy," should have an especial attraction for Kentish children, in that they tell of strange adventures, of fairies, witches, and animals in these southern parts of the county.

Crossing the East Stour near Smeeth station we can easily reach Aldington in the hilly district north of Romney Marsh, dealt with in the previous chapter. The fact that members of the poet's family were buried at Smeeth justifies us in claiming Gower as a Kentish worthy.

Following the course of the stream—decked in summer-time with white and yellow water-lilies—through level dyked meadows with all the character of marshland, we come to the little village of Mersham, with its southward extension beyond the Stour suggestively named Flood Street, and with the foot-path along a raised bank indicative of the flood-time state of the roadway in this high valley of the East Stour. The general level is over a hundred feet above the sea which lies but a few miles to the south beyond the Hythe to Appledore hills, for the stream, as has been said earlier, though it rises but a few miles from Hythe on this southern coast, flows north-westward to the Great Stour at Ashford, and reaches the sea in the neighbourhood of Sandwich.

To the south of Ashford lie various small hamlets, scattered about well kept farmlands, passing which we come to the broad woodlands north of the Romney Marshes, and so to

Ham Street, Warehorne, and Appledore. Westwards following the course of the Great Stour we come to the neat and attractive village of Great Chart, with its many cottage gardens rich in bright flowers, its typical grey stone towered church at the end of the rising street. Here Hadrian à Saravia, a famous divine, friend of the judicious Hooker as we have seen, was Rector during the closing years of his life, and here he died in 1613. He was a striking example of the cosmopolitan divine of the period ; his father was a Spaniard, his mother a Fleming, and he passed much of his life in the Channel Islands and England. To him we owe something for his share in the translation of the Bible, for he was nominated one of the translators in 1607, and was one of the committee to whom was entrusted the Old Testament from Genesis to the Second Book of Kings. He is also known as author of a Latin treatise on the Eucharist which he dedicated to James I., but which was not published until 1855.

To the north of Great Chart is one of the many beautiful parklands of the district, Godinton Park and Swinford Old Manor—the " haunt of ancient peace " in which Mr. Alfred Austin, the Poet Laureate, has long resided in a pleasant rambling house screened from the road by a wealth of flowering shrubs and trees. A seventeenth century worthy who lived at Godinton is said to have married five wives, and, on the death of the fifth, when he was ninety-three years of age, set out and walked to London in search of a sixth, but his zeal for matrimony was cut short by death. Park almost merges into park, and next we reach the beautiful and extensive one of Hothfield Place in the neighbourhood of which, according to one tradition, Alexander Iden slew the rebel Cade. The beautiful tract of Hothfield Heath is one to be lingered over and wandered about. Its grand clumps of pines, its sturdy beeches, with stretches of turf and innumerable patches of gorse and other shrubs make it very picturesque while from its higher portions are to be had beautiful views across the Weald in one direction, and of the wooded range of hills in the other. In one of the coppices of Hothfield, between the lake and the Ashford road, " the nodding foxglove " grows in splendid profusion—thousands of noble spikes being grouped in most admired disorder among the undergrowth where the trees have been cut down. From the

Heath in a couple of miles by the little hamlet of Westwell Leacon we may reach the comfortable looking village of Charing backed by the wooded downs with the steep and winding ascent of Charing Hill on the way to Faversham, the windmill silhouetted against the sky on top. From that bill a magnificent view across the upper valley of the Stour and the Weald is to be had, the flourishing farmlands being greatly diversified with clumps and stretches of woodland.

> " Dirty Charing lies in a hole,
> It had but one bell and that was stole."

This village, which strikes the present day visitor as anything but dirty, is one of the many places at which we come upon old-time residences of the Archbishops of Canterbury. Here for several centuries stood a splendid archiepiscopal palace, one of the most ancient possessions attached to Canterbury, taking us back to the early establishment of Christianity in England. In 757 it was seized by Offa but not long afterwards was returned to the Archbishop and remained one of his successors' most important possessions up to the time of Henry VIII. when Cranmer found it politic to hand it and others over to that grasping monarch. " Whilst Thomas Arundel filled the see, in the reign of Henry IV., the first capital execution for the crime of heresy occurred. He pronounced W. Sawtre a relapsed heretic, and those fires were kindled which at length consumed Cranmer, the last archiepiscopal tenant of the palace at Charing." The remaining ruins, partly formed into cottages, partly used as farm buildings, though considerable, suggest little of these old-time tragedies, or of the old-time splendour when Henry VIII. was entertained here en route for the Field of the Cloth of Gold. The ruins in which herring-bone masonry, tiles, and weather-worn carvings are to be seen stand by the gate leading to the handsome church which is the successor of an ancient one that was in 1590 " consumed by fire to the very stones of the building, which happened from a gun discharged at a pigeon, then upon the roof of it." The church has a sundial over the entrance.

Owing to the discovery long since of Roman remains,

Charing disputes with four-mile-distant Lenham the right to be considered the original Durolenum. Southwards towards the Weald we may visit Egerton, the great church tower of which village is seen prominently from the road; Pluckley, with its many delightful old houses, and good view across the Weald; and Little Chart, all set in pleasant country. Egerton, with some nice old cottages, and its church with a lofty buttressed tower is situated on a small hill and is said to mark one limit of that vague tract known as the Weald. Beyond it is another landmark in the Egerton windmill and below it by the infant Stour is the hamlet of Stonebridge Green. Another tiny hamlet near Egerton, in the opposite direction, and forming a detached portion of the parish of Little Chart, is Mundey Boys, worth more than passing mention in that a local story attaches to its quaint name. This story runs that a farmer here had several sons who were given to going out and enjoying themselves on Sundays so that they were loth to rise next morning, and their father had so regularly to rouse them with his cry of "Now, then, get up, get up,— it's Monday, boys," that the words came to be attached to the place. It needs but a simple story to win applause at the wayside inns in some of these quiet country spots. Pluckley station, from which this part of our district may well be explored, lies more than a mile to the south with near-by brickworks and smoke-belching chimney scarcely suggestive of the peaceful and lonely rustic places within easy reach; quiet woodlands, rich in the flora of the Weald, occasional ponds grown with reeds and rushes, and starred with water-lilies, lanes and footpaths along which we may walk for long without meeting another wayfarer.

North of Charing, too, among the higher hills leading up to the Faversham country, we may cross the old Pilgrim's Road which runs curiously parallel—at from less than half a mile to a mile and a half—with the high road, and find walks no less various, no less attractive. Here are wide stretches of woods in which the hop-grower's friend, the sweet chestnut, is plentifully seen. At Stalisfield, in a country of coppices, the church is to be visited for the sake of its carved oak screen. At Otterden dwelt an early electrical experimentalist, Stephen Gray (died 1736), whose labours assisted considerably in the advance of our knowledge of electricity. Climbing the steep Charing Hill and turning to the right beyond we come to the broad extent of Longbeech Wood and so reach the neighbourhood of Challock and its adjacencies touched upon in the earlier description of these places round and about Ashford.

Anglers.

R

CHAPTER XII

THOUGH it was of Sussex that Mr. Rudyard Kipling was singing when he wrote of

" Belt upon belt, the wooded, dim
Blue goodness of the Weald,"

and though a greater extent of the Weald belongs to Sussex than belongs to Kent our county may claim its share of the goodness ; for those who wander about the wooded belts there is as much to attract the attention in the things seen and as much to touch the imagination with bygone associations in the Kentish as in the Sussex Weald. It is still largely a country of retired villages, of much woodland, of quiet, winding ways. Though farms and tiny hamlets almost innumerable are scattered about it, and though branch railways now cross it from Headcorn by Tenterden to Robertsbridge, and from Paddock Wood by Cranbrook to near Hawkhurst the tract of country is one in which the lover of seclusion has not to travel far for his satisfaction.

Though changed much from the days when the Wealden Forest stretched from Hampshire and occupied a large part of the counties of Surrey, Sussex and Kent, though habitations in single spies and in battalions have invaded its privacy, yet enough remains to suggest how important a barrier its miles of hills, dense woods and clayey bogs made between the coast and the interior in the days when the best of the roads were probably no better than more or less indefinite tracks through the dense cover of various shrubs and trees, largely oak. The Wealden oak was indeed an important factor in the building up of Britain's supremacy as mistress of the seas. As that splendid utilitarian William Cobbett put it," Here the oak grows

finer than in any part of England.   The trees are more spiral
in their form.   They grow much faster than upon any other
land.   Yet the timber must be better ; for, in some of the Acts
of Queen Elizabeth's reign it is provided that the oak for the
Royal Navy shall come out of the Weald of Surrey, Sussex or
Kent."   Samuel Pepys in his "Memoires of the Navy" shocks
our prejudice about English oak by declaring that for the
larger vessels, foreign oaks—Prussian and Bohemian—yielded
better and more durable timber !   The shipbuilders took toll of
the woodlands and so also did the iron founders, yet still on

Headcorn Churchyard.

the whole the country that was in olden time Andredsweald, or
"the wood or forest without habitation," remains one of the
best wooded that we have of like extent.   Oaks are still to be
seen in plenty, occasionally in fine specimens and frequently in
coppices of younger growth and varied with other timber.   The
denuding of the Weald began early, and Michael Drayton three
hundred years ago made the forests, "daughters of the Weald,"
lament the change already wrought, the disregard of posterity
in the wholesale destruction of the timber trees :

    " 'Could we,' say they, 'suppose that any would us cherish,
   Which suffer (every day) the holiest things to perish ?

All to our daily want to minister supply
These iron times breed none that mind posterity.
'Tis but in vain to tell, what we before have been,
Or changes of the world, that we in time have seen ;
When, not devising how to spend our wealth with waste,
We to the savage swine let fall our larding mast,
But now, alas, ourselves we have not to sustain,
Nor can our tops suffice to shield our roots from rain.
Jove's oak, the warlike ash, vein'd elm, the softer beech,
Short hazel, maple plain, light asp, the bending wych,
Tough holly, and smooth birch, must altogether burn ;

Looking West from a point between Hawkhurst and Cranbrook.

What should the builder serve, supplies the forger's turn ;
When under public good, base private gain takes hold,
And we poor woful woods to rum lastly sold.' "

When Drayton wrote the Weald was already greatly changed
from its earliest character. In prehistoric times it is supposed
to have been the bed of a sea, and later a great river estuary on
the banks of which reptilian monsters "tare each other in the
slime." In the English Chronicle it is the " Mickle wood, that
we call Andred," and was "from west to east a hundred and
twelve miles long or longer, and thirty miles broad," while Bede

twelve hundred years ago described it as "thick and inaccessible, the abode of deer, swine and wolves," though it had long since been penetrated by several of the great roads which formed so important a factor in the civilising influence of the Romans. Centuries have gone since the last boar was hunted, the last wolf destroyed; great trees—survivals of the forest primeval— are comparatively few, but yet it is of the woods and coppices that we first think when we try to consider this great Wealden district as a whole. Over and over again we are reminded of

Between Goudhurst and Horsmonden.

it in the place-names of towns and villages and estates scattered about it, by the common termination of "hurst." Taking Cranbrook as our centre we have Staplehurst to the north, Hawkhurst to the south, Sissinghurst to the east, and Lamberhurst to the west, with "hursts" innumerable about the devious byways in between.

Though now quiet enough, picturesque Cranbrook was once a place of considerable importance, being the first centre of the cloth weaving industry in the days of Edward III. For centuries this manufacture was carried on here and in the sur-

Cranbrook.

rounding district, and when Fuller wrote " Kentish cloth at the present keepeth up the credit thereof as high as ever before," but it has now been supplanted by the manufacture of other districts, and to remind us of the bygone trade we have but the old gabled houses in which it was carried on, and such stories as that of Queen Elizabeth walking from Cranbrook to the neighbouring manor of Coursehorne entirely on a pathway of broadcloth made in the neighbourhood.   The church stand-

Staplehurst.

ing part hidden at an angle of the main street is an inter-esting building with many noticeable features, including a 'dipping place," constructed by a notable Anabaptist vicar here, known to those who read old works of controversial theology as "Johnson of Cranbrook."   Born at Frindsbury, and educated at Canterbury, the non-juring divine belongs very fully to our county for, successively or as pluralist, the Rev. John Johnson held the livings of Hardres, Boughton-under-

Blean, Herne Hill, Margate, Appledore, and lastly—1707-1725
—Cranbrook, where he was known as a diligent parish priest,
holding daily services in his church, and whence he issued
his various works on divinity. More famous names associated
with Cranbrook are those of Phineas Fletcher, the poet of "the
Purple Island"—"wise, tender, and sweet voiced old fellow"—
was born here when his grandfather was rector in 1582, and of
Sydney Dobell, the singer of "Balder," who was born here
in 1824.

To Willsley Green, a little north of Cranbrook, the infant
Douglas Jerrold was taken within a few weeks of his birth in
Soho; there he passed his earliest years, and thither I like to
believe his memory returned when he came to present the
idyllic spot described in "The Chronicles of Clovernook"—

"We will show every green lane about it; every clump of trees—every
bit of woodland, mead and dell. The villagers, too, may be found, upon
acquaintance, not altogether boors. There are some strange folk among
them. Men who have wrestled in the world, and have had their victories
and their trippings-up; and now they have nothing to do but keep their
little bits of garden ground pranked with the earliest flowers; their only
enemies, weeds, slugs and snails. Odd people, we say it, are amongst
them. Men, whose minds have been strangely carved and fashioned by
the world; cut like odd fancies in walnut-tree: but though curious and
grotesque, the minds are sound, with not a worm-hole in them. And these
men meet in summer under the broad mulberry-tree before the "gratis,"
and tell their stories—thoughts, humours; yea, their dreams."

There are in this neighbourhood many fine trees, particularly
grand conifers between Cranbrook and Sissinghurst.

Five miles to the north of Cranbrook is Staplehurst, with a
good view of the valley of the River Beult, one of the most
important tributaries of the Medway, and before reaching that
town we have Frittenden, a mile or so to the right, returning
from which attractive byroads lead to one of the old "stately
homes of England" at Sissinghurst, passing on our way the
Hammer Stream. This little tributary of the Beult as do other
names in the neighbourhood, reminds us of the days when
ironfounding was carried on extensively in the "hursts." But
northward the tide of manufacture has taken its way, and ironfounding and cloth-making must be looked for far from these
rural scenes.

The ruins of the Tudor Sissinghurst Castle, at some distance
from the village, are well worth visiting. Sir Roger de Cover-

ley we may be sure would have gone out of his way for the purpose, for he was a diligent reader of Baker's " Chronicle of the Kings of England," as Addison has told us, always keeping the volume in his hall window and quoting it with approval.

Frittenden Church.

Horace Walpole we know *did* go out of his way in 1752—and was not altogether gratified. " Yesterday," he wrote, " after twenty mishaps we got to Sissinghurst to dinner. There is a park in ruins, and a house in ten times greater ruins, built by sir John Baker, chancellor of the exchequer to queen Mary.

You go through an arch of the stables to the house, the court of which is perfect and very beautiful. . . . This has a good apartment, and a fine gallery a hundred and twenty feet by eighteen, which takes up one side : the wainscot is pretty and entire ; the ceiling vaulted and painted in a light genteel grotesque. The whole is built for show ; for the back of the house is nothing but lath and plaster." Nearly half a century later than Walpole's visit the place was utilised for keeping French prisoners, since which it has been reduced to mere ruins. It was at this Castle that the unhappy Sir Richard Baker was born, but the literary works by which he is remembered were destined to be written from the confinement of the Fleet Prison. It was Sir Richard's grandfather, Sir John Baker, ambassador to Denmark for Henry VIII., and Chancellor of the Exchequer under Queen Mary, who built Sissinghurst. Sir John is reported to have been a severe opponent of his Anabaptist neighbours at Cranbrook, and an unfounded tradition says that he was killed during a broil with them at a place in the vicinity still known as Baker's Cross. The historian was the eldest son of Sir John's disinherited eldest son, and though born at the Castle does not seem to have been long associated with it. At the age of sixty-seven he was forced to take refuge in the Fleet Prison, and there during the last ten years of his life he wrote various works, including the " Chronicles " by which he was once better remembered, and of which he himself said " it is collected with so great care and diligence, that if all other of our chronicles were lost, this only would be sufficient to inform posterity of all passages memorable, or worthy to be known." Contemporaries and successors passed far other judgments on the work, which has long since become obsolete. It is, however, with bitter feelings that we think of that son-in-law of his —" one Smith "—who destroyed the manuscript of Sir Richard's autobiography ; his devotional exercises and verses were little likely to do more than please his contemporaries, his " Chronicle " was doomed to be superseded, but from such of his works as we can judge we may well believe that the lost one might have had a lasting attractiveness. The destruction of a MS. book by any but the author thereof should rank with the worst of crimes. It is a kind of murder.

Northwards from Cranbrook we found the Wealden country gradually declining towards the Beult and its tributaries, southwards after rising to the small village of Hartley (near Cranbrook station) we go towards the Kent Ditch which for some distance forms the boundary between our county and Sussex. Not far from the boundary—beyond which the parish extends—is the extensive village of Hawkhurst in the midst of delightful country, with a number of Elizabethan residences and parks in the near neighbourhood.

The large church of Hawkhurst—at the southern end of the

Hawkhurst Moor.

village—is remarkable for its decorated east window, and for having parvis chambers over its northern and southern porches. In the church is an inscribed marble slab to the memory of Nathaniel Lardner, a celebrated nonconformist divine who was born in the Hall House, Hawkhurst, in 1684, spent most of his life in London and died in the house in which he was born on his annual visit to his native village in 1768. He is regarded as "the founder of the critical school of modern research in the field of early Christian literature, and he is still the leading authority on the conservative side."

The churchwardens' accounts for Hawkhurst during the sixteenth century include some curious items. For instance in 1548 we find there was twopence paid " to blast for kepyng the doggs out of the churche," while in 1549 we find the churchwardens lending money and accounting for the interests received, thus :—

> "Itm, of Thomas Seeeley for the ferme (loan) of Xⁱⁱ .   .   xiijˢ—iiijᵈ
> Itm, of John Hyckmote for the ferme of Vⁱⁱ. . . . . vjˢ—viijᵈ
> Itm, of John Keffynche for ferme of xxxˢ . . . . . ijˢ "

These sums were probably lent from the " Poor Men's Box " to poor men to purchase cows or other aids to a livelihood. A few years later we find

> " Pᵈ for the pformynge of the saxten's wags at Easter . .   11ˢ—vjᵈ

It would be curious to know what performance the " saxten's wags " indulged in—presumably one of the miracle plays or moralities in which the time was rich, though the performers being described as wags suggests that these performances may have been a drollery.

Sir John F. W. Herschel—the third member of one family to win wide fame as an astronomer—lived for thirty years at Collingwood just south of Hawkhurst Church; here he carried out his incessant work in widening the bounds of our knowledge of the stars—" every day of Herschel's long and happy life added its share to his scientific services "—and here in 1871 he died, but he is not buried here : Westminster Abbey claimed him—and there he was interred near to the grave of Sir Isaac Newton.

Hawkhurst was one of the neighbouring places which followed Cranbrook in the industry of clothmaking, and here also was another ironfounding centre—the furnaces being at one time the property of that " hero of peace," William Penn, whose beautiful and saintly wife, Gulielma Maria Springett, came from over the Sussex border.

East of Hawkhurst we may go by Benenden or Sandhurst into the Tenterden district, but immediately to the west is country no less attractive and still less inhabited where there stretches the broad extent of the Frith and Bedgebury Woods with good views and many miles of quiet walks for all who delight in woodland solitude. Frith Woods are sometimes Fright Woods—the term originally signifying rough, poorly grown, heathy woodlands, was as we have seen also used of Aldington Frith. Bedgebury Park is a noble estate lying to the north with some grand trees and with notable gardens and lakes. The great lake, a splendid sheet of water, is said to cover the site of the old moated manor house at which Queen Elizabeth stayed during one of her Kentish progresses. The

Goudhurst.

present house, since altered, was built in 1688 by Sir James Hayes—one time Secretary to Prince Rupert—out of his share of a recovered Spanish treasure ship. At the western side of the picturesque park is the hamlet of Bedgebury Cross from which we may reach the village of Kilndown in the modern and unattractive church of which Field-Marshal Viscount Beresford, one of Wellington's ablest lieutenants in the Peninsular War, is buried. Beresford has been much criticised for his conduct of the battle of Albuera, but Wellington declared that if he himself had been incapacitated he should

have recommended Beresford to succeed him, not for his
qualities of generalship, but because he alone could "feed an
army." The conqueror of Waterloo thus enforcing the truth
of the dictum that an army fights on its stomach.

Kilndown village is backed by Kilndown Woods and immediately beyond is Scotney Castle, the creeper-clad ruins of an
old moated residence by the little river Bewl.   Lamberhurst, a
little further to the west, is a large village among the well wooded
hills.   Here—as in so many of our "hursts"—iron smelting was
carried on extensively in past times ; it was indeed one of the
most important centres of the industry, providing the iron
railings which once surrounded, and now partially surround St.
Paul's Cathedral, and being also busied over cannon founding.
The St. Paul's railings were cast at the Gloucester furnace—so
named from Queen Anne's son who visited it in 1698—which
stood on the River Teise about midway between Lamberhurst
and Bayham Abbey.   These railings, according to an old writer
—Londoners please note when next passing through St. Paul's
Churchyard—"compose the most magnificent balustrade perhaps in the universe !"   The total weight of the rails and gates,
according to the same authority who fell from high falutin to
statistics, was over two hundred tons, and the cost upwards of
eleven thousand pounds.   Many of the rails which were moved
from the front of St. Paul's found their way to Canada.   The
vessel carrying them was wrecked, and some of them were only
recovered after considerable trouble and at much expense.
These now protect a tomb in High Park in Toronto, bearing
an inscription—which is quoted from memory—

> " St. Paul's Cathedral for 160 years I did enclose
> Stranger, behold with reverence !
> Man, unstable man,
> Twas thou that caused this severance ! "

East and north-east of Lamberhurst are Goudhurst and
Horsmonden, little more than a couple of miles apart with the
Teise flowing northwards between, and with roads "smooth
and handsome as those in Windsor Park."   Horsmonden is a
picturesquely situated village.   Its old church, which stands a
mile away near the river, with at its gate a grand walnut tree
the spreading branches of which are supported on many
"crutches," has some interesting features, including an excel-

lent fourteenth century brass of one de Grofhurst in ecclesias
tical vestments. The Grovehurst family was long resident at
the manor of the same name near the river here, but became
extinct some centuries ago. For a mural monument to the
Browne family a simile-seeking epitaph-writer produced the
following which is well worthy of standing with other punning
memorials of the dead :

> " Reader, stand still ; when the Almighties hand
> Had wrote these copies faire, then vnderstand,
> He strewed them ore with dust, that they might be

View from near Goudhurst.

> Secur'd from blots, discharg'd from injury :
> When God shall blow away this dust, they shall
> Be known to have been divinely pen'd by all."

On the oak screen on behalf of some unidentifiable Alice
Campion was carved an appeal for the prayers of the devout :
" Orate pro bono aestatu alecie campeon." A family of the
Campions is said to have resided in the neighbourhood in the
sixteenth century.

Near to the rectory, pleasantly situated in a little park on an
eminence, is a tower erected half a century ago by the late Rev.

Sir William Smith-Marriott to the memory of Sir Walter Scott
and within the tower is preserved a collection of the works of
the Wizard of the North.   An unique tribute it would seem to a
man of letters.   Besides the fine walnut by the church gate
there is, standing near the remains of an old moat, a grand old
tree known as the Big Oak.

Goudhurst again is a very picturesquely situated village,
having the advantage of its neighbour in the matter of height,
for it is on the summit of one of the loftiest ridges in the Weald
and all about it are to be had grand views—that from the church
to the south across the " Fright " woods and Bedgebury Park is
especially fine.   This view from the churchyard is said by one
with a liking for the particularity of figures to be "about
twenty-five miles in diameter."   In the church, much rebuilt
and restored, the tower of which forms a striking landmark,
are some curious old monuments while in the large village are
some of the ancient houses in which the clothmaking industry
was carried on in the palmy days of that manufacture in Kent.
"Some little wool staplery business " was continued here on
into the early nineteenth century.

In an old Kent guide we learn, of Goudhurst, that " there are
two schools in the parish, one for teaching grammar and the
Latin language, and the other English.   The former is under
the care of a master, who has a salary of thirty-five pounds
per annum, the latter is under the care of a widow woman,
who has a salary of five pounds per annum, and is full of poor
children."   The old grammar school has ceased to exist and
three college exhibitions are maintained with its funds.   The
poor widow woman who has long since laid aside the ferule,
and herself sleeps peacefully in the churchyard, must have
been such an one as inspired Shenstone's poem.

> " In ev'ry village mark'd with little spire,
> Embow'r'd in trees, and hardly known to fame,
> There dwells, in lowly shed, and mean attire,
> A matron old, whom we school-mistress name ;
> Who boasts unruly brats with birch to tame ;
> They grieven sore, in piteous durance pent,
> Aw'd by the pow'r of this relentless dame ;
> And oft-times, on vagaries idly bent,
> For unkempt hair, or task unconn'd, are sorely shent.

Some years after these munificently paid educators of the
people had been thus mentioned William Cobbett visiting

Goudhurst on one of those "Rural Rides" the account of
which forms one of the most bracing books of the kind we
have, thanks to the combined strong common sense and
dogmatism of the burly egotist, happened upon an opportunity
for enlarging upon another matter of education :

"I got to Goudhurst to breakfast, and as I heard that the Dean of
Rochester was to preach a sermon in behalf of the National Schools, I
stopped to hear him. In waiting for his Reverence I went to the Metho-
dist Meeting-house, where I found the Sunday School boys and girls
assembled, to the almost filling of the place, which was about thirty feet
long and eighteen feet wide. The 'Minister' was not come, and the
Schoolmaster was reading to the children out of a tract-book, and shaking
the brimstone bag at them most furiously. This Schoolmaster was a sleek-
looking young fellow ; his skin perfectly tight ; well-fed, I'll warrant him ;
and he has discovered the way of living, without work, on the labour of
those that do work. There were thirty-six little fellows in smock-frocks,
and about as many girls listening to him ; and I daresay he eats as much
meat as any ten of them. By this time the Dean, I thought, would be
coming on ; and, therefore, to the church I went ; but to my great disap-
pointment, I found that the parson was operating preparatory to the
appearance of the Dean, who was to come on in the afternoon, when I,
agreeably to my plan, must be off. The sermon was from 2 Chronicles,
Ch. xxi, v. 21, and the words of this text described King Hezekiah as a
most zealous man, doing whatever he did with all his heart. I write from
memory, mind, and, therefore, I do not pretend to quote exact words ;
and I may be a little in error, perhaps, as to chapter or verse. The object
of the preacher was to hold up to his hearers the example of Hezekiah,
and particularly in the case of the school affair. He called upon them to
subscribe with all their hearts ; but alas ! how little of persuasive power
was there in what he said. No effort to make them see the use of the
schools. No inducement proved to exist. No argument, in short, nor anything to move. No appeal either to the reason or to the feeling. All was
general, commonplace, cold observation ; and that, too, in language which
the far greater part of the hearers could not understand. This church is
about a hundred and ten feet long, and seventy feet wide in the clear. It
would hold three thousand people, and it had in it two hundred and fourteen, besides fifty-three Sunday School or National School boys ; and these
sat together in a sort of lodge, up in a corner, 16 feet long and 10 feet
wide. Now, will any Parson Malthus, or anybody else, have the impudence to tell me that this church was built for the use of a population not
more numerous than the present ? "

This question of the relative disproportion of the churches,
both in number and in size, to the population is one that crops
up again and again as we pass through many of our country
districts, and scarcely seems accounted for even by the growth
of Nonconformity and the "rural exodus." It may well

S

be believed that when the churches were erected "to the Glory of God" their size was conditioned more by the zeal of the builders and the wealth available than by the number of parishioners likely to worship in them.

Going from Goudhurst back to Cranbrook, which lies about four miles to the east, we pass Iden Green and cross-roads known locally as Four Wents, both of which names curiously enough are duplicated a short distance south of Cranbrook. At the first of these Four Wents we are reminded of a singular person of some importance in his day, one hundred years ago; an eccentric preacher known to notoriety as William Huntingdon, S.S. The natural son of a neighbouring farmer, this worthy was born in a cottage at the Four Wents and was baptized in the name of his putative father, William Hunt, at the age of five in 1750. Like a certain nobleman he was all things by turn and nothing long, though never statesman, fiddler or—at least in his own regard—buffoon. According to the "Dictionary of National Biography," after gaining the barest rudiments of education at the Cranbrook grammar school, Hunt "went into service as an errand boy, and was afterwards successively gentleman's servant, gunmaker's apprentice, sawyer's pitman, coachman, hearse-driver, tramp, gardener, coal heaver, and popular preacher." When at length he "found himself" as a preacher he should certainly have ac-quired such wide knowledge of men and matters as could not fail to prove serviceable. Having got into trouble which made it advisable for him to seek a new field for his labours, he changed his name from Hunt to Huntington, and having found a young woman to share his adventures, went off upon his wanderings from place to place—Mortlake, Sunbury, Kingston, Ewell, Thames Ditton—and from employment to employment. He suffered much from poverty, "and still more from conviction of sin." At length he was converted, saw Christ in a vision, and was brought "under the covenant-love of God's elect." Later he resolved to cease any work other than that of preaching the particular form of Calvinism which he evolved, depending for his subsistence entirely on faith (*i.e.* the contri-butions of his congregations). After spending some time as an itinerant preacher, he was afraid of the old Kentish scandal being brought up against him, and so confided the history to his staunchest supporters, and added the mysterious S.S. to his name. "As I cannot get a D.D. for the want of cash, neither can I get an M.A. for want of learning, therefore I am compelled to fly for refuge to S.S., by which I mean Sinner Saved" —which suggests that William Huntington was not entirely wanting in a sense of humour.   Later he removed to London, carrying on his eccentric preaching for thirty years in Providence Chapel, Titchfield Street, and on that being burned down, in New Providence Chapel Gray's Inn Lane—being enabled to build both of these owing to the confidence which he inspired in his adherents.   On the death of the woman with whom he had lived for over thirty years, Huntington married Lady Elizabeth Sanderson, widow of a Lord Mayor of London. He had become engaged in bitter controversy with various divines, and two years before his marriage published a collective edition of his works in twenty volumes.   He died in 1813 at Tunbridge Wells, a few miles from where he was born, and was buried at Lewes, having penned his own epitaph thus :

"Here lies the coal heaver, who departed this life July 1st, 1823, in the 69th year of his age, beloved of his God, but abhorred of men.   The omniscient Judge at the Grand Assize shall ratify and confirm this to the confusion of many thousands, for England and its metropolis shall know that there hath been a prophet among them."

When Lord Clive shortly before his death was spending many thousands of pounds over the building of Claremont, and the Surrey peasantry declared that he was building the walls so thick that he might keep out the devil who would one day carry him away bodily, according to Macaulay "among the gaping clowns who drank in this frightful story was a worthless ugly lad," our fugitive from Kent, and the historian goes on to declare of Huntington that "the superstition which was strangely mingled with the knavery of that remarkable impostor" derived support from the tales he had heard of Clive.

CHAPTER XIII

MAIDSTONE

If Maidstone were only one of the largest of our Kentish towns, and the capital of our county—its population is half as much again as that of Canterbury—it need not detain us long, but it is besides an ancient place with much in it and in its history of great interest, and if less full in these regards than the ecclesiastical capital, it is the centre of yet more interesting country—along the course of the Medway to the north and to the west, for the town is situated about the most easterly bend of the river—eastwards to Leeds and other places, southwards into orchards and hop gardens. In all these directions are spots intimately associated with men and events notable in our history, while about the chalk hills, the stone quarries and the Wealden district are innumerable villages and picturesque views typical of that pleasingly various thing which we term English rural scenery. Then, too, Maidstone is the chief centre of the hop and fruit growing in the county about which hop fields and orchards are observable in nearly all parts. Here as much as anywhere may be sung the stirring old song in praise of the hop :—

> " The hop that swings so lightly
> The hop that shines so brightly
> Shall still be cherished rightly
>   By all good men and true.
> Thus spake the jovial man of Kent
> As through his golden hops he went
> With sturdy limb and brow unbent
>   When autumn skies were blue."

Reckoned the third chief city of the ancient Britons the town became a Roman station and later the seat of a Saxon

castle. Its name has gone through various forms, from the
Saxon Medwegston; in the Domesday Survey it was
Meddestone and in local pronunciation it is still Medstun.
Incorporated by Edward VI. it was punished—we shall
see why—by losing its charter under that king's successor,
was granted a new charter by Elizabeth and several further
ones by succeeding monarchs; James I. incorporating it by

Maidstone.

the style of "the mayor jurats and commonalty of the King's
town and parish of Maidstone."

A clean, pleasant, prosperous town with broad main streets,
with some quaint old houses among its newer ones, with
important modern buildings, yet with an air of cherishing its
past—such is the present appearance of Maidstone to the
casual visitor; a town in which considerable manufactures are
carried on, in which troops are stationed, yet without becoming
stamped as either a manufacturing or a garrison town, and
through it runs the beautiful Medway the most important of all

our rivers, on which considerable carrying traffic is done hence to Rochester and the Thames.

Of the places to be seen in the town one of the principal is the Corporation Museum and that not only because a local museum is the best centre from which to start the tour of a locality but because the building itself is one best fitted to be turned to the purpose of housing precious relics connected with the past of the town and county. It is the ancient Chillington Manor House—a beautiful example of Tudor domestic architecture—acquired for its present purpose just half a century ago. Since then it has been added to and is now one of the chief provincial museums in the country. This is not the place in which to epitomise the contents but it may be said that the collection, while thoroughly representative of the archæology and natural history of Kent, includes also specimens and relics gathered from far afield.

At Maidstone the Archbishops of Canterbury had of old a palace —there were sixteen palatial residences at one time attached to the archiepiscopal see—preserved in a very good state. It dates from the fourteenth century, with additions and alterations, and is now utilised as the local school of science and art, having been purchased for public use to commemorate the Jubilee of Queen Victoria in 1887. Near the palace is the chief church of Maidstone, a large and handsome structure with, as might be imagined, many important monuments and other features, including, it is believed, one to the powerful Archbishop Courtenay, who erected the church in the fourteenth century. Courtenay, it may be said, is also buried at Canterbury.

Seeing how in recent times the value of the teaching of the "dead languages" has been discussed, it is interesting to find buried here William Grocyn, friend of Erasmus, and one of the principal revivers of the study of Greek at Oxford — he was, says the "Dictionary of National Biography," "among the first—if not the first—to publicly teach Greek in the university" (to adapt Byron, "the split infinitive's the dictionary's every line, for God's sake, reader, take it not for mine"). In 1506 Grocyn was appointed master of the collegiate church of All Hallows, Maidstone. Another notable man of Tudor times buried here is John Astley, Queen Elizabeth's master of the Jewel House, a great equestrian and author of a treatise setting forth

"The Art of Riding." His wife was chief gentlewoman of
the privy chamber to the Queen, who granted him a lease of
Allington Castle. Astley's son, Sir John, Master of the Revels
to Charles I., is also buried here. The churchyard has added
to the tale of epitaph humour the following: "In memory of
John Nettlefold, who died January 13, 1793, aged 80 years,
left issue a third wife and two daughters."

With the "College" founded here by Archbishop Courtenay
was incorporated the hospital of Newark for the use of
pilgrims on their way to Canterbury and other poor travellers,
which had been established towards the close of the thirteenth
century by his predecessor Boniface. The ruins near the church
on the bank of the river are well worth visiting. When we
turn from the things which we can see in the old town, reminding us mostly of its great past as an ecclesiastical centre, to
the events which we can consider, we find Maidstone noted
as the centre of two important episodes in history : one when
it was sought to restrain, in the interests of Protestantism,
Queen Mary from marrying King Philip of Spain, and one
when it was thought to uphold the forlorn hope of Charles's
cause against the triumphant Parliament. The first of these
movements was instigated by Sir Thomas Wyatt, son of the
Tudor poet, whom we may recall more fittingly at Allington.
Wyatt's rebellion, however, had Maidstone as its centre, though
the leader lived a few miles further down stream. Hatred
of Spain and all it stood for worked with zeal for the
Reformed religion to bring many adherents to the rebellion.
Unfortunately for the Kentish leader the affair got known ;
several of his allies were prevented from joining him, and he
with the Men of Kent had to rise and strike his blow with
unprepared suddenness. Despite several small successes, when
the force, the little army of four thousand receiving many
accessions on its way, reached London, its momentum was
destroyed, thanks to the courage—which the Tudors never
lacked—of Queen Mary herself. Wyatt was captured, and he
and many of his followers suffered that death which they must
have known was the penalty of failure. The very rigour of
the punishment meted out to the rebels had, however, the
opposite effect from that intended, so, though he paid with his
life, Wyatt forwarded the cause for which he suffered. One of
the finest scenes of Tennyson's "Queen Mary" is concerned

with the gathering of Wyatt's men in the neighbourhood of
Maidstone. As the messenger who roused Wyatt sonnetting
at Allington put it :

All Saints' Church, Maidstone.

> " They roar for you
> On Pennenden Heath, a thousand of them—more—
> All arm'd, waiting a leader."

"The mine is fired," says Wyatt, "and I will speak to
them," and he is then made thus to express the anti-Spanish
sentiment :

"Men of Kent ; England of England ; you that have kept your old customs upright, while all the rest of England how'd theirs to the Norman, the cause that hath brought us together is not the cause of a county or a shire, but of this England in whose crown our Kent is the fairest jewel. Philip shall not wed Mary ; and ye have called me to be your leader. I know Spain. I have been there with my father ; I have seen them in their own land ; have marked the haughtiness of their nobles ; the cruelty of their priests. If this man marry our Queen, however the Council and the Commons may fence round his power with restriction, he will be King, King of England, my masters ; and the Queen, and the laws, and the people, his slaves. What? Shall we have Spain on the throne and in the Parliament ; Spain in the pulpit and on the law-bench ; Spain in all the great offices of State ; Spain in our ships, in our forts, in our houses, in our beds ?

Crowd.—No ! no ! no Spain !

William.—No Spain in our beds—that were worse than all. I have been there with old Sir Thomas, and the beds I know. I hate Spain.

A Peasant.—But, Sir Thomas, must we levy war against the Queen's Grace ?

Wyatt.—No, my friend ; war *for* the Queen's Grace—to save her from herself and Philip—war against Spain. And think not we shall be alone—thousands will flock to us. The Council, the Court itself, is on our side. The Lord Chancellor himself is on our side. The King of France is with us ; the King of Denmark is with us ; the world is with us—war against Spain ! And if we move not now, yet it will be known that we have moved ; and if Philip come to be King, O, my God ! the rope, the rack, the thumbscrew, the stake, the fire. If we move not now Spain moves, bribes our nobles with her gold, and creeps, creeps snake-like about our legs till we cannot move at all ; and ye know, my masters, that wherever Spain hath ruled she hath withered all beneath her. Look at the new world—paradise made hell ; the red man, that good helpless creature, starved, maim'd, flogg'd, flay'd, burn'd, boil'd, buried alive, worried by dogs ; and here, nearer home, the Netherlands, Sicily, Naples, Lombardy. I say no more—only this, their lot is yours. Forward to London with me ! Forward to London ! If ye love your liberties or your skins, forward to London !"

The cry "a Wyatt ! a Wyatt !" was taken up by many as the little army went by Rochester, Gravesend, Dartford, and Blackheath to London and death. A folly the rising has been dubbed, but it was a splendid folly ; inspired by the highest motives, its foolishness was that which attaches to undertakings foredoomed to failure. In the Marian Persecutions which followed hard upon the gallant attempt to make such impossible, seven Protestants were burned for conscience' sake here at Maidstone.

Of the second rising which took place in Kent, that of 1648, we saw something at Canterbury, which may be looked upon as the centre of the movement ; but Maidstone had to bear the brunt of much of the fighting, and on June 1st General Lord Fairfax, with the Parliament's army cut off, a portion of the Royalist forces, about eight hundred men, drove them into Maidstone with much hard fighting, and then proceeded to storm, and take, the town, which, according to John Evelyn, he was enabled to do, thanks to the treachery of a gunner, who was to fire the ordnance of the bridge—which he did, but against the town instead of for it! It was a short and sharp conflict here, and the other portions of the " honorable though unfortunate expedition" passed into Essex, where they were finally overcome at Colchester by the triumphant Parliamentarians.

Despite earlier failures, another generation of representative Men of Kent, assembled at Maidstone in 1701, addressed a new Petition inspired by the general dissatisfaction at the slow proceedings of Parliament ; it was also said " that the King was not assisted, nor the Protestants abroad considered, and the country people began to say to one another, in their language, that 'they had sowed their corn, and the French were a-coming to reap it.'" The document was mild enough but was treated with severity which casts a strong light upon the political history of the time.

The five Kentish worthies—William Colepepper (chairman of the sessions), Thomas Colepepper, Justinian Champneys, David Polehill, and William Hamilton—who had the temerity to present this petition to the House of Commons, had the pleasure of hearing that it was voted " scandalous, insolent, and seditious," were placed under arrest and shamefully treated for about five weeks, being quietly released only on the prorogation of Parliament. On their return into their native county the gentlemen were hailed with public enthusiasm all along the way, and were feasted and made much of at Maidstone. Their perfectly loyal behaviour and unworthy treatment inspired Daniel Defoe with a strong political tract against " the conspirators and Jacobite party in a Parliament that are at present the nation's burthen, and from whom she groans to be delivered."

Turning from events to persons, there was born at Maidstone three-quarters of a century later one of the first of English essayists. In 1770 there came to the town as Unitarian minister of the Earle Street meeting-house a young Irishman named William Hazlitt, and on April 10th, 1778, "in a house no longer recognisable, in a lane once called Mitre and now Bullock " was born his younger son, *the* William Hazlitt. Though we can thus claim him technically as a native of Kent, Hazlitt has but little association with Maidstone, for he was only two years of age when, as Mr. Augustine Birrell puts it, " in consequence of one of those congregational quarrels which are the weakness of independency," the family left and returned to the minister's native Ireland.

Near to Maidstone is Pennenden Heath, the great county-gathering place for many centuries. Here as we have seen the people waited for Wyatt to lead them, but here long before, just ten years after the Conquest, a great cause was tried—one of the first of our recorded trials—when Lanfranc, Archbishop of Canterbury, sought to recover from Odo, Bishop of Bayeux and Earl of Kent, certain properties which he had seized. The trial lasted three days and the Archbishop won. As " King William sent Agelric, the venerable Bishop of Chichester, in a chariot, to instruct them in the ancient laws and customs of the land, our county may boast of affording the earliest instance of the ancient Itinera and the modern Circuits.". During the " No Popery " agitation which attended the removal of Catholic disabilities many meetings were held here, 1828–9, and then it is said arose that concerted clapping of hands and stamping of feet which has since become known as " Kentish fire."

Leaving talk about the many places to be visited by any one making Maidstone a centre for the next chapter, it may be well to say something about two of the most characteristic features of our county—its hop-gardens and its orchards—both of which are more noticeable around this town than elsewhere, except in the Sittingbourne and Faversham district. Cherry and apple orchards and hop-gardens or fields, as has been said earlier, are to be found all about the county, but it is in the Maidstone district that they occupy the greatest extent of ground, and in which they may be most fully examined. The May-time orchards, seas of white and pink-tinted blossoms, form a sight not easily to be forgotten, framed as they so frequently are by the fresh greenery of surrounding woodlands, or in the case of recently planted orchards before their branches have reached out from tree to tree, and made that shady whole

which is conjured up by the very name of orchard, the trees
show dazzlingly against the fresh spring turf.   And beneath the
trees may frequently be seen flocks of white-faced sheep with,
about blossoming time, their long-legged little lambs.   An
orchard in full bloom under a May sun, with sheep and lambs
feeding and resting under the trees, forms a perfect picture of
peace and restfulness, though frequently, alas! utility has to
step in and mar the picturesqueness when the boles of the
trees, as a protection against insect pests, are painted white with
a protecting wash.   When the petals have fallen and the fruit
is " set " the orchards are less attractive to the eye, less com-
pelling of the exclamatory " how beautiful ! "   All orchards are
beautiful in the time of bloom, but those of plum and pear less
strikingly so than those of cherry and apple : the pure white
of the former against its delicate young foliage ; the lovely pink
of the apple, whether seen in individual sprays or in a hillside
orchard, are possessed of beauty indescribable.   A walk about
our orchard districts is, then, a feast of delightful colour—nay,
some of us think that it would be far better worth while to take
a railway trip through the Maidstone and Sittingbourne districts in May than to journey to Bushey Park to see the chestnuts in bloom.   Two or three months later, when the branches
are set as with a myriad ruddy jewels, the freshness of youth
annually renewed has given place to quite another beauty—that
of maturity ; and, later still, when the foliage flames in autumn,
the cherry orchards especially take on yet another phase of
loveliness before passing into that seeming rest when all the
energies of sap and fibre are preparing for the next year's
sequence.

The wild cherry is occasionally to be met with in Kent, and
so unerringly does the true poet touch us with his description
of things seen and felt that it is impossible, knowing Mr.
George Meredith's "A Faith on Trial," to happen upon the
delicate tree in bloom without recalling his lines.   I remember
especially such a tree standing on the hedge bank towards
the top of a little hill near St. Mary Cray.

> " Now gazed I where, sole upon gloom
> As flower bush in sun-specked crag,
> Up the spine of the double combe
> With yew-boughs heavily cloaked,
> A young apparition shone :

Known, yet wonderful, white
Surpassingly : doubtfully known,
For it struck as the birth of light ;
Even Day from the dark unyoked.
It waved like a pilgrim flag
O'er processional penitents flown
When of old they broke rounding yon spine :
O the pure wild-cherry in bloom ! "

Although it was not until the sixteenth century that the cherry came to be cultivated extensively in Kent, Pliny has recorded that less than a hundred and twenty years after the fruit was introduced into Rome (by Lucullus, it is well to remember) "other lands had cherries, even so far as Britain beyond the ocean." Indeed they must have been grown for market more than a century before the time which John Evelyn gives as that of their first general planting in Kent. In John Lydgate's "London Lackpenny"—the narrative of an impecunious man of Kent who journeyed citywards only to find that Westminster and London were no places for the man who had no means to spend—we read

" Then unto London I did me hie,
Of all the land it beareth the prize.
' Hot peascods !' one began to cry,
' Strawberries ripe !' and ' Cherries in the rise !'
And bade me come near to buy some spice :
Pepper and saffron they gan me bede ;
But for lack of money I might not speed."

The disillusioned man then "conveyed" him into Kent, but his experiences as recorded by Lydgate show that cherries were sold in the London streets at the beginning of the fifteenth century even as they are at the beginning of the twentieth. "Cherries in the rise" is said to mean cherries on the branch, but it is more likely to mean cherries tied to a twig or "rise" as it is termed in many of our rural dialects. It was in the sixteenth century that Kent started its reputation as the county of cherry orchards if that great lover of trees John Evelyn is to be taken as a guide, for he has recorded that "it was by the plain industry of one Harris (a fruiterer to King Henry VIII.) that the fields and environs of about thirty towns in Kent only, were planted with fruit, to the universal benefit and general improvement of that county to this day."

If the cherry orchards are places of delight in the spring their uplifting beauty is soon followed by the green of the growing hops. According to Anne Pratt, a native of our county as we shall be reminded at Strood, "travellers who have beheld, in other lands, the various scenes of culture—the olive grounds of Spain or Syria, the vineyards of Italy, the cotton plantations of India, or the rose fields of the East,— have generally agreed that not one of them all equals in beauty our English hop gardens." There may be the element of exaggeration in this; there may be scenes of culture more beautiful, but often it is in a sense not meant by the poet that distance lends enchantment to the view, and a sight is pleasing because we have travelled far to see it, or have been taught to think it beautiful by the tales of other travellers our preceders. I confess that the first sight of vineyards in Northern Italy was a disappointing one compared with our Kentish hop-fields; of olive grounds, cotton plantations and the rose gardens of Persia I am unfortunately not qualified to speak, but I can readily believe that the mere addition of colour may render some of these scenes more beautiful than the slightly sombre green of our massed hops. The hop-fields to be enjoyed properly should be visited at three stages of their growth: when the bines are partly up their poles and strings, at the end of May; when the growth is completed and the topmost aspiring shoots have reached beyond their highest support in July, and again in the autumn when "hopping" has begun and the fields are busy with many workers—men, women and children—removing the hops from the bines. Then the scene does not lack colour, but it does not call for description, for every year as the hopping season comes round the scene is newly described in our newspapers, until it must be more or less familiar to all readers.

Seeing the extent of our hop-fields now it is curious to remember that the cultivation of the plant met with considerable opposition at various times. Though supposed to be indigenous it was not until five or six centuries ago that the plant was cultivated, for it is variously said to have been brought from Flanders in the reigns of Henry IV. and of Henry VIII., some authorities fixing an actual date at 1524. Though the common distich tells us of the arrival of the hop as a notable acquisition, yet Henry VIII. issued an edict against the mixing

of hops or sulphur in beer, but not, it would seem, with much
result, for in 1552 hop plantations were being formed, and in
the time of Queen Elizabeth the plant had come into general
use. In 1562 good old Thomas Tusser had much to say of its
cultivation in his " Five Hundred Points of Good Husbandrie "
and a dozen years later Reginald Scot published a treatise on
the subject in his " Perfite Platforme of a Hoppe Garden," so
that hop-growing must by then have become fairly general.
In another half century the City of London petitioned
Parliament against the hop on the grounds that " this wicked
weed would spoil the drink and endanger the lives of the people."
As a Commonwealth writer on agriculture said, " it was not
many years since the famous City of London petitioned the
Parliament of England against two anusancies or offensive
commodities, which were likely to come into great use and
esteem ; and that was Newcastle coals, in regard of their
stench, etc., and hops, in regard they would spoil the taste
of drink and endanger the people." Opposition not-
withstanding, the use of coals and hops went on flourishing
and to-day we may well wonder what we should do without
them.

John Evelyn joined the anti-hop crusade and wrote with
some vehemence and indignation against the squandering of
young trees, which might have grown into timber, by cutting
them down as supports for a deleterious plant.

" It is now little more than an age since, that hopps (rather a medical
than an alimental vegetable) transmuted our wholesome ale into beer,
which doubtless much alters our constitutions. That one ingredient, by
some not unworthily suspected, preserving drink indeed, and so by custom
made agreeable, yet repaying the pleasure with tormenting diseases and a
shorter life, may deservedly abate our fondness to it, especially if with this
be considered likewise the casualties in planting it, as seldom succeeding
more than once in three years, yet requiring constant charge and culture ;
besides that it is none of the least devourers of young timber. And what,
if a little care, or indeed one quarter of it, were for the future to be converted to the propagation of fruit trees in all parts of this nation, as it is
already in some for the benefit of cider ? "

The sylvan writer goes on to implore his Majesty Charles II.
and his loyal landowners to plant cider fruit "till the
preference of more wholesome and more natural drinks do
quite vanquish hopps, and banish all other drogues of that
nature." Cobbett, too, a century and a half later had much

to say of the cultivation of hops as being a "gambling concern"; but despite these sturdy critics the hop has gone on flourishing and of the fifty and odd thousand acres now grown in England Kent can boast of (or be reproached with !) having thirty and odd thousands.

The reproach of Evelyn that forests in the making were cut down for hop-poles has of course less point when it is remembered that the plantations of ash, sweet chestnut and other trees are grown for the very purpose, though less in demand now than they used to be since strings have largely taken the place of poles in most districts though now and again we may come upon hop-fields arranged with three poles to the hill even as they were described by Tusser—I recall one such field especially on the Pegwell Bay side of Minster. The introduction of strings has made it less necessary for any one to seek with Cobbett inclusion in the kalendar of Saints by discovering an everlasting hop-pole ; "if I could discover an everlasting hop-pole, and one that would grow faster even than the ash, would not these Kentish hop-planters put me in the Kalendar along with their Saint Thomas of Canterbury. We shall see this one of these days." Whether "this" is to be the everlasting hop-pole or the canonisation of William Cobbett the reader is left to determine.

A field of well grown hops is a beautiful place on a hot summer day, the "hills" placed with such regularity that stand where we may we see the radiating lines festooned with the handsome plants, for though strings have been largely substituted for poles the regularity is maintained and the lines are so even that they remind a reader of Crabbe of his wonder over the ploughman trying to write—

> " How strange the hand that guides the plough
> Should fail to guide the pen—
> For half a mile the furrows even lie,
> In half an inch the letters stand awry."

Of the various arrangements utilised in different districts it is unnecessary to speak here—of the three-pole hills and the two-pole hills, of the "umbrella" method of training the bines, the fastening of string from pegs in the ground, to wires criss-crossing from the tops of poles placed at some distance apart, or from lower wires placed from pole to pole at a short distance from the ground. These matters, and the special tools employed in the culture—hop-dogs, and hop-spuds,— the incessant work, from the ploughing or digging of the land (hop ground is best hand-dug), to the placing of the poles and strings, the continuous attention in the way of tying the growing crop, belong rather to a technical than a descriptive work : the hop-fields, especially where string is largely employed for the plants to climb, are protected by "lews" or shelters from the prevailing wind ; sometimes these are high, thin hedges of hawthorn or other shrubs, sometimes rows of trees cut down to about twelve or fifteen feet, and allowed to grow laterally, sometimes rows of "wild hops" on close-set poles and frequently they are formed of coarse canvas stretched from pole to pole along the whole side of the field.

In September, in a season now shortened to something under three weeks, is the great season of hopping, when thousands of poor Londoners invade the quiet country and get a healthful and profitable holiday helping to gather the clusters of delicate catkin-like cones. Men, women and children, of all ages and sizes, are to be seen at work, and the hop-fields for the time form scenes of striking picturesqueness. The aroma is said to be as healthful as it is pleasant, and a hopping holiday has been recommended as a pleasant simple-life "cure," indeed not long since a novel was published in which the hero (a young nobleman, if I remember rightly) went hopping incognito and met his "fate"—such are the ways of providence, or the novelist—engaged in the same romantic occupation. To those who have joined a hopper's camp for the "experience" or for the getting of "copy" there is romance, comedy and tragedy in these gatherings, and a large field for the study of character. The crowds of hoppers scattered about the "gardens" and surrounded by the ripened crop, take on a picturesqueness which could scarcely be imagined by those who have only seen them massed at the railway termini in London, as they go to catch the early morning hopping trains. There the picture is one of unrelieved greyness and sordidness.

A stranger passing through a hop-garden—and also sometimes through the cherry orchards—may find himself being honoured by having his shoes wiped with a bundle of hops, on which he

Hop-pickers at Work.

is expected to give "shoe-money;" in other words, to pay his footing. The shoe-money so collected is supposed to be used by the workers for a small feast of bread and cheese and ale, to be consumed on the ground when the hopping is over.

After being gathered by the hoppers into large bins or baskets the aromatic harvest is carried off to the cowled oast-houses to have about ten hours of drying over furnaces—in which the weight is reduced by nearly eighty per cent.—before being put up in "pockets" of a hundredweight and a half each, ready for the market.

If the details of hop culture as practised over thousands of acres of Kent belong rather to a practical treatise than to a gossipy book such as this, it is interesting to recall that culture as summarised in the monthly "abstracts" and "husbandries" of old Thomas Tusser, for his work is, unfortunately, not easily obtainable. In January, says Tusser, when wood cutting is being done : "save hop, for his dole, the strong, long pole," and again

> " Remember thy hop-yard, if season be dry,
> Now dig it and weed it and so let it lie.
> More fenny the layer, the better his lust,
> More apt to bear hops when it crumbles like dust."

In February : "Now every day set hops ye may," and then—

> " In March at the farthest, dry season or wet,
> Hop-roots so well chosen, let skilfull go set.
> The goeler and younger, the better I love ;
> Well gutted and pared, the better they prove.
>
> Some layeth them, cross-wise, along in the ground,
> As high as the knee, they do cover up round.
> Some prick up a stick in the midst of the same,
> That little round hillock, the better to frame
>
> Some maketh a hollowness half a foot deep,
> With fouer sets in it, set slant-wise asteep ;
> One foot from another, in order to lie,
> And thereon a hillock, as round as a pie.
>
> Five foot from another, each hillock would stand,
> As straight as a levelled line with the hand ;
> Let every hillock be fouer feet wide,
> The better to come to, on every side.

> By willows that groweth, thy hop-yard without,
> And also by hedges, thy meadows about,
> Good hop hath a pleasure to climb and to spread,
> If sun may have passage, to comfort her head.
>
> Get crow made of iron, deep hole for to make,
> With cross overthwart it as sharp as a stake,
> A hone and a parer, like sole of a boot,
> To pare away grass, and to raise up the root."

Month by month in his "abstract" Tusser puts into his terse advice hints to the hop grower showing that hops had become an important crop by 1572, and month by month he amplifies these hints in his "husbandry," and he even gives a special "Lesson where and when to plant a good hop yard"—

> "Whom fancy perswadeth among other crops,
> To have for his spending sufficient of hops ;
> Must willingly follow, of choices to chuse,
> Such lessons approved as skilfull do use.
>
> Ground gravelly, sandy and mixed with clay
> Is naughty for hops, any manner of way ;
> Or if it be mingled with rubbish and stone,
> For dryness and barrenness let it alone.
>
> Chuse soil for the hop, of the rottenest mould,
> Well dunged and wrought, as a garden plot should :
> Not far from the water (but not overflown)
> This lesson, well noted, is meet to be known.
>
> The sun in the south, or else southly and west,
> Is joy to the hop as a welcomed guest ;
> But wind in the north, or else northerly east,
> To hop is as ill, as a fray in a feast.
>
> Meet plot for a hop yard, once found as is told,
> Make thereof account, as of jewell of gold :
> Now dig it, and leave it the sun for to burn,
> And afterwards fence it, to serve for that turn.
>
> The hop for his profit, I thus do exalt,
> It strengtheneth drink, and it favoureth malt ;
> And being well-brewed, long kept it will last,
> And drawing abide, if ye draw not too fast."

In olden times, it may be recalled, the early shoots of the hop were cooked and eaten as asparagus and Anne Pratt recorded nearly seventy years ago " Kentish children can tell of pleasant hours spent among the hedges, in searching for the wild hop top, and of wholesome suppers made upon the well-earned treasure, ere they have learned to think their food the better for being rare and costly. Those who lead the "simple life" in cottage or in the increasingly popular caravan, please note ; and note also that the taking of cultivated hops is a felony !

High Street, Maidstone.

St. Leonard's Street, West Malling.

CHAPTER XIV

ROUND ABOUT MAIDSTONE

SOUTHWARDS towards the Weald from Maidstone we have
rich, cultivated lands well watered by some of the tributaries of
the Medway: hop gardens, cherry orchards, corn-fields and
broad stretches of varied farm crops dotted with farmsteads,
tiny hamlets and small peaceful and prosperous villages;
south-westward and north-westward along the Medway itself are
spots of sylvan beauty,—in the latter direction soon marred by
brick works and cement factories,—and more varied villages,
though here we are also close to the railway which for some
miles follows the course of the river; to the west are broad
woodlands; to the east stretch the higher downs, along which
the Pilgrims' Road may be followed by those who like, between
the heights and valleys, a lonely way which shall but rarely
touch at a village. In each of these directions are places of
interest and of beauty to be visited.

Immediately to the south of Maidstone Tovil, with its paper
mills, need not detain us, but beyond, on the right bank of the
Medway we come to East Farleigh,—a notable hopping centre—

with its spired church on a little hill by the river and with one of the many fine old stone bridges which span the chief of the Kentish streams.   It was over this bridge that Fairfax brought his army when he hurriedly descended on the Royalists and captured Maidstone.   West Farleigh, beyond, has little to hold our attention, though a pleasant view is to be had from its church across to East Barming, a village where the Rev. Mark Noble, biographer of Cromwell, was Rector for forty-two years—

East Farleigh.

in possession of a rich living in place of the two Warwickshire " starvations " as he termed them rather than " livings " which he had held before.   Here Noble died in 1827, and in the church he is buried ; his monument may draw the attention of devout Cromwellians who remember that he was one of the first to treat the Protector to a full biography.   Admirers of Carlyle visiting the place will, however, scarcely regard the " imperfectly educated, vulgar-minded man " in the light of the biographer as hero.   Carlyle summed up Noble's life of Cromwell as " bad dictionary gone to pie " and said " for Noble himself is a man of extreme imbecility, his judgment, for most part, seeming to lie dead asleep ; and, indeed, it is worth little when broadest awake. He falls into manifold mistakes, commits and omits in all ways ; plods along contented, in an element of perennial dimness, purblindness ; has occasionally a helpless, broad innocence of platitude which is almost interesting. A man, indeed, of extreme imbecility, to whom nevertheless let due gratitude be borne."

Southwards from West Farleigh we may go through rich hop country to Yalding and Hunton—what is described as the largest hop garden in the county is in this district—both by the Beult as it nears its confluence with the Medway. Forming a triangle with these villages, though belonging to the latter parish, is Burston, a farm once the seat of the Fane family, which had branches in various parts of Kent. The old place is beautifully situated on the hillside, with a good outlook over the Weald. Through many orchards the road goes south from Yalding to Goudhurst and Cranbrook, crossing the valley of the Teise, where one of the richest hop districts stretches to the right about Bockingfold and Peasons Green. Bockingfold is said to be a corruption of Buchins wald or beech wood, indicating a stretch of beeches among the more familiar oaks of the Weald. From Castle Hill, which rises rapidly to the south of Peasons Green, we have good views over the country through which we have been passing.

Returning to the Medway at one of its most beautiful stretches near Wateringbury we get back to the road—from Maidstone to Mereworth—which won a notable tribute from Cobbett as being the finest seven miles he had ever seen in England or anywhere else. In Wateringbury churchyard is buried Sir Oliver Style, sole survivor of a large dinner party at Smyrna which was effectually broken up by an earthquake that killed all his companions. Here, too, lies Thomas Clampard, a further illustration of Theodore Hook's

> " It seems as if Nature had curiously plann'd
> That men's names with their trade should agree,"

for he was a blacksmith, and, dying in 1748, was honoured with one of those punning epitaphs in which the eighteenth century seems especially to have delighted—

"My sledge and anvil I've declined,
My bellows, too, have lost their wind ;
My fire's extinct, my forge decayed,
And in the dust my vice is lay'd ; .
My coals are spent, my irons gone ;
My nails are drove, my work is done.'

Mr. Thomas Clampard, who died in 1748, is an interesting personage as having been the last deputy for the Dumb Borsholder of Chart. The " Borsholder " was the headborough, or chief of each tithing in a hundred, and at the manor of

A wayside pond near West Farleigh.

Chart, in Wateringbury, it was the custom to elect in place of a man the "dumb borsholder," a man acting for it and answering for it at the Court. " The Dumb Borsholder of Chart (wrote a former vicar of Wateringbury) is a staff of wood that by age has become perfectly black ; it is three feet and half an inch long, and has an iron ring on the bottom. It once had four more by the sides near the top ; three of these, however, are now wanting, though the marks remain where they were inserted. The circumference is greater at some places than at others, and it has a square iron spike fixed in the top, four-and-a-half inches long, which perhaps was used to break a door open upon occasion, which was done without a warrant from a justice of the peace, when it was suspected that persons or things were unlawfully concealed " in any of the twelve houses over which the Dumb Borsholder had jurisdiction.   A most efficient substitute for Dogberry ! The twelve householders of Chart took turns in acting as Deputy for a year, receiving from each of the eleven others the sum of one penny.

From Wateringbury a young unmarried lady of the Twysden family wrote in the early part of the eighteenth century many engagingly unaffected letters of gossip to a married friend near Wingham.   Her correspondence—a dozen long letters were given in an early volume of the *Archaeologia Cantiana*—is full of talk about friends and their doings, of births, marriages, rumours of marriages and deaths, of visits to Tunbridge Wells and other places.   Miss Isabella Twysden was beautifully disregardful of the grace of spelling, but her letters help us to realise the time in which she lived far more intimately than more laboured histories.   Here is a bit dealing with one of the changes of fashion that came in with the first of the four Georges in 1714.

"I sopose they are in full content with their new King, who I think has incouraged their intriest with most surprising zeal, whether 'tis to his own he may hereafter be a better judge ; but this is a topick far beyond my sphere, the alteration of fashions (wch is the reigning descourse amongst us at present) is much more suteable to my capacity ; and, to tell you the truth, makes a much greater impression upon my spirits. Pray how can you reconcile yr self to the odious Hanover cutt?   I sopose you saw the Princes at Canterbury.   We hear she took perticular notice of the dress of Mrs Marsham's head and the beauty of Mrs. (but I can't think of her name) 's face. I flattered myself a great while yt the Princess wou'd find out that we dress'd after a much genteeler way than her highness, but I hear all the Town have paid her the compliment of dressing their heads half as ugly as her own, and without doubt we must all follow the example within this half year or submitt to be hollow'd at.   Mrs. Rider and her daughter are the only people have had the courag to put one on hear abouts, except some of the country Town Ladys.   I did not see her in it, but the discription is most tirible, and indeed it sutes so ill with my pockett to buy two yds where I used to buy one, and that only to make me ugler than Nature has done allready, that yt I think to walk off into another Land, or ells content my self with a good warm sute of nightcloths in my chamber, and intirely have done with all the vainities of dress.   But Lord, Madam, if you shou'd be gott into one of these heads after I have been railing at it without that consideration, may I hope you will forgive me? Upon my word, I believe if I were to see you in one I shou'd not think it one quarter so disagreeable as I have represented it to myself.

Teston, a village on the east side of Wateringbury, is a particularly attractive place; near it is Barham Court, where Hannah More and William Wilberforce used to visit, and where the latter probably first turned his attention to the abolition of slavery, for it was here in 1783 that he met the rector of Teston, an old time naval chaplain in the West Indies. The Rev. James Ramsay had already enlisted the active assistance of Lady Middleton of Barham Court in the cause, and the publication in 1784 of his "Essay on the Treatment and Conversion of African Slaves in British Sugar Colonies" had been described as the most important event in the early history of the Anti-Slavery movement. Ramsay who was consulted by Wilberforce, Clarkson, Pitt and other leaders in the movement, is buried at Teston. Pitt, Wilberforce and "Abolition" we shall meet again in another part of our county.

Leaving the Medway, which here flows from the south by Yalding, we may follow the road which won the enthusiastic praise of Cobbett, who delighted in well cultivated land, varied by woods, and so come to Mereworth, passing on our way the eighteenth century Italianate Mereworth Castle—curiously contrasting with other of our stately homes. Set in a very picturesque country of hilly parkland and woods Mereworth is regarded as one of the show places to be visited either from Maidstone or Tonbridge, and unlike some show places and beauty spots, it is little likely to disappoint the visitor, though the Castle itself will appeal chiefly to those with a taste for the exotic. Horace Walpole, visiting it in 1752—four years after the Castle was built, waxed enthusiastic.

"Since dinner, we have been to Lord Westmoreland's at Mereworth, which is so perfect in a Palladian taste, that I must own it has recovered me a little from Gothic. It is better situated than I had expected from the bad reputation it bears, and has some prospect, though it is in a moat, and mightily besprinkled with small ponds. The design, you know, is taken from the Villa del Capra by Vicenza, but on a larger scale; yet, though it has cost an hundred thousand pounds, it is still only a fine villa: the finishing of in and outside has been exceedingly expensive. A wood that runs up a hill behind the house is broke like an Albano landscape with an octagon temple and a triumphal arch; but then there are some dismal clipped hedges, and a pyramid, which by a most unnatural copulation is at

once a grotto and a greenhouse. Does it not put you in mind of the
proposal for your drawing a garden-seat, Chinese on one side and Gothic
on the other? The chimneys, which are collected to a centre, spoil the
dome of the house."

North of Mereworth stretch grand woods through which we

Malling Abbey.

can readily reach Ightham or Offham and other of the attractive
villages scattered about the southern slope of the northern
range of hills.   Leaving these places for the present we may go
by the hamlet of Kent Street through a part of the pleasant
Mereworth Woods to West Malling, sometimes named Town

Malling, with its attractive ruins of a Benedictine abbey founded
here by Bishop Gundulf, the architect-ecclesiast who did so
much for Rochester Cathedral,—he who built the Great Keep
of the Tower of London. The remains of the Abbey include
some fine Norman fragments and good examples of herring-
bone work, and have features very similar to the good Bishop's
work at Rochester.

To the east of Town Malling is a group of villages, East
Malling, Leybourne, and Ditton, each with attractions for those
who seek the story of a neighbourhood in its church. In
Leybourne church is a curious heart niche for the reception of
the hearts of people whose bodies were buried elsewhere. Only
one of the two shrines was ever used, and it contains, it is believed, the heart of Sir Roger de Leyburn, who died in 1271,
probably when engaged in one of the Crusades with Prince
Edward. Leybourne was the centre of the domains of a rich
and powerful Kentish family—whose castle was situated near
by the church—that died out in the reign of Edward III in the
person of Juliana de Leybourne, known as " the Infanta of Kent "
Juliana, as heiress of the Leybournes and wife successively of
three powerful barons, became the owner of almost illimitable
lands and riches—all of which she made over to various religious
houses or to the King at her death—at which time she had no
fewer than twelve manors in Kent alone.

The country here, coming gradually down to the Medway, is
richly varied with corn, hops, woodland and pasture, and
turning out of the main road beyond Ditton we may reach
the river near one of the most notable of historic places on its
banks. This is Aylesford, its red and many gabled roofs and
the tower of its church appearing finely grouped among elm
trees with the rising chalk downs beyond. Here before recalling some of the lore attaching to the place we may pause
at the very picturesque old bridge which spans the Medway,
for the march of improvement threatens it with early destruction.
The narrow way across the bridge forms a pleasant approach
to the old town, while the bridge itself, with its pointed arches
and triangular buttresses, is one of the many beautiful ones which
are to be found crossing the Medway—contrasting with that
at Maidstone and with that acme of hideousness, the railway
bridge at Rochester. The old bridge has already been
" improved " owing to the demands of the navigation by the

forming of the wide central span, but now it seems probable
that it will have to be replaced by one better suited to modern
traffic.

Aylesford.

Aylesford is an ancient place that grew up about an important ford, the lowest across the Medway, on an ancient track-
way.   Here the Jutes under Hengist and Horsa came to find a

way over the river to pursue their British enemies, and here was fought a stubborn battle, the invaders winning a notable victory, though in the moment of success Horsa fell and is said to have been buried at a place called Horsted, more than halfway on the road to Chatham. The ancient chronicler gives us no details of the decisive battle, as Green puts it : "we hear only that Horsa fell in the moment of victory ; and the flint heap of Horsted, which has long preserved his name, and was held in aftertime to mark his grave, is thus the earliest of those monuments of English valour of which Westminster is the last and noblest shrine." Below Aylesford, also on the right bank of the river, was an ancient Friary—the remains of which have largely been overlaid and incorporated in the present residence—belonging to the first Carmelite Monks who came to England. A Kentish worthy known in the Calendar of Saints as St. Simeon Stock, had lived in a tree stump or stock—hence his name—for twenty years from the age of twelve, and at the coming of the Carmelites into England he "quitted his oak, and advanced forward to meet them, as of whom, though he had no sight, he had a vision before, which is probably as true as that he was fed seven years with manna on Mount Carmel. He was chosen the general governor of their order all over Europe ; and died in the hundredth year of his age, anno domini 1265, and was buried at Bordeaux in France." The Christian Diogenes who had for his tub the stock of a hollow tree is said to have foretold the coming of the Carmelites out of Syria even as another Simeon had a revelation that he should see Christ, whereon Fuller comments, "reader, behold here how the roaring lion hath translated himself into a mimical ape, endeavouring a mock parallel betwixt this Simon and Simeon in the Gospel."

North of Aylesford about a mile and a half, on the lower chalk hills from which may be had a fine view of the valley of the Medway, stands the famous Cromlech known as Kits Coty House, "that old grey cairn which seems like a monument erected by Time, to perpetuate the memory of his flight into far eternity"! This relic of an unknown past set on a close cut green in the midst of a cornfield consists of four great irregular slabs of stone, three upright and the fourth and largest balanced above them, the total weight of the four being

estimated at about thirty tons. How they were erected by
primitive man must puzzle everyone who sees them. The
stones were probably taken from the neighbouring hills to
mark the grave of some noted chieftain, but how, when, and
why they were erected can only be conjectured ; the tradition
that they mark the grave of Katigern, a British leader slain in
fight with the Saxons, being easily dismissed in that sepulchral
monuments of this character probably belong to a period far
anterior to the coming of the Saxons. Going down to the
Aylesford road from this finest relic of the kind which we
have to show we can see in a field on the left the " Countless
Stones," presumably the remains of a more complicated
cromlech, while numerous less noted relics of the same
nature abound in the immediate neighbourhood. The Countless Stones owe their name to a not uncommon tradition in
regard to such remains that the accurate counting of them is
not possible. Extending further half a dozen miles to the
west—as we shall see—are other relics of the stone ages, and
in the hills about here are many deep shafts or pits descending
to hollowed chambers utilised either by cave-dwellers or as
places of refuge by pre-historic man.

One of the best known of cromlechs or dolmens, Kits Coty
House, is protected from impious visitors by a stout iron
railing, for not all people who go to see such relics of the past
have so worthy a feeling as that of an old time owner of this
one, " who would not for one hundred guineas part with as
much of the stone as would serve to set in a ring." In 1723
the monuments were described as having a very different
appearance from that of the present, the Upper Coty being
partly in a barrow and the Lower Coty—the Countless Stones
—as having been pulled down within the memory of people
then living. Then, too, there was about eighty yards north of
Kits Coty House a fallen megalith traditionally known as the
General's Tombstone. The relation of these stones to ancient
dwellers in Kent and the various theories as to their purpose
are recorded in many works. The consideration of these
points would take us too far into the byways of archæology,
but visitors to the district will find much information in Mr.
F. J. Bennett's " Ightham, the Story of a Kentish Village and
its Surroundings." It may, however, be said that according
to an old story " rife among the simple and untaught country-

men " of the neighbourhood the stones forming the Dolmen were brought from lands beyond the sea and placed as they now stand by a famous witch. Seventy years ago a no less astounding and much more original accounting for them was hazarded :—

"A friend of ours, riding from Chatham to Maidstone in the van, entered into conversation with a lady, whose appearance and manners bespoke a situation certainly somewhat above that of the middle classes, and not a little surprised was he to receive from her fair lips the following solution of a great mystery. Those immense blocks of stone which now excite our wonder as to the means by which they were raised and placed in their present position, were, at the time of their erection, comparatively speaking, mere trifles ; but being of a very porous nature, they absorb a vast quantity of rain and other humid matter, to this adheres the dust blown from the road, and all sorts of atmospheric impurities, which being baked by successive suns becomes hard as the stone itself, of which in fact it forms a portion ; and thus ' Kits Coty House' has attained its present gigantic size. Hear this, oh, ye fishers in muddy waters—ye diggers in the mines of antiquity—ye men of historical research. Listen to this simple— this satisfactory explanation, and confess how vain are all your theories, about Cromlechs and Druidical altars, and resting places for the bones of Saxon Kings ! "

Returning to the Medway at Allington Castle—midway between Aylesford and Maidstone—we may pass on our way the Elizabethan Cobtree Hall, overlooking the river, a place which is of interest to devout Dickensians through having been unhesitatingly identified by the late Mr. F. G. Kitton as the original of the Manor House at Dingley Dell—though the sceptical will point out that Dickens places the " Dell " at fifteen miles from Rochester, while Cobtree is but little more than half that distance.

Allington Castle, beautifully situated among the water meadows on the left bank of the Medway, half circled by a bend of the river, is notable as having been one of the seven chief castles of Kent. Part of the wide possessions of the Conqueror's half-brother, Odo, Bishop of Bayeux, it passed through various hands and was altered from time to time, until towards the close of the thirteenth century it was embattled by royal license and some of the original brickwork of that period is to be seen in the extensive remains. The chief traditions of Allington are associated with the Wyatt family, successive members of which gave a legend to the Tower of

U

London, a remarkable poet to English letters, and a martyr to Protestantism. Sir Henry Wyatt, who had bought the Castle in 1492, opposed the pretensions of Richard III. and suffered imprisonment in the Tower, where he was succoured by a cat, which daily brought to his window a pigeon from a neighbouring cote and so saved him from starvation ; after his release it is recorded that he " would ever make much of cats, as other men will of their spaniels or hounds." On the accession of Henry VII. Sir Henry became *persona grata* with that monarch, and continued in favour with his successor until his death in 1537.

Sir Thomas Wyatt the elder, son of the lover of cats, who won his place to an honourable position in English poetry, had a romantic career. Sir John Russell, having been appointed Ambassador to the Pope, was journeying down the Thames when he met Thomas Wyatt : " after salutations, was demanded of him whither he went, and had answer, ' to Italy, sent by the King.' ' And I,' said Wyatt, ' will, if you please, ask leave, get money and go with you.' ' No man more welcome,' answered the Ambassador. So, this accordingly done, they passed in post together." With Wyatt's subsequent services as Ambassador we are not here concerned, but it was probably from his hastily-decided upon journey to Italy that he brought back into England the art of sonnet-writing, an art which was to have some remarkable English exponents before the century closed. Though Wyatt is now recognised as occupying an important place in English poetry, nothing from his pen was published during his lifetime, and for a while he seemed more or less eclipsed by his " disciple " the Earl of Surrey ; some authorities, indeed, credit them jointly with the introduction of the sonnet, but the balance of evidence seems to show the elder as the true pioneer. Wyatt, however, has his definite place as the first of those who, as Warton puts it, " corrected the roughness of our poetic style." Here where he was born we may recall a couple of his poems, remembering that " He has too much art as a lover, and too little as a poet. His gallantries are laboured, and his versification negligent." The first brief piece describes " the one he would love," the second is entitled " Disdain me not : the Lover prayetn not to be disdained, refused, mistrusted, nor forsaken."

" A face that should content me wondrous well
  Should not be fair, but lovely to behold ;
Of lively look, all grief for to repel
  With right good grace, so would I that it should
Speak without words, such words as none can tell ;
  Her tress, also, should be of crispèd gold ;
With wit, and these, perchance, I might be tried,
And knit again with knot that should not slide."

   " Disdain me not without desert,
     Nor leave me not so suddenly,
  Since well ye wot that in my heart
     I mean ye not but honestly.

Refuse me not without cause why,
   Forethink me not to be unjust,
Since that by lot of fantasy
   This careful knot needs knit I must.

Mistrust me not, though some there be
   That fain would spot my steadfastness ;
Believe them not, since that ye see
   The proof is not as they express.

Forsake me not till I deserve,
   Nor hate me not till I offend ;
Destroy me not till that I swerve ;
   But since ye know what I intend

Disdain me not that am your own,
   Refuse me not that am so true,
Mistrust me not till all be known,
   Forsake me not, me for no new."

Whether the lady addressed in these poems was the fair
Anne Boleyn of Hever Castle, some miles to the west, cannot
now be determined, but certain it is that he to whom we owe
the first step in the smoothening of our versification was a lover
of Sir Thomas Boleyn's daughter before the bluff eighth Henry
had become her wooer and she could be described as saying
" *Noli me tangere* : I Cesar's am." Sir Thomas Wyatt, owing
to his relations with Anne, was for a time prisoner in the Tower,
but was later restored to the King's highest favour. In a
poetic epistle to a friend Wyatt described his life here at
Allington—

  ' This maketh me at home to hunt and hawk,
    And in foul weather at my book to sit ;
    In frost and snow then with my bow to stalk ;

No man doth mark whereso I ride or go,
In lusty leas at liberty I walk ;
And of these news I feel nor weal nor woe. . . .

I am here in Kent and Christendome
Among the Muses where I read and rhyme ;
Where if thou list, mine own John Poins, to come,
Thou shalt be judge how I do spend my time."

Sir Thomas Wyatt, the poet, was bewailed in verse by his disciple, the Earl of Surrey, thus—

" A visage stern and mild where both did grow
    Vice to contemn, in virtue to rejoice ;
Amid great storms, whom grace assurèd so,
    To live upright, and smile at Fortune's choice.

A hand that taught what might be said in rhyme,
    That reft Chaucer the glory of his wit ;
A mark the which (unparfited of time)
    Some may approach, but never none may hit."

According to most critics Surrey himself was the first to "hit" the perfectness of Wyatt. It was Wyatt (Wiat, as it was sometimes written) who devised the anagram " Wiat, a Wit."

Sir Thomas Wyatt, the younger son of the poet, was the leader of the Kentish rebellion against Queen Mary's marriage with Philip of Spain, mentioned in the preceding chapter, and it was from Allington that he set out—

" Ah, grey old castle of Allington, green field
    Beside the brimming Medway, it may chance
That I shall never look upon you more—"

when he led the Men of Kent to tragic defeat. After this last of the Wyatts the estate was granted to John Astley, Master of the Jewel House to Queen Elizabeth.

East of Allington is another possession of the Wyatts at Boxley, where in Boxley Abbey, lying midway between the two villages, was a notable seat of the Cistercian monks, founded in 1146 by William de Ypres by way of penance for earlier sacrilegious attempts on a monastery. William de Ypres was a very powerful person in Kent, and something of a terror to his adopted country until he went blind and became devout. To him, presumably, Rye owes its old Ypres (" Wipers ") Tower. At some time or another Boxley Abbey acquired precious relics in the form of a miracle-working Holy

Rood and a stone figure of St. Rumwald, which could only be lifted by those of clean lives, or—as Lambarde and Fuller suggest—by those who had made sufficiently liberal offerings to the monks ; as the former put it : "such who paid the priest well might easily remove it, whilst others might try at it to no purpose .... chaste virgins and wives went away with blushing faces, whilst others came off with more credit because with more coin—though with less chastity."

The Rood shall be described in the words of old Lambarde, who was a child at the time of its dramatic destruction—

"It chanced (as the tale is) that upon a time a cunning carpenter of our countrie was taken prisoner in the warres between us and France, who (wanting otherwise to satisfie for his ransome, and having good leisure to devise for his deliverance) thought it best to attempt some curious enterprise, within the compas of his own art and skill to make himself some money withall ; and therefore getting together fit matter for his purpose, he compacted of wood, wyre, paste and paper, a Rood of such exquisite art and excellencie, that it not only matched in comlynesse and due proportion of the parts, the best of the common sort ; but in strange motion, varietie of gesture, and nimbleness of joints passed all other that before had been seen : the same being able to bow down and lift up itself, to shake and stirre the hands and feet, to nod the head, to rolle the eyes, to wag the chaps, to bend the brows, and finally to represent to the eye both the proper motion of each member of the body, and also a lively, express, and significant show of a well contented or displeased minde ; byting the lipp, and gathering a frowning, froward, and disdainfull face, when it would pretend offence ; and shewing a most milde, amiable, and smiling cheere and countenance when it would seem to be well pleased."

The cunning carpenter brought his wonderful piece of work to England and putting it "upon the back of a Jade that he drave before him," set out for Rochester ; while he was refreshing himself at an alehouse the horse made off to Boxley Abbey, where "he so beat and bounced with his heels" that the monks had to open the door, when the beast "rushed in and ran in great haste to a pillar (which was the very place where this Image was afterwards advanced) and there stopped himself and stood still." The carpenter arrived, but nor force nor persuasion would make the horse budge a bit ; and so the man was fain sell his handiwork to the Abbey, and then the Image allowed itself to be taken off the horse's back and the horse consented to be led away. The Rood remained a great wonder and miracle-worker until on the break-up of the monasteries it was, in 1538, removed, and after being exhibited in Maidstone on a market day that all might see its working was taken to London, where it was destroyed by an irate congregation who had listened at St. Paul's Cross to a sermon by the Bishop of Rochester of which it formed the "text." It is recorded in a document in the Cottonian MSS.—"on. . . Sonday did the bisshop of Rochester preche at Polles Cross, and hed standyng afore hym alle his sermon tyme the pictur of the roode of grace in Kent, that had byn many yeres in the Abbey of Boxley in Kent, and was gretely sought with pilgrymes, and when he had made an ende of his sermon, the pictor was toorn alle to peces."

Near Boxley Abbey a spring which leaves a calcareous deposit upon objects lying in it has long been an object of curiosity : these are not petrified as by certain dripping wells, but are coated with what is known as calcareous tufa. In the third dialogue of Sir Humphry Davy's " Consolations in Travel " may be found a discussion of the tufa-depositing lake near Paestum, and an account of the chemical process which takes place in such waters. Similar tufa deposit is found in the Ightham district.

At Boxley village, situated on the lower slope of the chalk near the ancient Pilgrims' Road, Alfred Tennyson stayed in 1842, taking long walks along the old way of the Canterbury Pilgrims. To Edmund Lushington, of the Park House, nearer the Medway, the poet's sister Cecilia was married, and the present Lord Tennyson in his biography of his father tells us that " the park round the house is described in the prologue to ' the Princess.' " The occasion described was presumably a fête of the Maidstone Mechanics' Institute.

> " We went. . . .
> Down thro' the park ; strange was the sight to me ;
> For all the sloping pasture murmur'd, sown,
> With happy faces and with holiday.
> There moved the multitude, a thousand heads :
> The patient leaders of their Institute,
> Taught them with facts. . . . so that sport
> Went hand in hand with Science ; otherwhere
> Pure sport : a herd of boys with clamour bowl'd
> And stump'd the wicket : babies roll'd about
> Like tumbled fruit in grass ; and men and maids
> Arranged a country dance, and flew thro' light
> And shadow, while the twangling violin
> Struck up with Soldier-laddie, and overhead
> The broad ambrosial aisles of lofty lime
> Made noise with bees and breeze from end to end."

Though written nearly seventy years ago the picture might stand for a country festival of to-day, when " the park " is thrown open and the neighbouring folk enjoy themselves. Men of the early 'forties were perhaps more given to " improving the occasion " and " teaching the people with facts " ; now games, sports and feeding form the features of such a day's entertainment. One of the closing passages of the same poem, in describing Sir Walter Vivian, gives us a portrait that might well stand as type of the Kentish squire :

> " In such discourse we gain'd the garden rails,
> And there we saw Sir Walter where he stood,
> Before a tower of crimson holly-oaks,
> Among six boys, head under head, and look'd
> No little lily-handed Baronet he,
> A great broad-shoulder'd genial Englishman,
> A lord of fat prize-oxen and of sheep,
> A raiser of huge melons and of pine,
> A patron of some thirty charities,
> A pamphleteer on guano and on grain,
> A quarter-sessions chairman, abler none ;
> Fair-bair'd and redder than a windy morn ;
> Now shaking hands with him, now him, of those
> That stood the nearest—now address'd to speech—
> Who spoke few words and pithy, such as closed
> Welcome, farewell, and welcome for the year
> To follow : a shout rose again, and made
> The long line of the approaching rookery swerve
> From the elms, and shook the branches of the deer
> From slope to slope thro' distant ferns, and rang
> Beyond the bourn of sunset : O, a shout
> More joyful than the city-roar that hails
> Premier or king ! Why should not these great Sirs
> Give up their parks some dozen times a year
> To let the people breathe ? So thrice they cried,
> I likewise, and in groups they stream'd away."

Detling, Thornham (or Thurnham), Broad Street and Hollingbourne, are pleasant villages on the side of the chalk hills, all of them on that old Pilgrims' Road, along which such places are generally infrequent. After Hollingbourne we may follow the ancient way for many miles before touching at anything more than an occasional cottage, the villages, Harrietsham, Lenham, Charing, lying the usual half a mile or so away on the highroad, with which it keeps roughly parallel. At Thornham are the remains of an old " minor " castle perched on the hill

with a grand outlook over Maidstone and the Medway valley.
It is sometimes named Godard's Castle, and according to one
account was built by a Saxon named Godardus on the site of
a Roman watchtower.   The tradition is no doubt based on the
fact that the Roman remains have been found in the neighbourhood, but no authentic history of the castle has come
down to us.   In the churchyard of Thornham is buried one of

Hollingbourne Church, near Maidstone.

Kent's many famous cricketers, Alfred Mynn (born at
Goudhurst), a batsman whose chief feat (in 1836) was the
scoring 283 runs—twice not out—in four consecutive innings,
remembered as the first eminent bowler to use the fast round-
arm delivery and as one who has had few if any superiors
among his successors.   Mynn, who lived for many years at
Thornham, came of a Kentish family renowned for their great
stature and physical strength, and on the cricket field he could
" maintain a terrific pace for hours without fatigue."

South of Thornham a mile or so, and appearing as though bowered in trees, is Bearsted, with a church tower at three angles of which are figures said to represent the lion of St. Mark, the ox of St. Luke, and the eagle of St. John ; at the fourth angle is an octagonal tower turret.

Hollingbourne is a pretty village with a church in which are many monuments of the Colepeper or Culpeper family — celebrated in Kentish annals. William Colepeper of the Hollingbourne branch of the family who gained some fame as poet and politician was one of the five gentlemen whose Petition in 1701 was so unhandsomely treated. The beautiful marble monument of Lady Elizabeth Culpeper (1638) is especially worthy of notice. Here there was born, "a landed man and a true labourer," one Nicholas Wood who suffered from a disease, happily rare, known in Greek or Latin, as Boulimia or Caninus Apetitus, " insomuch that he would devour at one meal what was provided for twenty men, eat a whole hog at a sitting, and at another time thirty dozen of pigeons. . . . Let us raise our gratitude to the goodness of God, especially when he giveth us appetite enough for our meat, and yet meat too much for our appetite ; whereas this painful man spent all his estate to provide provant for his belly, and died very poor about the year 1630." Fuller's words might very well have inspired the good Scot's grace

> " There's some hae meat and canna eat,
> An' some hae none who want it ;
> But we hae meat, an we can eat,
> An' so the Lord be thankit."

John Taylor, the Water Poet, was a great eater and was, it is recorded, once very near engaging the voracious Nicholas Wood in a contest " to eat at one time as much black pudding as would reach across the Thames at any place to be fixed upon by Taylor himself between London and Richmond." Maybe it was Wood's inordinate appetite that gave rise to the saying " a Kentish stomach." Apropos of which saying it is recorded that a gentleman of this county who took his Bachelor of Arts degree at Cambridge when he was asked the question "quid est abyssus ? " promptly answered "Stomachus Cantianus." Readers of Sir Thomas Browne's works may recall that he has an interesting scrap on a poor Yarmouth woman aged 102 who suffered from Boulimia.

At Hollingbourne we are within easy reach of Leeds Castle but leaving that historical centre for awhile we may glance at the chalk-hill country, which may be reached by many lanes and roads going upward from the Pilgrims' Way. Climbing Hollingbourne Hill we have a magnificent view from the summit, shortly after enjoying which we may turn left to Hucking and Bicknor or right to Wormshill and Frinsted, by picturesque ways. The largest of these villages has probably fewer than two hundred inhabitants, but each has its old church with—despite restorations—various interesting features. From here the hills trend downwards towards the Faversham and Sittingbourne districts, and those who explore this part of our country on bicycles may be recommended to follow the plan of pushing up the hills from the abrupter Pilgrims' Way side that they may have the more gradual slopes for descent.

Coming down to the Ashford and Maidstone Road we have along it Lenham and Harrietsham (locally " Harrisham ") — quiet villages each with some attractive old timbered houses, but each more attractive as a point for reaching the beauties of the chalk hills north and of the greensand Quarry Hills south than for anything in itself. Lenham Church has, however, many monuments, old oaken stalls and other things worthy of inspection, and in the churchyard the tomb of one of the hundred and fourteen grandchildren of " the truly religious matron, Mary Honeywood," who at the time of her decease had living " lawfully descended from her three hundred and sixty-seven children." This prolific lady—who died in 1670 " in the ninety-third year of her age and the forty-fourth year of her widowhood "—was born at Lenham, married an esquire of Charing, but died and was buried in Essex, where her epitaph duly set forth the tale of her descendants. Fuller in mentioning her as one of the worthies of Kent said that she had already in his time " been much outstripped in point of fruitfulness." " This worthy matron (in my mind) is more memorable on another account, viz. for patient weathering out the tempest of a troubled conscience, whereon a remarkable story dependeth. Being much afflicted in mind, many ministers repaired to her, and amongst the rest the Rev. Mr. John Fox, than whom no more happy instrument to set the joints of a broken spirit. All his counsels proved ineffectual, insomuch that in the agony of her soul, having a Venice-glass in her hand, she broke forth into this expression, ' I am as surely damned as this glass is broken : ' which she immediately threw with violence on the ground. Here happened a wonder ; the glass rebounded again, and was taken up whole and entire. I confess it is possible (though difficult) so casually to throw as brittle a substance, that, lighting on the edges, it may be preserved ; but happening immediately in that juncture of time, it seemed little less than miraculous." Later Mistress Honeywood happened upon faith and, " led the remainder of her life in spiritual gladness."

Leeds Church.

" Ah, sir, poor Lenham," was, according to Hasted, the old time reply of the inhabitants to the traveller asking the name of the place. This, says one tautological writer, was because of its " damp and moist situation owing to the springs which rise near it." Jane Austen staying at Godmersham Park wrote that the clergyman of Lenham had called in to breakfast—" on his way from Ramsgate, where is his wife, to Lenham, where is his church, and to-morrow he dines and sleeps here on his return. They have been all the summer at Ramsgate for her

health ; she is a poor honey—the sort of woman who gives me
the idea of being determined never to be well, and who likes
her spasms and nervousness, and the consequence they give
her, better than anything else."

Hence·flows the infant Stour to the east and the Len
to the west to join the Medway. South of Lenham beyond
Chilstone Park—"a sweetly watered place" as Evelyn describes it—is Boughton Malherbe (locally pronounced Bawton
and anciently spelt Bocton) consisting chiefly of the church and
the old Place now a farm house ; for the parish is a scattered
one.   Here was the seat of the Wottons—a family several
members of which won fame in the past—one as Dean of
Canterbury, and another (the one of whom we think most here
at his birthplace) Sir Henry Wotton, the witty ambassador who
defined ambassadors generally as honest men sent to lie abroad
for the good of their country.   Incidentally, it may be said, Sir
Henry got into some disgrace with his Royal Master James the
First for uttering this coin of wit, which has had three centuries'
currency, and is as bright and welcome as when first minted.
Sir Henry Wotton was poet as well as diplomatist, and he
deserves to be known as one of the first of our literary letter-
writers.   The house standing somewhat behind the church is a
picturesque and interesting old place, and from it is to be had
a magnificent view across the Weald—as Izaak Walton was
aware when he wrote the life of his angling friend.   From the
road just below the farm, in front of which is a great grey stone
barn, the view is yet more extensive, looking down on the hamlet of Grafty Green set amid orchards.   A similar view, too, is
to be had from the yew-grown yard around the lichened grey
stone church.

Boughton Malherbe, mansion and church, said Izaak Walton,
are neither remarkable for anything so much " as for that the
memorable Family of the Wottons have so long inhabited the
one, and now lie buried in the other."   The most famous of
them was that Sir Henry Wotton whose life his friend Walton
was writing.   The master of the art of concise biography, as of
that which is the contemplative man's recreation, Walton referred
to Wotton's connection thus

" Sir *Henry Wotton* . . . was born in the year of our Redemption
1568 in *Bocton hall* (commonly called *Bocton*, or *Bougton*-place, or Palace)
in the Parish of *Bocton Malherb*, in the fruitful Country of *Kent: Bocton-*

hall being an *ancient* and *goodly Structure*, beautifying, and being beautified by the Parish Church of Bocton Malherb adjoyning unto it; and both seated within a fair Park of the *Wottons*, on the brow of such a *Hill*, as gives the advantage of a large Prospect, and of equal *pleasure* to all Beholders."

When Essex got into trouble Sir Henry Wotton had been taken into his "serviceable friendship," and on the Earl's being committed to the Tower, Wotton, "knowing *Treason* to be so comprehensive as to take in even circumstances and out of them to make such positive conclusions as Subtle Statesmen shall project, either for their revenge or safety; considering this, he thought prevention by absence out of England a better security than to stay in it and there plead his innocency in a *Prison*. Therefore did he, so soon as the Earl was apprehended, very quickly and as privately glide through Kent to Dover, without so much as looking towards his native and beloved *Bocton*, and was by the help of favorable winds and liberal payment of the Mariners, within sixteen hours after his departure from London set upon the *French* shore."

Born in what is now a farm house amid farm fields, but in what was then a noble residence in a park, Sir Henry Wotton ended his life as Provost of Eton College, and is buried in the College Chapel. When not abroad he paid annual visits to Boughton Place, and his will directed "If I shall end my transitory days at, or near Eaton, to be buried in the Chappel of the said College, as the Fellows shall dispose thereof, with whom I have liv'd (my God knows) in all loving affection; or If I shall dye near Bocton Malherb in the County of Kent, then I wish to be laid in that Parish Church, as near as may be to the Sepulchre of my good Father, expecting a joyful Resurrection with him in the day of Christ." He further directed, as Walton tells us, that his monument should be inscribed: "Hic jacet hujus Sententiae primus author Disputandi pruritus, Ecclesiarum scabies, Nomen alias quaere. Which may be Englished thus, Here lies the first Author of this Sentence. The itch of Disputation will prove the Scab of the Church. Inquire his name elsewhere."

Before turning from Boughton Malherbe we may recall one of the happiest of Wotton's poems, that "Character of a Happy Life" which, though it has found its place in many collections, may form fitting reading where his happy life began.

> " How happy is he born and taught,
> That serveth not another's will?
> Whose Armour is his honest thought,
> And simple truth his utmost Skill?
>
> Whose Passions not his Masters are,
> Whose Soul is still prepar'd for Death;
> Unti'd unto the World by care
> Of publick Fame, or private Breath.
>
> Who envies none that chance doth raise,
> Nor Vice hath ever understood;
> How deepest Wounds are given by praise,
> Nor Rules of State, but Rules of good.
>
> Who hath his Life from Rumours freed,
> Whose Conscience is his strong retreat;
> Whose State can neither Flatterers feed,
> Nor Ruine make Oppressors great.
>
> Who God doth late and early pray,
> More of his Grace than Gifts to lend:
> And entertains the harmless day
> With a Religious Book or Friend.
>
> This man is freed from servile hands,
> Of hope to rise, or fear to fall:
> Lord of himself, though not of Lands,
> And having nothing, yet hath all."

A little way out of Boughton Malherbe on the road towards Lenham is something which must puzzle most of the casual passers by—of whom it is easy to believe there are but few on the quiet byway; this is a large old yew tree growing on a mound of earth enclosed—as though in a gigantic, square "flowerpot"—in stone walls. Local enquiry elicits the tradition, first, that "it had something to do with Queen Elizabeth—or one of the queens," and, secondly, that underneath the "flowerpot" is a chamber communicating by means of an underground passage with Boughton Place. Perched on the top of the hill the yew is visible from some distance.

Another noted member of the Wotton family was Dean Nicholas Wotton, who served as ambassador for Henry VIII. and Queen Mary, and is buried in Canterbury Cathedral. When, in the reign of Mary, Thomas Wotton had newly come into his estate at Boughton Malherbe, he would have joined in Sir Thomas Wyatt's Rebellion, but his uncle the Dean, then ambassador in France, dreamed that his nephew was in danger of being party to such project, and so wrote to the Queen asking that Thomas should be committed to some favourable gaol on some plausible charge. This was done, and Wotton only released when the rebellion was over—some years later to become father of *the* Sir Henry Wotton in 1568, the very year after the death of that diplomatic dreamer Dean Nicholas.

South of Boughton Malherbe through the country which we overlook from near the church we can go to Headcorn and Smarden, both on the River Beult, and so into the Weald. West by shady lanes and tortuous byroads we may go to the small and very picturesque old-world places of Ulcombe and the Suttons—East Sutton, Sutton Valence (or Town Sutton) and Chart Sutton—and see pretty old cottages and Elizabethan houses. At East Sutton Place lived Sir Robert Filmer, the political writer, author of "Patriarcha; or, the Natural Power of the Kings of England asserted," who would have put back the clock and have restored a patriarchal system of government. He had to pay for his views, for it is said that his house at East Sutton was plundered ten times on account of his Royalist sympathies. His views on monarchy were strongly answered from west Kent by Algernon Sidney.

It was at East Sutton Park, still occupied by the Filmer family, that, according to a recent book of reminiscences, some years ago a certain passage at arms took place which resulted in a sketch being sent to *Punch*: After dinner one evening the noise from the housekeeper's room became so pronounced that Lady Filmer sent for the housekeeper, and complained.

"' Really Mrs.—, I must beg you to keep a little more order downstairs ; the noise is quite annoying.'

'I can assure your ladyship that the noise which comes from the drawing room is quite as annoying to us as ours can possibly be to your ladyship,' was the impudent reply. A daughter of the house made a sketch of the scene and sent it to *Punch*, where it appeared under the heading of 'Flunkey-ana.'"

At Sutton Valence, near the modern church of which are trifling remains of an old castle, probably built in the twelfth

century, was born William Lambe, a sixteenth century London
Merchant who founded the famous grammar school and
certain almshouses in his native village ; he was buried in old
St. Paul's Cathedral, his tomb being destroyed in the Great
Fire. The following punning lines, fixed up it is recorded by
himself in his lifetime, formed part of his epitaph :

> " Oh Lamb of God, which sin didst take away,
>   And (as a Lamb) wast offered up for sin ;
> Where I (poor Lamb) went from thy flock astray,
>   Yet thou, good Lord, Vouchsafe thy Lamb to win
>   Home to thy fold, and hold thy Lamb therein,
> That at the day when Goats and Lambs shall sever,
> Of thy choice lambs, Lamb may be one for ever."

Chart Sutton, or Chart next-Sutton-Valence to give it the
dignity of its full name, shares the picturesqueness of its
neighbour, but has no special story to detain us. It may be
said, however, that the word chart—which as a place name
occurs in many parts of Kent—signifies a rough common
grown with gorse and bracken. Systematic enclosing of waste
lands has, however, in most instances made of the name
a misnomer, for in past years many people found it convenient
to ignore the more serious charge in the old saying.—

> " It is a fault in man or woman
> To steal a goose from off a common—
> But it admits of less excuse
> To steal a common from a goose."

The whole extent of country here is well varied with great
breadths of hop lands and orchards, woods and fields, stretching west by Boughton, Monchelsea and Linton to Cox Heath
and the Medway valley. As we are here on the Quarry Hills,
it may be pointed out that it is from this district that so much
of the Kentish ragstone used in churches and other buildings
was taken. Much of this stone, indeed, was employed in the
building of Westminster Abbey, and it was commanded at the
time that until the Abbey was completed no stone from the
Kentish quarries should be taken to London for any other
purpose. Its use in London goes back to the time when
a Roman temple was built of it on the site where St. Paul's
Cathedral now stands. At one time this hard stone was

extensively utilised for the making of cannon balls and other missiles.

Linton is an interesting place which readers of Walpole's letters will remember as the residence of the Manns, and as the place where his correspondent, Sir Horace Mann (who died in Florence in 1786) is buried. In the church are several monuments to the Mann and Cornwallis family—including a tawdry one designed, and thought much of, by Horace Walpole himself. Linton Place—which passed from the possession of the Manns to the Cornwallis family—is a beautiful seat, the park comprising one of the grandest collections of conifers in the country. It won the cordial commendation of Walpole, who said "the house is fine and stands like the citadel of Kent. The whole county is its garden." Often as we may feel disposed to object to the "Wardour Street" taste of the lord of Strawberry Hill, that his enthusiasm is here justified few visitors will be inclined to dispute.

From Linton we may return to Maidstone through the village of Loose, pleasantly situated on a hill of the same name, or by the hamlet of Boughton Green and the ragstone quarries, through land still rich in hops and fruit trees, to Otham and Langley— the church of the former place with some curious monuments— and so on to Leeds, a picturesquely irregular village the seat of an old abbey of which scanty traces remain. This abbey was founded in 1119 by Robert de Crevecœur, member of a family to which Leeds Castle belonged for several generations. It was from Leeds Abbey that John Mulso, in 1744, began an interesting correspondence with his friend Gilbert White, later the famous naturalist of Selborne. "I am at Mrs. Meredith's at Leeds Abbey in Kent: · The house extremely large, but it has few traces of an abbey. . . a large garden well stock'd with fruit and adorn'd with fountains, cascades and canals ; a most romantic wood behind it with large fish ponds ; large stables with a complete set of foaming horses for a coach that has a prodigious easy corner, and riding nags that I am in love with. But Oh ! Gil, here is a loss ye most severe that can be : this house had a fine library, which not falling by will to the lady of it, had been sold off, and nothing remains but ye skele-ton cases. I really believe that my brain will be moss'd over like our old walls, for here is very little company, and those come so seldom that it is all form and starchedness."

A pleasant footpath skirting the southern side of the finely
wooded park goes to Broomfield, immediately north of which
stands the ancient Leeds Castle in its great moat ; a splendid
pile even as seen in passing along the main road which borders
the park for more than a mile.   The extensive moat, formed by
the River Len, which flows through the park, must have made

Leeds Castle from the Road.

the castle well-nigh impregnable in the mediæval days, when it
was one of the chief strongholds of Kent.   The noble pile was
for many reigns the property of the Queens of England, and remained a royal castle until the time of Edward VI., when it was
granted to Sir Anthony St. Leger, who, as Lord Deputy of
Ireland, had inaugurated a new epoch in that country, and who
summed up the Irish Question of his day by saying that the
island was easier to be won than to be kept, " for onelesse it be

peopled with others than be there already, and also certen fortresses there buylded and warded, if it be gotten the one daye it is lost the next." He died at Ulcombe—three miles to the south-east of Leeds Castle—and is buried in the parish church there. His grandson sold Leeds Castle in 1608 and joined Sir Walter Raleigh in his expedition to Guiana Some years later the property passed to the Culpepers, and afterwards to the famous Yorkshire family of Fairfax. The castle was frequently used as a prison for persons of consequence. Here Eleanor Duchess of Gloucester was imprisoned in 1441, charged with ' necromancy, witchcraft, heresy and treason " ; here the unhappy

Leeds Castle from the Park.

Richard II., was brought secretly, disguised as a forester ; later Henry IV.'s Queen Joan was confined here : and here the Irish leader Desmond was held prisoner in Elizabeth's time by Sir Warham Leger For over two years—1665-7—John Evelyn records in his "Diary" he with the other commissioners had charge of 500 French and Dutch prisoners in Leeds Castle ; he hired the castle of Lord Culpeper for the purpose, having been earnestly desired "to spare Maidstone from quartering any of my sick flock."

The castle, despite many modern additions, is a fine and impressive building—though Walpole, in his mania for the Gothic, sneered at it, declaring that the only thing worth seeing were a portrait of the Duchess of Buckingham and the moat

The Len, which forms the moat, flows on to beautiful Milgate Park, and soon does its share of work for some of the paper mills of the Maidstone district, and so on to the grand park of the Mote where it forms a large lake. This park, which is noted for its many magnificent beeches and oaks, has been successively the property of such important families as the Woodvilles (Lord Rivers), the Wyatts, and the Marshams (Lord Romney).

Leybourne.

CHAPTER XV

"THE WELLS" AND TONBRIDGE

"Tunbridge [Wells] is the same distance from London that Fontaine-bleau is from Paris, and is, at the season, the general rendezvous of all the gay and handsome of both sexes. The company though always numerous, is always select; since those who repair thither for diversion ever exceed the number of those who go thither for health, everything there breathes mirth and pleasure; constraint is banished, familiarity is established upon the first acquaintance, and joy and pleasure are the sole sovereigns of the place. The company are accommodated with lodgings in little, clean, and convenient habitations that lie straggling and separated from each other, a mile and a half all around the Wells, where the company meet in the morning: this place consists of a long walk, shaded by spreading trees, under which they walk while they are drinking the waters: on one side of this walk is a long row of shops, plentifully stocked with all manner of toys, lace, gloves, stockings, and where there is raffling, as at Paris, in the Foire de Saint Germain; on the other side of the walk is the market, and, as it is the custom here for every person to buy their own provisions, care is taken that nothing offensive appears on the stalls. Here young, fair, fresh-coloured country girls, with clean linen, small straw hats, and neat shoes and stockings, sell game, vegetables, flowers, and fruit; here one may live as well as one pleases; here is, likewise, deep play, and no want of amorous intrigues. As soon as the evening comes every one quits his little palace to assemble on the bowling green, where, in the open air, those who choose dance upon a turf more soft and smooth than the finest carpet in the world."

THUS wrote Anthony Hamilton a couple of centuries ago, and already the Wells had enjoyed nearly a century of reputation as a place at which Society could combine its search after enjoyment with its search after health, for it was in 1606 that a nobleman first found the value of the chalybeate springs and so in course of time started the hilly village upon its transformation into a centre of fashionable life. Dudley, Lord North, the nobleman to whom Tunbridge Wells is indebted in the first place for its fame, was reported to be entirely cured of "the lingering consumptive order he laboured under" by the use of the waters, and they long continued famous for their efficacy "in cold chronical distempers, weak nerves and bad digestion." The Earl of Abergavenny had the springs enclosed and sought to popularise the resort, the success of which was such that it was many years before the accommodation for visitors could be made to equal the demands.   In 1630 Queen Henrietta Maria attended by a large suite journeyed to the Wells for her health's sake but was obliged to camp on the Downs, while a generation later many visitors who wished to take the waters had to seek accommodation in neighbouring villages two or three miles away.   Charles the Second's Queen took up her residence here—Pepys again and again tells us the Queen has gone to Tunbridge Wells—and henceforward the fashionable popularity of the place was assured.   In the eighteenth century it rivalled Bath as a social resort and everybody who was anybody made a point of being seen at the Wells.   Already when Defoe wrote the first volume of his "Tour Thro' the whole Island of Great Britain" (published 1724) he could say "the coming to the Wells to drink the water is a mere matter of custom ; some drink, more do not, and few drink physically ; but company and diversion is in short the main business of the place ; and those people who have nothing to do anywhere else, seem to be the only people who have anything to do at Tunbridge."   On the walks (the Pantiles) he tells us any gentleman of decency and good manners could talk with any lady, and he gives a lively account of the place as the resort of fashion and of beauty.

It was here that Mr. Henry Esmond Warrington from Virginia improved his acquaintance with his aunt, the wonderful Madame de Bernstein (née Beatrice Esmond), having ridden over the wooded and hilly ways from Westerham with Mr. Wolfe. It was here, too, to turn to the work of another master of fiction, that Beau Beamish reigned and the fair Chloe came to her tragic end, and we seem to get a flavour of the mixture of rusticity and fashion in the ballad of "The Duke and the Dairymaid," "ascribed with questionable authority to the pen of Mr. Beamish himself in a freak of his gaiety" :—

    " Sweet Susie she tripped on a shiny May morn,
      As blithe as the lark from the green-springing corn,

When, hard by a stile 'twas her luck to behold
A wonderful gentleman covered with gold !

There was gold on his breeches and gold on his coat,
His shirt-frill was grand as a fifty-pound note ;
The diamonds glittered all up him so bright,
She thought him the Milky Way clothing a Sprite !

' Fear not, pretty maiden,' he said with a smile ;
' And pray let me help you in crossing the stile.'
She bobbed him a curtsey so lovely and smart,
It shot like an arrow and fixed in his heart.

As light as a robin she hopped to the stone,
But fast was her hand in the gentleman's own ;
And guess how she stared, nor her senses could trust,
When this creamy gentleman knelt in the dust ! ''

The Tunbridge Wells of the past lives again in the pages of
Thackeray and Meredith but it may also be found in hints and
scraps in many of the memoirs and correspondence of the
eighteenth century literary and fashionable folk. References
from such works would suffice to make a large book about
Tunbridge Wells alone ; here we may get a glimpse of the place
as it appeared of old, may seek to repeople the walks with
beaux and belles of a past. Lord Boyle, who visited the town
in the summer of 1728, wrote a lively description in which
he showed how closely everyone followed the lead of the reigning notable at the Wells :

" We are honoured here with the Presence of Princess Emilia, to whome
the Tunbridgians leave no method untried to pay their Court. If she
laughs (and sometimes princesses laugh at nothing) we all grinn, remembering the good old Saying, ' the frightfull'st Grinner, be the Winner.' If she
looks grave, we put on countenances more sorrowfull than the Mutes at a
Funeral. When She walks, the Lame and the Blind hobble after Her.
If she complains of the Toothache, the ugly Faces of the Women of
Quality are wrop'd up in Flannel. In all reasonable Pleasures, nay in
Pains as far as the Toothache and the Vapours, we humbly imitate Her.
. . . Under the Rose, I believe these renowned Wells are not of any
great use. We are ordered down here commonly *pour la Maladie
Imaginaire*, for the Spirits and the melancholy to which our whole Nation
are too subject. The Diversions and Amusements of the Place send us
home again chearfull, and the foggy Air of London with the common
Disappointments of Life urge our Return the following Year. The Water
has a brackish taste never palatable. "

His lordship then went on to give the following entertaining
account of an eccentric person whose doings must have varied,
if not always agreeably, the ordinary daily round.

"Among the infinite variety of People now here there is a Madman, surnamed Drapier, who strikes us all with pannick Fear, and affords us Diversion at the same time. He has raised a Regiment and enlists his Soldiers in a manner not a little extraordinary. He fixes on any Gentle-

The Pantiles, Tunbridge Wells.

man whom his wild Imagination represents as fit for martial Exploits, and holding a Pistoll to the pore Captive's Breast obliges him to open a Vein and write his Name in Blood upon the Regimental Flag. Some have leap't out of Window to escape the Ceremony of bleeding, but many others have tamely submitted, and they march every morning in Military Order at his Heels. He has in his Suite an Irish Viscount, an English Baronet, three Jews, five Merchants and a supercargo. These are the Cheife, but the whole Regiment consists of Twenty-Seven. All agree he should go to Bedlam, but none dare send Him there. The unbelieving Jews tremble at the Sight of Him, and the sober Citizens of London turn pale when he enters the Room. To his natural heat he adds the strength of Liquor, and is a most terrible Hector. I wish he was chained up, for the Women are all frightened out of their Wits about Him ; thank Heaven I have not the Honour of his Acquaintance."

Half a century later and Mrs. "Blue Stocking" Montagu met here the author of "The Complaint : or Night Thoughts on Life, Death and Immortality"—to give the poem its neglected full title ; the lady described how they rode, walked, and took sweet converse together, he carrying her to places "suited to the genius of his muse, sublime, grand, and with pleasing gloom diffused over them." In our more self-conscious age Genius and its admirers are both more fearful of seeming ridiculous. Mrs. Montagu was "in the vapours" at Dr. Young's departure, though the presence of other literary lights soon consoled her for his absence and with Mrs. "Epictetus" Carter, Lord Lyttelton and others "wit flowed more copiously than the springs," and the "wits" became annoyed when a mere newspaper "intelligencer"—we should call him a reporter nowadays—said that the noblemen were attracted more to ladies of fashion than to the "blues," Mrs. Carter and Mrs. Montagu ! The former lady wrote—

"It is true that my Lord Bath does sometimes draw his chair, in a sort of a kind of an edgeway fashion, near my Lady A. But pray consider the difference. It is by mere dint of scratching and clawing that Lady A. can draw Lord Bath—poor man—a few plain steps across the Pantiles, while we, by the natural power of sober attraction, draw him quite up 'Tug Hill' to the top of Mount Ephraim, and keep him there till we are quite afraid he will endanger his life in returning. Well ; but my Lord Lyttelton ? Let any impartial person ask Lord Lyttelton's postillion, and his horses, and his dog 'Pert' whether many a long evening's attendance upon Mount Ephraim has not given them good reason to wish there was no body that detained his Lordship longer than Lady A."

Mrs. Montagu also wrote of the round of life at the Wells : "so many glasses of water to be drunk, so many buttered rolls to be eaten, so many turns on the walk to be taken, so many miles to be gone in a post chaise or on horseback, so much pains to be well, so much attention to be civil." Early in the season there were people of quality of "extremely bourgeoise"

behaviour, and they were followed by proud and impertinent
citizens aping the persons of quality. Still the good lady
thought as Providence made the system for the multitude the
life led by the generality must be the happiest, then added,
with smug self-satisfaction and the pride that apes humility,
speaking for the intellectual minority, " though as fortune's
elder children we are best portioned, I know not if we are
best beloved ; I hope not."

A celebrated old engraving fully described in Mr. Austin

Tunbridge Wells from Southborough Common

Dobson's " Samuel Richardson " shows many celebrities of
1748 grouped along the public walk here and that picture
might well have suggested the scene in Thackeray's
" Virginians " where Harry and his companions, after their
athletic competition, look out upon the assembled company.—

"There was, indeed, a great variety of characters who passed. M.
Poellnitz, no finer dressed than he had been at dinner, grinned, and
saluted with his great laced hat and tarnished feathers. Then came

by my Lord Chesterfield, in a pearl-coloured suit, with his blue ribbon and star, and saluted the young men in his turn.

' I will back the old boy for taking his hat off against the whole kingdom, and France, either,' says my Lord March. ' He has never changed the shape of that hat of his for twenty years. Look at it. There it goes again. Do you see that great, big, awkward, pock-marked, snuff-coloured man, who hardly touches his clumsy beaver in reply. D —— his confounded impudence—do you know who that is?'

' No, curse him ! Who is it, March?' asks Jack, with an oath.

' It's one Johnson, a dictionary-maker, about whom my Lord Chesterfield wrote some most capital papers, when his dictionary was coming out, to patronise the fellow. I know they were capital. I've heard Horry Walpole say so, and he knows all about that kind of thing. Confound the impudent schoolmaster.'

' Hang him, he ought to stand in the pillory,' roars Jack.

' That fat man he's walking with is another of your writing fellows,—a printer,—his name is Richardson ; he wrote *Clarissa*, you know.'

' Great Heavens, my Lord, is that the great Richardson ? Is that the man who wrote *Clarissa?*' called out Colonel Wolfe and Mr. Warrington in a breath.

Harry ran forward to look at the old gentleman toddling along the walk with a train of admiring ladies surrounding him.

' Indeed, my very dear sir,' one was saying, ' you are too great and good to live in such a world ; but sure you were sent to teach it virtue.'

' Ah, my Miss Mulso, who shall teach the teacher,' said the good fat old man, raising a round, kind face skywards. ' Even he has his faults and errors. Even his age and experience does not prevent him from stumbl——, heaven bless my soul, Mr. Johnson, I ask your pardon if I have trodden on your corn.'

' You have done both, sir. You have trodden on the corn and received the pardon,' said Mr. Johnson, and went on mumbling some verses, swaying to and fro, his eyes turned towards the ground, his hands behind him, and occasionally endangering with his great stick the honest, meek eyes of his companion author.''

Since the days of which Thackeray wrote, Tunbridge Wells has lost something of its eminence as a fashionable place, though it remains a delightful health-resort surrounded by inexhaustibly attractive country. Indeed Thackeray found it changed much between his schooldays and his age as he shows in that delightful autobiographical essay in the " Roundabout Papers " dealing with " Tunbridge Toys." Set upon hills with magnificent views over the Sussex forests, it is so near the border that Mr. E. V. Lucas quietly annexed it to his county when writing of " Highways and Byways in Sussex." Those who once fall under the fascination of the place return to it again and again, not as of old, for the waters or for the company, but for the health-giving air of the Kentish hills, the beautiful walks and drives through lanes and byways to quaint old villages and stately parks. The chief park is that of Eridge to the south, in the neighbour county—but visitors need be less troubled than topographers by such arbitrary delimitations. The town itself, despite its hilly ways, suggests ease and comfort, its famous Pantiles—avenued with limes—still attract many visitors, and the local Tunbridge-ware (beech or sycamore inlaid with other woods) still provides pleasant souvenirs, as it has done for several generations. Though the beautifully situated town finds favour with many visitors and residents—its population is greater than that of Canterbury, and nearly equal to that of Maidstone—it has not for various reasons appealed to everyone. Cobbett, with all his love of country divided between woodland and cultivation, disliked it, apparently for little reason beyond that of its being frequented by Londoners—"by making a great stir in rousing waiters and 'boots' and maids, and by leaving behind me the name of 'a d—d noisy troublesome fellow,' I got clear of 'the Wells' and out of the contagion of its wen-engendered inhabitants."

An earlier writer had far other views, for it was at a house on Mount Sion, that Richard Cumberland, poet and prolific playwright, passed the last twenty-seven years of his life, and there he died, in 1811, having written of his Kentish home that it was not altogether a public place, yet at no period of the year a solitude, and that during his long residence there, he had never experienced a single hour's indisposition that confined him to his bed. The dramatist was honoured with burial in Westminster Abbey, but his poems have ceased to be read, his plays to be acted. His "Memoirs" should be worth reprinting, for the entertainment of those who like to read intimate gossipy records of the past.

A couple of years ago an interesting custom was revived by the Mayor of Tunbridge Wells. Having discovered an old statute requiring the mayor of the town to send corn to the parish church at the conclusion of each year's harvest, he purchased a large quantity, and sent it to St. John's Church to be used in connection with the harvest festival there.

The fine extent of hilly common, well-nigh surrounded by the growing town, is one of the notable features of Tunbridge Wells, to be visited after we have walked the Pantiles, and dutifully taken a draught of the waters—less curative, perhaps,

now that springs further afield have become so easily accessible. On Rusthall Common, beyond, the Toad Rock is to be
seen and puzzled over while the High Rocks, now sophisticated
into a show place, and therefore largely spoiled, lie a mile or so to
the south-west ; these rocks, the "surprising cliffs and chasms"
and "narrow gloomy passages" of which awed our grandparents of the eighteenth century, just over the boundary in
Sussex, should be visited if for no other reason than that rocks
are uncommon features of our southern scenery of wooded
hills and rounded downs.

Along the Sussex border from Tunbridge Wells to the west
until our county merges into Surrey, about nine miles away, are
Groombridge and Ashurst, Fordcombe and Cowden—the first
mainly in Sussex, and the second the most westerly place on the
Medway, which for a short distance, where it flows to the north,
forms the boundary between the two counties, until it is joined
by the Kent Water near to Fordcombe paper mills. In the
churchyard of the modern church of Fordcombe, which he had
been mainly instrumental in building, is buried Field-Marshal
Lord Hardinge, one of the most notable of Wellington's
lieutenants in the Peninsular War, who later gained fame as
Governor-General of India ; one of the governors to leave the
finest record. Hardinge resided at South Park, between here
and Penshurst. Cowden, on the Kent Water, with a large
" furnace pond " in the neighbourhood, is another of the quiet
little villages within easy reach of any of these West Kent
centres. The country all about is woodland and parkland,
diversified by hops and corn, with a certain rich sameness
about the scenery, but offering again and again glimpses of
pleasant houses and quaint cottages to those who pass through
the shady lanes. Here, as in other rural parts, one is struck
again and again by the few people who are met, the few even at
work in the fields, except during the hopping season, or when the
hay is a-making. The meeting with a group of flower-gathering
or playing youngsters is quite an event in a long walk, except
when passing through villages. North of Cowden is the high
hamlet of Markbeech, with splendid views across this corner
of our county—both into the valley from which we have
come, and on the further side of the ridge to that of the
river Eden. Turning easterly again, leaving for the present
the tempting signposts which tell us that Hever and Penshurst

are within easy reach, and taking retired byways we go by woodlands of oak and pine, by one of the many Coldharbours our county knows — surely the very commonest of place-names— to the Medway, about a couple of miles below the point at which its waters have been joined by those of the Eden. Just beyond are Speldhurst, Bidborough, and Southborough, bringing us near to "the Wells" again. The two first are

Tonbridge **Castle.**

beautifully situated old villages, while the other is quite a town which has risen with its neighbour, and also boasts of chalybeate springs, though it never attained fashionable vogue.

Tonbridge, or Tunbridge, lies about five miles north of the Wells to which it gave its name. It is a place that was of importance in mediæval times, owing to its strong castle, and, thanks to its situation at the head of the navigable waters of the Medway and to the fact that it is an important railway junction, it has acquired a new modern importance as a market and manufacturing centre, with its corn mills, powder mills, and breweries. It is, too, a capital centre from which to explore West Kent, owing to its being a kind of railway

Old Chequers Inn, Tonbridge.

four-cross roads along each of which are to be found characteristic scenery and many places of special beauty and interest. A pleasant, prosperous town with some quaint timbered buildings—notably the well preserved three hundred years old Chequers Inn, which is strikingly picturesque from the street, and the internal arrangement of which shows the spacious arched rooms—now divided up by partitions—in which our forefathers took their rest within their inn in days presumably before the refinement of separate rooms for guests had been reached. There are other ancient houses to be seen in the old market town but new offices and factories and the railway have combined to modernise the place while giving it an air of substantial prosperity.

The ruined Castle in its beautiful grounds—now a well-planted place for public recreation—was at one time an important Kentish stronghold. It is situated in the middle of the town, its shrub-grown grounds reaching to the bank of the river. The remains are full of interest. Dating back to Norman times the Castle was besieged on many occasions and passed through the possession of various owners during the troubled centuries that followed. After having been put in a state of defence on behalf of the Parliamentarians in the Civil War it was dismantled and gradually fell into the ruined state in which it has now been arrested. The mound on which the ancient keep stood is regarded as a prehistoric earthwork. From the remaining creeper-clad towers an admirable view is to be had over the town and along the valley which the Castle guarded. An old visitor objected to the removal of ivy from the ruins—a present-day one may well complain of the coloured lights with which they are hung.

At Somerhill, or Summerhill, a beautiful park to the south-east of Tonbridge and for a mile alongside which runs the road to the Wells, we have a place to which the public are allowed access. The fine Jacobean house occupies the position of one once belonging to Sir Philip Sidney—brought as part of her dower by his wife the daughter of Sir Francis Walsingham. The present house, which was built in 1614 by one of the earls of Clanricarde (who sit in the House of Lords, by the way, as Baron Somerhill), was among the properties given to John Bradshaw, the President of the Court which condemned Charles I., but before the close of the same century it had returned to the Lord Clanricarde of that time and then passed by his daughter's marriage to Lord Muskerry. The four courts in which the house was enclosed afforded magnificent views, from that on the east the distant Barham Downs between Canterbury and Dover being dimly shown. The hill to the south of the house perhaps offers the best view; from this point, as an old writer puts it, " a stranger may

behold at leisure a valley equal to Tempe, Andalusia, or
Tinian." Here "la Belle Hamilton" stayed when the Court
was at the Wells. Presumably the neighbourhood of the
fashionable place proved costly to the local nobility, for we
learn that "Lady Muskerry having, by her expensive way of
life, wasted her estate, she, by piecemeal, sold off a great part
of the demesnes lying mostly on the southern side of South
Frith, to different persons; and, dying in great distress, was
buried accordingly, about the year 1698." Behind the gaiety
and colour of life at the Wells this gives us a hint of the note
of tragedy. When Horace Walpole visited the place in 1752
it was of the romantic visitor, "Grammont's princess of
Babylon," that he thought rather than of the ruinous hospitality,
and he said there was scarce a road to it and the house was
little better than a farm. The house has long been restored
and enlarged, the roads made good, while the fine old trees
and the views over a vast landscape remain.

North of Tonbridge on the road to Sevenoaks is the quiet
village of Hildenborough, famous on many cricketing fields as
a place where some of the best bats and balls are made. In
the last few years, however, Hildenborough has won something
of a new celebrity, for here for several winters village players
have performed specially written dramatic pieces. The project
was first devised about five years ago to afford winter evenings'
amusement for the men of the village and many of them
proved apt actors in the little plays of old Kentish life written
for them by Mr. Dagney Major. An interesting fact about the
Hildenborough performance is that—apart from the costumes
—everything is "home made" by local talent. Not having had
an opportunity of seeing that performance I cannot describe
it, but I have heard it referred to as an extremely interesting
experiment in training the minds of the men and boys who are
members of the village institute and giving them employment
in winter evenings. "It has done all this and much more.
It has shown that men can be easily drawn from the inanities
of the taproom, and that even in a little community like this
there exists a strong natural talent for reproducing the drama
of life. The village green has been the cradle of county
cricket; is it possible also that the real school of acting may
be discovered in the village institute?" A representative "cast,"
included two gardeners, three cricket-ball makers, two black-

smiths, two carmen, a saddler, a dairyman and a worker at the gunpowder mills. Hildenborough's success may well give rise to similar experiments and the players become as common in village, as pageants are becoming in City, history.

At Hildenborough we have north of us the high range of hills on which Sevenoaks is situated—westwards Ide Hill and Toys Hill show prominently—but keeping to the south of them we may turn more eastwards to visit Shipborne, Hadlow and the Peckhams, going through the wooded higher lands of the Medway valley. Shipborne is interesting as being the birthplace of Christopher Smart, the eighteenth century poet whose "Song to David" has much in it of real poetic beauty and not a little of baldness—and as the burial place of Sir Henry Vane the younger. This ardent Republican, "Vane, young in years, but in sage counsel old," as his friend Milton put it, is perhaps most often remembered by Cromwell's outcry on the expulsion of the Long Parliament, "O Sir Henry Vane, Sir Henry Vane; the Lord deliver me from Sir Henry Vane." He was an able and incorruptible leader of the Parliament and had to suffer for it on the Restoration when he was one of the few excluded from the Act of Indemnity, and was executed on Tower Hill, bearing himself so hiavely that Pepys, who was present, recorded it as miraculous. His body was given to his relatives and he was buried here at Shipbourne not far from Hadlow, his father's native place. According to a local tradition he was wont to haunt o' nights the neighbourhood of the Fairlawn yews, between here and Plaxtol, strolling about with his head under his arm.

From the neighbouring country a conspicuous object is the tall tower of the modern Hadlow Castle in a park containing some noble cedars, and going north-easterly from here, with the grand extent of the Hurst and Mereworth Woods—in which wild swine still flourished in Elizabeth's reign—occupying the high ground in front of us, we get to West and East Peckham; the villages are pleasant places neighbouring Mereworth and in the same lovely wooded district. At East Peckham is buried Sir Roger Twysden in whose journal—printed in the earlier volumes of the *Archæologia Cantiana*—we get much information about social life and public affairs in the days of the triumphant Parliament. He lived at Roydon Hall here and suffered as some other men of like opinions in Kent did

during the whole of the Civil War and Commonwealth periods;
for some years indeed he was imprisoned, with but occasional
intervals of freedom on bail; the whole story of his relations
with the Parliament, and of the spoliation of his estate is set
forth in his "Journal." Sir Roger Twysden and Sir Edward
Dering were summoned to the bar of the House of Commons
as early as 1642 for being concerned in a petition against
the conduct of Parliament, and a minor poet of the time
wrote :

> "Ask me not why The House delights
> Not in our two wise Kentish Knights;
> Their counsel never was thought good
> Because they were not understood."

Poor Sir Roger had continuous trouble with the " House "
and its agents, had his woods felled, his goods taken, and
large sums to pay before he got clear. Here is his list of
"things caryed out of my house in East Peckham by ye
Troopers" on one occasion.

" A saddle.
2 or 3 byts, gyrts, snaffles, styrrops, and all of yt kind they met with.
Nurse her lased handkerchiefe.
Wm. Sparks' shirts, 3 bands, 4s 8d in money, a boxe in sylver out of my
wive's closet.
Captayn Vaughan's two-handed sword.
A glove of male.
A booke and a payr of compasses.
A payr of Pystol cases, a combe, and a book or two of Ward's.
A little dagger, two belts, and gyrdles.
2 little bookes of waxe candles."

Going down to the Medway again we may, after passing
through Hale Street, turn to the right by way of a number
of scattered hamlets near the left bank, and crossing the
little Shode which flows from the neighbourhood of Ightham
through the pretty break in the downs known as the Shode
valley, pass Hadlow and Golden Green, and so come again
to the Tonbridge Road. This shows us part of a very
attractive stretch of the Medway valley rich in orchards and
hop gardens, giving evidence of the fertility of the land, that it
is sometimes known as " The Garden of Eden," to suggest
perhaps that it is the finest portion of that Garden of England,
which is Kent. Crossing the Medway to the south of Hale

Street we may make for Paddock Wood, a more or less new town grown up about the railway junction. It was here, according to Canon Benham, that Carker met with his terrible death as told in " Dombey and Son," the station being then a lonely place, " the small town that was nearest being some miles away." That " small town " would have been Brenchley, a delightful village with picturesque timbered cottages, a place presumably of some importance in the long past as the site of an old castle of which nothing now remains beyond the mound

Brenchley.

on which it stood, not far from the landmark clump of tall trees locally known as Brenchley Toll. Brenchley was particularly unfortunate in the destructive storm of 1703 for as one Mr. Thomas Figg wrote at the time :—

"A stately steeple, whose altitude exceeded almost, if not all in Kent, the height whereof, according to various computations, it never in my knowledge being exactly measured, did amount at least to 10 rods, some say 12, and others more ; yet this strong and noble structure, by the rage of the winds, was levelled with the ground, and made the sport and pastime of boys and girls, who to future ages, though perhaps incredibly, yet can boast they leaped over such a steeple ; the fall thereof beat down great part of the church and porch, the damage of which to repair, as before, will not amount to less than £800 or £1,000. This is the public loss ; neither does private and particular much less bemoan their condition, for some houses and some barns, with other buildings, are quite demolished ; though blessed be God, not many lives or limbs lost in the fall, and not one house but suffered greatly by the tempest."

On the wooded byways between here and the Wells—with views to the north over our lovely Medway valley and southward to the woods of Sussex about Bayham Abbey—are the hamlets of Matfield Green (where Harrison Weir lived) and Kippings Cross and the old village of Pembury. Turning back towards the Medway the main road will take us along the grand extent of the Pembury Woods to Somerhill and Tonbridge ; but for the pedestrian, or for those cyclists who prefer the generally greater beauty of the byways before the smoothness of the highways there is metal more attractive through well farmed country and diversified woodlands to Capel, Five Oak Green and Crockhurst Street and Tudeley. In both Capel and Tudeley churches are altar tombs to the Kentish Fanes—a branch of the same family we saw as Vanes in the north of this district at Hadlow and Shipbourne.

With noblemen's and gentlemen's seats where rank and fashion, wit and beauty gathered during the hey-day of the Wells, the whole of this district is dotted, and its hillsides are covered with grand woodlands, while " marvelus fair ground champain and fruteful ground of corn " mark the course of the Medway through this western part of Kent. People brought up among loftier hills and wide moorlands tell me that they tire of this rich scenery as of vast parklands and gardens, but to those who have come under its spell it has a perennial charm in its round, timber-grown hills, its well farmed valleys, its shady lanes and unfrequented footpaths.

CHAPTER XVI

THE very name of Penshurst, even to those who do not know the pleasant village and the stately pile of Tudor buildings, is redolent of memories : it brings up thoughts of various members of that great and gracious family which has given many interesting and picturesque figures to our history—of poets, statesmen and soldiers, fair women and brave men ; above all, it reminds us of that romantic Crichton, the author of the "Arcadia," the hero of Zutphen—Sir Philip Sidney—of the martyred Algernon Sidney, of Waller's "Sacharissa," and of the lady elegised by William Browne or Ben Jonson—

> " Underneath this sable hearse
> Lies the subject of all verse,
> Sidney's sister, Pembroke's mother,
> Death ! ere thou hast slain another
> Learned, fair and good as she,
> Time shall throw a dart at thee."

Easily to be reached from Tonbridge or The Wells, Penshurst has a station of its own about two miles north of the village, but whether approached from that direction or from the Tonbridge road we get a good view of the grand old castellated house. From the former direction we see the north front and western side over the sunk fences which divide the park from the road and the lawns surrounding the house from the park. The best way of approach for those who are influenced by the "spirit of place" is by the road coming down the hill from the further side of Medway, past the remnant of the Ashover Wood of which Ben Jonson sang as providing for the Sidneys' " open table,"

" The purpled pheasant with the speckled side."

Coming up from the Medway bridge into attractive Penshurst—a place which seems to rest comfortably in an atmo-
sphere of antique distinction—we reach at once the
beginning of the village, the entrance to the churchyard and
the footpath way to the mansion, for village, church, and
mansion lie in close and friendly proximity. A couple of old-
style stone and timber cottages (one of them the village post
office) stand at the top of some steps on the right bank ; between
them is the gnarled remnant of a mighty elm and the path
to the churchyard under part of a really beautiful old timbered
cottage. The glimpse of the churchyard through this opening
is peculiarly pleasant when the sun is shining on the turf and
tombs and formal yews, while the way through which we look
is cut off by deep shadow. Entering this small but impressive " acre " we see that it is divided from the gardens of
Penshurst Place by a wall immediately on our right, with a
gateway through which generations of Sidneys have passed to
worship in the church of which their tombs form one of the
most notable features. To the left of the church goes a footpath giving access to the park, passing near to the western
side and leading to a fine view of the great crenellated grey
stone front close-covered with ivy, above which show many
irregular Tudor chimneys. Approaching by the park entrance
we reach the old gateway over which is a stone inscribed with
the story of the acquisition of " Pencester," as it was anciently
named.—

" The most Religious and Renowned Prince Edward *the sixt*, Kinge
Of *England, France* and *Ireland*, gave this House of *Pencester* with
The Mannors, Landes, and Appurtenances thereunto belonginge
Unto his trustye and welbeloved servaunt Syr *William Sydney*, Knight
Banneret, serving him from the tyme of his Birth unto his
Coronation in the Offices of Chamberlayn and Steward of his
Household ; in commemoration of which most worthie and famous Kinge
Sir Henrye Sydney, Knight of the most Noble Order of the Garter,
Lord President of the Councill, established in the Marches of
Wales, Sonne and Heyre to the aforenamed Syr *William*
Caused this Tower to be buylded, and that most excellent
Princes Armes to be erected—*Anno Domini*, 1585."

Before being acquired by the Sidneys the place was about two hundred years old, having been built by that famous citizen of London, Sir John de Pulteney, four times Lord Mayor, and having changed owners earlier, while earlier still the estate had belonged to the Penchester or Pencestre family. To-day, however, it is with Sir John de Pulteney that the interest in the place begins for us, as amid all the changes and additions which the mansion has undergone his great hall remains unchanged, one of our most perfectly preserved examples of its kind in the country. In it we see the " Hall " of feudal times ; here is still the raised dais with the table for the family, in front of it the open hearth with its great andirons on which huge logs blazed, the smoke passing away through an opening surmounted by a turret—now done away with—in the high timbered roof ; down either side long oaken tables for the retainers, and at the eastern end the minstrels' gallery and entrances to the buttery and kitchens. With nothing but these plain ancient furnishings and a few horns on the wall above the dais it is easy to picture it as the centre of mediæval feudal life,—to see the floor rush-strewn, the gaily garbed people, the cook and his henchmen entering with the boar's head and other steaming dishes and passing to where the lord sat at the raised table with his family and honoured friends. Here, runs the tradition, the Black Prince and his wife, the Fair Maid of Kent, once held their Christmas feast.

The hall, as has been said, is the original centre of the place, but around it successive generations of owners have grouped building after building—much of the long north front was added little more than half a century ago—but the work has always been carried out with careful regard to tradition, and the result is a magnificent and pleasing whole. It is easy to believe that the most romantic of the Sidneys had this his birthplace in view when he described the home of Kalander :

"The house itself was built of fair and strong stone, not affecting so much any extraordinary kind of fineness as an honorable representing of a firm stateliness ; the lights, doors and stairs rather directed to the use of the guest than to the eye of the artificer, and yet as the one chiefly heeded, so the other not neglected ; each place handsome without curiosity, and homely without loathsomeness ; not so dainty as not to be trod on, nor yet slubbered up with good fellowship ; all more lasting than beautiful, but that the consideration of the exceeding lastingness made the eye believe it was exceeding beautiful."

Other descriptive passages in "The Arcadia" may well have been inspired by Penshurst and its surroundings.

The galleries of Penshurst Place with their many portraits of famous people by Vandyck, Zucchero, Douw and other great

Penshurst.

artists, their old furniture, carved panellings, and tapestries are almost too crowded with matters of interest for the visitor to get more than a confused idea of their richness; curious cabinets and wonderful china—one small room has the walls entirely covered with priceless porcelain—are pointed out, all things having an association with the historic past of the mansion. For details of such the visitor must consult a special guide-book. From the end of the gallery in which hang portraits of Sir Philip Sidney and of Queen Elizabeth is to be had a beautiful view of the formal flower gardens.

In itself and in its associations Penshurst has been the inspiration of more poetry than perhaps any similar place—Ben Jonson, Waller, Southey, Elizabeth Barrett Browning, Mr. Swinburne, these are but some of those who have sung of the Sidneys and their beautiful Kentish home. If the famous epitaph, already cited, was not written by "Rare Ben Johnson"[1] there is no doubt about the authorship of his tribute to the place where the lady elegised belonged. He sang of the lavish hospitality of Penshurst as one who had enjoyed it.

> " Thou art not, Penshurst, built to envious show
> Of touch or marble ; nor canst boast a row
> Of polished pillars or a roof of gold :
> Thou hast no lantern, whereof tales are told ;
> Or stair, or courts ; but stand'st an ancient pile,
> And these grudged at, are reverenced the while.
> Thou joy'st in better marks, of soil, of air,
> Of wood, of water ; therein thou art fair.
> Thou hast thy walks for health, as well as sport :
> Thy mount, to which thy Dryads do resort,
> Where Pan and Bacchus their high feasts have made,
> Beneath the broad beech and the chestnut shade ;
> That taller tree, which of a nut was set,
> At his great birth, where all the muses met.
> There, in the writhed bark, are cut the names
> Of many a sylvan taken with his flames ;
> And thence the ruddy satyrs oft provoke
> The lighter fauns to reach thy lady's oak. . . .
> Now, Penshurst, they that will proportion thee
> With other edifices, when they see
> Those proud ambitious heaps, and nothing else,
> May say, their lords have built, but thy lord dwells."

Of the trees which Jonson mentions, that which was said to mark the birth, "at a quarter before five of the clock," of Sir Philip Sidney on the morning of November 30th, 1554, has probably long since gone. It was presumably a chestnut which stood near what is now known as " Sir Philip Sidney's oak," a tree the starting of which dates further back than Sidney's birth,

---

[1] I quote from the wall of Westminster Abbey, and not from misquoters innumerable.

and properly known as the Bear Oak, as the Hon. Mary Sidney
tells us—"the retainers wore sprigs of this tree in their hats
when they went to meet the Earl of Leicester at the entrance
of the Park at Leigh on their return from London."[1]

Edmund Waller's poetic adoration of the Lady Dorothy
Sidney, his "Sacharissa," in the generation following that of Jonson, gives us further tributes to Penshurst—two different poems
are entitled "At Pens-Hurst," though quotations from them are
frequently run together as though they came from one. In the
first piece Waller declared that when the Lady went into a wood
it became a garden at once "embroider'd so with flowers,"
while

> "If she sit down, with tops all tow'rds her bow'd
> They round about her into arbors crowd :
> Or if she walks, in even ranks they stand
> Like some well-marshal'd and obsequious band. . . .
> Ye lofty beeches, tell this matchless dame,
> That if together ye fed all one flame,
> It could not equalise the hundredth part,
> Of what her eyes have kindled in my heart.
> Go, boy, and carve this passion on the bark
> Of yonder tree, which stands the sacred mark
> Of noble Sidney's birth."

The lofty beeches which long retained the name of "Sacharissa's
Walk" have gone, but another notable avenue still existing is
that of the Lime Walk from the eastern end of the lawns down
to the stables—magnificent trees supposed to have been planted
by Robert, Lord Leicester, nephew of Sir Philip Sidney. This
avenue, the inner branches meeting overhead, the outer sweep-
ing nearly to the turfy sides, humming with myriad bees, and
offering deep shade when the park is brilliant in sunshine and
the air is to be seen quivering with heat above the gravel drive,
is a lovely monument to the father of "Sacharissa." The
artificiality of the poet is seen in sending his boy to carve the
letters on the tree—Sidney would not thus have delegated the
honouring of his lady.

After Waller's time Sir Philip was restored to his place as
the central figure in the associations of Penshurst. As Southey
asks—

[1] *Historical Guide to Penshurst Place*, 1903. The Warwick device of
the Bear and Ragged Staff will be noticed as occurring frequently in
Penshurst decorations ; it was adopted by Sir Henry Sidney on his
marriage in 1552 with Lady Mary Dudley.

> " Are days of old familiar to thy mind,
>   O reader ?   Hast thou let the midnight hour
> Pass unperceived, whilst thou in fancy lived
> With high-born beauties, and enamoured chiefs,
> Sharing their hopes, and with a breathless joy,
> Whose expectation touched the verge of pain,
> Following their dangerous fortunes ?   If such love
> Hath ever thrilled thy bosom, thou wilt tread,
> As with a pilgrim's reverential thoughts,
> The groves of Penshurst.   Sidney here was born,
> Sidney than whom no greater, braver man
> His own delightful genius ever feigned
> Illustrating the groves of Arcady
> With courteous courage and with loyal love."

To Elizabeth Barrett Browning it was Sir Philip and Sacharissa
who appealed when she visited here and wrote " The Picture
Gallery at Penshurst,"—

> " There, I beheld the Sidneys :—he, who bled
> Freely for freedom's sake, bore gallantly
> His soul upon his brow ;—he, whose lute said
> Sweet music to the land, meseem'd to be
> Dreaming with that pale face, of love and Arcadie."

Mr. Swinburne too, in that wonderful word-music of his, has
sung of " Astrophel "—

> " O light of the land that adored thee
>   And kindled thy soul with her breath,
> Whose life such as fate would afford thee,
>   Was lovelier than aught but thy death,
> By what name, could thy lovers but know it,
>   Might love of thee hail thee afar,
> Philisides, Astrophel, poet
>   Whose love was thy star ? "

A rich anthology might be made of the poems inspired by
Penshurst and its people.

It is impossible to tell of all the Sidneys associated with the
place but Sir Philip belongs peculiarly to it not only as the
most famous owner, as the one whose name, as typical of all
that is noble and chivalrous, has become familiar in our mouths
as household words, but in that it was here that he was born
and here he probably passed his earliest days.   Of those early
days there is unfortunately no record, but amongst the Penshurst
MSS. is an account kept by one Thomas Marshall showing that
at Shrewsbury school during nine months 1565–6 the twelve-

year-old boy's expenses amounted to £40 0s. 3d. The account is kept with minute carefulness and includes such items as the following :

"For a yard of cloth to make Mr. Philip a pair of boot-hose, having none but a pair of linen which were too thin to ride in after his disease, 3*s*. 4*d*.

For making these boot-hose and for stitching silk, 1*s*. 6*d*.

For a pen and inkhorn and sealing-wax, 6*d*.

For two quires of paper for example books, 8*d*.

For an ounce of oil of roses and another of calomel to supple his knee, which he could not ply or bend, 6*d*.

For wax to burn in the school a-morning before day, 4*d*.

For perfumes to air his chamber with after the young gentlemen were recovered, 12*d*."

The story of Sir Philip's after life—he was an "ubiquitary" said Fuller—his position at the Court of Elizabeth, his interest in the New World expeditions, his death on the field of Zutphen before completing his thirty-second year, does not belong here, nor does an appreciation of his writings, his long and fascinating romance of "Arcadia," his sonnet sequence- "Astrophel and Stella," or his other poems. Men in those spacious days seem to have had "crowded hours of glorious life"; Sir Philip having but reached early manhood had won lasting fame in many fields, and then even by his death added yet other claims on our remembrance—by his foolhardy throwing off of his armour that he might not be better protected than his friend in the fight ; by his passing on of a cup of water to a wounded soldier, "Friend, thy need is greater than mine" ; by his dying words, "I would not change my joy for the empire of the world." Here at the home of the Sidneys we cannot but regret that this man in whom were focussed the family gifts was not buried in Penshurst Church ; but St. Paul's Cathedral claimed him and his tomb was destroyed in the Great Fire of London. "Rest, then, in Peace, Oh, Sidney, we will not celebrate your memory with tears but admiration ; whatever we loved in you, whatever we admired in you, still continues, and will continue in the memories of men, the revolutions of ages and the annals of time." The *Vale* of Camden expressed the sentiment which the name of Sir Philip is likely long to evoke.

Another noted Sidney was the patriot Algernon, who was not born at Penshurst like his great uncle but unlike him is buried there. Algernon Sidney as a convinced Republican sided with the Parliament in the great struggle of his time and bore an active part in it. When the trial of Charles I. took place Algernon Sidney was appointed one of the commissioners to try him, but bore himself so independently that it is a wonder that he continued to stand as well as he did during the Protectorate. His own account of the matter was given in a letter to his father written nearly a dozen years later—

"I was at Penshurst when the act for the trial passed, and, coming up to town, I heard my name was put in, and that those who were nominated for judges were then in the Painted Chamber. I presently went thither, heard the act read, and found my own name with others. A debate was raised how they should proceed upon it, and, after having been sometimes silent to hear what those would say who had the directing of that business, I did positively oppose Cromwell, Bradshaw and others, who would have the trial to go on, and drew my reasons from these two points : First, the King could be tried by no court ; secondly, that no man could be tried by that court. This being alleged in vain, and Cromwell using these formal words, 'I tell you we will cut off his head with the crown upon it,' I replied, 'You may take your own course, I cannot stop you, but I will keep myself clear from having my hand in this business. And immediately went out of the room and never returned."

A man of extraordinary courage and consistent sincerity Algernon Sidney was suspected during the Commonwealth, and after the Restoration his known anti-monarchical opinions led to his being arrested on the flimsiest excuse after he had come from abroad and to his execution on Tower Hill in 1682 for alleged complicity in the Rye House Plot. A less sincere man would probably have returned to the Royalist ranks after his quarrel with the regicides, or would have sought to make his peace on the Restoration. When it was complained that his scruples were extravagant and overstrained he replied " I cannot help it if I judge amiss. I walk in the light God hath given me ; if it be dim or uncertain I must bear the penalty of my errors." The "unconquered patriot" met his fate with extraordinary heroism and after his execution the body was given to his family and was duly interred in the Sidney vault in Penshurst Church.

Algernon Sidney's brother, Henry, Earl of Romney, became Master of the Ordnance to William III., and it is said that his family heraldic charge, the pheon, is the origin of the now familiar "broad arrow." The story runs that in his official position he found so many public stores, &c., going astray for want of a uniform stamp that he used his heraldic pheon for the purpose, and since, conventionalised, this has become the common Government mark. The wanderer about country places will come across broad-arrow inscribed stones in all manner of places, the mark having been placed by officials engaged in the Ordnance Survey. Another account, however, says that the mark arose from a broad barbed arrow or javelin being carried before royalty, while yet another says that the mark as employed by the Survey is a kind of hieroglyphic to de-note the points from which trigonometrical measurements have been made. At Penshurst we may well believe the first version.

The church which, as has been said, stands close to the Place in a small but beautiful churchyard has been much restored (by Sir Gilbert Scott), but a small portion of it, being more than a century older than Sir John de Pulteney's great hall, is probably part of the church built by one of the Penchesters about 1200. Within are a number of interesting monuments and brasses, the Sidney tombs claiming, as might be expected, a goodly share of attention. Here, as in a few other old places in our county, there is a surviving link with the past in the custom of ringing the Curfew bell each evening from Michael-mas to Lady Day.

Before leaving the staid and comfortable village the tasteful new stone Village Hall and Club should be visited, as this seems a model of what such places should be—simple yet dignified and pleasing in architectural appearance.

Just to the north of Penshurst Park, on the further side of the railway, is Leigh—pronounced locally " Lie "—a village with a pleasant green and many neat cottages built in the olden manner. At the mansion of Hall Place here lived for some years, and died in 1886, Samuel Morley, a politician and philanthropist, summed up as one who "had all the busi-ness talents of a man of this world and all the warmth of heart and piety of a man of the next." In the church is an undated brass of a character sufficiently unusual to call for mention here ; it represents the half figure of a female rising from an altar tomb in which the body is shown clad in a shroud. She is saying, " Behold, o lord, I com willingly," while the tomb is inscribed, " Farre well all ye Tell you come to me."

Immediately to the west of Penshurst Park is the estate of Redleaf, long celebrated for its beautiful gardens, with the Eden —here considerably widened—flowing along its western side. The confluence of the Eden and the Medway is a little below the Penshurst bridge. Further west again is the beautiful little village of Chiddingstone, one of the most unmodernised of old places we have to show. Its line of timbered houses near the church is unspoiled by the close contiguity of any new ones, and its butchers' shop, with an opening in the side wall up an alley way, by way of a "shop front," is an interesting survival. In the Park at the back of this attractive village "street" is a great boulder of sandstone known as the Chiding Stone, traditionally the source of the name of the parish, and said to have been a Druidical judgment-seat. Those matter-of-fact folk who would destroy all our cherished illusions point out that the rock is probably in its natural position though admitting that it may have been utilised as a gathering-place for the neighbourhood at important crises.

Beyond Chiddingstone the branching road may be followed north across the Eden, and by the hamlet of Bough Beech above the long, deep railway cutting, towards the wooded Sevenoaks range, from which the clump of trees on eight-hundred-feet-high Toy's ("Ties") Hill shows out as a bold landmark, or south-westerly to Markbeech. In either case the next point of special attraction to most people will be Hever Castle of romantic memories.

Long left more or less neglected, and partly used as a farmhouse, Hever, a few years ago, was purchased by Mr. William Waldorf Astor, and has been so restored and added to, that it starts upon a renewed lease of life as one of the noblest old residences that Kent has to show. I do not propose to discuss the general question of the restoration of ancient buildings, though the thick-and-thin opponents of all such architectural restoration would apparently let a thing crumble to nothing rather than allow the renewal of decayed portions and the whole thus to last for future generations. It is a struggle between sentiment and common-sense, and certainly common-sense seems to have the better argument. Hever Castle was a more or less neglected ruin ; it is a restored mansion full of interest, the restoration being carried out with careful attention to the history of the structure. So careful, indeed, has the attention to detail been, that the modern transverse oak flooring of a corridor was not allowed to remain, because in the olden days such timbers were never put any way but longitudinally. Now the Castle has been restored, and the new owner has built a veritable village of "guest houses" in its immediate neighbourhood. These are all designed in the Tudor style, and are connected by a bridge and subway with the old stone main edifice. The River Eden has here been widened into a lake, and an extensive tract of land enclosed as a deer park.

Hever Castle was built in the days when the nobleman's strongly fortified residence was gradually giving way to the fine mansion—Penshurst marked a further stage in this evolution— and thus its main defence was in its broad moat and its embattled entrance and portcullis. But little remains of the castellated house built by Sir William de Hevre in the reign of the third Edward, and our interest in the place begins with the purchase of the estate and commencement of the present castle, in the thirty-seventh year of the reign of Henry VI., by Sir Geoffrey Boleyn, who had been Lord Mayor of London. From him it descended to his grandson, Sir Thomas Boleyn, whose daughter Anne was born just four hundred years ago. What was that fateful woman's birthplace has not been ascertained, but Hever is one of the places claiming that distinction. There seems no doubt, however, that here she passed her childhood, and here she may have been wooed by Sir Thomas Wyatt, before the poet had to give way to the Prince, and here, certainly, Henry VIII. visited her during the years of their strange courtship; indeed one tradition says that it was in the Castle gardens that Henry and Anne first met. Certainly here he addressed to her some of those love-letters breathing a fervid strain to which the tragic close of Anne's life seems an impossible sequel. Here are two of those letters, the one accompanying a present, the second acknowledging one—

" My mistress and friend, my heart and I surrender ourselves into your hands, beseeching you to hold us commended to your favour, and that by absence your affection to us may not be lessened : for it were a great pity to increase our pain, of which absence produces enough and more than I could ever have thought could be felt, reminding us of a point in astronomy which is this : the longer the days are, the more distant is the sun, and nevertheless the hotter ; so is it with our love, for by absence we are kept a distance from one another, and yet it retains its fervour, at least on my side ; I hope the like on yours, assuring you that on my part the pain of

absence is already too great for me ; and when I think of the increase of
that which I am forced to suffer, it would be almost intolerable, but for the
nrm hope I have of your unchangeable affection for me : and to remind
you of this sometimes, and seeing that I cannot be personally present with
you, I now send you the nearest thing I can to that, namely, my picture
set in a bracelet, with the whole of the device, which you already know,
wishing myself in their place, if it should please you. This is from the
hand of your loyal servant and friend.

H. R."

" For a present so beautiful that nothing could be more so (considering
the whole of it), I thank you most cordially, not only on account of the
fine diamond and the ship in which the solitary damsel is tossed about, but
chiefly for the fine interpretation and the too humble submission which
your goodness hath used towards me in this case : for I think it would be
very difficult for me to find an occasion to deserve it, if I were not assisted
by your great humanity and favour, which I have always sought to seek,
and will seek to preserve by all the kindness in my power, in which my
hope has placed its unchangeable intention, which says, *Aut illic, aut
nullibi.*

The demonstrations of your affection are such, the beautiful mottoes of
the letter so cordially expressed, that they oblige me for ever to honour,
love, and serve you sincerely, beseeching you to continue in the same firm
and constant purpose, assuring you that, on my part, I will surpass it
rather than make it reciprocal, if loyalty of heart and a desire to please
you can accomplish this.

I beg, also, if at any time before this I have in any way offended you,
that you would give me the same absolution that you ask, assuring you
that henceforward my heart shall be dedicated to you alone. I wish my
person was so too. God can do it, if He pleases, to whom I pray every
day for that end, hoping that at length my prayers will be heard. I wish
the time may be short, but I shall think it long till we see one another.

Written by the hand of that secretary, who in heart, body, and will is,
\our loyal and most assured servant,

H. aultre  ne cuerse R."

Of Anne herself the most varied accounts are given. To
some writers she owed her fate to the ambition of her father,
which led him to sacrifice his daughter to the passion of a
rapacious tyrant ; to others she was just an ambitious woman
herself, sacrificing everything to becoming Queen ; then, again,
she is sometimes referred to as a most beautiful woman, while
the Venetian Ambassador wrote of her—with the license, let us
hope, of one sent to lie abroad for the good of his country—

that "Madame Anne is not one of the handsomest women in the world. She is of middling stature, swarthy complexion, long neck, wide mouth, bosom not much raised, and has in fact nothing but the King's great appetite and her eyes, which are black and beautiful." Against this may be set the description of "the rare and admirable beauty of the fresh and young lady" by her avowed admirer Wyatt, from which we may gather that it was not so much regularity of features and delicacy of colouring as the *je-ne-sais-quoi* of beauty which captivated her various admirers. " In this noble imp," says he, "the graces of nature graced by a gracious education seemed even at first to have promised bliss unto hereafter times. She was taken at that time to have a beauty not so whitly clear and fresh, above all we may esteem, which appeared much more excellent by her favour passing sweet and cheerful, and these both also increased by her noble presence of shape and fashion, representing both mildness and majesty more than can be expressed."

Seeing the destiny of the young beauty of Hever—long wooed by a king already married, then raised to the dizzy height of Queen, only after a brief reign to lose her head on Tower Hill—it is not to be wondered at that a local superstition declared that her ghost haunted the place of her happy girlhood. The ghost was said to cross the bridge over the Eden each Christmastide. I have not heard of any recent appearance. Hever Castle too is said to have had another ghost—the shrouded spirit of a farmer named Humphrey who had been robbed and killed in the neighbourhood ; this uncanny manifestation—so runs the story—was effectually laid by the Rector with the aid of a bowl of Red Sea water !

Hever was, on the death of Anne's father, taken over by the King, who bestowed it on his ill-favoured and repudiated Queen Anne of Cleves, who is said by unsupported tradition to have died here. The most conclusive proof that she did so was that her death chamber was long pointed out.

Hever Church stands, as a number of our Kentish churches do, at an angle of the road in the village and near it is the ugly red-brick entrance to the drive leading down to the renovated Castle. The church is on a small eminence so that its spire forms a landmark for some distance round. In the Boleyn Chapel is the ornate brass to the memory to Anne

Boleyn's father, the unhappy man whose ambition was so realised that he saw his daughter crowned only to see her shortly afterwards, and his son also, executed. He survived them less than two years, the inscription on his tomb running, " Here lieth Sir Thomas Bullen Knight of the Order of the Garter Erle of Wilscher and Erle of Ormunde wiche decessed the twelve dai of Marche in the iere of our Lorde 1538." It must have been a melancholy ending for the man who had shone so long at courts, though his faithful steward wrote that "he made the end of a good Christian man, ever remembering the goodness of Christ."

A couple of miles or so west of Hever is Edenbridge, near to the Surrey border, where another Kent Brook, before its junction with the Eden, forms the county boundary. Edenbridge is a small, unattractive town mostly scattered along the high road ; south and north of it the country rises through varied and well wooded scenery, in the one direction to Markbeech, Cowden and the Sussex border, in the other to Crockham and its wooded hill, at the further side of which lies Westerham. From the summit of Crockham Hill we have an extensive view not only of the valley from which we have risen but across it into Sussex and westerly into Surrey.

CHAPTER XVII

AT Westerham we are at the head of the valley of the Darent, coming over into which from that of the Eden we can cross the range of sandstone hills at its highest part—the whole of it from the county boundary at Kent Hatch to beyond Sevenoaks. being rarely less than five hundred feet above the sea, and the highest point, a couple of miles to the south-west of Westerham, being just over eight hundred feet and the highest bit of our county. This is Toy's Hill, from which a rapidly descending road to Brasted may be followed over The Chart—properly so named, for though we have many " Charts "[1] in the county, this is the most extensive—or a delightful footpath way may take us by the strangely named hamlet of French Street and Chartsedge to Westerham. At Chartsedge lived for many years, and died in 1848, a zealous delver into Kentish history, the Rev. Thomas Streatfield, who had projected a large " History of Kent," to be published in ten folio parts at two guineas each, had amassed much material for this work, but did not live to write it. Those materials—forming fifty-two volumes—are now in the British Museum. From the less lofty Crockham Hill we cross pine-grown commons to Westerham. Before going down into the valley a visit should be paid to the ragstone quarries here.

Westerham is a clean-looking pleasant town with narrow approaches giving on to a broad main street above which

---

[1] Chart—"a rough common, overrun with gorse, broom, bracken." Parish and Shaw's *Dictionary of Kentish Dialect*.

stands the church, a centre of interest for several reasons. Here, from the eastern end of the edifice, is to be had a beautiful view along the narrow valley which is bounded on the north by the hilly country of the chalk and on the south by that of the sand with their markedly different characters. Within, the church has brasses and other monuments to show the curious in such matters, and a local memorial to Westerham's acknowledged most famous son, General James Wolfe, the

Westerham Church.

conqueror of Quebec.   The Westerham folk m the inscription recognise Wolfe's pre-eminence in their town annals—

> " With humble grief inscribe one artless stone,
>   And from thy matchless honours date our own. "

Wolfe was born at the vicarage house here, on January 2nd, 1727, and a cenotaph in the grounds of Squerryes Court marks the spot on which he received his first commission.   It was hither that Mr. Henry Esmond Warrington rode from

Oakhurst with Colonel Lambert ; here he stayed the night with Colonel Wolfe's people and hence he rode on the following morning to Tunbridge Wells with that brilliant young officer—"that tallow-faced Put with the carroty hair," as vinous Jack Morris described him—as is pleasantly set out in the twenty-fourth chapter of the romance of " The Virginians," already referred to in the previous chapter.

Other famous folk born at Westerham were John Frith, the friend of Tyndale, burned at Smithfield on July 4th, 1533, and the worthy and wordy Bishop Benjamin Hoadley (1676). In fiction too the town has a place besides that in Thackeray's romance, for near here, as Jane Austen's admirers may like to be reminded, was the parsonage of Mr. Collins—a kind of clerical Uriah Heep—whose courting is recounted in some of the amusing early chapters of " Pride and Prejudice " and at whose humble residence Elizabeth Bennett visited him and the friend who, on her refusal, had caught his heart at the rebound.

The little Darent, Spenser's

"still Darent, in whose waters clean
Ten thousand fishes play, and deck his pleasant stream,"

rises in the grounds of Squerryes Court, and flows easterly by Brasted, Sundridge and Chipstead until it turns north and passes through a break in the chalk hills by Otford.

North of Westerham, across the valley, is the steep Westerham Hill crossed near its foot by the Pilgrims' Way—with hedges festooned by the Travellers' Joy. A chalk pit in the hillside forms a striking landmark all along the valley. To the north of this hill, on ground but a few feet lower, is the high-perched Cudham Church, centre of a widely scattered parish which has at its southern extremity a lonely place of gruesome memories from its association with a notorious tragedy of a generation ago. The westerly part of the parish, a few years since as quiet and retired a place as could be found within eighteen miles of London, has been invaded by suburban villadom. Cudham church dominates a wooded district, its spire a landmark for some distance, and a very extensive view is afforded from its churchyard in which are some magnificent old yews. On one occasion the vicar of Cudham was called upon to baptise four children " of the

same birth "—twinned twins—and the story runs that a boy
being sent to the clergyman to come and baptise "a parcel
of children," the Vicar inquired how many there were, and
the boy answered, "three when I came, but God knows how
many there may be before you get there!" The four were all
buried four days later.

Not far from Cudham on the higher part of the chalk overlooking the valley from which we have come is Knockholt, a
pleasant little village chiefly notable for its clump of tall
beeches (770 feet above sea level) occupying a small hollow
on the hill-top. In clear weather it is said that the dome of
St. Paul's Cathedral may be seen from this spot—but my
visits have never been in weather sufficiently clear for that. It
is also claimed that the dome-like clump itself has been
recognised—in like favourable climatic conditions—by westerly
observers from Leith Hill, in Surrey, and by northerly
observers from Harrow-on-the-Hill. The derivation of the
name of Knockholt, as of other places, has exercised the wits of
various people. Hasted suggested that it means, Noke or corner,
and holt or wood, while another ingenious person describes
the word as deriving from Ock-holt or Oak-wood, thus North
Ockholt = N. Ockholt = [K]nockholt!

Coming down into the valley again from Knockholt we
reach the fine expanse of Chevening Park once crossed by
the Pilgrims' Road, but at the lodge gate of which the modern
pilgrim is told that he may not pass but must go by the road
skirting the park—in other words, he must take three sides of a
square, and walk over two miles instead of little more than
half a mile to the small village of Chevening, the first village
on the ancient road, now a little used byway between wide
farmlands, since leaving the Surrey boundary near Titsey Hill.
The old way was closed by an Act of Parliament obtained by
the owner, Lord Stanhope, in 1780. At the time that that Act
was passed there was at Chevening the owner's little daughter
(who had been born there four years earlier) destined to make
a notable appearance in the world and to be remembered by
posterity as a clever eccentric. This was Lady Hester
Stanhope, whose childhood was passed here at Chevening.
When she was seven-and-twenty her uncle, the great William
Pitt, asked her to keep house for him and made her his
trusted confidant, though her eccentric ways and ready speech

caused comment on the part of some of Pitt's friends. His reply to such comment was, " I let her do as she pleases ; for if she were resolved to cheat the devil she could do it." Pitt's death in 1806 destroyed all Lady Hester's ambitions. In 1810 she, "Chatham's fiery granddaughter," went abroad, and four years later settled in a strange home on the slopes of Mount Lebanon, where she died "in proud isolation" in 1839, and where she was visited by A. W. Kinglake, as recorded in one of the most attractive chapters of that fascinating travel book, " Eothen."

Chevening Place, where this eccentric lady was born, was originally designed by Inigo Jones but has been greatly altered. The church, near the eastern entrance to the park, one of the few churches built actually on the course of the Pilgrims' Road, has many features of interest. Dunton Green, a little further east, is mostly a new place near the junction whence starts the branch railway to Westerham.

Returning to the south side of the Darent at the foot of the hills along which the stream flows we come a couple of miles from Westerham to Brasted, the place at which Napoleon III. stayed, and whence he set out in 1840 to make his descent upon France, a descent doomed to failure from the first and rendered ridiculous by the carrying with the expedition of a tame eagle. The difference between the symbolic eagle of Napoleon the Great and the tame eagle of his successor was the difference between the two men as seen in the light of history.

Sundridge, next along the road which here runs closely parallel with the Darent—thus early in its course utilised for serving a mill—is a pleasing little village. From Brasted to Sundridge the Darent flows through the lovely park of Combe Bank conspicuous for its noble trees. There used also to be an estate south of the village belonging to the Isley family—to several members of which there are old monuments in the church—but this was forfeited when the Isleys joined in Wyatt's Rebellion. Here lived an enthusiastic angler who made fish-ponds at this and other seats he owned, and he even went so far as to have fish-ponds made at the top of his house at Sundridge, as was set forth in a poem on " The Genteel Recreation," by John Whitney in 1700. When Walton wrote his book half a century earlier angling was the "Contemplative man's recreation"—the change from contemplation to gentility seems to mark the change between the mid-seventeenth century and the early eighteenth. The church with some fine trees about it stands near Sundridge Place above the village.

Combe Bank was long a seat of the Campbell family, and the Duke of Argyll sat in the House of Lords as Baron Sundridge until in 1892 Queen Victoria made him a Duke of the United Kingdom. Bishop Tenison of Ossory—not to be confused with his cousin the Archbishop—was rector here for a time and presented the brass chandelier to the church. Another cleric associated with the place was Beilby Porteus, Bishop of London, who was wont to retire here for the summer, and on his death in 1806 was, by his own request, buried here. At the age of twenty-eight Porteus won the Seatonian Prize for a poem on "Death" in which he lauded George II. in so fulsome a fashion that a century later he came in for severe castigation from Thackeray when the novelist was reviewing the unlovely days of "The Four Georges." This is how the future bishop wrote of "one who had neither dignity, learning, morals, nor wit—who tainted a great society by a bad example, who, in youth, manhood, old age, was gross, low, and sensual ":—

> " While at his feet expiring Faction lay,
> No contest left but—who should best obey ;
> Saw in his offspring all himself renewed ;
> The same fair path of glory still pursued ;
> Saw to young George Augusta's care impart
> Whate'er could raise and humanise the heart ;
> Blend all his grandsire's virtues with his own,
> And form their mingled radiance for the throne—
> No further blessing could on earth be given—
> The next degree of happiness was—heaven."

The most ardent upholder of the divine right of kings would admit that young Mr. Porteus *did* indulge in flattery, but at his grave we may remember rather his earnest work in the anti-slavery cause, his zeal for religious observance, his attempts to ameliorate the condition of the poorer clergy.

Perhaps a more attractive figure recalled by a visit to Sundridge Church is that of the Hon. Mrs. Anne Seymour Damer, the daughter of Horace Walpole's great friend, Field-

Marshal Conway, and herself a great "pet," and finally residuary legatee, of the famous dilettante and letter-writer. A granddaughter of the fourth Duke of Argyll, Mrs. Damer is not only buried here but she is represented by several evidences of her talent as sculptor, including the monument to her mother. As an "amateur fine lady" Mrs. Damer was overpraised by her contemporaries for her sculpture ; her best known work—the heads of Thames and Isis on the bridge at Henley-on-Thames—was especially lauded, and two of her busts were eulogised by Erasmus Darwin in—of all things—his " Economy of Vegetation "—

> " Long with soft touch shall Damer's chisel charm,
> With grace delight us and with beauty warm ;
> Foster's fine form shall hearts unborn engage,
> And Melbourne's smile enchant another age."

When Anne Seymour Conway was a child she was reproved by David Hume for laughing at the work of an Italian street sculptor, the philosopher adding that she should not laugh at that which she could not do. The girl was piqued and immediately modelled a head in wax and then proceeded to carve it in stone. One critic declared that her whole life as sculptor was spent in persistently trying to refute Hume's doubts of her ability !

Before the lady sculptor's time Mary Bellenden, the beautiful and lively Maid of Honour, who was offered and scorned the love of a Prince of Wales, and married one of the Grooms of his Bedchamber, Colonel Campbell, resided here and wrote hence some of those frank and spirited letters which admirably represent their time though they offended the sensitive John Wilson Croker. One of her letters may be given as showing the interest which the Court beauty took in home affairs.

"COMBE-BANK, *April* 10*th* (1723).

" How do you do, Mrs. Howard ? that is all I have to say—if my brain could have produced anything sooner, you should have heard from me. This afternoon I am taken with a fit of writing ; but as to matter, I have nothing better to entertain you with but to tell you the news of my farm. I therefore give you the following list of the stock of eatables that I am fatting for my private tooth. It is well known to the whole County of Kent, that I have four fat calves, two fat hogs fit for killing, twelve promising black pigs, four white sows big with child, for whom I have great compassion, ten young chickens, three fine geese, sitting with thirteen eggs under each (several being duck eggs, else the others do not come to maturity)—all this, with rabbits and pigeons, and carp, in plenty, beef and mutton at very reasonable rates—(this is writ very even). Now, Mrs. Howard, if you have a mind to stick your knife in anything I have named, say so. Nothing has happened here since I came worth mentioning in history, but a bloody retaliation committed on the body of an Owl that had destroyed our pigeons."

The beautiful Mary Bellenden, afterwards Campbell, died before she was forty, and her husband, quarter of a century after her death, succeeded to the Dukedom of Argyll. Her correspondent, "Mrs. Howard," was afterwards George the Second's Countess of Suffolk.

Chipstead is a pretty village on the Darent, just south of Chevening. Beyond, on the main London to Sevenoaks road, is Riverhead, where turning to the right past the parkland of Montreal, we may follow the road to Sevenoaks, the principal town of our district situated on high ground, though some distance below the summit of the range of hills. Montreal received its name from Sir Jeffrey Amherst, the conqueror of Canada, and capturer of Montreal in 1760.

Sevenoaks in itself has no special attractiveness apart from its position, but as a centre for beautiful walks it may vie with any others in the county. South and west are the wooded hills along the northern foot of which we have been coming— Sevenoaks Hill, Hubbard's Hill, Bayley's Hill, Ide Hill, Toy's Hill, Crockham Hill. This series of heights offers endless variety of quiet walks and magnificent views over the Weald, with only occasional retired hamlets, such as Goathurst and Ide Hill. Of the last named place, I have heard a Kentish servant girl speak when referring to a cake in which, as she thought, the currants were scanty, " I should think the baker stood on the top of Ide Hill and threw the currants in the dough." Eastwards the hills run at gradually lower elevations, broken by the valley through which the Ightham-born Shode runs southwards to join the Medway.

"Story! God bless you, I have none to tell, sir," has been the reply of Sevenoaks to topographical inquirers, and a century ago the town was described as " chiefly remarkable for the many good houses throughout it, and the respectability of the inhabitants," a character which may be endorsed by the latest visitors.

Despite its importance, Sevenoaks has no greater event recorded in its history than a fight between Jack Cade and his men in 1450, against a detachment of the King's army, fifteen hundred strong, when the rebels triumphed, and for a time sent dismay into the hearts of their opponents. Shakespeare makes the scene of the defeat of Sir Humphrey Stafford and his brother a part of Blackheath, but the success of Cade was really scored in the neighbourhood of this town, and that " headstrong Kentish man " enjoyed his brief hour of triumph here :

" *Cade.* Where's Dick, the butcher of Ashford ?
Dick. Here, sir.
Cade. They fell before thee like sheep and oxen, and thou behavedst thyself as if thou hadst been in thine own slaughter-house : therefore thus will I reward thee, the Lent shall be as long again as it is ; and thou shalt have a licence to kill for a hundred lacking one.
Dick. I desire no more.
Cade. And, to speak truth, thou deservest no less, this monument of the victory will I bear (putting on Sir Humphrey's brigandine) ; and the bodies shall be dragged at my horse's heels till I do come to London, where we will have the mayor's sword borne before us.
Dick. If we mean to thrive and do good, break open the gaols and let out the prisoners.
Cade. Fear not that, I warrant thee. Come, let's march towards London."

William Lambarde tells us that "about the latter end of the reign of King Edward the Third there was found (lying in the streets at Sennocke) a poor childe whose parents were unknown, and he (for the same cause) named, after the place that he was taken up, William Sennocke." This " wafe " came to be Sir William Sevenoke, Lord Mayor of London (1418), and a very wealthy man, who gratefully remembered the place of his origin by founding the Grammar School and almshouses there (rebuilt in the eighteenth century).

In a black-letter pamphlet of 1592, by Richard Johnson, which tells the stories of " The Nine Worthies of London," the third worthy is " Sir William Sevenoake, grocer, in the time of Henrie the Fift," and he is made to tell of his strange beginning, of his work as a grocer, of his joining Henry V. in his French wars and fighting with the Dauphin, of his return to grocerdom, and of his death. Three out of the sixteen stanzas may allow him to speak for himself in his native town—

Some monster that did envie nature's worke
(When I was borne in Kent) did cast me foorth
In desert wildes, where though no beast did lurke
To spoyle that life, the heavens made for woorth ;
　Under seaven oakes yet mischief flung me downe,
　Where I was found and brought unto a towne.

Behold an ebbe that never thought to flowe,
　Behold a fall unlikelie to recover ;
Behold a shrub, a weed, that grew full lowe,
　Behold a wren that never thought to hover :
　Behold how yet the Highest can commaund,
　And make a sand foundation firmelie stand. . .

By testament, in Kent I built a towne,
　And briefly calde it Seavenoake, from my name ;
A free schoole to sweete learning, to renowne,
　I placde for those that playde at honour's game ;
　Both land and living to that towne I gave,
　Before I took possession of my grave."

Mr. Johnson credits his "worthy" with building Sevenoaks, which is an exaggeration, for Sir William, by his testament, built but the free school and almshouses in the town.

The author of the " Perambulation of Kent," though he was born in London, died and was first buried at Greenwich, lies in Sevenoaks Church, whither his body was transferred by his son. Lambarde's will is a lengthy and interesting document, one notable feature of which brings home to us how slowly social observances change. Many people nowadays protest against funeral black, and here is Lambarde in 1597 saying :—

"my bodie I yeild to the earthe whereof yt is, to be buryed by the discretion of such as shall take the care thereof, but with this desire that my funerall be performed without blacke or feastinge."

The church in which the first of county historians lies is near the southern end and highest part of the town, forming a conspicuous landmark. The Lambarde chancel contains memorials to many other members of the family associated with Sevenoaks for three and a half centuries. An old seeker after the humour of tombstone inscriptions has recorded this one of Sevenoaks :

"Grim death took me without any warning,
I was well at night, and dead at nine in the morning."

Never was the uncertainty of human life put with more matter-of-fact simplicity. Another Kentish gravestone, which I have not been able to localise, was said a century ago to bear this inscription, made by a husband on the death of his second wife who happened to be buried next to his first one :

> ' Here lies the body of Sarah Sexton,
>   Who was a good wife, and never vext'd one :
>   I can't say that for her at the next stone."

Nearly opposite Sevenoaks church is the principal entrance to Knole—the magnificent park is about six miles in circumference, and has in its splendid mansion in the centre one of the noblest Tudor residences and one of the richest private treasure-houses in the Kingdom. Since Queen Elizabeth in 1566 granted the reversion of Knole to Thomas Sackville, Lord Buckhurst, afterwards first Earl of Dorset, the place has been famous, for it was on that nobleman's coming into the property in 1603 that the house was largely rebuilt, a couple of hundred men being engaged for two years over the work. Before coming to the Sackvilles, Knole had been one of the many palaces possessed by the Archbishops of Canterbury, having been purchased by Archbishop Bourchier in 1456 and attached by him to the see. Here successive primates entertained Henry VII. and Henry VIII. until Cranmer found it advisable to make it an item in the series of palatial presents which he made to his King.

Though considerably added to by the first of the Sackville owners much of the ancient edifice remains—including Bourchier's Chapel—in the picturesque pile of buildings with its many gables. It is a fitting centre to the grand park, some of the fine trees of which nearly neighbour the mansion. On certain days the chief treasure rooms of Knole are opened to the public and then the visitor may see it much as Horace Walpole saw it in 1752 :

" The outward court has a beautiful, decent simplicity that charms one. The apartments are many, but not large. The furniture throughout, ancient magnificence ; loads of portraits, not good nor curious ; ebony cabinets, embossed silver in vases, dishes, etc., embroidered beds, stiff chairs, and sweet bags lying on velvet tables, richly worked in silk and gold. There are two galleries, one very small ; an old hall, and a spacious great drawing-room. There is never a good staircase. The first little room you enter has sundry portraits of the times, but they seem to have been bespoke by the yard, and drawn all by the same painter ; one should

be happy if they were authentic ; for among them there is Dudley Duke of
Northumberland, Gardiner of Winchester, the earl of Surrey the poet,
when a boy, and a Thomas duke of Norfolk ; but I don't know which.
The only fine picture is of Lord Goring and Endymion Porter by Vandyke.
There is a good head of the queen of Bohemia, a whole length of duc
d'Espernon, and another good head of the Clifford countess of Dorset. . . .
In the chapel is a piece of ancient tapestry : saint Luke in his first profession. . . . Below stairs is a chamber of poets and players, which is proper
enough in that house ; for the first earl wrote a play, and the last earl was
a poet, and I think married a player."

Knole, it may be worth recalling, has been identified as the
" original " which Lord Beaconsfield had in mind when
describing Vauxe, the seat of Lord St. Jerome, in " Lothair."
It was in the gardens of Vauxe that, on Clare Arundel presenting
him with some violets and saying she could have brought him
primroses but did not like to mix the flowers, St. Jerome sapi-
ently remarked, " They say primroses make a capital salad."
In that line some historians see the germ that has converted
the anniversary of the death of the author of " Lothair " into
Primrose Day ! A striking piece of prophecy in this novel,
which has not so far as I am aware been noted, is that where
Clare Arundel, speaking as a Roman Catholic, says, " Had I that
command of wealth of which we hear so much in the present
day, and with which the possessors seem to know so little what
to do, I would purchase some of those squalid streets in Westminster, which are the shame of the metropolis, and clean a
great space and build a real cathedral." Little more than thirty
years after " Lothair " was written the beautiful Westminster
Cathedral was in existence.

It is not necessary here to give a guide to the " ancient magnificence " of Knole, but it is interesting to recall the two earls
mentioned in the closing words of the passage from Walpole's
description. The first, to whom Knole as it now is owes so
much, was famous as a statesmen and diplomatist, a man who
died at the age of eighty in 1608, leaving, as Robert Southey
tells us, " an unblemished memory in murderous times." It was
as statesman, as Lord High Steward and Lord Treasurer, that
Sackville was known by his contemporaries, but by posterity
he is recognised as the author of poems which, though few, are
singularly important. His " Induction to a Mirroure for Magistrates " has been described by Mr. Sidney Lee as having no
rival among the poems issued between Chaucer's " Canterbury

Tales " and Spenser's " Faerie Queue." Spenser, indeed, recognised Sackville's position and his own indebtedness to him, addressing one of the seventeen dedicatory sonnets prefixed to "The Faerie Queene " " to the Right Honourable the Lord of Buckhurst, one of her Majestie's Privie Counsell "—

> " In vain I thinke, right honorable Lord,
>   By this rude rime to memorize thy name,
> Whose learned Muse hath writ her own record
>   In golden verse, worthy immortal fame :
> Thou much more fit (were leasure to the same)
>   Thy gracious soverains praises to compile
> And her imperiall Majestie to frame
>   In loftie numbers and heroicke stile.
> But, sith thou maist not so, give leave a while
>   To baser wit his power therein to spend,
> Whose grosse defaults thy daintie pen may file,
>   And unadvised oversights amend.
> But evermore vouchsafe it to maintaine
> Against vile Zoilus backbitings vaine."

Sackville's " Induction " was written long before he was inducted into Knole but three stanzas may be given as taste of the quality of the first of the two poets associated with the place. The stanzas personify—as Spenser, Phineas Fletcher and other poets were later given to personifying—Misery, Sleep and Old Age.

> " His foode for most, was wylde fruytes of the tree,
> Unles sumtimes sum crummes fell to his share.
> Which in his wallet long, God wote, kept he,
> As on the which full dayntlye would he fare.
> His drinke the running streame : his cup the bare
> Of his palme closed : his bed the hard colde grounde.
> To this poore life was Miserie ybound. . . .
>
> By him lay heavy Slepe the cosin of death
> Flat on the ground, and still as any stone,
> A very corps, save yelding forth a breath.
> Small kepe took he whom Fortune frowned on,
> Or whom she lifted up into the trone
> Of high renowne, but as a living death,
> So dead alyve, of lyef he drewe the breath. ..
>
> And next in order sad Old Age we found
> His beard all hoare, his iyes hollow and blynde,
> With drouping chere still poring on the ground,
> As on the place where nature him assinde

> To rest, when that the sisters had untwynde
> His vitall threde, and ended with theyr knyfe
> The fleeting course of fast declining life."

The poet is also remembered as being part author, with one Thomas Norton, of the earliest English tragedy known to us, " Ferrex and Porrex " or " Gorboduc" (1562), a play the leading motive of which has been summed up as being a protest against discord as the chief curse of the lives of both rulers and ruled, a subject which not unnaturally interested the statesman who succeeded in holding an even course in troublous times. The closing words of his " Complaynt of Henry Duke of Buckingham " convey something of the same significance—

> " Byd Kynges, byd Cesars, byd all states beware,
> And tell them this from me that tryed it true :
> Who reckless rules, right soone may hap to rue."

Charles Sackville, sixth Earl of Dorset (great-great-grandson of the first earl and second poet-owner of Knole) is remembered as a notable wit, courtier and poet in days when poets, courtiers and wits were many about the saturnine looking Merry Monarch.

> " Dorset, the Grace of Courts the Muse's pride
> Patron of arts,"

as Pope described him, is now chiefly remembered by his lyrical masterpiece—

> " To all you ladies now on land,
> We men at sea indite ;
> But first would have you understand
> How hard it is to write.
> The muses now, and Neptune, too,
> We must implore to write to you.
> With a fa la, la, la, la."

Something of a romance attaches to the fourth Earl, who in 1613—eleven years before coming into his inheritance—fought a desperate duel with Edward Bruce, Lord Kinloss, near Bergen-on-Zoom, and, himself thrice wounded, killed his opponent. The story is set forth by Steele in two numbers of the " Guardian " with the preliminary correspondence and Sackville's full relation of the contest.

The noble park, to which the public are allowed access, is "sweet " as it was in Walpole's day and has many magnificent trees in it, including some splendid beeches, which some of us vastly prefer to the sycamores which won his " love." Southwards the park extends along the Tonbridge road for over a mile ; to the east it extends to Fawke Common, and northwards to near the lower extension of Sevenoaks known as St. John's. From the north-east side we may go through woodland—the parks almost join—by the attractive hamlet of Godden Green to the park of Wilderness by Seal and so to the fascinating Ightham district.

South of Sevenoaks, near the end of the tunnel—close upon two miles long—by which the railway here pierces the hills, is the village known as the Weald, or Sevenoaks Weald, from which some pleasant miles of zig-zagging byways may be taken down to the Medway in the neighbourhood of Penshurst, or turning eastward we may go by the hamlet of Under River through quiet farmlands to Shipborne and so into that part of the district described in the Tonbridge chapter, or taking the wooded roads up through the hills again may make for Ightham and the district reserved for the next chapter. Here it is that we are in that extensive tract which according to the old quatrain is at once the healthiest and wealthiest our county possesses—

> " Rye, Romney and Hythe for wealth without health,
> The Downs for health with poverty,
> But you shall find both health and wealth
> From Foreland Head to Knole and Lee."

Whether the "Lee" is that near Blackheath or Leigh to the west of Tonbridge it is not easy to determine—in either case we may believe the saying equally accurate.

Here, overlooking the Weald, before we turn back again to the chalk and sand country, it may be well to recall one of its most famous sons, the great printer William Caxton, who has recorded, " I was born, and learned myne English, in Kente, in the Weeld, where English is spoken broad and rude." The place of his birth is not, unfortunately, more exactly known. Before Caxton's time the men of Kent were noted for their provincial speech—" It seemed by his langage that he was borne in Kent "—now, however, the general speech is less provincial than that of other southern counties though many dialect words remain in use. Another old writer referred to the " broad and rude " speech of his county—

> " And though mine English be sympill to mine entent
> Have me excused, for I was borne in Kent."

CHAPTER XVIII

OTFORD, situated on the Darent where that stream has turned in a northerly direction through a break in the chalk downs, is a place with a past that is of interest to the student of history, not only for its remains of one of the splendid palaces belonging to the Archbishops of Canterbury, but because it was the scene of one of the early decisive battles recorded in our history, when Offa, King of Mercia, won a great victory in 775 by which, presumably, he got control of Kent, London, and Essex. Another fight took place when Edmund Ironside had his fifth battle with Cnut and gained "a most honorable victorie, and pursued him (flying towards Shepey) untill he came to Ailesforde : committing upon the Danes such slaughter and bloody havock, that if Edric the traitor had not by fraudulent Counsell witholden him, he had that day made an end of their whole army." The sixth battle was fought out in Essex when the flower of the English race was destroyed and the stubborn Edmund was compelled by his fellows to arrange a division of the land with the no less stubborn Danes. The place "at the ford "—for so the old form of the name, Otteford, is translated—has nothing to show of the ancient sanguinary engagements, though late in the eighteenth century roadmakers are supposed to have come across relics of the slain, but it has evidence of its later importance as one of the most princely seats of the Archbishops of Canterbury. It had already belonged to the see for several centuries when Warham in the reign of Henry VIII. built the palace of which a fine ruined octagonal tower, and other portions since built into cottages now remain. To à Becket's stay here three legends are attached. Firstly, it is said that as he walked in the park, engaged in devotional exercises, he was much disturbed by the singing of a nightingale and therefore "in the might of his holiness he injoyned, that from thence forth no bird of that kinde should be so bold as to sing thereabout." Secondly, a blacksmith having cloyed or pricked the primate's horse in shoeing it the irate Archbishop uttered a curse that should prevent any smith from ever flourishing in the parish. Thirdly, there being no proper water supply for his palace à Becket "strake his staffe into the drie ground" and immediately a plentiful flow of water gushed forth. The nightingales and the blacksmiths have presumably long since found the curse weakened by lapse of centuries, but St. Thomas's Well is alive at this day to testify, therefore deny it not.

Another miracle worker at Otford was St. Bartholomew, before whose image pregnant women offered a cockerel or a pullet according to their desire that their child should be a boy or a girl.

It was Archbishop Warham in the early part of the sixteenth century who made of Otford the splendid palace which it long was, spending upwards of thirty thousand pounds upon re-building nearly the whole—this sum he had intended spending over the palace at Canterbury, but a quarrel with the citizens made him divert it to Otford. In some of his many letters which are extant the powerful Churchman frequently subscribed himself with the pride that apes humility, "at my poor house of Otford," "my poor lodging at Otford," "my poor place at Otford." The splendid palace of Warham was visited by Henry VIII. and was duly handed over to him by Cranmer with various other archiepiscopal properties. All that now is to be seen is a group of picturesque ruins near the church overlooking the Darent where the old-time Pilgrims' Way crossed the stream and backed by the rapidly rising, tree-topped downs. Approaching the railway station from the south the nearer spur of those downs looks not unlike Box Hill as seen from the Dorking road.

Along the old Pilgrims' Road, keeping, as usual, to the hillside, roughly midway between the higher ground and the valley, we may pass in comparative solitude for some miles, meeting but few people, and seeing but few cottages, for as usual the inhabited road passes parallel with the old way at

a short distance – here sometimes less than quarter of a mile —
to the south. Shortly after leaving Otford, however, the spire
of Kemsing church is seen, and here we are at a very attractive
little village lying half a mile or so from the railway station.
The small church is dedicated to a St. Edith who is said
to have been born here, and a well bearing her name —which
to the consternation of the villagers ran dry a few years ago —
is an important local feature; its water being still considered
locally a cure for bad eyes. In the churchyard an image
of the saint used to be much frequented for the preserving
of corn "from blasting, myldew, brandeare, and such other
harms as commonly doe annoy it." Old Lambarde, who
generally waxed indignant in recording the miracles that took
place in his county, says :

"The manner of the which sacrifice was this : Some silly body brought
a peck, or two, or a Bushel of Corn, to the Church : and (after prayers
made) offered it to the Image of the Saint : of this Offering the Priest used
to toll the greatest portion, and then to take one handfull, or little more of
the residue (for you must consider he would be sure to gain by the bargain)
the which after aspertion of holy water, and mumbling of a few words of con-
juration, he first dedicated to the Image of St. Edithe, and then delivered it
back to the party that brought it : who then departed with full perswasion,
that if he mingled that hollowed handfull with his seed Corn, it would
preserve from harm, and prosper in growth, the whole heap that he should
sowe, were it never so great a Stack or Mough. . ..
How much that God of the Romans, and our Gods of Kemsing
differed in profession, let some Popish Gadder after strange Gods make the
accompt, for I myselfe can finde no odds at all."

"Kemsing is yet the Mother Church (as they say), and Scale
is but a child (or Chappell) of it," according to the old writer.
Seal is a pleasant little village backed by the tree-grown hills
of Wilderness, Knole and wooded commons towards Ightham.
Its church with some Early English features is mainly Perpendicular, is built of the local stone, and has several monuments
and other memorials of the dead interesting to antiquarians,
the most notable being a large and beautifully preserved brass
(dated 1395) to Sir William de Bryene.
From Seal to Ightham a beautiful four-mile walk may be
taken nearly all through fine woods, either directly following
the road over the hill, or turning to the left half a mile beyond
Seal a lower way may be taken by Styants' Bottom. For a

cyclist I would recommend the main road, for I can recall on one occasion having to push my machine along rutty, stony ways for a considerable distance only then to have to turn back and rejoin the open road.   Either way takes us to Oldbury Hill, a famous spot owing to the extensive pre-Roman camp here, the entrenchments enclosing more than one hundred and twenty acres.   Near the rough steps leading up to the camp on the eastern side about two hundred years ago a murder was committed and the murderer was duly hanged in chains on a gibbet erected close by the scene of his crime. The place was long known as Gibbet or Gallows Field, and when the neighbouring mill was burnt down two or three years ago, the iron cage in which the murderer's body had been hung was unearthed.   A crude traditional verse about the crime runs :

> ' I, Oldbury, of a bloodthirsty mind,
>   Prompt by the Devil to thieving,
> To murder was inclined ;
>   When with Will Woodin I did meet,
> And bore him company,
>   Surely then I did him greet,
> But full of treachery.
>   I cut his throat from ear to ear,
> Cruel and inhumanly ;
>   And for that crime I suffer here
> And die upon a tree."

The making of the murderer's name Oldbury would seem to be an error of memory, for the place-name if not as old as murder is far older than the specific crime.

The slopes of Oldbury have been described as one of the finest, if not the finest, of terminal moraines in this country. Readers who would learn the geological minutiæ of the district should read the deeply interesting if somewhat inchoate volume, " Ightham : The story of a Kentish Village and its Surroundings," written by Mr. F. J. Bennett with the assistance of several other zealous students of the district.[1]

Part of Oldbury Hill has been extensively quarried for stone for " metalling " roads, and especially was this done when much of the stone was taken in 1844 for macadamising the Edgware

---

[1] Published (1907) by the Homeland Association, Ltd., the various local guides of which have done much to stimulate interest in home-travel.

road. Much of the famous hill, overgrown with pine woods
and chestnuts, is enclosed and on the northern slopes are
wide strawberry fields, but it has been suggested not un-
reasonably that the Hill, so rich in evidences of our past,
should be bought for the nation and systematic search made
for its relics. The whole district is so interesting, both from
the geological and archæological points of view, that such
a consummation is devoutly to be wished. On the north side
of Oldbury Hill are remarkable crags known as Rock
Shelters from beneath which we have a very fine view across to
the chalk hills. These " shelters "—though much destroyed
by the stone taken for road metalling and other utilitarian purposes—are almost without parallel in the south of England,
and are as picturesque from their situation as they are interesting from the history which the geologist is able to piece
together about them. We are told, for instance, that deep water
at one time flowed about these hills, while bones recovered in
the neighbourhood testify to the prehistoric monsters that
ranged about it in the days of palæolithic man. To the south-
east of Oldbury, in what is known as Rose Wood, are many
ancient Pit Dwellings which have been partially explored by
Lord Avebury and other students of primitive man—these
" dwellings " are " some forty circular, basin-like pits, symmetri-
cally made and resembling inverted cones, five to ten feet deep
and fifteen feet in diameter."

The little Shode which rises a mile and a half north of
Ightham and flows through a lovely valley south past that
village down to Plaxtol, Hadlow and the Medway, small as it
is, is particularly interesting for the deep gorges formed in
its course in the neighbourhood of Ightham. These gorges
have set geologists a-theorising, but if we are unable to
account for them we may at least enjoy the beauty which
they offer—sometimes steep and well-wooded, and sometimes
with their sides rounded by centuries of denudation. The
picturesque village of Ightham itself, with its timbered houses
and its interesting old church, is the delightful centre of a
district which is not excelled in varied attractiveness by any
other in the county.

A notable inhabitant of Ightham, a man who has investi-
gated his " world," as he describes the county within a few
miles' radius of his place, is Mr. Benjamin Harrison, a student

of geology and natural history whose zeal and labours have won for him a position which may best be recognised, as has been suggested, by describing him as the Gilbert White of Ightham. To Mr. Harrison students of prehistoric man owe it that investigations into human antiquities have been pushed much farther back, so that he may be described as the father of eolithic man—beside whom, if the present theories are correct, palæolithic man is comparatively recent, and neolithic man a creature of the day before yesterday. Mr. Bennett, in the work already referred to in describing a typical walk round Ightham, has given us a charming sketch of the veteran geologist :

" Starting from the bottom of the village, we walk up its steep and quaint street. Just before where the roads fork we come to an old-fashioned grocer's shop front, and notice that one of the windows is filled up with antiquities of various kinds, fire backs, etc., and noticing also some flint implements we at once look at the name, and are, of course, prepared to see that of Harrison. We now know we are before the residence of—we may say—the hero of this book. So we at once enter, and find that as soon as he understands that we seek to interview him for scientific purposes we receive a hearty welcome. We note that he is a thick-set veteran, full of vigour and intellect, and most interesting in every way. We may find him, perhaps, earnestly gazing on a flint implement ; or, may be, completing a most skilfully and artistically coloured sketch of one ; or serving a customer. Hearing that we wish to plan out a walk he is alert at once, turns quickly round and gets out a sheet of sugar-paper, and very quickly and accurately turns that into a map of the proposed walk ; full of instructions of all that we should see. Most likely we are told to visit the Rock-shelters and the Celtic Camp at Oldbury. We thank him and proceed on our archæo-geological quest with our sugar-paper map as a guide. It may also be a botanical ramble, for Mr. Harrison is well up in the plants of his district ; indeed, when anyone in the village, whether gentle or simple, wants any information, they generally come to Mr. Harrison, and usually find what they want."

In 1315 a royal licence was granted giving one William de Inge the right of holding a weekly market and a yearly three days' fair in Ightham. The fair—reduced to one day—still survives, being held annually on the Wednesday in Whitsun week. It is locally known, why I have not been able to ascertain, as " Cockscomb Fair."

Ightham, peaceful little village as it now is, was twice deeply stirred by civil strife in the long past. When Jack Cade was forming his large Kentish army the local constables formally summoned to his banner John Thrope, baker, Richard Thrope, John Mercer, Will Godewyn, Will Sawyer, John Smith and other folk of the village and they presumably all went to swell the formidable army on Blackheath. Then again we have an intimate old account of the way in which the popular feeling was stirred up here to aid Wyatt and his fellow leaders :

" The sheriff continued on the alert, and from time to time kept the privy council informed of the movements of the rebels. He forwarded a deposition of one William Colman, a blacksmith at Ightham, who stated that William, the eldest son of Sir Henry Isley, came to his shop two hours before daylight to have his horse shod, and told him ' the Spaniards were coming into the realm, with harness and handguns, and would make the English worse than conies, and viler : ' and as he left the forge, he said with a loud voice—' Smith, if thou beest a good fellow, stir and encourage all thy neighbours to rise against these strangers. I go to Maidstone, and return again shortly.' ' Why,' quoth the smith, ' these be marvellous words : We shall be betrayed if we stir.' ' No,' said Isley, ' we shall have help enough, for the people are already up in Devonshire, Cornwall, Hants, and other places.' " The people were not " up " and Kent had to suffer sadly by being left to rebel alone.

The church though modernised has a number of interesting monuments, the most attractive one to the curious being that inscribed as follows :

"D. D. D.

To the Precious Name and Honour
of
DAME DOROTHY SELBY,
the relict of
Sir William Selby, Knt.,
the only daughter and heir of
Charles Bonham, Esq.

She was a Dorcas,
Whose curious needle turned the abused stage
Of this lewd world into the golden age :

Whose pen of steel and silken ink enrolled
The acts of Jonah in records of gold.
Whose art disclosed that plot, which, had it taken,
Rome had triumphed, and Britain's walls had shaken,
In heart a Lydia, and in tongue a Hannah,
In zeal a Ruth, in wedlock a Susannah ;
Prudently simple, providently wary
To the world a Martha, and to Heaven a Mary.
Who put on immortality   { of her Pilgrimage 69.
        in the year   { of her Redeemer 1641."

The "plot" which Dame Dorothy is credited with disclosing
was the Gunpowder Plot, and a story runs that she disclosed it
by means of her "curious needle," as set forth some years ago
by one of her descendants. An anonymous letter had been
delivered telling of the intentions of Guy Fawkes :

"The letter is stated in Rapin's History of England to have been
delivered to Lord Monteagle's servant by an unknown person (26th
October, 1605) with a charge to give it into his master's own hand, and the
writing was unknown and somewhat 'unlegible.' Lord Monteagle carried
the letter to Cecil's Earl of Salisbury, who either thought, or pretended to
think, little of it ; and the affair was dropped till the King, who had been
at Royston, returned to town, when the letter was further considered, and
the plot was scented. Most authors attribute this to the sagacious timidity
of James, who was fond of the reputation of this discovery, and publicly
assumed the credit of it.
    There is an old tradition that it was Dame Dorothy Selby who dis-
covered the meaning of the anonymous letter ; and a report, less well
founded, adds that she discovered it by working it on a piece of tapestry.
I cannot vouch for this latter report, but the following facts are beyond
dispute. My great-great-grandmother, Dorothy (the daughter of Sir Henry
Selby, Knt., second son of George, cousin of Sir William Selby, the
husband of Dame Dorothy), handed down this tradition to her children,
and as such it was stated to me by my grandmother, the late Mrs. Selby, of
the Mote, who died in 1845 at the age of 90."

For nearly three centuries—until within the past twenty
years—Ightham Mote or the Mote House as it is variously
termed, belonged to the Selby family. It stands over two
miles to the south of the village on the further slope of the
hills, more or less hidden by surrounding trees ; the last portion
of the delightful journey from the small hamlet of Ivy Hatch
being through a tree-grown gorge well representative of much
of the wooded scenery of the greensand hills. To visitors staying in the Sevenoaks district, Ightham Mote is one of the show
places to which they will inevitably be taken ; it has long been

Ightham Mote.

one of the objectives of cycling and sketching clubs' excursions, and few who journey thither will be found to deny that it justifies the interest taken in it. In the first place it is situated in the centre of lovely country with a tiny tributary of the Shode diverted to form its once protective but now merely ornamental moat. Then, too, the building is as perfect a mansion of its kind as the country has to show. It was originally built about the middle of the fourteenth century by Sir Thomas Cawne—whose effigy is in Ightham Church—and was added to in Tudor days. The ragstone castellated tower is believed to be Tudor, as is much of the timber work and the gables with their carved barge-boards of the portion giving on to the beautiful courtyard. A visitor to the ancient residence in 1837 when "huge timber logs placed on andirons still blazed in the capacious chimney of this most venerable hall," going to the chapel said "one could have fancied that one saw. Sir Richard Haut returned from Bosworth's bloody fray offering up his praises in this his own family oratory, to the arbiter of battles, for the event of that which had restored to him his home and patrimonial possessions."

East of the Mote is the village of Plaxtol, beyond which we cross the Shode near a spring known as Plaxtol Spout, and so reach Allen's Farm near to which in 1857 were dug up a number of Roman remains, including a beautiful bronze statuette of Minerva. A little beyond again, backed by the grand extent of the Hurst Woods, is a remarkable survival of domestic architecture in the remains of Old Soar, a fortified manor house dating back perhaps as early as the earliest part of the Mote. The place bears evidence of having been built at a period when, if every Englishman's house was his castle, it was a castle which he might at any time be called upon to defend.

A good walk is that from Old Soar, by the hamlets of Crouch and Bastead, to Ightham—giving us beautiful views across the little Shode valley to Oldbury Hill, a close view of the curious Shode gorge and a fine view northwards again, with Ightham church standing on its knoll boldly ahead. It would not be easy to find a more attractive and interesting walk of eight or ten miles than that from Ightham to Oldbury Hill, the Mote, Plaxtol, Old Soar, and Crouch, back to the starting-point. Indeed, each of the "hams" of this neighbourhood may be made an attractive centre for pedestrians of the most varied powers of endurance.

A little to the south of Ightham is a tumulus, from which

many stone implements have been recovered, while another is near Borough Green, anciently Barrow Green, by Wrotham station—the railway centre of a fascinating district. Wrotham, to the north of Ightham, is a place scarcely less interesting than its neighbour. Here, near to the large church—rich in memorial brasses—stood one of the many, and one of the early, palaces of the Archbishops of Canterbury. It was mostly pulled down in the time of Archbishop Islip that its materials might go to the completion of the palace at Maidstone. Wrotham, situated on an old Roman way, has not much in itself to tell us of a romantic past except in its associations with the risings of Jack Cade and of Sir Thomas Wyatt. The hundred of Wrotham seems to have entered with spirit into Cade's attempt, the Constable of the place summoning the men of the district to rebellion. Possibly Lord Say, the Lord Lieutenant, who lived at Knole, and his son-in-law, William Crowmer the Sheriff—Sir James Cromer according to Shakespeare—were unpopular magnates; if so, they paid for it with their lives during the brief success of the rebels. These constables, John Thorpe and John Wyberne, formally called upon various people of their district to join the army of Cade, and the success with which they did so may be gauged from the fact that to Cade's army Kent contributed some twenty thousand men.

A century later when Sir Thomas Wyatt called upon Kent to prevent the Spanish marriage and all the dire consequences prognosticated, Wrotham was the scene of actual fighting. The battle took place in Blacksole Field when the Queen's troops under the Sheriff, Sir Robert Southwell and Lord Abergavenny met and put to flight Wyatt's men under the Isleys and one Anthony Knyvett.

Just beyond Wrotham the Pilgrims' Road takes a northward bend—seemingly for the purpose of keeping at its usual middle distance between the hills and valley; but following the road above it up Wrotham Hill we get magnificent views to the southwards over the Hurst and Mereworth Woods to the left and the woods and parks on the hills about Sevenoaks while between we have the break of the Shode valley. Here we are on the chalk with roads running north to the Thames by Gravesend and Dartford, the nearest villages being the small Stansted with its thousand-year-old yew, Ridley, and

Kingsdown with its plain little church in the woods.   Returning to Wrotham we have within three or four miles to the east
—near to our Maidstone district at the Mallings—Trotterscliff,
Birling, Ryarsh, Addington and Offham, a small group of

Birling.

places particularly attractive to those interested in megaliths, or
rude stone monuments of pre-historic people.
    Trotterscliff, the nearest of these at the foot of the chalk
downs, is especially notable for having on a hill to the north
the Coldrum cromlech, wanting only its capstone.   Here half
a century ago were found many Romano-British remains.
Nearly six miles to the east on the other side of the Medway

valley we saw Kits Coty House and the Countless Stones, at one time connected, it is conjectured, with Coldrum by a great avenue of stones ; about six miles to the north are many Sarsen stones, a supposed ancient circle, in a hollow in a wood named Cockadamshaw, while a mile or so south is the Stone Circle or fallen cromlech in Addington Park.   Mr. Bennett in his " Story of Ightham," to which reference has already been made,

Quintain on Village Green at Offham.

gives some interesting particulars of the relations of these old monuments to the lives of those who designed them, and suggests the nature of their secular and religious use.   To the student of such things this district thus affords many opportunities for investigating megaliths, but even the least studious traveller finds something attractive in these strange evidences of man's activity in the long past ; as Thomas Wright —that literary Briareus as he has been termed—put it in " The

Celt, the Roman and the Saxon," the whole district is one of our hallowed sites, owing to these strange survivals of a savage past among rich scenery of diversified woodlands, pastures, corn-fields, and hop gardens of the present. It has been pointed out that many of the sarsen stones are built into some of the local churches. An ingenious suggested derivation of the word " sarsen " is that sar in Saxon signified grievous or troublesome, and hence sarstan or stone, the removal of which must have been a very long and troublesome work !

Ryarsh is a pleasant little village, near neighbour to Birling, the old manor house of which is now a farm, Birling Manor being a modern residence. Here we are near the foot of the chalk hills with the Medway ahead of us to the east. A delightful footpath takes us through the attractive Leybourne Park, leaving which we pass Malling at the north-western extremity of our Maidstone district and come to Offham, an attractive village set amid hopfields and backed by the broad Mereworth Woods.

On the green at Offham is a curious survival of one of the games of our ancestors in the shape of a quintain, which has been maintained for centuries at the cost of the estate on which it stands ; this is a tall post with a cross-piece pivoted at the top, broad at one end, and pierced with holes. At the further end of the cross-piece hung a bag of sand, and the agile youth of the neighbourhood up to the end of Tudor times used to exercise themselves and their horses in tilting at the broad piece of wood " he that by chance hit it not at all, was treated with loud peals of derision ; and he who did hit it made the best use of his swiftness, lest he should have a sound blow on his neck from the bag of sand, which instantly swung round from the other end of the quintain. The great design of this sport was to try the agility of the horse and man, and to break the board, which whoever did, he was accounted chief of the day's sport." It would be a healthier exercise for the youth of to-day than watching other youths play football.

Offham Church, a small Early English and Norman (restored) edifice, stands some distance from the village, nearly half-way to Addington, a little scattered place, with its church pictur-esquely situated on a mound. Addington Church has some brasses, but has lost its most remarkable feature, a wall inscription which, when Hasted wrote, was still to be seen declaring not only the date of the edifice, but the time it took a-building—

> " In fourteen hundred and none
> Here was neither stick nor stone ;
> In fourteen hundred and three
> The goodly building which you see."

CHAPTER XIX

COMING from the small, variedly picturesque and crowdedly interesting bit of country that lies south of the chalk downs, between Darent and Medway, we find the northern portion between those rivers a far larger tract, bordered on the north by the Thames, with a greater air of sameness in the wide stretching undulations of its orchards, hop and fruit gardens and fields. Though there is an air of sameness about the country stretching east and west of the little Darent, yet there are leafy lanes, overlooking wide extending orchards, there are frequent copses primrose-starred in spring and blue with abundance of wild hyacinths later, and, especially in an easterly direction, there are long miles that may be followed by the lover of quiet ways without touching at anything more than small retired villages. To the west, by orchards and strawberry-grown hillsides, we soon come to the sophisticated places forming a portion of the belt of outer suburbs—or places which, if they may not yet be described as suburban, have already over them the shadow of coming events that shall convert them to that state.

Following at first the course of the Darent along its narrow valley through the chalk, we come to Shoreham, backed to the west by the height through which is bored the Polehill Tunnel, from Knockholt to Dunton Green stations. From here, old and new companion each other down to the Thames—the old in the shape of remains of castles and ancient ecclesiastical foundations stimulating to the imagination and gratifying to the sense of antiquity; the new in the shape of paper mills and other useful but unlovely factories. Following the river we come to Lullingstone, Eynsford, Farningham, Horton Kirby, Sutton-at-Hone, Darenth, and so to Dartford itself, the principal town on the river, a gradual change from the rurality of the Westerham Valley to the business of the manufacturing towns near to the Thames. Certain of these Darenth-side places have been hit off in a jingling quatrain by some local rhymester of the past—

> " Sutton for mutton,
>   Kirby for beef,
>   South Darne for gingerbread,
> And Dartford for a thief."

Lullingstone's old church, with various brasses and sixteenth century monuments, situated at the edge of the beautiful Lullingstone Park, is a capital place from which an admirable walk may be taken by road and footpath over the western hill to Chelsfield and thence through a rich bit of orchard country by Crockenhill to Swanley Junction—a new town in the midst of a fruit-growing district. Or a pleasanter route over the hill to the south of Chelsfield would be that by Green Street Green and High Elms to Downe—by the residence of one distinguished scientist to a place long the home of another. At flowering time the fruit country about Swanley Junction is beautiful enough, but it lacks colour and variety at other seasons. Beyond, bowered in orchards, is the parent village of Swanley itself. Returning to the Darent—a large portion of the valley of which is given up to cherry orchards and other fruit growing, we have at Eynsford the small representative of a place at one time of considerable importance owing to its ford. Here was a large castle the ruins of which are to be seen on the right bank of the river, ruins made interesting from the fact that it was a dispute between the then owner and à Becket which led to the quarrel with the King and so indirectly to the great tragedy of Canterbury Cathedral. A road hence going to the south-eastward over the chalk hills to Kemsing may be followed by those whose enjoyment is to be found in wide prospects—and an extensive view is one of the best features of a country ramble, a thing worth walking for.

From Eynsford to Farningham the beauty of the orchard is varied by the unbeautifulness, as the children put it, of paper mills. Farningham itself is a village along the high

road from London to Tonbridge, picturesquely situated in a
valley, with the air about it of an old coaching village. From
Farningham there is choice of two roads, one each side of the
Darent—linked, a mile or so away, by a connecting road past
the interesting Elizabethan manor house of Franks. The road
to the right is the more attractive, as following it brings us shortly
to Horton Kirby, its thirteenth century cruciform church possessing many beautiful Early English features, and with, by the
river-side, the remains of an ancient castle. South Darenth,
beyond, is a modern village near to old Sutton-at-Hone, at
which the Knights of St. John of Jerusalem established a
Commandery in the reign of King John. The scanty remains
have long since been converted to domestic uses. At
Sutton Place, near the four cross roads, lived and died a
merchant prince and navigator of the times of Elizabeth and
James, Sir Thomas Smith, or Smythe. He was a director of
the East India and Muscovy Companies, and treasurer of the
Virginia Company, so that the wealth which he amassed came
from all parts of the world. He was a promoter of expeditions
in search of the North-West Passage and his name was given
by Baffin to Smith's Sound. His monument may be seen in
Sutton Church.

Darenth—or Darne as it is sometimes locally shortened—
is a small, scattered place with a particularly interesting old
church, portions of which are thought to date back to the time
of St. Dunstan. It is a small edifice and the fact that many
Roman bricks are worked into the walls indicates its age. It
has also a font with a series of carved figures that have been
variously described as Anglo-Saxon and Norman, as representing a succession of incidents from the life of St.
Dunstan and as being mere insignificant fancies of the
sculptor.

Along the valley of the Darent, along the hilly ground
about Swanley, by South Darenth and near the woods to the
east of Darenth itself, are various great charitable establishments
and public institutions—convalescent and other homes,
schools, hospitals and asylums—erected in this district, it may
be believed, for its healthfulness.

Beyond Darenth the river from which it takes its name is
more and more given up to manufacture as we near Dartford,
passing on the way extensive powder mills. Dartford itself

is not particularly attractive. It is about three miles from where the Darent, on which it is situated, flows into the Thames opposite Purfleet and is now the centre of a large paper-making industry and other manufactures. Here, indeed, Sir John Spielman, jeweller to Queen Elizabeth, is said to have established the first paper mill in England, and as he died in 1607 Dartford has been a centre of the industry for over three centuries. He is also said to have brought over to England in his portmanteau the first two young lime trees ever seen in these parts, and to have planted them in front of his mill, where they flourished for close upon two centuries. The lime was, it may be said, already known in England in Chaucer's time. It was a generation after Spielman's death that Lord Leicester planted the stately avenue of these trees at Penshurst. Spielman's monument is to be seen in the church, in which are fragments of a fresco depicting St. George and the Dragon and a number of fifteenth century brasses. At Dartford there was a Priory of Augustinian nuns which on the dissolution of the monasteries Henry VIII. had converted into a palace for his own use; later it was the residence of Anne of Cleves.

Dartford is associated with one of the most notable incidents of the Peasants' Revolt of the fourteenth century. The unpopular poll-tax had set the people agog in various parts of the country and the preaching of John Ball inflamed them to the point of rebellion. Then a certain Tiler of Dartford, John or Wat, whose daughter had been brutally assaulted by the collector of the obnoxious impost, beat out the offender's brains, and thus brought matters to a crisis on June 5th, 1381. According to one story the Dartford man was John the Tiler, while Wat the Tiler—now familiar in all the history books as Wat Tyler—the leader, was said to be a Maidstone or an Essex man. The popular version of the story makes the vengeful Dartford man and the leader of the peasants' movement one and the same Wat Tyler—and certainly the demands of romance seem thus to be better suited. The revolt was short and sharp, the men of Kent and the men of Essex moving parallel along the Thames towards London, where a sudden fracas during an interview with the young King Richard led to Lord Mayor Walworth's killing of Tyler. (The Fishmongers' Company has the very dagger with which, according to tradition, he did the deed.) That which Tyler and his fellows were doing on

either side the Thames Jack Straw was doing in the eastern
counties and all were seemingly inspired by the one-time
priest of York, John Ball, whose letters, as Green puts it,
began for England the literature of political controversy.   In
a biography of Richard II., "by a Person of Quality,"
published in 1681, half-a-dozen of Ball's brief addresses are
given in black letter, and help to indicate the spirit which
animated the " Revolt."

" John Bell S. Mary Prist gretes wele all manner men, and byddes them
in the Name of the Trinity, Fadur and Son and Holy Ghost, stond manlyche
togedyr in trewthe, and helps trewthe, and trewthe shall helpe yowe : Now
regneth Pride in prise, and Covetous is hold wise ; and Lechery without en
shame, and Glotony without en blame.   Envie regneth with treason, and
slouthe is take in grete sesone.   God do bote, for now is the time, Amen,
in Esex, Southfolc, and Northfolc.

Jack the Miller's Epistle.

" Jakk Mylner asket help to turn his Mylne aright.   He hath Grounden
small, small, The Kings Son of Heven he shall pay for all.   Look thy Mylne
do a right, with the four Sailes, and the Post stand in stedfastnesse.   With
right and with might, with skill and with will, lat might help right, and
skill go before will, and right before might, than goeth our Mylne aright.
And if might go before right, and will before skill than is our Mylne
mysadyght.

Jack the Carter's.

" Jakk Carter pryes yow all, that yee make a gode end of that yee have
begunnen, and doth wele, and ay bettur and bettur, for at the even men
heryth the day : for if the end be wele than is all wele.   Lat Peres the
Plowman my Brother duele at home, and dyght us Corn, and I will so with
yow, and help that yee may so dyght your mete and your drynk, that yee
none fayle.   Lokke that Hobb Robbyoure be wele chastised for lesing of
your Grace, for yee have grete nede to take God with yow in all yowr dedes,
for now is time to beware.

Jack Trewman's Scroll.

" Jakk Trewman doth yow to understand, th t falseness and gile havith
regned to long, and trewth hath been sett under a Lokke, and falsneth and
gile regneth in everylk Flokke.   No man may come trewth to, both syng
Si dedero, Speke, spend, and speed quoth John of Bathon, and therefore
sinn fareth as wilde flode, trew love is a way that was so gode, and
Clerks for welth worth hem wo.   God do bote, for nowze is time."

John Ball was in prison at Canterbury when the trouble
came to a head at Dartford and the first thing that the risen

people did was to free him before marching in their thousands on London.

Dartford has given its name to one of the rarest of British birds, the Dartford warbler, first found in this neighbourhood in 1773 by the naturalist Latham. The little singer has since been found in various parts of the country, but never plentifully. Unlike the other warblers it remains in England all the year round and it is supposed that the severe winters kill so many as to prevent any continued increase of their number, the stock only being maintained by migrants from over Channel.

To the south-west of Dartford is the rising ground of Dartford Heath, from which there are wide views, especially that Thameswards over the marsh through which runs Dartford Creek, as the short navigable stretch of the Darent is sometimes named. On the Heath there are a number of hollows in the chalk which are by some archæologists thought to be ancient pit-dwellings, and similar things are to be seen at Crayford, less than a mile to the north-west.

On Dartford Heath nearly two centuries ago was played a cricket match which led to a quarrel between the sides, the taking of their trouble to the Law Courts, and the referring back of the trial to the cricket field. The story was told in a 1726 newspaper thus—" On Monday is to be determined a Suit of Law on Dartford-Heath by a Cricket Match between the Men of Chinkford, and Mr. Steed's Men: they had a hearing about two Years ago before the Lord Chief Justice Pratt, when the Merits of the Cause appear'd to be, that at a Match between the above-said Players, the Chinkford Men refused to play out the Game at a time the other Side had the Advantage; but the Judge, either not understanding the Game, or having forgot it, referr'd the said Cause back to Dartford Heath, to be play'd on where they left off, and a rule of Court was made for it accordingly." Most wise Chief Justice Pratt! The result of the trying of the " referr'd back Cause " is not recorded.

South-east of the Heath is the village of Wilmington set, as so many of these places between the Rivers Cray and Darent are set, amid cherry orchards ; a place that was once the manor of Warwick, the Kingmaker. South through orchards and fields lie Swanley and various scattered hamlets, while west a most attractive walk by footpath may be taken through Joyden Wood to Bexley or North Cray. Through Dartford ran of old the Roman Watling Street; following this in the easterly direction we pass over the small heath of Dartford Brent where the local martyrs were burnt during the Marian persecutions. "Brent," however, does not here signify burnt, as might be imagined, but is a dialect word meaning steep. Following the Watling Street takes us to some of the higher country giving us good views and quiet ways. Three miles from Dartford it will be found that the road has been deflected, south is a curve to Betsham and Southfleet amid their cherry orchards, the straightness of the Roman way being represented by a footpath crossing the higher part of Swanscombe Park or Wood, crossed by another path leading to Swanscombe Church. In this wood is a great cavern which has long had the local name of "Clabber-Napper's Hole." It has been suggested, with doubtful authenticity, that Clabber is a perversion of "Caer l'arbre," or the dwelling in the wood or trees, but it does not seem reasonable that the ancient namer of the spot should have drawn upon French as well as Welsh. The cavern is traditionally referred to as the lair of a great freebooter and kidnapper who came to be regarded as the local "bogey." The old Roman Road passes within two or three hundred yards of the home of this mysterious evil-doer. The footpath along the eastern side of the wood takes us down to Swanscombe Church in which are some interesting monuments to the Weldon family associated with this neighbourhood. Several of the Weldons distinguished themselves in the Civil Wars in the Parliament's cause, the most notable being Sir Anthony Weldon, author of "The Secret History of the first two Stuart Kings," and of "A Catt may look at a King; or a Brief Chronicle and Characters of the Kings of England from William the Conqueror to the Reign of Charles I." Sir Anthony, who occupied the position of Clerk of the Kitchen to James I., was dismissed from his post for having libelled the nation to which the King belonged. The old mansion of the Weldons having fallen into decay was taken down over a hundred years ago. It was from Swanscombe that the assembled Men of Kent set out with boughs in their hands to meet William of Normandy and dictate their terms to the Conqueror, as recorded by Lambarde in a passage quoted at the beginning of this book.

Though cement works and river-side trades do not make a picturesque appearance, there are attractive bits to be found along the Kent side of the Thames here by the searcher after such — quaint old cottages and houses, interesting churches and rustic scenes, though the chimney stacks disfigure the country, and nearly everything is tinged with their smoke. Having come down near the river again at Swanscombe, Milton Street, Greenhithe and Stone its near neighbours to the west towards Dartford may be visited.

People who pass in pleasure steamers and ocean-going vessels down the Thames from London, along the winding of the channel, get but a poor and inadequate impression of the country near the river bank, but here and there a place may appear a somewhat picturesque group of buildings backed by attractive looking country. Greenhithe is one of these places, for it still may be said to justify its name. The grounds of Ingress Abbey, to the east of the town, afford a pleasant background, as the town is seen by those coming down stream. This place was originally attached to Dartford Priory—the present mansion having been built partly of stones from the demolished London Bridge[1] by Alderman Harmer, in the first half of the nineteenth century. At Ingress Abbey Sir Henry Havelock passed the early years of his childhood.

It was from Greenhithe, on May 18th, 1845, that Sir John Franklin set out on his last tragic expedition in command of the " Erebus " and " Terror " to search for the North-West Passage. The expedition passed hence down the Thames to be lost before many months in the unknown. Fourteen years were to elapse before Franklin's fate was revealed, and then it was ascertained that he had died just over two years after leaving Greenhithe. In the river near here are naval training ships, where youths are fitted for the profession which Franklin strikingly adorned—since Nelson's time no officer had so touched the popular imagination as Franklin, who

---

[1] Some of these stones travelled far ; part of the balustrading is at the land end of Herne Bay Pier, and some of the stones were until a few years ago outside Garrick's Villa at Hampton-on-Thames. They were removed when tramway invasion necessitated the widening of the road.

as a lad yet in his 'teens fought under the great captain at Trafalgar.

Stone, near to Greenhithe,—frequently referred to as Stone-near-Dartford,—is chiefly interesting for its beautiful church, known as "the lantern of Kent," a church of which George Street, the architect, when engaged in restoring it in 1860, said that in France it would be classed as a national monument, and preserved as such at the public cost. In 1638 this church was badly damaged by fire in consequence of being struck by lightning, and the Rector, Mr. Richard Chase, who had already come to loggerheads with his parishioners, dismissed his curate and left the place without any spiritual guidance. Before the fire he never "came himselfe above once or twice in a twealve month, and then only to reccon for tythes or pick quarrels," and after the fire the parishioners had to lay their piteous position before Parliament. Mr. Richard Chase seems to have been a worthy companion of his contemporary at Minster.

"And, now, since our Church hath bynn burnt, wee have had neyther prayers nor any other function ner thes two yers : and he would have dismist his Curat assone as the Church was burnt, which had bynn one to us, wee having noe use of him ; but nowe, of late, wee have none resident in our parish to bury our deed. Soe that as Mr. Chase leves our soules cure to the neighbouring ministers, soe our bodies to lye as noysom carrion, unless the dead will bury ther dead."

It was ten years after this petition that the living of Stone was sequestered, but presumably in the interval the Rector was made to see the reasonableness of putting it into a fit state for use. The building was reverently restored by Street and remains one of those best worth visiting, its full story, so far as that can be ascertained—with the evidence showing it to have been erected by the builder of Westminster Abbey—is given by the architect named in the third volume of the *Archæologia Cantiana*.

The name of the "lantern of Kent" is attached to Stone Church in accordance with an ancient joke recorded by Reginald Scot, "It is a common jest," said the enlightened "discoverer" of witchcraft, "among the watermen of the Thames to show the parish church of Stone to the passengers, calling the same by the name of the 'lanterne of Kent,' affirming and that not untruly, that the said church is as light (meaning in weight and not in brightnesse) at midnight as at noonday."

Two hundred years ago, when most East Kentish folk who had occasion to go to London went by water from Gravesend, a loaded tilt-boat was wrecked here in the Long Reach, owing to the "desperate obstinacy and rudeness" of the steersman. He would "tack again and stand over upon a wind," though his rowers told him it blew a storm ; "he called them Fools bid the Wind Blow-Devil (a rude Sailor's Proverb) the more Wind the better Boat." In consequence the boat shipped a sea and foundered, himself and fifty-three passengers being drowned, only five of those aboard succeeding in swimming ashore. The extent to which these tilt-boats—or boats with canvas shelters at the end—were utilised may be gathered from the fact that early in the seventeenth century they went from "Lion Key" twice a day with the tide in each direction " betwixt London and the towns of Deptford, Greenwich, Woolwich, Erith, and Greenhithe in Kent," while "at Billingsgate are every tide to be had Barges, Light Horsemen, Tilt-boats and Wherries, from London to the towns of Gravesend and Milton in Kent, or to any other place within the same bounds ; and as weather and occasions may serve beyond and further." The fare in the tilt-boat was sixpence in the time of Defoe.

As the approach to Rochester along the Medway is given over to lime and cement works, so all along this stretch of Kent where the chalk comes down near the river the trade in lime-making and exporting and in the quarrying of chalk for the purpose of sending it to less favoured districts is carried on as it has been carried on for a couple of centuries. It was so when Defoe perambulated the country, for even then the "chips" which crumbled where the large chalk was quarried for lime were carried away in hoys and lighters in prodigious quantities to be sold to the farmers of Norfolk, Suffolk, and Essex, who sent to fetch it from the boats by land carriage ten or fifteen miles, "Thus the Barren Soil of Kent, for such the Chalky Grounds are esteemed, make the Essex Lands Rich and Fruitful, and the mixture of Earth forms a Composition, which out of two Barren Extreams, makes One prolifick Medium ; the strong Clay of Essex and Suffolk is made Fruitful by the soft meliorating melting Chalk of Kent which fattens and enriches it." The whole of this tract of our

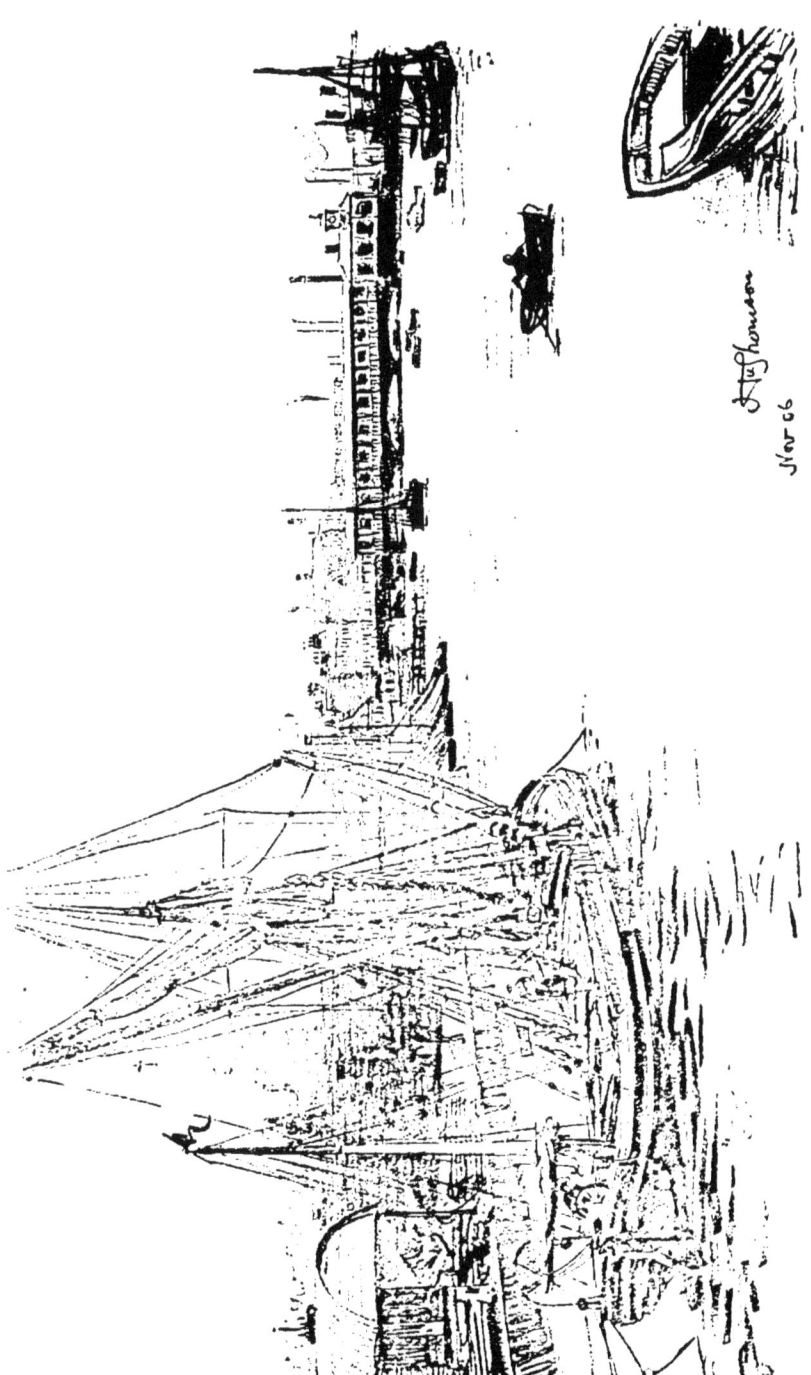

Stephenson
Nov 06

Gravesend.

county bordering the Thames shows evidence of the extent to which the chalk has been removed, in great pits—sometimes now converted into gardens—giving a scarred appearance to the river-side county.

Gravesend, as we approach it coming up or down the Thames, has a certain picturesqueness, especially perhaps in the eyes of those who have been down to the sea in ships and return after a long voyage, to whom it is often the first home town of which they get an intimate view. Its buildings show diversified with trees and backed by the rising chalk hills. It is a place of considerable importance for its shrimp fishery fleet, and from the fact that it is practically the limit of the Port of London—the point at which in-coming vessels are visited by the Customs officers, the point at which the river pilots are taken on board. The old part of the town has a certain picturesqueness in its narrow ways, but it has not much to hold the attention of visitors. Opposite, on the Essex coast, is Tilbury, a famous old place in the scheme of Thames defences, where Queen Elizabeth reviewed her army when the Spanish Armada threatened her dominions.

In Gravesend Church was buried the romantic Indian Princess, Pocahontas, who married John Rolfe—the first tobacco cultivator of Virginia, as smokers may like to be reminded—visited England and died in 1617, when arrangements had been made for her to return with her husband to Virginia. Recently attention has been drawn once more to her story by the discovery, during building operations near the church, of remains supposed to be hers. According to the church register, however, the beautiful young Indian "was buried in ye chauncell," so it is scarcely likely that the peculiar skull found last summer is that of Pocahontas.

On a wall near a Gravesend bowling-green a local eighteenth century celebrity was commemorated in the punning fashion admired at the time :—

> " To the Memory
> of Mr. Alderman Nyun
> An honest Man and an excellent Bowler.
>
> Cuique est sua Fama.
>
> Full forty long years was the Alderman seen,
> The delight of each Bowler, and King of this Green :
> As long be remembered his art and his name,

Whose hand was unerring,—unrivalled his fame.
His BIAS was good, and he always was found
To go the right way, and take enough ground.
The Jack to the uttermost verge he would send.
For the Alderman lov'd a full-length at each end.
Now mourn ev'ry eye that has seen him display
The Arts of the Game, and the wiles of his Play,
For the Great Bowler, DEATH, at one critical cast,
Has ended his Length, and close rubb'd him at last.

                F. W. posuit.   MDCCLXXVI."

Rosherville Gardens, laid out largely amid disused chalk quarries which stretch along the river-side west of Gravesend, have long been famous as one of the places in which the Cockney takes his pleasures anything but sadly. The " Gardens," which were originally established by one Jeremiah Rosher—hence the name—lie between Gravesend and North fleet. The latter place is worth visiting on account of its very large church, from which are to be had good views up and down stream. All about these places are wide fruit gardens and nursery grounds—the district being particularly noted for its rhubarb and asparagus The railway from Gravesend to Rochester runs for some distance closely parallel with the old Thames and Medway Canal, which was completed a few years before the coming of the railways, only to fall into early disuse.

CHAPTER XX

LEAVING Gravesend we have choice of ways to the triple towns of Strood, Rochester, and Chatham. First we reach Chalk, its landmark church notable for curious carvings over the doorway. Here Dickens spent his honeymoon and here he wrote the beginning of his perennially amusing " Pickwick." Passing Chalk we may go by Gadshill ; going south to the Watling Street we can take the beautiful road by Cobham Park, or crossing that highway can take a very pleasant round—through the chalk country, of hops, orchards, and woodlands—by Nurstead and Meopham. Here we should pause to remember that in this village was born in 1608 John Tradescant the younger, the famous botanist and traveller whose " Closet of rarities " forms part of the Ashmolean Museum at Oxford. Tradescant and his father deserve our grateful remembrances for the many trees and plants they introduced into this country, trees and plants so familiar now that it is difficult to realise what our gardens (and especially our suburban gardens) would be without them, for among the trees which we owe to them are the acacia, the plane, and the lilac.

From Meopham to Wrotham we may go over a picturesque bit of the Downs by following the south road, or by yet more attractive roundabout ways through well-wooded country, touching at many retired hamlets, may come down to the Medway at Snodland or Halling and thence follow the river to the triple towns. The whole of this tract with its up and down lanes, its wide woodlands, its hillside hopfields is full of beauty. Turning east after passing Meopham Church an attractive route over Foxen Down takes us to Luddesdown

Church and thence to Cobham at the western end of the beautiful park.

The clean and neat old village is a famous point of pilgrim-

The Leather Bottle, Cobham.

age for Dickensians, the quaint old "Leather Bottle" inn being familiar to all readers of "Pickwick." Was it not here that the misanthropic Tracy Tupman retired? Was it

c c

not here that Pickwick and Winkle found him? And above all was it not here that the enthusiastic Pickwick bore in triumph his archæological treasure so strangely inscribed "+BILSTUMPSHIS.MARK"? The Dickens' room is crowded with pictures and other matters associated with the Master.

Cobham Church, restored, has much to interest the visitor :

Cobham Church.

especially is it rich in monumental brasses from the thirteenth to the sixteenth centuries. Here was an ancient college of which there are but scanty remains, the New College—dating from the modernity of Elizabeth's time—consisting of twenty almshouses. Cobham Park with its undulating turf, its broad stretches of bracken, its grand oaks, ashes, limes, and chestnuts, is one of the most attractive as it is one of the most extensive in the county. The most notable of the trees is a great chestnut known as "The Four Sisters." Cobham Hall, a noble red brick Elizabethan mansion with a magnificent collection of pictures representing many schools, is open to visitors on Fridays. Hither Charles I. and his Queen came just after their marriage "all the high-waies strewed with roses and all maner of sweet flowrs." The grand park, in which are many deer and a large heronry, may be crossed and Strood reached by footpath, which passes the high-placed, ugly and costly Mausoleum which was raised in 1783 but has never been utilised. The way takes us first through the park with glimpses of the red brick mansion, then through woodlands, with many very tall hornbeams and birches, to an outlook over the Medway valley, and so by hopfields to Strood.

The road from Cobham passing between the park and the open Ashenbank Wood is as attractive as the park itself; where it joins the Watling Street we might easily imagine ourselves in the New Forest. To the north of the main road is the little village of Shorne, the church of which has brasses and other monuments and a sculptured font not dissimilar from that at Northfleet. From the neighbourhood of the post office is to be had a splendid view of the shipping-dotted reach of the Thames known as the Lower Hope. A vague Sir John Shorne, supposed to have belonged to this village in mediæval times, was looked upon as a kind of uncanon-ised saint "who achieved fame by the curing of ague and gained notoriety as the custodian of the devil, whom, it is alleged, he imprisoned in a boot, with the result that shrines were erected to his memory." "Maister John Shorne" had a shrine here and was also worshipfully regarded in other places. His village is much uglified by red brick since Charles Dickens thought it one of the most beautiful in Kent.

From Shorne we come out on to the Gravesend road and turning to the right soon reach that place of many memories—Gadshill. Here Prince Hal and Poins played their trick on the fat knight until—

"Falstaff sweats to death
And lards the lean earth as he walks along,"
                                        C C

only to tell a different story of his own behaviour, how he was
"at halfsword with a dozen of them two hours together."
The fooling of genius is familiar to all, and Falstaff's connection
with the hill is appropriately perpetuated in the name of an inn.

Shorne Churchyard.

Gadshill—the summit of which is broad highway between
shrub grown gardens—was notorious as a scene of robberies
for centuries, but the most romantic episode attaching to it is
the robbery effected at four in the morning "by one Nick on
a bay mare just on the declining part of the hill on the west

side." The highwayman got away to Gravesend, ferried over the river and galloped helter-skelter, reaching York the same afternoon. Changing his dress Nick went to the Bowling Green where he met the Lord Mayor of York, entered into talk with him—and so, when charged with the crime, proved an alibi and got off on the strength of his Worship's evidence, the jury considering it impossible that a man who played at bowls at York one afternoon could have been at Gadshill on

The Sir John Falstaff Inn, Gadshill

the morning of the same day! Nick's exploit probably suggested to Harrison Ainsworth that ride to York of Dick Turpin's which has come to be better known than Turpin's actual doings. On the south side of the road on the top of the hill, masked by greenery, is Gadshill Place, which was bought by Charles Dickens in 1856 and where he died in 1870. The story has often been told how, as a boy, Dickens fixed his affections on this house, and how, as a man, his dream of possessing it was realised. Many as were the homes associated with the novelist this is the one likely longest to be the shrine which his admirers will visit : here in his pleasant home Boz spent his later years and here he suddenly passed away on June 9, 1870. His affection for the house grew with his stay in it. Shortly after he had entered into possession he wrote to a friend :

> " At this present moment I am on my little <entish freehold (not in top-boots, and not particularly prejudiced that I know of), looking on as pretty a view out of my study window as you will find in a long day's English ride. My little place is a grave red brick house, which I have added to and stuck bits upon in all manner of ways, so that it is as pleasantly irregular, and as violently opposed to all architectural ideas, as the most hopeful man could possibly desire. The robbery was committed before the door, on the man with the treasure, and Falstaff ran away from the identical spot of ground now covered by the room in which I write. A little rustic alehouse, called the Sir John Falstaff, is over the way—has been over the way ever since, in honour of the event. Cobham Park and Woods are behind the house : the distant Thames in front ; the Medway, with Rochester, and its old castle and cathedral on one side. The whole stupendous property is on the old Dover road.'

Gadshill Place has come to be regarded very appropriately as the centre of Dickens land—over the Medway are Rochester and Chatham associated both with his life story and with his novels, north by the marshes is Cooling with its reminders of " Great Expectations," south-west is Cobham as we have seen, and south-east the supposed Dingley Dell, with further afield Canterbury familiar to David Copperfield. Dickens loved this quarter of Kent associated with his early childhood as it was to be with his latest life, and many people love it the more for its association with him. On the Higham side of the hill are many pine trees and an obelisk—falling to pieces—erected to the memory of a citizen of Rochester.

Strood and Frindsbury, Rochester and Chatham, Brompton and Gillingham—all grown together but that the Medway sepa-rates the first two from the others—form a congeries of towns with curious nooks and corners of old buildings and tiled and gabled roofs—(especially as seen from the railway). By the river they are given over to cement works and other manufac-tures ; on the heights Chatham is given over to the military and on the river side to the naval works and dock-yards. Things have not changed very much—if we allow for the coming of tram-cars, the growth of the cement industry, and the extension of building operations—since Mr. Samuel Pickwick summed

up the four towns of Strood, Rochester, Chatham and
Brompton thus : " The principal productions of these towns
appear to be soldiers, sailors, Jews, chalk, shrimps, officers and
dock-yard men. The commodities chiefly exposed for sale in
the public streets, are marine stores, hard-bake, apples, flat-
fish, and oysters."
Of these towns Rochester is by far the most interesting both
for what it has to show and for the story it has to tell—the
others, with their long streets of new houses spreading by the

*View from the Chatham Recreation Ground, looking over the Barracks and
Dockyard to Brompton.*

riverside and up the chalk hill with their unpicturesque busyness need not detain us long, unless curiosity impels to a visit
to the great Dock-yards. At Strood we may recall however
that Anne Pratt, who did so much to popularise the study of
wild flowers, was born in 1806, being the daughter of a wholesale grocer.
According to an old saying certain Kentish folk are born with
tails, and that caudal addition is supposed to be a privilege
peculiarly attaching to those who hail from Strood. It was all
owing to the way in which their rude forefathers behaved to

Thomas à Becket when the Primate and the King had fallen
out, or so at least says Polydore Virgil when honouring "his
great God Saint Thomas." "When as it happened him upon
a time to come to *Stroude* the Inhabitants thereabouts (being
desirous to dispite that good Father) sticked not to cut the tail
from the horse on which he road, binding themselves thereby
with a perpetuall reproach : for afterward (by the will of God)
it so happened, that every one which came of that kinred of men
which plaied that naughty prank, were born with tails, even as
brute beasts be." Lambarde, to whom we owe the story, points
out that the same legend attaches to St. Augustine and his relations with some unmannerly Dorsetshire folk.

Strood and Rochester are connected by a bridge—running
closely parallel to the most hideous of all railway bridges—
successor after a long interval, to one of wood that crossed the
Medway here as early as 1300, for in that year Edward I. paid to
a citizen of Rochester twelve shillings in lieu of a horse which
had been hired and which had been blown off the bridge into
the river. Apparently this old bridge afforded but a hazardous
crossing, for in the British Museum is an ancient manuscript
poem in old French telling of the "Harpur a Roucestre," and
of how when midway over the bridge a violent wind blew him
over into the Medway (the pun is the minstrel's), of how he called
on the Virgin for assistance and still harping her praises was
carried a league down the stream where he landed in safety, and
duly offered up thanks for his miraculous preservation. By the
reign of Elizabeth the old wooden bridge had given place to "a
very Fayer Bridge of Stone," and that again has long since been
replaced by an iron structure.[1]

Its position on the road from Dover to London has made
Rochester an important place ever since the time of the Roman
occupation, and a native of the city forty years ago had the
curiosity to collect all references to remarkable visitors in old
manuscripts and printed records and contributed an entertaining
miscellany of such to the *Archælogia Cantiana*.[2] Some of
these visits were of distinguished Continental travellers passing
to or from London, others were of English monarchs journey-

---

[1] The stone bridge had at one time high, iron railings,—"that drunkards,
not uncommon here, may not mix water with their wine," as a French
gentleman put it,—but these were replaced by a stone balustrade in the
18th century.   [2] Vol. VI. pp. 43–82.

The Medway at Rochester.

ing thither to see their navy. Then too, the city was a stage
on the road for pilgrims from London to Canterbury—" Lo
Rouchester standeth here faste by "—and the century that saw
pilgrimages go out of fashion saw the navy rise into greatness
and the shore of the Medway become the chief of places for
the building and fitting out of ships.

Though the seat of a Roman castrum, it is by the remains
of its Norman castle and its interesting Cathedral that
Rochester chiefly appeals to the visitor now. The massive
keep and the Cathedral are the most prominent objects seen
over a medley of old gabled roofs as we reach the place by
train and each is worthy a visit for that which it has still to
show, and for that which it has to suggest of the past. The
Bishopric dates back to the beginning of the 7th century, when
it was one of the two first sees founded by St. Augustine. The
building, in which there are remains of the original Saxon and
the Early Norman churches, is full of architectural interest and
beauty and contains a number of remarkable old tombs and
monuments, notably that of Bishop Gundulf, the famous
monkish architect to whom London owes its White Tower and
who did much for Rochester, including the building of the
Castle. The Cathedral was also long celebrated and much
frequented for the shrine of St. William the patron saint of
the city. St. William was a baker from Perth who was
bound as pilgrim for the Holy Land when (it is believed
in 1201) he was murdered outside the walls of Rochester
and came to be associated therefore with this city.

Ernulf was another of its bishops to whom Rochester Cathedral
owed much improvement. He is the worthy who will be
remembered by readers of " Tristram Shandy " as author of
the portentously long and forceful curse which was read out by
Dr. Slop at Mr. Shandy's request the while my Uncle Toby
whistled " Lillabullero "—" May the Holy and Eternal Virgin
Mary, mother of God, curse him —May St. *Michael*, the
advocate of holy souls, curse him—and may all the angels,
and archangels, principalities and powers, and all the heavenly
armies, curse him. (Our Armies swore terribly in *Flanders*
cried my Uncle *Toby*,—but nothing to this.—For my own
part I could not have a heart to curse my dog so)."

Besides its monuments to ecclesiastical dignitaries Rochester
Cathedral has others that will appeal more intimately to most

people in the neighbouring memorials to Richard Watts the 16th century philanthropist, and to Charles Dickens, the novelist who has made the philanthropist familiar to thousands of readers. It is not necessary to do more than refer to "The Seven Poor Travellers," the reading of which must alone make many people desirous of visiting the quaint hostel in

The Crypt, Rochester Cathedral.

the High Street over the doorway of which runs the inscription

"Richard Watts, Esq.
by his Will, dated 22 Aug., 1579,
founded this Charity
for Six poor Travellers,
who not being Rogues, or Proctors,
May receive gratis for one Night,
Lodging, Entertainment,
and Fourpence each."

The small gabled house thus inscribed, which was rebuilt in

1771 and again "renewed and inscribed" in 1865, represents but a small portion of Watts' charities, the annual value of which is considerable, supporting almshouses and contributing to hospitals and other local institutions. At the time that Richard Watts left certain lands in the neighbourhood for the good of his townsfolk he could have little idea of the way in

The Bull at Rochester.

which the growth of the city would increase the value of his bequest, now said to reach the amount of seven thousand pounds a year. The quaint inscription which suggested Dickens' story was but one of the many features of old Rochester which appealed to the novelist. "The old High Street of Rochester is full of gables, with old beams and timbers carved into strange faces. It is oddly garnished

with a queer old clock that projects over the pavement out of
a grave, red-brick building, as if Time carried on business
and hung out his sign." Time has changed the city much,
but his " sign " still projects, and if the High Street is no longer
"full of gables" there is still much to be seen reminding us of
its past, the Guildhall, associated with Pip and Joe Gargery,
Eastgate House (the Nuns' House of " Edwin Drood "),
"Satis House," and the Bull still attract Dickensian
pilgrims.

In the year 1732 Hogarth and four friends set out on a
" Five Days Peregrination by Land and Water " down the
Thames and reached Rochester, where they enjoyed a two
hours' dinner "on a dish of soles and flounders, with crab
sauce, a calf's heart, stuffed and roasted, the liver fried and the
other appurtenances minced, a leg of mutton roasted, and
some green peas, all very good and well dressed, with good
small beer, and excellent port." After dinner rest a while, says
the proverb, and after such a dinner rest would certainly have
seemed advisable to most people, but the peregrinators were
apparently equal to anything, and at once sallied forth when
" Hogarth and Scott stopped and played at hop-scotch in the
colonnade under the Town-hall ; and then we walked to
Chatham, bought shrimps and ate them." The walk was not
a very long one for, as has been said, the towns are clustered
together here, a fact which is well put in the Hudibrastic
versifying of the " peregrination " made by the Rev. W. Gostling
when he told of the five surveying the scene from the top of
the castle :

> " All roundabout us then we gaze,
> Observing, not without amaze,
> How towns here undistinguished join,
> And one vast One to form combine.
> Chatham with Rochester seems but one,
> Unless we're shown the boundary-stone.
> That and its \ards contiguous lie
> To pleasant Brompton standing high ;
> The Bridge across the raging flood
> Which Rochester divides from Strood
> Extensive Strood, on t'other side,
> To Frindsbury quite close ally'd :
> The Country round and river fair,
> Are prospects made beyond compare,
> Which quite in raptures we admire ;
> Then down to face of earth retire."

Visitors should follow the jovial peregrinators in getting the wide view which is obtainable from the battlements of the Keep, a view of the broad stretching Medway, its course marked by the clustering chimney shafts of cement works, of the wooded hills, of the mass of slate-roofed grey houses which is Strood, and of the other towns now spread about this bit of the old Watling Street. When Pepys was here in 1665 he found little pleasure presumably in the climb—" to Rochester, to visit the old castle ruins which have been

Rochester Castle.

a noble place : but, Lord, to see what a dreadful thing it is to look upon the precipices, for it did fright me mightily." Here and there on the old walls may still be seen the beautiful wild pink, though no longer in such profusion as when Anne Pratt wrote of the castle as " bathed, though in ruins, with a flush of flowers," and when a local rhymer sang in about a hundred lines of

> " The Castle Pink !   The Castle Pink !
>   How wildly free it waves,
> Exposed to every blast that blows,
>   And every storm that raves."

The grand old ruined Keep forms the most prominent object in the view of the visitor approaching Rochester. After long being the chief stronghold in this part of Kent, and the scene of various sieges, it fell into a state of disuse until nearly a quarter of a century ago it was secured by the city and the grounds laid out as a place for public recreation. Its massy walls, stout pillars and bold carvings tell of the days when such a place could be held long against a foe, of the time when Odo, Bishop of Bayeux, owner of so large a portion of Kent, sought unavailingly on the death of the Conqueror to hold it on behalf of Robert of Normandy, its besieging by King John, and its subsequent capture by the Dauphin, of the fruitless siege by the barons when it was held by Simon de Montfort. It is true that the present structure did not witness all these changes, for the existing Keep was built early in the 12th century; use being made of the earlier one which in turn had incorporated something of the old Roman castrum, built according to unsupported legend by Julius Cæsar. Time in carrying on his " business " here has made the grim building of many memories the centre of a beautiful public pleasance, where young Rochester seems ever to be feeding the numerous pigeon-tenants of the Keep.

It was at Rochester that Charles II. rested for the night on his way to London when he had "come into his own again" in May, 1660, staying at what has since come to be known as Restoration house, a handsome, Elizabethan residence, and it was at Rochester that his brother James II. stayed twice during that time when, loth to stay and unwilling to fly, he was playing weakly into the strong hands of William of Orange. It is said that it was from 47 High Street that James made his final escape, stealing from the house by the back entrance at the dead of night with a single companion, and making for the river, where a small skiff was in waiting. When day broke the abdicating monarch was upon a smack in the Thames and a few hours later reached the French coast and the safety of ignominious exile.

Chatham and Brompton are mainly attractive for their military and naval establishments. The great Dock-yard with its reputation of over two centuries is a wonderful hive of impressive busyness which attracts and fascinates many visitors.

Here many ships have been launched from the days of Elizabeth; here was much building and work in the days when Mr. Samuel Pepys was Secretary to the Admiralty, and here in those days, too, befell the Dutch attack when De Ruyter brought his fleet up Medway and Thames and did considerable damage to the English navy. There seems to have been a good deal of bungling in high places, and a scapegoat being called for, the unhappy lot fell on Peter Pett, Commissioner of the Navy at Chatham and member of a family the name of which was represented in the Dock-yards for a couple of centuries. Pett was removed from his position, impiisoned in the Tower and threatened with impeachment. A contemporary satirist, Andrew Marvell it has been suggested, dealt with the matter in stinging fashion :

> " After this loss, to relish discontent,
> Some one must be accus'd by Punishment.
> All our miscarriages on *Pett* must fall ;
> His name alone seems fit to answer all.
> Whose Counsel first did this mad War beget ?
> Who all Commands sold thro' the Navy ? *Pett.*
> Who would not follow when the Dutch were bet ? . . . .
> Who to supply with Powder did forget
> *Languard, Sheerness, Gravesend* and *Upnor* ? *Pett.*
> Who all our Ships expos'd in *Chatham's* Net ?
> Who should it be but the *Phanatick Pett* ?
> *Pett*, the Sea Architect, in making Ships
> Was the first cause of all these Naval slips ;
> Had he not built, none of these faults had bin ;
> If no Creation, there had been no Sin."

East of the Dock-yards on the further sides of hills in which a large part of Chatham is basined are Gillingham and Grange, the latter close to the marshes, the former at the beginning of the broad stretch of fruit-growing country extending from here to Faversham. It is a far cry from the cherry orchards of Gillingham to the cherry orchards of Japan but Gillingham deserves mention on another account, for here was born William Adams, destined to be the first Englishman to reside in Japan, where he lived from 1600 until his death in 1620. Adams' letters are the earliest news which we have from the far eastern Empire, and it is interesting to recall that he " buylt " ships for the country that has now become a great naval power, and also to know that our adventurer's summing up of the Japanese, was so sure that it might—except in the matter of spelling—be that of the latest globe-trotter ; " This Iland of Iapon is a great land . . . The people of this Iland of Iapon are good of nature, curteous above measure, and valliant in warre ; their iustice is severely executed without any partialitie upon transgressors of the law. They are governed

Old Road, Chatham (Watling Street).

in great ciuilitie. I meane, not a land better governed in the world by ciuill policie."

East of Chatham on the broad Watling Street is Rainham with an interesting church, and southwards are many quiet wooded ways up the rising chalk land with but few and small hamlets, as at Bredhurst and Lidsing from which we can go

D D

through woods to Kits Coty House and so to the Medway again. Returning to the river at Rochester, a pleasant rising road may be followed through Borstal, and keeping to the higher way it affords us again and again views over the Medway valley, and an especially beautiful one when we near the great chalk pits overlooking Burham. Descending to the river opposite Snodland we can cross to that place and so return to Strood by Halling and Cuxton. Most of the names of these Medway-side villages are associated with cement, the little lines for carrying the chalk from the hill-side quarries are familiar objects, and the chimney shafts go far to destroy the beauty of these reaches of the river, yet there is much that is attractive about the scene on a bright day when barges with ruddy brown sails are passing along, but we must go far up the stream to find the Medway as Spenser describes it.

> " Like silver sprinkled here and there,
> With glittering spangs that did like stars appear."

To the north of Rochester spread the broad-stretching marshes lying between the Medway and the Thames. Here are various small villages and old churches, with many retired farms scattered on the flats, and about the lower hills into which the land rises as we near the Gravesend district. This peninsula formed by the river Thames and Medway is probably but little visited. I have zig-zagged over it without seeing anyone beyond villagers and field labourers except at the beautifully situated golf-links below Higham Upshire. Yet there is much pleasant country to be seen in the wooded hills and cornlands stretching across the central part of the peninsula and a charm in the broad marshes going down to the river. The villages have not much to detain us except that of Cooling (or Cowling), the old castle of which, part hidden by trees, is well worth visiting. Besides some portions of the walls there remains a fine flint and stone 14th century machicolated gatehouse almost perfect. Through the entrance is seen a modern house strangely contrasting with the ancient gateway. On the right-hand tower the visitor will notice an old enamelled inscription with seal duly attached. This runs :

> " Knoweth that beth and shall be,
> That I am made in help of the contre,
> In knowing of which thing,
> This is Chartre and witnessing."

The castle was built by John Lord Cobham, a powerful noble of his time, who was succeeded by his granddaughter, one of whose five successive husbands was that Sir John Oldcastle, the Lollard martyr, whose name first appeared in Shakespeare's " Henry IV." in place of that of Sir John Falstaff. Oldcastle shut himself up in Cooling and refused the Archbishop's citations, but was finally arrested and, after escaping from the Tower of London, was re-captured, tried, and executed for opinions which little more than a century later he would have been executed for denying. When Wyatt was seeking to raise Kent on behalf of Protestantism he unavailingly attacked Cooling, but the Lord Cobham of that day defended it so stubbornly that the siege had to be raised.

To the west of the castle beyond wide fields given up to the cultivation of vegetables is the interesting little village of Cliffe, a place of importance in the early times of the Church, overlooking wide marshes. Here Mr. J. Holland Rose thinks that when Napoleon contemplated the invasion of England he probably "hoped to effect a landing near the mouth of the Thames (perhaps on the Cliffe peninsula between Sheerness and Gravesend)." East of Cooling by winding lanes we may go to High Halstow, St. Mary's Hoo, Allhallows and Stoke, by fields of radish and other seed crops, and so down to the marshland pastures and the end of the peninsula at the Isle of Grain,—cut off by Yantlet Creek—with its restored little church noticeable for a castellated tower lower than the body of the building. Coming down off the higher ground towards Grain we see on our left over broad saltings, or marshes partly under water at high tide, the shipping of the Thames, and on the right that of the Medway. Going down to the shore by Grain Tower we have, over half a mile away across the mouth of Medway, the Dockyard of Sheerness.

The country here has changed a good deal since the old distich was written,

" He that rideth in the Hundred of Hoo
Besides pilfering Seamen shall find dirt enow."

CHAPTER XXI

LEAVING Rochester and Chatham with the strange mixture of past and future—the past of an ancient cathedral, a Norman castle, old houses and a fiction-master's creations, the future which the great dock-yards are concerned in safeguarding.—we come to a long stretch of country largely given over to the cultivation of fruit; cherry orchards appear to predominate, but are varied with tracts of plums, pears and apples, with fields upon fields of bush fruit, while there are also many of those hop-gardens which form our county's most persistent characteristic from the Weald to the marshes and "isles." To the railway traveller the journey from Chatham to Faversham in spring seems to be through "orchards, orchards all the way," and the fruit country may be followed northward to the marshes about the Medway estuary, and southward up the hills that lie between Maidstone and Ashford. The railway traveller gets but a "sample," and, beautiful as it is in blossoming and lambing time, not the best sample of this part of the country. The same may be said of the journeyer along the highway,—the old Watling Street, with which the railroad keeps closely parallel for most of the distance,—who gets but a glimpse of "the Cherrie Garden and Apple Orchard of Kent." It was in the Sittingbourne district that the first cherry orchard is reported to have been planted, so we may believe that it was hereabouts "our honest patriote Richard Harrys (fruiterer to King Henrie the 8) planted by his great cost and rare industrie the *sweet cherrie* temperate *pipyn* and the golden *renate* . . . about the year of our Lord Christ 1533." Of the coming of the cherry and of the "honest patriote" we saw something in

an earlier chapter, here it must suffice to say that from Gillingham to Faversham, zig-zagging north and south of the Watling
Street, we may pass by mile after mile of well kept orchards,
may be struck again and again by the radiatings which always
make the spectator a centre, thanks to the commonly adopted
quincuncial arrangement of the trees.

  The popularity of the cherry in Fuller's time is made plain
by that writer's enthusiastic testimony—" No English fruit is

Sittingbourne.

dearer than those at first, cheaper at last, pleasanter at all times ;
nor is it less wholesome than delicious . . . We leave the
wholesomeness of this fruit both for food and physic, to be
praised by others, having hitherto not met with any discom-
mending it. As for the outlandish proverb, ' He that eateth
cherries with noblemen, shall have his eyes spurted out with the
stones,' it fixeth no fault in the fruit ; the expression merely
being metaphorical, wherein the folly of such is taxed, who
associate themselves equal in expense with others in higher
dignity and estate, till they be losers at last, and well laughed

at for their pains." Even in a cherry stone the moraliser may find his text.

Rainham, or Renham as it was anciently spelt and is now frequently pronounced, has no special attractiveness beyond some curious monuments and brasses in the church, but from it we may find pleasant ways by orchards and fields to Upchurch, Lower Halstow—High Halstow we saw dominating the Thames marshes—and the marshes. The little Halstow church is worth visiting for it contains some Roman masonry reminding us that here we are in a neighbourhood where the Romans had an important centre and where it is believed they had their most extensive British potteries. Many pieces of such pottery and other remains have been recovered in this district on both sides of that highway, which is the most enduring mark the Romans left us. Some of the best remains of native glass of the Roman period have also been recovered hereabouts.

The marshes are broken much by broad creeks or inlets, and though there is something of a sameness about them there is a distinct charm in the wide, grassy stretches when seen under a bright sky, and a quiet that should please the greatest of solitudinarians. Here, too, the lover of birds may sometimes see some unusual visitors, but until such visitors are brought under an all-the-year-round Protection Act it seems unwise to specify either the birds or the localities in which they have been seen. The way in which rare birds are shot must have been newly brought home to many readers by Mr. W. J. Davis's interesting compilation on "The Birds of Kent," and must have suggested that collectors and indiscriminating "sportsmen" should not be allowed to welcome such visitants with a charge of shot "pour encourager les autres." It would be well if the shooting of our rarer birds could be made an offence against the law, as it is one against good taste; any one convicted of the offence twice might be made ineligible for having a gun license.

From the little marsh-land village of Wade may easily be reached the toll (and railway) bridge leading into Sheppey, the only link of the kind between the mainland and the Isle. Leaving Sheppey for a while we may return by the small village of Bobbing—where having "slipped into orders" the "execrable Titus Oates" was for a brief while vicar—to the main road and to the pleasantly situated Newington, a village surrounded by hop-gardens and orchards, lying mostly to the north of the high road. Its station is a good centre from which to reach the marsh district, affording within a walk of a few miles the most varied scenery, where hoplands and orchards gradually give place to the marsh meadows and saltings.

To the south by further stretches of hops and orchards, as we rise towards the chalk ridge are the villages of Hartlip and Stockbury, a little to the west of the former are the remains of an extensive Roman villa opened up and closely explored in the middle of the last century. Other Roman remains were found at about the same time at Sutton Baron (or Barne) about two miles east of Stockbury. Near here, too, are the orchard-surrounded villages of Bredgar, Tunstall and Borden. At Sutton Baron was born and died the antiquary Robert Plot, first custodian of the Ashmolean Museum at Oxford, historiographer royal, secretary to the Royal Society, and friend of our two great diarists, Pepys and Evelyn. Plot produced such "natural histories" of Oxfordshire and Warwickshire that Evelyn wished he might continue the work throughout all the counties. Later critics have been less kind. "Pliny, who wrote what he believed to be true, though too often assumed upon the credit of others, has been called a liar, because he knew nothing of experimental philosophy: and Dr. Plot, because he did not know enough of it." Plot is buried at Borden and there his widow erected a monument to his memory.

Returning to the high road again by the hamlets of Chestnut Street and Key Street we come out opposite the road to Bobbing and Wade, and turning to the right have Sittingbourne about a mile and a half away. The hamlets through which we pass here are chiefly notable for their names. Chestnut Street reminds us of the numbers of sweet chestnut trees seen in this district, descendants it is suggested of those originally introduced by the Romans, who fondly hoped to establish the tree for the sake of its food nuts, but the fruit it bears in this country is rarely anything but insignificant. It remains, however, one of the notable trees of our well-wooded county, though mostly grown in coppices as game cover, and for hop poles. Key Street takes its name from Keycol Hill—between it and Newington—which, according to Hasted, derives from Caii Collis or Caius Julius Cæsar's Hill!

Sittingbourne, reached by a navigable creek from the Swale, claims the distinction of being a sea port. It is one of the principal centres of the fruit-growing country, and forms with its near neighbours Milton and Murston an important place for the manufacture of cement, paper and bricks. It is too the railway junction for reaching the Isle of Sheppey. Sittingbourne church, having been destroyed by fire in the eighteenth century, has little beyond a curious monument to an unknown lady and infant, but Milton church has Roman and herring-bone work in its masonry. Milton—Milton Royal as it claims to be named—is one of the chief centres of the oyster fishery, and has long shared with Whitstable association with that delicate bivalve the reputation of which on this coast goes back to the days of the Romans. Here we overlook the marshes extending to the Swale, and going past the church may follow a footpath to an old quadrangular earthwork known as Castle Rough near to Milton Creek, where tradition says the Danish chieftain Hasting made a fortress in 894, after bringing eighty of his ships up the Swale.

These Swale marshes and the country adjacent seem indeed to have had great importance in olden times. On the further side of the creek and near to Sittingbourne is Bayford Castle, first erected—"a pre-conquest earthwork"—in the same year as Hasting formed his camp at Castle Rough, by King Alfred for the purpose of keeping watch upon the Danish invaders. It subsequently underwent conversion into a Norman castle, and centuries since fell from its high estate to being a mere farm house, and its ditch-surrounded enclosure to being an orchard. A mile and a half to the east of Bayford is the mound—amid cherry orchards—on which stood another of our Kentish castles, that of Tonge or Tong, anciently, if old Geoffrey of Monmouth is to be accepted as a veritable historian, Thong. The story runs that Hengist asked permission of Vortigern to send over for more Saxons to oppose the British king's enemies, and, that conceded, then pointed out that he ought to have some town or city granted him, to which Vortigern did not agree. "'Give your servant,' said Hengist, 'only so much ground in the place you have assigned me, as I can encompass with a leathern thong for to build a fortress upon as a place of retreat if occasion should require. For I will always be faithful to you, as I have been hitherto, and pursue no other design in the request which I have made. With these words the King was prevailed upon to grant him his petition ; and ordered him to despatch messengers into Germany, to invite more men over speedily to assistance. Hengist immediately executed his orders, and taking a bull's hide, made one thong out of the whole, with which he encompassed a rocky place that he had carefully made choice of, and within that circuit began to build a castle, which, when finished, took its name from the thong wherewith it had been measured."

Then came eighteen ships full of Saxons bringing with them Hengist's beautiful daughter Rowena, and at a feast at the new " Thong " Castle Vortigen fell in love with and married her. The romantic story has been set amid other scenes, but—allowing for the dropped h—seems fittingly to belong, and may well be recalled, here, though some writers who have no liking for the " flowers " of history dismiss the whole matter as an idle tale. On the main road just south of Tonge Mill near the place where the old castle stood is another of the orchard villages, Bapchild, with an Early English and Norman Church, while Rodmersham, another of them, is a little farther south. All along the road and a couple of miles on either side we may visit villages and hamlets among the cherries—places which are at their best at the Maytime of the year. Northwards, however, we soon get through the fruit tree country to the marshes bordered by the Swale and its creeks. Where these are given over to sheep-pasturing they have a distinct attractiveness, but in the neighbourhood of Teynham they are marked and marred by unlovely brick fields. Of an old rhyme concerning this bit of country there are two contradictory versions, one of which says

> If you'll live a little while,
>   Go to Bapchild
> If you'd live long
>   Go to Teynham or Tong."

This sounds satisfactory for those compelled to live in the marsh country, but then comes the pessimistic rendering

> " He that would not live long,
>   Let him dwell at Murston, Teynham or Tong."

Incidentally, perhaps, it illustrates the fact that such place-rhymes are produced not so much with the view of enunciating a truth as with the object of making an easily remembered jingle.   Perhaps the first version was made by a marsh-dweller and the revision by one who preferred the hills.   Healthful or not there is nothing about Teynham now to remind us that at one time the archbishops of Canterbury had a vineyard here. Kent had several vineyards in the 13th century, but they long since passed out of cultivation, giving place to other fruit and to the ubiquitous hops.   Here and there we come across vine

Faversham from the Creek.

covered cottages, but then it may be believed that the vine is more ornamental than fruitful.

Faversham, which Cobbett commended as "a very pretty little town" is a mixture of old and new, of the comfort of a substantial place with traditions, and the sordidness which belongs to so many creekside towns ; it had old time importance owing to the fact that the Watling Street from Dover first touched an inlet of navigable water where a creek comes inland from the Swale.   That it was a place of importance in Roman times has been shown by the discovery of many remains which have found their way into various collections, notably the

Gibbs collection in the British Museum. Later it was favoured as a Royal residence, being described in the 9th century as "the King's little town of Fevresham," and his "royal villa." Here in 930 Athelstane held a wittenagemote. The mediæval progress of the place was as usual marked by the establishment of an Abbey. This was founded by King Stephen and his Queen, who were buried here with their son. Abbey Farm, to the north of the town, not far from the creek, is on the site of the Abbey, of which there are but scanty remains.

Faversham Abbey has however an important place in our literary history, for in the middle of the 16th century it and its lands belonged to one Thomas Arden, or Ardern, one time mayor of the town, who on Sunday, February 15, 1550–1 was, as the "Wardmote Book of Faversham" records, "heynously murdered in his own parlour, about seven of the clock in the night, by one Thomas Morsby, a tailor of London, late servant to Sir Edward North, Knight, chancellor of the augmentations, father-in-law unto Alice Ardern, wife of the said Thomas Ardern." The "heynous" murder is chiefly marked out from other domestic tragedies by the way in which it touched the popular imagination so that Holinshed devoted five pages of his "Chronicle" to recording it, and a great dramatist—by some critics recognised as William Shakespeare —wrote a great tragedy on the theme. According to the chronicler and the dramatist Alice Arden and her paramour made incessant attempts on Arden's life only to be foiled again and again. The woman took all and sundry into her confidence, making them accessories, and various attempts were made on the goodman—now at Rainham as he journeyed homewards, an attempt frustrated by an arrival on the scene of "Lord Cheiny"; and now as he went to visit that nobleman in Sheppey, when a kindly fog fell. In the end the poor man was done to death in his own home, which was presumably near the Abbey, behind which the body was thrown and promptly discovered, the murderers having no time to cover up their tracks:

> "I fear me he was murdered in this house
> And carried to the field; for from that place
> Backwards and forwards may you see
> The prints of many feet within the snow.
> And look about this chamber where we are,

And you shall find part of his guiltless blood ;
For in his slipshoe did I find some rushes,
Which argueth he was murdered in this room."

The play which recounts the horrible story in all its details up
to the close, where five of the principals are ordered off to
execution, was first claimed for Shakespeare by a Faversham
critic, Edward Jacob, in 1770, and since then various writers
have taken sides, but the matter remains not proven. The
most notable counsel on behalf of the Shakespearean authorship being Mr. A. C. Swinburne, who says "Considering the
various and marvellous gifts displayed for the first time on our
stage by the great poet, the great dramatist, the strong and
subtle searcher of hearts, the just and merciful judge and
painter of human passions, who gave this tragedy to the new born
literature of our drama . . . I cannot but finally take heart to
say, even in the absence of all external and traditional testimony,
that it seems to me not pardonable merely or permissible, but
simply logical and reasonable, to set down this poem, a young
man's work on the face of it, as the possible work of no man's
youthful hand but Shakespeare's."

It is not possible to visit Faversham and forget the horror
which inspired one of the most Shakespearean of pre-Shakespear-
ean plays, but though there are references to a local inn, the
Flower-de-Luce, and to a farm at Bolton (*i.e.* Boughton) and
to Harty Ferry, there is little of local colour in the tragedy,
which is a crude story of greed, lust and punishment, in
the central character of which, the wife, it is not easy to
realise the great woman whom Mr. Swinburne sees—her
"penitential breath" seems rather the common cry of one
who had been found out—

" Pale and great,
Great in her grief and sin, but in her death
And anguish of her penitential breath
Greater than all her sin or sin-born fate,
She stands the holocaust of dark desire,
Clothed round with song for ever as with fire."

Where the Abbey once stood now spreads a large orchard
and the name remains only as attached to the neighbouring
farm, but much of the history of the town may be found in the
large cruciform tall-spired church in which are to be seen some
curious old paintings dating, it is believed, from the time when

the building was first erected in the Early English period. The church, which has monuments, brasses and other things of interest which well repay careful examination—including a brass to King Stephen, who was however probably buried in the long-gone church attached to the Abbey—was at one

Town Hall, Faversham.

time much frequented by pilgrims because it had a chapel dedi- cated to St. Thomas of Canterbury and altars to St. Crispin and St. Crispianus, who are looked upon as Faversham's special saints in that according to one tradition they fled hither from Rome during the Diocletian persecutions and set up as cobblers. The "Golden Legend" however makes them exercise their craft and suffer martyrdom at Soissons in France. Perhaps

they visited Faversham first.   It would not be pleasant to think
that they were entreated here as the legend tells us, for "these
holy men being sought of Rictius Varius, were founden amend-
ing and clouting poor men's shoes, which were taken and
bounden with chains and brought unto him.   And after many
interrogations and questions, they, refusing to sacrifice to the
idols, were stretched and bounden unto a tree, and were commanded to be beaten with staves, and after, awls such as shoes
be sewed with, were threaden and put under the ongles or nails
of their fingers, and lainers or latchets of their skin were cut
out of their back.   Who among these sharp and strong pains
praying, the awls sprang from their ongles and nails, and smote
the ministers that pained them and wounded them cruelly."
Millstones were hung round their necks, and they were thrown
in the river but swam easily ashore ; they were to be cast into
molten lead but it spurted into their persecutor's eye and
blinded him ; they were placed in boiling "pitch oil and
grease" but were led out of it by an angel unscathed.   Then
they prayed that they might come to the Lord and the swords
did not refuse to behead them.   We may be sure that the
martyrs' shrine at Faversham was much visited after the Battle
of Agincourt—

> "This day is call'd the feast of Crispian :
> He that outlives this day and comes safe home,
> Will stand a-tip-toe when this day is named
> And rouse him at the name of Crispian."

The saints are said to have carried on their shoemaking
trade "at a house in Preston Street, near the Crosse well, now
the sign of the Swan," and that house, even after the
Reformation had done away with their altar in the parish
church, was long a place of pilgrimage for other workers in the
craft of which St. Crispin is the special patron.

Faversham Grammar School is a famous foundation first
established in 1527 and later re-established by a royal charter
of Queen Elizabeth in 1576.   After standing for three hundred
years near the church, it was rebuilt thirty years ago and is to
be seen on the left by the railway traveller approaching the
town from London.

The central part of Faversham consists of narrow streets of
old houses, and has an air of comfortable prosperity, but as a

busy commercial centre it has spread southwards to Preston
and Ospringe and, northwards to Davington—each of which
places has a church with interesting monuments. At Preston
is a monument to Roger Boyle, father of the first Earl of Cork.
Ospringe church, which has been carefully restored, is a very
old edifice, presumably of earlier date than the Benedictine
Priory to which it was attached, which was founded in 1153.
This priory belonged to the "poor nuns of Davington"—to
the wrecking of two of whom beyond Herne Bay we owe the
twin towers of the church of Reculver. What remains of the

"Maison Dieu." Old House, Ospringe.

Priory is now a private residence. Near Ospringe again, we
have ecclesiastical remains in all that is left of Stone church—
fenced-in ruins with much Roman material in the masonry.
Here, too, is Judd's Hill, or Judde Hill, with remains of a
Roman camp, to which it has been suggested the old church
was attached. Hasted records that many coins and other
Roman relics were discovered here and at Davington. To the
west of Ospringe and just south of the main road is the small,
scattered parish of Norton—with an old ghost story attached
to Norton Court. The story runs, as jotted down from the
account of one present, that on the last day of August, 1719, a
couple of men were sent out rabbiting and returning in the

evening were near the house when their dog crept close and the men took to their heels and rushed to the gate. Then the following conversation took place.

"Are not you prodigiously frightened?"

·"I was never so frightened in all my life."

"What was it you saw?"

"Nay, what was it that frightened you so?"

"I saw a coffin carried, just by us, on men's shoulders."

"I saw the same, as plain as I ever saw anything in my life."

There was staying at Norton Court at the time an improvident divine, one-time secretary of the Royal Society, Dr. John Harris. Harris scoffed at the men's tale and, at the eating of the rabbits the next day, said "if the devil had had a hand in catching them he was sure they were good." On the Wednesday, talking of dreams at breakfast, the Doctor said he thought they were always recounting their dreams and talking of apparitions, and that he would make a collection of them and have them published; "for my part," added he, "if I ever took notice of a dream, it should be of one I had last night. I dreamed that the Bishop of ——, in Ireland, sent for me to come over to him, and I returned answer that I could not—for I was dead; when methought I laid my hands along by my sides, and so died." On the following Monday, just one week after the coffin-apparition, Dr. Harris died. He projected a "History of Kent" of which only one volume, "inaccurate and incomplete," was published.

South of Faversham we may go by beautiful ways towards the hilly country, through woods and lanes, to Throwley, Sheldwich and Selling, and so to Charing and Ashford or to Chilham, in districts described earlier. At Sheldwich is the grand park of Lees Court—the mansion built by Inigo Jones—with tragic memories. Here in the Commonwealth time lived Sir George Sondes, a Royalist whose loyalty cost him imprisonment and about thirty thousand pounds. A few years after he returned to Lees Court the younger of his two sons murdered the elder as he lay asleep, and was duly hanged at Maidstone a fortnight after the crime. A couple of miles to the west of Lees Court is Belmont Park, the seat of the first Lord Harris, conqueror of Seringapatam in 1815, and now the residence of his descendant the present Lord Harris who has won new laurels for the family in piping times of peace on the cricket field.[1]

Following the main road through Faversham brings us in a couple of miles to Boughton Hill, and one of the most extensive views over the well-cultivated and wooded country, across the grassy marshes to the boat-dotted estuary of the Thames. By orchards and hop gardens, through the little village of Good-nestone with its tiny church and Graveney, we reach the pasture marshes stretching along by Whitstable Bay to Whitstable, passing on the way near the disused church of Seasalter, which parish is now amalgamated with its neighbour. Though largely protected by a defensive bank the marshes are here, it is reported, being gradually encroached upon, and at low tide there is a wide stretch of muddy sand exposed on which are often to be seen large numbers of sea and shore birds.

A hundred years ago a collector of curious notices gave the following one as belonging to this neighbourhood. A famous post was erected by the direction of the surveyor of the roads of Kent inscribed " This is a bridle-path to Faversham, if you can't read this, you had better keep the main road." To this was given as parallel the Irish wayside bull : " On the edge of a small river in the Co. Cavan, there is a stone with the following strange inscription—' N.B.—When this stone is out of sight it is not safe to ford the River.' " I have looked in vain for the bridle path notice ; ridicule perhaps prevented its mainten-ance.

Leaving Faversham by Davington Hill we get, from the small village of Oare, a good view of the "crick" by which boats reach the town. West in the marsh is Luddenham church. Going on to Harty Ferry we pass across the marsh where many sheep pasture, and reach the embankment by which the land has been reclaimed. The ferry house is at the other side of the Swale on the Isle of Sheppey, and a patient wait will at length be rewarded by the arrival of the boat across the three-quarters of a mile of high-tide water   At low tide there are innumerable gulls, curlews and other birds, and these the wayfarer may well have time to watch if delayed as I have been for over an hour

---

[1] Lord Harris has recently issued a full " History of Kent County Cricket " tracing the game as played by Men of Kent and Kentish men from the beginning up to their winning for the county the position of " Champion " in 1906.

by thunder, hail and wind, that made the return of the boat impossible, a squall which washed boats and barges from their moorings, and even swept the gulls like large snow flakes down the wind. It was August, and the sun was shining brightly but an hour after the country had been shadowed by grey-edged clouds of inky blackness.

Harty Ferry is the best crossing for those who would visit Sheppey from end to end, afoot or awheel; for others there is a light railway from Queenborough which may be reached by ferry steamer from Port Victoria or by train or road from

Queenborough.

Sittingbourne. It was near Harty Ferry, by the way, that Thomas Arden was temporarily saved from his pursuers by fog, his murderers being hidden in "a certain broom-close betwixt Faversham and the ferry." There is still, it may be mentioned, a Broomfield to the west of Oare which may have been on the way to the old course of the ferry—a fact which seems to have escaped the annotators of the tragedy.

In its southern and eastern parts the island is largely marsh on which sheep pasture—it is Sheppey or Sheep isle—with wide corn fields on the higher ground, but as we get nearer the north side the country becomes hillier and more diversified with trees —mainly side-lopped elms—with wooded combes on the north.

From the higher ground, between the villages of Eastchurch and Minster, are beautiful distant views across the Swale and its marshes to the district from which we have come and in the other direction over the wide estuary of the Thames to the Essex shore, the water ever dotted with shipping. It is by its marshlands and its views that the isle appeals to me, its villages and its great town of Sheerness have little that is attractive, though those who look for the varied life and movement of a busy seaport and dockyard town will find them in plenty in the latter place Its fronts to the Thames and Medway are always lively with varied shipping from the sombre vessels of the Navy to the barges with their red-brown sails, the fishing smacks and trawlers, fussy tugs and smaller craft, gadding about between the pier and the various moored ships.

Queenborough—which owes its name to the Queen of Edward III.—was the site of a strong castle destroyed in the 17th century, of which but part of the moat and well, still in use, remain. Now the place is chiefly notable as a port of embarkation for the Continent. When Hogarth and his fellows were here they found it like "a Spanish town, viz., there is no sign of any trade," could get no fresh meat or poultry to eat, and noted a curious epitaph on "Henry Knight Master of a Shipp to Greenland and Herpooner 24 voyages—

> In Greenland, I Whales Sea horses, Bears did Slay
> Though Now my Body is Tutombe in Clay."

At Sheerness the veritable historian of the outing tells us Hogarth was laughed at, as well he might be, "for sitting down to cut his toe-nails in the garrison"!

Minster Church standing high with grand views over the busy river and the mainland, is interesting on account of various monuments and brasses, notably the monument to Sir Robert de Shurland, one-time Lord Warden of the Cinque Ports, the romantic tradition of whose death is set forth with humoristic details by Barham in his legend of "Grey Dolphin." The Hogarthian company were also told the story—with a difference. Summarised, the tradition is that Shurland, finding a monk would not bury a corpse that had been washed ashore, had him buried also! King Edward I. or Queen Elizabeth—accounts vary thus widely—being on board ship off the Nore, Shurland mounted his horse, swam out to the vessel, got royal pardon for his crime, and swam back again. On landing he met a mysterious old woman, who said that though the horse had saved his life then it would yet be the cause of his death. Shurland, to disprove her prophecy, dismounted, and slew his steed.   Years later, walking on the shore, he kicked the horse's

The highest point in the Isle of Sheppey.

skull, injured one of his toes, and died.   In proof of the truth of tradition a horse's head forms part of the monument.
    Near to Minster Church was a nunnery, founded in the seventh century by Sexburga, of which there are but few remains ; it was destroyed by the ravaging Danes, and only re-established four

or five hundred years later, then to flourish until the Dissolution, when it was given to the Cheyneys of Shurland—a fine old mansion now a farm house, beautifully situated to the east of Eastchurch.

Along the foot of the clay cliffs at the north side of Sheppey —as along the similar strip between Whitstable and Reculver— are found quantities of iron pyrites. This was presumably the "certaine stone" used by "one Mathias Falconer (a Brabander)" for the making of copperas when Lambarde saw his furnace at Queenborough in 1579.

CHAPTER XXII

LONDON, properly a Middlesex city, has so spread into the neighbouring counties of Essex, Kent, and Surrey that miles of their highways have become but parts of the capital. Village after village has been brought under the great central influence until it is difficult to say where, despite City limits and County limits, London ends in any given direction. Daniel Defoe, early, and Horace Walpole later, in the 18th century, commented on the way in which London was reaching to the outlying villages, marvelled over its growth, and foretold the absorption of places many of which were annexed in the 19th century, and now, at the beginning of the twentieth, the spread of Suburbia has reached from fifteen to twenty miles in many directions, and further spreading is indicated by the cutting up of estates, the advertising of " eligible building sites," far into what was a generation or two ago still the heart of the country. This change means the destruction of much beauty, for the notice-board of the builder is too often the shadow of coming events which mean the transmogrifying of country into suburb, of suburb into town. Such notice boards are common objects of the wayside south as far as Westerham and east as far as Gravesend, though happily the big section of our county comprised in such a triangle still includes wide stretches of unspoiled commons, parks, and farmlands. Its whole extent, too, is so brought into touch with town by trains and trams that anywhere within it may be explored on a " half-holiday " excursion.

Though London has absorbed so much of our county we may well glance at those places which have become part of the

"Great Metropolis" or of its greater Suburbia. Going down the Thames we reach the division between Surrey and Kent at Deptford, a place that became one of naval importance in Henry VIII.'s time, when there was established here " The Corporation of the Elder Brethern of the Holy and Undivided Trinity "—the original of that body, now known as Trinity House, which regulates and manages lighthouses and buoys around the shores of England. It was here at Deptford that Elizabeth honoured Drake on board the *Golden Hind* after his circumnavigation of the world, and it was here that Tsar Peter the Great came to learn the art of ship-building, and where he grieved John Evelyn by driving wheelbarrows through the beautiful holly hedges of Sayes Court—but hedges, the trees which the diarist recorded planting, and the mansion to which they were attached, have long since gone. Evelyn, indeed, had given up Sayes Court a few years before his death, on inheriting the stately domain of Wotton in Surrey. Now Deptford has little about it to suggest its past, for the naval establishments have removed otherwhere, the site of Sayes Court is occupied by a Workhouse, and the headquarters of the Trinity House Brethren are on Tower Hill. It is a dingy, busy river-side district where engineering and other works are carried on.

It was at Deptford—in the churchyard of St. Nicholas—that there was buried on June 1st, 1593, that singer of brave translunary things, Christopher Marlowe, a poet who, had life been granted him, might, it has been conjectured, have rivalled the greatness of his contemporary of Stratford-on-Avon. He was, however, but thirty when a tavern brawl here in Deptford—following on a visit to Drake's *Golden Hind*—brought his life to an end. Had Shakespeare died at Marlowe's age Marlowe would rank as the greater poet.

A little further down the river is Greenwich, a place that, backed by its fine park and with the noble Hospital on the river-side, has more to attract the visitor than any other of our Thames-side places. Here the Danes brought their vessels, and inland, on the height of Blackheath, formed one of their camps Here, later, were stately palaces of the nobility and monarchs ; for the first Edward is believed to have lived here, and the Good Duke Humphrey—whose bad wife we met at Leeds Castle—built a magnificent mansion to which he gave the name of Placentia, formed the park and built in it a high tower. After many changes and rebuildings Placentia has become Greenwich Hospital and Naval Museum, the tower has been replaced by the Observatory, though much of the park remains. In Tudor times Greenwich was a place of great importance ; Henry VIII. was born and was twice married here, and here his daughters Mary and Elizabeth were born and his son Edward VI. died.

In the splendid times of Henry VIII. and of his younger daughter it was the centre of much courtly pageant—at Greenwich ambassadors were received in pomp and circumstance, and the Court was wont to enjoy its Christmas festival. The river was then the great highway and was frequently gay with the coming and going of the nobles or with stately processions, as when Henry set out from Greenwich for Westminster with his second bride, after her long courtship, for the beginning of her short triumph and her coronation at Westminster. Something of the state which was kept here may be gathered from Paul Hentzner's account of the pomp which attended Queen Elizabeth on her passage from her private apartments to the Chapel. On his journey down to Greenwich the German lawyer was first impressed by " The ship of that noble pirate, Sir Francis Drake, in which he is said to have surrounded this globe of earth." (There is a lawyer-like safeguarding in the " said to have.")

" We were admitted, by an order Mr. Rogers had procured from the Lord Chamberlain, into the presence chamber, hung with rich tapestry, and the floor, after the English fashion, strewed with hay, through which the Queen commonly passes on her way to chapel. At the door stood a gentleman dressed in velvet, with a gold chain, whose office was to introduce to the Queen any person of distinction that came to wait on her ; it was Sunday, when there is usually the greatest attendance of nobility. In the same hall were the Archbishop of Canterbury, the Bishop of London, a great number of Councillors of State, officers of the Crown, and gentlemen, who waited the Queen's coming out, which she did from her own apartment when it was time to go to prayers, attended in the following manner :—

First went gentlemen, barons, earls, Knights of the Garter, all richly dressed and bareheaded ; next came the Chancellor, bearing the seals in a red silk purse, between two, one of whom carried the Royal sceptre, the other the sword of state, in a red scabbard, studded with golden *fleurs de lis*, the point upwards : next came the Queen, in the sixty-fifth year of her age, as we were told, very majestic ; her face oblong, fair, but wrinkled : her eyes small, yet black and pleasant ; her nose a little hooked ; her lips narrow and her teeth black (a defect the English seem subject to, from their too great use of sugar) ; she had in her ears two pearls, with very

rich drops ; she wore false hair, and that red ; upon her head she had a
small crown, reported to be made of some of the gold of the celebrated
Lunebourg table ; her bosom was uncovered, as all the English ladies have
it till they marry ; and she had on a necklace of exceeding fine jewels ;
her hands were small, her fingers long, and her stature neither tall nor low ;
her air was stately, her manner of speaking mild and obliging. That day
she was dressed in white silk, bordered with pearls of the size of beans,
and over it a mantle of black silk, shot with silver threads ; her train was very
long, the end of it borne by a marchioness ; instead of a chain she had an
oblong collar of gold and jewels. As she went along in all this state and
magnificence, she spoke very graciously, first to one, then to another,
whether foreign Ministers, or those who attended for different reasons, in
English, French, and Italian ; for, besides being well skilled in
Greek, Latin, and the languages I have mentioned, she is mistress of
Spanish, Scotch, and Dutch. Whoever speaks to her, it is kneeling ; now
and then she raises some with her hand."

With the growth of docks, the spread of manufactures, the
smoke-gloom which hangs over London and follows far down
the Thames, the incessant passage of steamboats of all kinds,
from the black fussy little tug to the large ocean-going vessels,
it is not easy to picture the river as it must have appeared in
the olden days before the colour of all things had been deadened
by smoke, when the air was clearer, the barges of the nobles
were gaily decked with colours, and colour still played a
large part in the national costume. With the coming of the
Commonwealth, Greenwich fell from its high estate, and though
the Merry Monarch had the decayed Placentia demolished and
a new palace designed by Inigo Jones, it was never completed.
Then in the time of William and Mary (who was born here),
after the naval battle off La Hogue, the Queen had the happy
idea of converting the palace into a hospital for maimed sailors.
The necessary alterations were begun, but little was done until
after Mary's death, when William completed it as a memorial to
his consort. As Macaulay says :

"A plan was furnished by Wren : and soon an edifice, surpassing that asylum which the magnificent Lewis had provided for his soldiers, rose on the
margin of the Thames. Whoever reads the inscription which runs round the
frieze of the hall will observe that William claims no part of the merit of the
design, and that the praise is ascribed to Mary alone. Had the King's life been
prolonged till the works were completed, a statue of her who was the real
foundress of the institution would have had a conspicuous place in that court,
which presents two lofty domes and two graceful colonnades to the multi-
tudes who are perpetually passing up and down the imperial river. But
that part of the plan was never carried into effect ; and few of those who now

gaze on the noblest of European hospitals are aware that it is a memorial of the virtues of the good Queen Mary, of the love and sorrow of William, and of the great victory of La Hogue."

For over a century and a half the Greenwich Pensioner, "that strange composition of battered humanity and blue serge," was a familiar object. Then, about forty years ago, it was found that the pensioners preferred having their pensions and living in their own homes to being congregated at the Hospital, and the magnificent building was put to appropriate new uses as a Naval College, Sailors' Hospital, and Naval Museum. Wren's handsome Painted Hall should be visited for its fine series of naval pictures, while the Hospital as a whole—to which Inigo Jones, Sir Christopher Wren, and Sir John Vanbrugh all contributed—should be seen from the splendid river terrace, and again from the slopes of the park which, with its deer, its undulating ground of nearly two hundred acres; its splendid trees, is one of the most beautiful places of the kind near London. According to Horace Walpole, compared with Greenwich, "even the glories of Richmond and Twickenham hide their diminished heads." I do not fancy that many people would now say ditto to Mr. Walpole.

The Observatory, where all manner of astronomical, meteorological, and magnetical observations are continuously being carried on, erected by Charles II. on a hill in the middle of the park in place of Good Duke Humphrey's tower, is of world-wide fame. Through here runs the meridian from which all measurements east and west are made, and from which our time is calculated. "Greenwich time" stands for unexceptionable accuracy.

Just south of Greenwich and adjoining the park is Blackheath, an open space which has been a popular gathering place for centuries since the northernmen formed their camp upon it. A great cave suggests that pre-historic man made use of it; tumuli long since opened, and the discovery of numerous Roman relics all round the neighbourhood, show its old importance. In 1381, 1450, 1497, and 1554, when the flag of rebellion was raised under the successive leadership of Wat Tyler, Jack Cade, Lord Audley, and Sir Thomas Wyatt, it was on Blackheath that the insurgents camped before marching on London. Here, in the first of these rebellions, the "prest of S. Mary,"

John Ball, preached his famous incendiary sermon on the
text

> " When Adam delved and Eve span,
> Who was then the gentleman ? "

to the assembled multitude of a hundred thousand followers
whom his words had largely recruited to Wat Tyler's banner.
When Cade was here he had with him "infinite numbers"
according to Shakespeare.   Four scenes of the second part of
" Henry VI." are laid on Blackheath, and in the first of them
we get an idea of the unruly multitude—and in the "asides" a
hint of the coming downfall of the leader.

" *Holland.*   I see them.   I see them.   There's Best's son, the tanner of
Wingham—·

Bevis.   He shall have the skins of our enemies, to make dog's-leather
of.

Holl.   And Dick the butcher—

Bevis.   Then is sin struck down like an ox, and iniquity's throat cut like
a calf.

Holl.   And Smith the weaver—

Bevis.   Argo, their thread of life is spun.

Holl.   Come, come, let's fall in with them.

*Drum.   Enter Cade, Dick Butcher, Smith, the Weaver, and a
Sawyer, with infinite numbers.*

Cade.   We, John Cade, so termed of our supposed father—

Dick.   [*Aside*] or rather, of stealing a cade of herrings.

Cade.   For our enemies shall fall before us, inspired with the spirit of
putting down kings and princes—Command silence.

Dick.   Silence !

Cade.   My father was a Mortimer—

Dick.   [*Aside*] He was an honest man, and a good bricklayer.

Cade.   My mother a Plantagenet—

Dick.   [*Aside*] I knew her well ; she was a midwife.

Cade.   My wife descended of the Lacies.

Dick.   [*Aside*] She was, indeed, a pedler's daughter and sold many laces.

Smith.   [*Aside*] But now of late, not able to travel with her furred pack,
she washes bucks here at home.

Cade.   Therefore am I of an honourable house.

Dick.   [*Aside*] Ay, by my faith, the field is honourable ; and there was
he born, under a hedge, for his father had never a house but the cage.

Cade.   Valiant I am.

Smith   [*Aside*] A' must needs ; for beggary is valiant.

Cade.   I am able to endure much.

Dick.   [*Aside*] No question of that ; for I have seen him whipped three
market-days together.

Cade.   I fear neither sword nor fire.

Smith.   [*Aside*] He need not fear the sword ; for his coat is of proof.

Dick. [*Aside*] But methinks he should stand in fear of fire, being burnt i' the hand for stealing of sheep.

Cade. Be brave, then ; for your captain is brave, and vows reformation. There shall be in England seven halfpenny loaves sold for a penny ; the three-hooped pot shall have ten hoops ; and I will make it felony to drink small beer ; all the realm shall be in common ; and in Cheapside shall my palfry go to grass ; and when I am King, as King I will be—"

This was in June ; in July the King-to-be was wounded and captured by Alexander Iden, and died in a cart on the way to London.

Audley's brief rebellion, which is less well known than the others, and was occasioned by heavy taxation, had started in Cornwall. On June 17, 1497, the day after they reached Blackheath, the rebels were defeated and before the end of the month their leader, "clothed in a paper coat," was beheaded on Tower Hill. Bishop Latimer, in preaching before Edward VI. half a century later, gave a pleasant scrap of autobiography. "My father was a yeoman, and had no lands of his own, only he had a farm of three or four pound by year at the uttermost, and hereupon he tilled so much as kept half a dozen men. He had walk for a hundred sheep ; and my mother milked thirty kine. He was able, and did find the King a harness, with himself and his horse, while he came to the place that he should receive the King's wages. I can remember that I buckled his harness when he went unto Blackheath Field."

But Blackheath has seen the pageantry of peace as well as the panoply of war, having been the great meeting place to which the King or his nobles journeyed for the welcoming distinguished visitors, the place to which official London went to meet the monarch returning from victorious war. The neighbourhood of the heath boasted many notable mansions in the 17th and 18th centuries—here the dramatist-architect Sir John Vanbrugh, the polite Lord Chesterfield, the brave General Wolfe, and the unhappy Queen Caroline successively dwelt. Vanbrugh "Castle" and Vanbrugh House, still standing, were built by that dramatist-turned-architect, for whom a fellow wit proposed the epitaph :—

> "Under this stone, reader survey
> Dead Sir John Vanbrugh's house of clay :—
> Lie heavy on him, earth, for he
> Laid many heavy loads on thee."

At Vanbrugh House, Thomas Hood stayed for a short time during the last few months of life, and to Blackheath Felix Wanostrocht—the Nicholas Felix of the cricket field—removed the school which he had at Camberwell—the school which Hood as a boy had attended and of which he sang in his "Ode on a distant Prospect of Clapham Academy." Black-heath, Lee, Lewisham—these contiguous places have become part of the great suburban London. Lewisham was the birth-place of an eminent divine, Brian Duppa, and the burial place of the unhappy young Irish poet Thomas Dermody, who boasted, " I am vicious because I like it."

Woolwich, the next great centre beyond Greenwich along the Thames, which between them takes a northerly bend by Blackwall and Bugsby's Reaches, is not a place to detain long anyone who is not interested in military and naval matters; such can gain permission to inspect the ·Arsenal and other " sights." Kent, which for centuries claimed the privilege of leading the van in battle, may well be proud of having within its confines such establishments as Woolwich, Sheerness, and Chatham—all concerned in the consolidation of national de-fence. At Woolwich was born that sweetest of Cavalier singers Richard Lovelace.

Charlton, near Woolwich, was long—until about forty years ago—the scene of a more or less unruly " Horn Fair" every October on St. Luke's day. According to tradition the Fair originated in the time of King John owing to that monarch having an amour with a miller's wife in the neighbourhood. The gathering place was Cuckold's Point, near Deptford, from which the mob, bearing and wearing all kinds of horns, marched in procession through Deptford and Greenwich to Charlton ; the men at one time attending in women's clothes—which suggests that King John may have forestalled the disguise of Sir John Falstaff.

In 1642 there was seen " the strange appearance of a Man-Fish about three miles within the River Thames, having a musket in one hand and a petition in the other." The story of the apparition seems to have been a hit at the readiness of the Men of Kent to " petition," and the promptness with which they were prepared to back their appeals with force. It seems also to have suggested to some ingenious person of Woolwich a " fake " for the wonderment of Londoners, for shortly after-

wards a pamphlet was published giving " a Relation of a terrible
Monster, taken by a Fisherman near Wollage, July 15, 1642,
and is now to be seen in King Street, Westminster, the shape
whereof is like a Toad and may be called a Toad-fish ; but
that which makes it a Monster is that it hath hands with
fingers like a man, and is chested like a man, being neere five
foot long and three feet over, the thickness of an ordinary
man."

Beyond Woolwich, by the open Bostall Common and woodland overlooking the marshes of Plumstead and Erith, largely
reclaimed in Elizabeth's time, we come to Erith, passing on the
way Abbey Wood, which takes its name from Lessness Abbey,
an establishment of which there are a few remains. Erith,
a place of many manufactures and of old maritime importance,
has yet a certain rural attractiveness in many of its surroundings ;
south of it, by market gardens and orchards, we come to Crayford, situated on the little River Cray not far from its junction
with the Darent. Here Hengist overthrew the Britons so
that, as the " English Chronicle " has it, they "forsook Kent-
land and fled with much fear to London." London is now
extending with its suburban villa-building so far in this dirce-
tion that it is interesting to learn that the River Cray was in
the middle ages the bound of the citizen's right of chase.
Near Crayford are several of those pits in the chalk, over the
ancient use of which archæologists have puzzled.

At this town the Watling Street crossed the Cray, and following
it Londonwards we come to Bexley Heath and Welling. The
old village of Bexley, on the Cray, a little south of its residential
" expatiation," is still a pleasant-looking place, with park-like
surroundings backed by Dartford Heath and the extensive
Joyden Woods, which we approach yet nearer at North Cray.
At Blendon Hall lived for a time William Camden, to
whom directly or indirectly all students of archæology and
topography owe much. At Bexley an ingenious student of
moths and butterflies has started a " farm " for the breeding of
those insects, an enterprise likely to be successful in days when
"collectors" of such find it simpler to buy than to capture
their "specimens." Crossing the Cray at Bexley a very
pleasant journey may be made by the road which, with the
stream mostly on our right, takes us to the Crays and Orpington, through country rich in fruit and hop gardens and still

well diversified with trees.   At North Cray "carotid-artery-
cutting Castlereagh " committed suicide.   North, Foot's, St.
Paul's, and St. Mary's Crays are all ancient places, mostly with

The Parish Church, Bromley.

unlovely modern additions, with old churches possessing notable features, that **at** St. Paul's being the most interesting
building, that at St. Mary's rich in monumental brasses.

Orpington—where the Cray starts on its eight-mile flow to the Darent—is an old village the centre of an extensive fruit and hop-growing district which spreads far into the surrounding parishes. Few travellers by railway passing through Orpington Station can fail to be struck by the wide hillside fields of straw-berries, as further on by the tracts of black currants—gayzels as they are sometimes termed in this county—and other bush fruit. The wonderful neatness with which a many acred field of strawberries is kept would have gladdened the heart of that good Bishop who, as reported by Izaak Walton, declared of the strawberry that "doubtless God could have made a better berry, but doubtless God never did."

In the southern part of this district of Kent near London, to which following the course of the Cray has brought us, there are still beautiful commons, handsome parks and wide woodlands, though some of the commons are getting built around and sophisticated. Farnborough, Keston and Hayes, however, re-main as rural as any district within fourteen miles of London. Farnborough has nothing particular to claim our attention, but a pleasant road or pleasanter footpath across the fields by quaintly named Farthing Street takes us to Downe, where the great investigator Charles Darwin lived for many years and carried on those studies which revolutionised natural history. It is, perhaps, appropriate that the home of the man who taught us so much should now be converted into a school. In the field opposite his house Darwin is said to have pursued those observa-tions which resulted in his important work on the earthworm.

West of Farnborough, on high ground, is the fine extent of Holwood Park, from the footpath crossing which from Keston to Downe are to be had some grand views through the trees; while from the higher ground of "Cæsar's Camp" a more ex-tensive landscape may be seen. Here is believed to have been an ancient British town, and here, as villa and other remains have testified, the Romans had an important station. Outside the park on the north is the small but lovely Keston Common, one of the most attractive "playgrounds" within easy reach of London; on the common is a spring traditionally known as Cæsar's Well, the water from which supplies a series of three beautiful, tree-shaded lakes, and from the last of them emerges the little Ravensbourne that, passing through Bromley and Lewisham, reaches the Thames at Deptford.

Holwood Park was long the residence of "the heaven sent minister" William Pitt, and to his ownership attaches a story similar to that of Dickens and Gadshill, for, born in the neighbourhood, it is recorded that Pitt as a child "longed to call the wood of Holwood his own ;" a desire he was able to gratify shortly after becoming Prime Minister. It was here that he concerted with William Wilberforce the campaign against slavery. On the footpath through the park already referred to is a stone seat, placed there nearly half a century ago to commemorate a history making conversation. It is inscribed with a passage from one of Wilberforce's letters : " I well remember, after a conversation with Mr. Pitt, in the open air, on the root of an old tree at Holwood, just above the steep descent into the Vale of Keston, I resolved to give notice, on a fit occasion, to bring forth the abolition of the slave trade." Leaving the park by a series of steps surmounting the park paling, the road to the right will take us pleasantly by Keston Mark and Bromley Common—which is no common—to Bromley, but a more attractive way is over the corner of Keston to the old windmill and pretty little Keston village, happily placed between two wooded commons, for coming through it we are on the broad, gorse-grown tract of Hayes. Dinah Maria Craik, author of that ever popular story " John Halifax, Gentleman," is buried at the old Keston church which stands near the south-western corner of Holwood Park.

Hayes Common in spring time, with its wide prospect, its gorse and hawthorn, its fine trees at the northern end, is one of the most beautiful bits of country easily accessible from London. Hayes village, a quiet little place north of the common, is chiefly memorable in that it was here that the great Lord Chatham lived for many years. It was to Hayes Place, which he had built, that he was removed after his collapse in the House of Commons, and there a month later he died. At Hayes, in 1759, the second William Pitt, a man who made history, was born, and at neighbouring Pickhurst, exactly a century later, died Henry Hallam, a man who wrote history. Near Hayes is West Wickham—close on the Surrey border—with, a mile from the village, Wickham Court, a handsome Tudor manor house traditionally associated with Henry VIII.'s courtship of Anne Boleyn, for here it is said that the lady stayed during some part the time that the

F F

King was planning to clear her way to the throne; Anne Boleyn's Walk is still pointed out in the grounds.

Just north of West Wickham Station is Langley Park, long the residence of the Style family. Here in the 16th century lived Sir Humphrey Style, cupbearer to Charles I., and his half-brother, William Style, a distinguished writer on law. A long letter from Sir Humphrey to his wife (February, 1632) gives interesting particulars of the preparations necessary for attending the Assizes in state in the olden time. There is much instruction as to the horses to be utilised, "well dressed, fed, and trimmed," and how they are to be taken "softely" to Dartford to meet Sir Humphrey. The latter half of the letter may be given as illustrating the thought which had to be taken when a Kentish gentleman desired to make a brave appearance in Stuart days :

" On Saturdaye morninge, before you goe out of towne, send Snelgar to Sir John Spralie, to fetch the horse hee hath lent me, and let him be wel looked to at my stable in London, till I coom thither on Mundaye ; then I will dispose of him, and would have Mr. Brookes to fit the boyes shute to him, and if there be ever an ould laced band of mine past my wearing, let the boye have it. If the Croidon shoemaker hath not brought my boots and the boy's, let him be sent for with all speede. I woold have the Cochman, if thou canst spare him, to goe to Langlie for a daye or two, and let him take oile with him to oile the great Coche, and let him bee sure it bee well mended and [clea]ne, for I wolde have that Coche brought to mee on Shrove Sundaie to London, to be theare in readinese. I would have thee send for Sir Cornelius Fairemedu, to desier him not to faile to be ready according to his promis, on Tewesdaye morning, to goe along with mee ; allso that he speak to Sir John Ashfield and Mr. Braye, and any one gallant man like himselfe, that maye make the better showe. Let Mr. Brooke be spoken to [that] my satten shut bee in readines, and, if I have never a silver hatband, that he bespeake mee a curius neate one. I wold have brought from Langley the felt hat laced with satten, and my damask night bagg and cloth.

" This is all, Sweete hearte, I can remember for this time. I pray thee bee merry, and make mutch of thy self, and take the coch and go brode this fayre wether ; it will do thee good. So, with my best love to thee, and my kind remembrance to my sister and all our friends, in great haste by reason of the spedie departure of the bearer, who hath promised me safely to deliver this letter, I rest
            Thy trewly loveing husband."

North of Langley Park are Beckenham and Bromley, and even in Cobbett's time it could be said, "when you get to Beckenham, which is the last parish in Kent, the country begins to assume a cockney-like appearance." A brass to Lady

Style's " trewly loveing husband " may be seen in Beckenham
Church.   Beckenham is a large, residential, suburban town,
and Bromley—which in recent years has been granted the
dignity of a municipal borough—has become the same.   Here
was long a palace of the Bishops of Rochester—built by Gun-

Beckenham.

dulf—and in the parish church we are reminded of Dr. Johnson, for his wife is buried here, with a Latin inscription which
he wrote, and here also lies his friend Dr. John Hawkesworth.
In the neighbourhood of Bromley are still pleasant walks by
Sundridge and Bickley Parks, and still some fairly rustic lanes

F F 2

but great are the changes within the past quarter of a century. Just beyond Bickley is Chislehurst, with its beautiful common, its wooded hills dotted with villa residences.

On the west side of Chislehurst common is Camden Place—named after the Elizabethan antiquary who died here in 1623. More recent memories attaching to the mansion are those of the exiled Napoleon III. and the Empress Eugenie. Here Napoleon died in 1873, and here half a dozen years later was

Beckenham.

brought the body of his gallant young son the Prince Imperial, killed in Zululand. The procession along the beauteous common was a sight the impressiveness of which is little likely to be forgotten by anyone present when the last hope of the French Imperialists, killed in a foreign war, was brought to be laid by his father, near the home of their exile. The bodies of the Emperor and Prince have both been removed from the Roman Catholic chapel where they rested to the

Mausoleum prepared for them by the Empress Eugenie at Farnborough in Hampshire.

In Camden Park and other places about Chislehurst are many of those pits excavated by prehistoric man, such as are to be seen on Dartford Heath and elsewhere, and facilities have been made—even to the lighting of them with electricity —for their investigation. The spired church of Chislehurst, picturesquely situated at the south-east corner of the common, has a number of interesting old monuments—notably of the Walsingham, Warwick, and Townsend families. From Chislehurst we may easily reach the Crays and Sidcup, or turning northwards may go by Mottingham to Eltham. At Mottingham the curious in such phenomena may like to know that, on August 4, 1585, "in a field which belongeth to Sir Percival Hart, betimes in the morning the ground began to sink, so much that three great elm trees were suddenly swallowed into the pit, the tops falling downward into the hole; and before ten o'clock they were so overwhelmed that no part of them might be discerned, the concave being suddenly filled with water. The compass of the hole was about 80 yards, and so profound that a sounding line of fifty fathoms could hardly find or feel any bottom."

At Eltham we reach a place of old time splendour, for here several of our Kings had a grand palace, in which they frequently resided until Henry VIII. migrated to Greenwich and Eltham fell into desuetude. The old banqueting hall with its grand oak roof—which George III. wished to transfer to Windsor—is all that remains of the palace long a favourite residence of Plantagenet and Tudor Kings, where Parliaments were held and foreign visitors received, where, as the records tell, the Court often passed the festive season of Christmas, and where Wolsey drew up the Statutes of Eltham for the practical guidance of those responsible for the good order of the Royal Household.

In the time of the Commonwealth Eltham Palace was the residence of the Earl of Essex, the Parliamentarian General who died there in 1646; later it was bestowed by Charles II. on one Sir John Shaw who had lent him much money when in exile. Shaw seems to have been well rewarded for his timely assistance, for after the Restoration he was described as "a miracle of a man," holding more places than any other man in England.

The old palace is Eltham's chief attraction, but its church is also worth visiting. In it is buried Thomas Doggett, the comedian who died in 1722, having established five years earlier the Thames Watermen's race for " Doggett's coat and badge." He was one of the most popular actors of his day, and was described by a contemporary thus, in Elian fashion, " on the stage he's very aspectabund, wearing a farce on his face, his thoughts deliberately forming his utterance congruous to his looks. He is the only comic original now extant." Here, too, is buried Bishop George Horne, whose " Commentary on the Book of Psalms" was much read a century ago.

A letter which a Mrs. Amy Owen of Eltham sent to her friend John Evelyn ("Mon Amy—that is My Friend," as he punningly addressed her) is interesting for the glimpse it affords us of the old tulip craze.

" HONOURED SIR,
        " I am heartily sorry that I forced you to buy tulips for your fine garden. I must confess your guineas look more glorious than now these tulips do; but, when they come to blow, I hope you will be better pleased than now you are. I have sent you some of my ordinary sort, and, sir, when mine are blown, if you please to come and see them, Mr. Evelyn shall buy no more, but have what he pleases for nothing. I am so well pleased with those that I have, that I shall neither buy more, nor part with any, unless it be to yourself.

        I cannot, sir, send my husband's service to you, because I do not acquaint him with my trading for tulips."

We may see beautiful gardens all through our county, but the traffic in tulips—"a traffic which is so innocent, so laudable, and so frequent even among very great persons"—has long since ceased to be a fashionable hobby.

Though midway between such great suburban centres as Bromley and Woolwich, Eltham offers pleasant rurality in some of the country walks around, and especially in the direction of Bexley and North Cray. To the north of it rises Shooters Hill, and a couple of miles to the west of it is Lee, and here, within the bounds of the county of London, we may bring to an end our wanderings in the highways and byways of Kent. It has been pointed out how, standing anywhere in one of our hopfields, the avenues of poled bines always radiate from us, and so it may be said that in this rich county, start where we may, we are in a centre from which beautiful or interesting places are within reach of us in every direction.

INDEX

R. CLAY AND SONS, LTD., BRUNSWICK ST., STAMFORD ST , S.E.

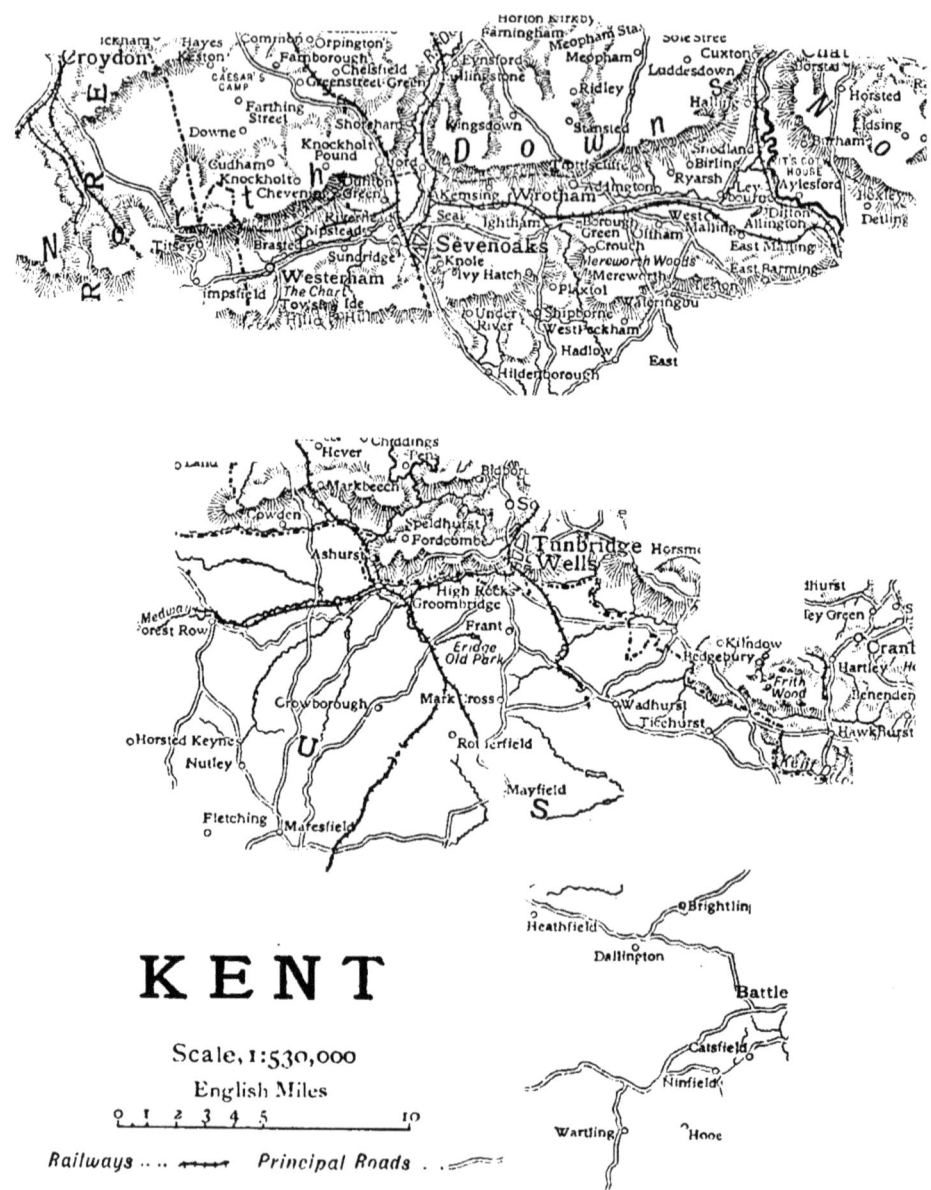

KENT

Scale, 1:530,000

English Miles

0 1 2 3 4 5   10

Railways ... ⤛⤜⤛   Principal Roads . . ⤜⤛

NORTH SEA

Westgate on Sea Margate
Herne   Kingsgate
Street Stones   North Foreland
Swale   Broadstairs
                         Ramsgate
                    Farm
                    Pegwell
                    Bay
Stourmouth Stour
As
ordwich Wickhambreux
olck um
terbury Wingham Ash ich gh The Goodwin
Milton Nackington Fixbourne Staple Wordnesboro Sands
Chartham Bridge Beakesbourne Goodnestone Eastry SANDWICH CASTLE Downs
Garlinge Adisham Chillenden Shot n Deal
Denge Green Lower Hardres Bishopsbourne Knowlton Walmer
Molash Petham Kingston Nonington Northbourne Kingsdown
iteHill omersham Upper Hardres Womenswold Barfreston Great Mongeham Ringwould
Solestreet Barham Tilmanstone Little Mongeham Hope Point
Crundale Wolvage Green Eythorne Studdal Margaret's at Cliffe
Wye Waltham Stephenswell St.Margaret's Bay
ithersdane Sibling Minnis Denton Coldred West Langdon South Foreland
Hastingleigh Wootton Waldershare Park East Langdon
Elham Lydden Whitfield Guston Strait of Dover
Brabourne Herise Swingfield Alkham Copt Hill
Smeeth Hurst Park Paddlesworth Capel Dover
Sellinge Etchinghill le F rne Shakespeare Cliff
ast Stour Stanford Postling Ferry Garden Abbot's Cliff
ington Newing n Cheriton East Wear Bay
Court oat Street Sal r Folkestone
L mney West Sandgate
litary oldenhurst Fm Hythe Sandcliffe Camp
Canal Asri
m n e y Dymchurch
Ho.
l r s h
church
Little Stone
Romney

Dungeness

LISH CHANNEL C. Gris Nez

FRANCE

THE
HIGHWAYS & BYWAYS
SERIES.

Extra crown 8vo, gilt tops, 6s̄. net each.

London. By Mrs. E. T. Cook. With Illus-
trations by Hugh Thomson and Frederick L. Griggs.

GRAPHIC.—"Mrs. Cook is an admirable guide; she knows her
London in and out; she is equally at home in writing of Mayfair and of
City courts, and she has a wealth of knowledge relating to literary and
historical associations. This, taken together with the fact that she is a
writer who could not be dull if she tried, makes her book very delightful
reading."

Middlesex. By Walter Jerrold. With
Illustrations by Hugh Thomson.

EVENING STANDARD—"Every Londoner who wishes to mul-
tiply fourfold the interest of his roamings and excursions should beg,
borrow, or buy it without a day's delay."

DAILY TELEGRAPH.—"A model of its class, for it is difficult to
see how descriptive work of the kind could be performed with a more
sympathetic and humane touch."

Hertfordshire. By Herbert W. Tompkins,
F.R.Hist.S. With Illustrations by Frederick L. Griggs.

WESTMINSTER GAZETTE.—"A very charming book. . . .
Will delight equally the artistic and the poetic, the historical and the antiquarian, the picturesque and the sentimental kinds of tourist."

ST. JAMES'S GAZETTE.—"Cram full of interest and entertainment.
The county is singularly rich in material for gossip and comment, and Mr.
Tompkins has made a very charming book from it. Nothing more can
well remain to be said, yet all that is said in these pages is to the point."

Buckinghamshire. By Clement Shorter.
With Illustrations by Frederick L. Griggs.

WORLD.—"A thoroughly delightful little volume. Mr. Frederick
L. Griggs contributes a copious series of delicately graceful illustrations."

OBSERVER.—"A very full, pleasant, and informing book. . . .
Mr. Griggs again gives us of his best."

Surrey. By Eric Parker. With Illustrations
by Hugh Thomson.

DAILY TELEGRAPH.—"Author and artist have combined to give
us one of the very best books on the most variedly beautiful of the home
counties."

SPECTATOR.—"A very charming book, both to dip into and to read
. . . Every page is sown with something rare and curious."

Kent. By WALTER JERROLD. With Illustrations by HUGH THOMSON.

PALL MALL GAZETTE.—"A book over which it is a pleasure to pore, and which every man of Kent or Kentish man, or 'foreigner,' should promptly steal, purchase, or borrow. . . . The illustrations alone are worth twice the money charged for the book."

Sussex. By E. V. LUCAS. With Illustrations by FREDERICK L. GRIGGS.

WESTMINSTER GAZETTE.—"A delightful addition to an excellent series. . . . Mr. Lucas's knowledge of Sussex is shown in so many fields, with so abundant and yet so natural a flow, that one is kept entertained and charmed through every passage of his devious progress. . . . The drawings with which Mr. Frederick Griggs illustrates this charming book are equal in distinction to any work this admirable artist has given us."

Berkshire. By JAMES EDMUND VINCENT. With Illustrations by FREDERICK L. GRIGGS.

DAILY CHRONICLE.—"We consider this book one of the best in an admirable series, and one which should appeal to all who love this kind of literature."

Oxford and the Cotswolds. By H. A. EVANS. With Illustrations by FREDERICK L. GRIGGS.

DAILY TELEGRAPH.—"The author is everywhere entertaining and fresh, never allowing his own interest to flag, and thereby retaining the close attention of the reader."

Shakespeare's Country. By The Ven. W. H. HUTTON. With Illustrations by EDMUND H. NEW.

PALL MALL GAZETTE.—"Mr. Edmund H. New has made a fine book a thing of beauty and a joy for ever by a series of lovely drawings."

Hampshire. By D. H. MOUTRAY READ. With Illustrations by ARTHUR B. CONNOR.

STANDARD.—"In our judgment, as excellent and as lively a book as has yet appeared in the Highways and Byways Series."

Dorset. By Sir FREDERICK TREVES. With Illustrations by JOSEPH PENNELL.

STANDARD.—"A breezy, delightful book, full of sidelights on men and manners, and quick in the interpretation of all the half-inarticulate lore of the countryside."

Wiltshire. By Edward Hutton. With
Illustrations by Nelly Erichsen.

Somerset. By Edward Hutton. With
Illustrations by Nelly Erichsen.

DAILY TELEGRAPH.—"A book which will set the heart of every West-country-man beating with enthusiasm, and with pride for the goodly heritage into which he has been born as a son of Somerset."

Devon and Cornwall. By Arthur H.
Norway With Illustrations by Joseph Pennell and Hugh Thomson.

DAILY CHRONICLE.—"So delightful that we would gladly fill columns with extracts were space as elastic as imagination. . . . The text is excellent ; the illustrations of it are even better."

South Wales. By A. G. Bradley. With
Illustrations by Frederick L. Griggs.

SPECTATOR.—"Mr. Bradley has certainly exalted the writing of a combined archæological and descriptive guide-book into a species of literary art. The result is fascinating."

North Wales. By A. G. Bradley. With
Illustrations by Hugh Thomson and Joseph Pennell.

PALL MALL GAZETTE.—"To read this fine book makes us eager to visit every hill and every valley that Mr. Bradley describes with such tantalising enthusiasm. It is a work of inspiration, vivid, sparkling, and eloquent—a deep well of pleasure to every lover of Wales."

Cambridge and Ely. By Rev. Edward
Conybeare. With Illustrations by Frederick L. Griggs.

Also an *Edition de Luxe.* Limited to 250 copies. Royal 8vo, 21s. net.

ATHENÆUM—"A volume which, light and easily read as it is, deserves to rank with the best literature about the county."

GUARDIAN—"Artist and writer have combined to give us a book of singular charm."

East Anglia. By William A. Dutt. With
Illustrations by Joseph Pennell.

WORLD.—"Of all the fascinating volumes in the ' Highways and By-ways ' series, none is more pleasant to read. . . . Mr. Dutt, himself an East Anglian, writes most sympathetically and in picturesque style of the district."

Lincolnshire. By W. F. Rawnsley. With
Illustrations by Frederick L. Griggs.

PALL MALL GAZETTE.—"A splendid record of a storied shire."

Nottinghamshire. By J. B. Firth. With
Illustrations by Frederick L. Griggs.

Northamptonshire and Rutland. By
Herbert A. Evans. With Illustrations by Frederick
L. Griggs.

Derbyshire. By J. B. Firth. With Illustra-
tions by Nelly Erichsen.

Yorkshire. By Arthur H. Norway. With
Illustrations by Joseph Pennell and Hugh Thomson.

PALL MALL GAZETTE.—"The wonderful story of Yorkshire's
past provides Mr. Norway with a wealth of interesting material, which
he has used judiciously and well; each grey ruin of castle and abbey he
has re-erected and re-peopled in the most delightful way. A better guide
and story-teller it would be hard to find."

Lake District. By A. G. Bradley. With
Illustrations by Joseph Pennell.

ST. JAMES'S GAZETTE.—"A notable edition—an engaging
volume, packed with the best of all possible guidance for tourists. For
the most part the artist's work is as exquisite as anything of the kind he
has done."

The Border. By Andrew Lang and John
Lang. With Illustrations by Hugh Thomson.

STANDARD.—"The reader on his travels, real or imaginary, could
not have pleasanter or more profitable companionship. There are charming
sketches by Mr. Hugh Thomson to illustrate the letterpress."

Galloway and Carrick. By the Rev. C. H.
Dick. With Illustrations by Hugh Thomson.

Donegal and Antrim. By Stephen Gwynn.
With Illustrations by Hugh Thomson.

DAILY TELEGRAPH.—"A perfect book of its kind, on which
author, artist, and publisher have lavished of their best."

Normandy. By Percy Dearmer, M.A. With
Illustrations by Joseph Pennell.

Lightning Source UK Ltd.
Milton Keynes UK
UKHW020610110119
335177UK00005B/316/P